Rick Steves'

POCKET

ROME

Rick Steves & Gene Openshaw

Contents

Introduction

Rome is magnificent and brutal at the same time. It's a showcase of Western civilization, with astonishingly ancient sights and a modern vibrancy. But with the wrong attitude, you'll be frustrated by the kind of chaos that only an Italian can understand. On my last visit, a cabbie struggling with the traffic said, *"Roma chaos."* I responded, *"Bella chaos."* He agreed.

Two thousand years ago, when the ancient city dominated Europe, the word "Rome" meant civilization itself. Today, Rome is Italy's political capital, the heart of Catholicism, and the enduring legacy of the ancient world. As you peel through the city's fascinating layers, you'll find Rome's monuments, cats, laundry, cafes, churches, fountains, traffic, and 2.6 million people endlessly entertaining.

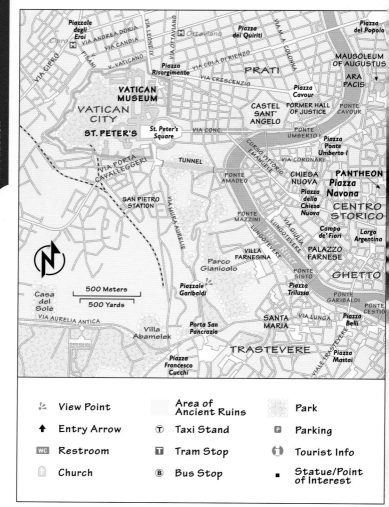

View Point		Area of Ancient Ruins		Park	
Entry Arrow		Taxi Stand		Parking	
Restroom	WC	Tram Stop		Tourist Info	
Church		Bus Stop	B	Statue/Point of Interest	

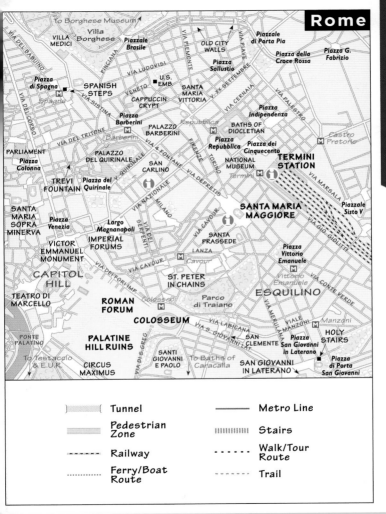

Rome

) (	Tunnel	————	Metro Line
▬▬	Pedestrian Zone	|||||||||	Stairs
- - - - -	Railway	· · · · ·	Walk/Tour Route
··············	Ferry/Boat Route	- - - - -	Trail

About This Book

With this book, I've selected only the best of Rome—admittedly, a tough call. The core of the book is seven self-guided tours that zero in on Rome's greatest sights and neighborhoods. Do the "Caesar shuffle" through ancient Rome's Colosseum, Forum, and Pantheon. Take a night walk from Campo de' Fiori to the Spanish Steps, lacing together Rome's Baroque and bubbly nightspots. Visit St. Peter's, the greatest church on earth, and learn something about eternity by touring the huge Vatican Museum. Savor the sumptuous Borghese Gallery.

The rest of the book is a traveler's tool kit. You'll find hints on saving money, avoiding crowds, getting around Rome, finding a great meal, and more.

Rome—A City of Neighborhoods

Sprawling Rome actually feels manageable once you get to know it.

The historic core, with most of the tourist sights, sits in a diamond formed by Termini train station (in the east), Vatican City (west), Villa Borghese Gardens (north), and the Colosseum (south). The Tiber River runs through the diamond from north to south. In the center of the diamond sits Piazza Venezia, a busy square and traffic hub. It takes about an hour to walk from Termini train station to Vatican City.

Think of Rome as a series of neighborhoods, huddling around major landmarks.

Ancient Rome: In ancient times, this was home for the grandest buildings of a city of a million people. Today, the best of the classical sights stand in a line from the Colosseum to the Forum to the Pantheon.

Pantheon Neighborhood: The Pantheon anchors the neighborhood I like to call the heart of Rome. It stretches eastward from the Tiber

Rome's Neighborhoods

VATICAN MUSEUM
VATICAN CITY
ST. PETER'S

PIAZZA DEL POPOLO

NORTH ROME
VILLA BORGHESE
BORGHESE GALLERY

"SHOPPING TRIANGLE"
SPANISH STEPS

TERMINI
NAT'L. MUSEUM   TRAIN STATION

PANTHEON NEIGHBORHOOD

PIAZZA VENEZIA

CAPITOL HILL
FORUM
ANCIENT ROME
COLOSSEUM

PILGRIM'S ROME
SAN GIOVANNI IN LATERANO

Tiber River

STA. MARIA
TRASTEVERE

TESTACCIO
SOUTH OF TESTACCIO
SOUTH ROME
APPIAN WAY
E.U.R.

Not to Scale

River through Campo de' Fiori and Piazza Navona, past the Pantheon to the Trevi Fountain.

North Rome: With the Spanish Steps, Villa Borghese Gardens, and trendy shopping streets (Via Veneto and the "shopping triangle"), this is a more modern, classy area.

Vatican City: Located west of the Tiber, it's a compact world of its own, with two great, huge sights: St. Peter's Basilica and the Vatican Museum.

Trastevere: This seedy, colorful wrong-side-of-the-river neighborhood is village Rome. It's the city at its crustiest—and perhaps most Roman.

Daily Reminder

Sunday: These sights are closed—the Vatican Museum (except for the last Sunday of the month, when it's free and even more crowded), Villa Farnesina (except the first Sun of the month), and the Catacombs of San Sebastiano. In the morning, the Porta Portese flea market hops, and the old center is delightfully quiet. The Via dei Fori Imperiali and much of the Appian Way are closed to traffic and fun to stroll.

Monday: Many sights are closed, including the National Museum of Rome, Borghese Gallery, Capitoline Museums, Catacombs of Priscilla, Museum of the Imperial Forums (includes Trajan's Market and Trajan's Forum), Castel Sant'Angelo, Ara Pacis, Montemartini Museum, E.U.R.'s Museum of Roman Civilization, Etruscan Museum, some Appian Way sights (Tomb of Cecilia Metella; Circus and Villa of Maxentius; and the San Sebastiano Gate and Museum of the Walls), Ostia Antica, and Villa d'Este (at Tivoli). Many of the ancient sights (e.g., Colosseum and Forum) and the Vatican Museum, among others, are open. Churches are open as usual.

Tuesday: All sights are open.

Wednesday: All sights are open, except for the Catacombs of San Callisto. St. Peter's Basilica may close in the morning for a papal audience.

Thursday: All sights are open.

Friday: All sights are open.

Saturday: Most sights are open, except the Synagogue and Jewish Museum.

Termini: Though light on sightseeing highlights, the train-station neighborhood has many recommended hotels and public-transportation connections.

Pilgrim's Rome: Several prominent churches dot the area south of Termini train station.

South Rome: South of the city center, you'll find the gritty/colorful Testaccio neighborhood, the 1930s suburb of E.U.R., and the Appian Way, home of the catacombs.

Planning Your Time

The following day-plans give an idea of how much an organized, motivated, and caffeinated person can see. Start with the Day 1 plan—the most important sights—and add on from there.

Day 1: The Colosseum is the ultimate place to begin your tour of ancient Rome. Then continue to the Forum and Pantheon. After a siesta, have dinner on atmospheric Campo de' Fiori, then take the Night Walk Across Rome to the Trevi Fountain and Spanish Steps. If all you have is this one day, skip the Night Walk and see Day 2's sights in the afternoon and evening. Crazy as it sounds, many people actually "do" Rome in a day.

Day 2: See St. Peter's, climb its dome, and tour the Vatican Museum. In the evening, join the locals strolling the Via del Corso from Piazza del Popolo to the Spanish Steps.

Day 3: See the Borghese Gallery (reservations required) and the Capitoline Museums.

Day 4: Take a side trip to Ostia Antica (closed Mon), the Appian Way, and the Catacombs of Priscilla, or Tivoli.

Day 5: Visit the National Museum of Rome and walk through Trastevere.

Key to Symbols

Sights are rated:
- ▲▲▲ Don't miss
- ▲▲ Try hard to see
- ▲ Worthwhile if you can make it
- No rating Worth knowing about

For opening times, if a sight is listed as "May-Oct daily 9:00-16:00," it's open from 9 A.M. until 4 P.M. from the first day of May until the last day of October.

If you'd like more information than this Pocket Guide offers, I've sprinkled the book liberally with web references, including my own website. For updates to this book, feedback from fellow travelers, in-depth travel tips, and much more, visit **www.ricksteves.com**.

Rome at a Glance

▲▲▲**Colosseum** Huge stadium where gladiators fought. **Hours:** Daily 8:30 until one hour before sunset: April–Aug until 19:15, Sept until 19:00, Oct until 18:30, off-season closes as early as 16:30. See page 13.

▲▲▲**Roman Forum** Ancient Rome's main square, with ruins and grand arches. **Hours:** Same hours as Colosseum. See page 27.

▲▲▲**Pantheon** The defining domed temple. **Hours:** Mon–Sat 8:30–19:30, Sun 9:00–18:00, holidays 9:00–13:00, closed for Mass Sat at 17:00 and Sun at 10:30. See page 55.

▲▲▲**National Museum of Rome** Greatest collection of Roman sculpture anywhere. **Hours:** Tue–Sun 9:00–19:45, closed Mon. See page 147.

▲▲▲**Borghese Gallery** Bernini sculptures and paintings by Caravaggio, Raphael, and Titian in a Baroque palazzo. Reservations mandatory. **Hours:** Tue–Sun 9:00–19:00, closed Mon. See page 119.

▲▲▲**Vatican Museum** Four miles of the finest art of Western civilization, culminating in Michelangelo's glorious Sistine Chapel. **Hours:** Mon–Sat 9:00–18:00. Closed on religious holidays and Sun, except last Sun of the month (when it's open 9:00–14:00). May be open late some Fri nights in summer by online reservation only. Hours are notoriously subject to constant change. See page 63.

▲▲▲**St. Peter's Basilica** Most impressive church on earth, with Michelangelo's *Pietà* and dome. **Hours:** Church—daily April–Sept 7:00–19:00, Oct–March 7:00–18:00, often closed Wed mornings; dome—daily April–Sept 8:00–18:00, Oct–March 8:00–16:45. See page 93.

▲▲**Palatine Hill** Ruins of emperors' palaces, Circus Maximus view, and museum. **Hours:** Same hours as Colosseum. See page 135.

▲▲**Capitoline Museums** Ancient statues, mosaics, and expansive view of Forum. **Hours:** Tue–Sun 9:00–20:00, closed Mon. See page 141.

▲▲**Ara Pacis** Shrine marking the beginning of Rome's Golden Age. **Hours:** Tue–Sun 9:00–19:00, closed Mon. See page 153.

▲▲**Catacombs** Layers of tunnels with tombs, mainly Christian. **Hours:** Generally open 10:00–12:00 & 14:00–17:00 (Priscilla is closed Mon; San Sebastiano closed Sun and mid-Nov–mid-Dec; San Callisto closed Wed and Feb). See pages 155 and 165.

▲**Arch of Constantine** Honors the emperor who legalized Christianity. **Hours:** Always viewable. See page 24.

▲**St. Peter-in-Chains Church** with Michelangelo's *Moses*. **Hours:** Daily 8:00–12:30 & 15:00–19:00, until 18:00 in winter. See page 136.

▲**Trajan's Column** Tall column with narrative relief, on Piazza Venezia. **Hours:** Always viewable. See page 138.

▲**Museum of the Imperial Forums** Includes entry to Trajan's Market. **Hours:** Tue–Sun 9:00–19:00, closed Mon. See page 138.

▲**Capitol Hill Square** Hilltop piazza designed by Michelangelo, with a museum, grand stairway, and Forum overlooks. **Hours:** Always open. See page 139.

▲**Trevi Fountain** Baroque hot spot into which tourists throw coins to ensure a return trip to Rome. **Hours:** Always flowing. See page 52.

▲**Baths of Diocletian** Once ancient Rome's immense public baths, now a Michelangelo church, Santa Maria degli Angeli. **Hours:** Church—Mon–Sat 7:00–18:30, Sun 7:00–19:30. See page 149.

▲**Santa Maria della Vittoria** Church with Bernini's swooning *St. Teresa in Ecstasy*. **Hours:** Mon–Sat 8:30–12:00 & 15:30–18:00, Sun 15:30–18:00. See page 150.

▲**Victor Emmanuel Monument** For a 360-degree city view, take the **Rome from the Sky** elevator to the top. **Hours:** Monument—daily 9:30–18:30; elevator—Mon-Thu 9:30–18:30, Fri-Sun 9:30–19:30. See page 142.

▲**Cappuccin Crypt** Decorated with the bones of 4,000 Franciscan friars. **Hours:** Daily 9:00–19:00. See page 152.

▲**Castel Sant'Angelo** Hadrian's Tomb turned castle, prison, papal refuge, now museum. **Hours:** Tue–Sun 9:00–19:30, closed Mon. See page 156.

▲**Galleria Doria Pamphilj** Aristocrat's ornate palace shows off paintings by Caravaggio, Titian, and Raphael. **Hours:** Daily 10:00–17:00. See page 147.

Day 6: Visit the four churches of Pilgrim's Rome and the Cappuccin Crypt.

Day 7: You choose—South Rome sights, St. Peter-in-Chains, Ara Pacis, Victor Emmanuel Monument viewpoint, Trajan's Column, shopping...or peruse the Sights chapter for more options.

These are busy day-plans, so be sure to schedule in slack time for picnics, laundry, people-watching, shopping, hiding from the summer heat, and recharging your touristic batteries. Slow down and be open to unexpected experiences and the friendliness of Romans. Budget time for Rome after dark. Dine well at least once.

Here are a few quick sightseeing tips to get you started: Consider the handy €30 Roma Pass (✪ see page 214), which covers admission to several sights plus a three-day transportation pass. Reservations are recommended for the Vatican Museum and mandatory at the Borghese Gallery. Avoid lines at the Colosseum, St. Peter's, and elsewhere by following my suggestions. Since Rome's opening hours are notoriously variable, get the latest information from tourist information offices (TIs) when you arrive. For more sightseeing tips, ✪ see page 213.

And finally, remember that Rome has hosted visitors for 2,000 years with the same level of inefficiency, improvisation, and apathy you'll find today, so... be flexible.

Buon viaggio!

Colosseum Tour

Colosseo

Start your visit to Rome with its iconic symbol—the Colosseum. Fifty thousand Romans could pack this huge stadium and cheer as their favorite gladiators faced off in bloody battles to the death.

This self-guided tour brings that ancient world to life—the world of Caesars, slaves, Vestal Virgins, trumpet fanfares, roaring lions, and hordes of rabid fans. Prowl the arena like gladiators, climb to the cheap seats for the view, see the underground "backstage" where they kept caged animals, and marvel at the engineering prowess that allowed these ancient people to build on such a colossal scale.

For its thrilling history and sheer massiveness, the Colosseum gets a unanimous thumbs-up.

ORIENTATION

Cost: €12 combo-ticket also includes Roman Forum and Palatine Hill; ticket valid two consecutive days—one entry per sight. Admission is also covered by the handy €30 Roma Pass; if you're planning to visit the Colosseum, the Roma Pass might be worthwhile for you (✪ see page 214).

Hours: The Colosseum, Roman Forum, and Palatine Hill are all open daily 8:30 until one hour before sunset: April–Aug until 19:15, Sept until 19:00, Oct until 18:30, off-season closes as early as 16:30; last entry one hour before closing.

Getting There: The Colosseo Metro stop on line B is just across the street from the monument. Bus #60 is handy for hotels near Termini train station, and bus #87 goes from Largo Argentina (Pantheon-area hotels).

Avoiding Lines: Avoid long ticket-buying lines by getting your combo-ticket or Roma Pass in advance. They're both sold at the less-crowded Palatine Hill entrance, 150 yards south of the Colosseum on Via di San Gregorio. Roma Passes are also available at the Colosseo Metro station's *tabacchi* shop, and combo-tickets are sold online at www.ticketclic.it (€1.50 booking fee, good for two consecutive days, not changeable). If you take a guided tour, you can skip the line. Armed with your combo-ticket or Roma Pass, you can bypass the Colosseum's ticket-buying queue and go directly to the turnstile. However, everyone must first wait in line to pass through a security check.

Tours: Official 50-minute guided tours in English depart hourly (€5 plus your €12 ticket). To join, pass through security, then tell a guard, who

Endless lines in the Eternal City

Goofy gladiators get two thumbs down

will usher you to the tour booth, allowing you to skip the long ticket-buying line. Private tour guides lingering outside the Colosseum offer two-hour tours of the Colosseum, Forum, and Palatine Hill that let you to skip the line (€15 plus the €12 ticket). Tours of the underground passageways and third level must be reserved through a private company at least a day in advance (€8 plus €12 Colosseum ticket, 1.5 hours, tel. 06-3996-7700, www.coopculture.it).

Audioguides: The Colosseum rents a dry but fact-filled audioguide (€5.50) and a handheld videoguide of video clips (€6). My free Colosseum audio tour is available from iTunes, Google Play, or at www.ricksteves .com.

***Caveat Viator*—Tourist Beware:** The Colosseum's exterior is a happy hunting ground for pickpockets, con artists, and the incredibly crude modern-day gladiators. For a fee, these plastic-helmeted goofballs snuff out their cigarettes and pose for photos, then intimidate timid tourists into paying too much. €4–5 for one photo usually keeps the barbarians appeased.

Information: Tel. 06-3996-7700.

Length of This Tour: Allow an hour.

Restoration: A multi-year renovation project to clean the Colosseum and add a visitors center may affect your visit.

Modern Amenities in the Ancient World

The area around the Colosseum, Forum, and Palatine Hill is rich in history, but pretty barren when it comes to food, shelter, and WCs. Here are a few options:

The Colosseum has a few, crowded **WCs** inside, but don't count on them being available. A nice big WC is behind (east of) the structure (facing ticket entrance, go right; WC is under stairway). If you can wait, the best WCs in the area are at Palatine Hill—at the Via di San Gregorio entrance, in the museum, or in the Farnese Gardens. The Forum also has one WC at the entrance and another near the Temple of Vesta (⭐ see #8 on map on page 28).

Because there are limited **eateries** in the area, consider assembling a small picnic. The Colosseo Metro stop has €5 hot sandwiches. Snack stands on street corners sell drinks, sandwiches, fruit, and candy. If you prefer to dine in, you'll find a few restaurants behind the Colosseum (with expansive views of the structure), a few recommended places a block away (no views but better value—⭐ see page 194), and a cluster of places near the Forum's main entrance (where Via Cavour spills into Via dei Fori Imperiali).

To refill your **water** bottle, stop at one of the water fountains found along city streets, as well as inside the Forum and Palatine Hill.

A nice oasis is the free tourist center, **I Fori di Roma,** with a small café, a WC, and a few exhibits. It's located between the Colosseum and the Forum entrance, on Via dei Fori Imperiali.

If your sightseeing takes you as far as **Capitol Hill,** you'll find services at the Capitoline Museums, including a nice view café (⭐ see page 141).

1 Colosseum Entrance
2 Palatine Hill Entrance
3 Forum Entrance
4 I Fori di Roma
   Visitors Center

F Food

THE TOUR BEGINS

Exterior

▶ *View the Colosseum from the Forum fence, across the street from the Colosseo Metro station.*

Built when the Roman Empire was at its peak in A.D. 80, the Colosseum represents Rome at its grandest. The Flavian Amphitheater (the Colosseum's real name) was an arena for gladiator contests and public spectacles. When killing became a spectator sport, the Romans wanted to share the fun with as many people as possible, so they stuck two semicircular theaters together to create a freestanding amphitheater. The outside (where slender cypress trees stand today) was decorated with a 100-foot-tall bronze statue of Nero that gleamed in the sunlight. In a later age, the colossal structure was nicknamed a "coloss-eum," the wonder of its age. It could accommodate 50,000 roaring fans (100,000 thumbs).

The Romans pioneered the use of concrete and the rounded arch, which enabled them to build on this tremendous scale. The exterior is a skeleton of 3.5 million cubic feet of travertine stone. (Each of the pillars flanking the ground-level arches weighs five tons.) It took 200 ox-drawn wagons shuttling back and forth every day for four years just to bring the stone here from Tivoli. They stacked stone blocks (without mortar) into the shape of an arch, supported temporarily by wooden scaffolding. Finally, they wedged a keystone into the top of the arch—it not only kept the arch from falling, it could bear even more weight above.

The exterior says a lot about the Romans. They were great engineers, not artists, and the building is more functional than beautiful. (If ancient Romans visited the US today as tourists, they might send home postcards of our greatest works of "art"—freeways.) While the essential structure of the Colosseum is Roman, the four-story facade is decorated with mostly Greek columns—Doric-like Tuscan columns on the ground level, Ionic on the second story, Corinthian on the next level, and at the top, half-columns with a mix of all three. Originally, copies of Greek statues stood in the arches of the middle two stories, giving a veneer of sophistication to this arena of death.

Only a third of the original Colosseum remains. Earthquakes destroyed some of it. The pock-marks you see are the peg-holes for iron rods that stapled larger stones together. Most of the Colosseum's missing stone

Colosseum

Not to Scale

was carted off during the Middle Ages and Renaissance—pre-cut stones that were re-used to make other buildings that still adorn Rome today.

▶ To enter, line up in the correct queue: the one for ticket buyers or the one for those who already have a ticket or Roma Pass. The third line is for groups. Once past the turnstiles, there may be signs directing you on a specific visitors' route, but eventually you'll be free to wander.

Interior

Entrances and Exits

As you walk through passageways and up staircases, admire the ergo-nomics. Fans could pour in through ground-floor entrances; there were 76 total, including the emperor's private entrance on the north side. Your ticket was a piece of broken pottery marked with entrance, section, row, and seat number. You'd pass by concession stands selling fast food and souvenirs, such as wine glasses with the names of famous gladiators. The hallways leading to the seats were called by the Latin word *vomitorium*. At exit time, the Colosseum would "vomit" out its contents, giving us the English word. It's estimated that all 50,000 fans could enter and exit in 15 minutes.

▶ *Soon you'll spill out into the arena. Wherever you end up—upstairs or downstairs, at one side of the arena or the other—just take it all in and get oriented. The tallest side of the Colosseum (with the large Christian cross) is the north side.*

Arena

The games took place in this oval-shaped arena, 280 feet long by 165 feet wide. The ratio of length to width is 5:3, often called the golden ratio. Since the days of the Greek mathematician Pythagoras, artists considered that proportion to be ideal, with almost mystical properties. The Colosseum's architects apparently wanted their structure to embody the perfect 3-by-5 mathematical order they thought existed in nature.

When you look down into the arena, you're seeing the underground passages beneath the playing surface. (Note: These underground areas may be open to tourists.) The arena was originally covered with a wooden floor, then sprinkled with sand (*arena* in Latin). The new bit of reconstruct-ed floor gives you an accurate sense of the original arena level, and the subterranean warren where animals and prisoners were held. As in modern stadiums, the spectators ringed the playing area in bleacher seats that slanted up from the arena floor. Around you are the big brick masses that supported the tiers of seats.

A variety of materials were used to build the stadium. Look around. Big white travertine blocks stacked on top of each other formed the skeleton. The pillars for the bleachers were made with a shell of brick, filled in

Column capital of marble

The top story once held an awning

with concrete. Originally the bare brick was covered with marble columns or ornamental facing, so the interior was a brilliant white (they used white plaster for the upper-floor cheap seats).

The Colosseum's seating was strictly segregated. At ringside, the emperor, senators, Vestal Virgins, and VIPs occupied marble seats with their names carved on them (a few marble seats have been restored, at the east end). The next level up held those of noble birth. The level tourists now occupy was for ordinary free Roman citizens, called plebeians. Up at the very top (a hundred yards from the action), there were once wooden bleachers for the poorest people—foreigners, slaves, and women.

The top story of the Colosseum is mostly ruined—only the north side still retains its high wall. This was not part of the original three-story structure, but was added around A.D. 230 after a fire necessitated repairs. Picture the awning that could be stretched across the top of the stadium by armies of sailors. Strung along horizontal beams that pointed inward to the center, the awning only covered about a third of the arena—so those at the top always enjoyed shade, while many nobles down below roasted in the sun.

Looking into the complex web of passageways beneath the arena, you can imagine how busy the backstage action was. Gladiators strolled down the central passageway, from their warm-up yard on the east end to the arena entrance on the west. Some workers tended wild animals. Others prepared stage sets of trees or fake buildings, allowing the arena to be quickly transformed from an African jungle to a Greek temple. Props and sets were hauled up to arena level on 80 different elevator shafts via a system of ropes and pulleys. (You might be able to make out some small rectangular shafts, especially near the center of the arena.) That means there were 80 different spots from which animals, warriors, and stage sets could pop up and magically appear.

The games began with a few warm-up acts—dogs bloodying themselves attacking porcupines, female gladiators fighting each other, or a dwarf battling a one-legged man. Then came the main event—the gladiators.

"Hail, Caesar! *(Ave, Cesare!)* We who are about to die salute you!" The gladiators would enter the arena from the west end, parade around to the sound of trumpets, acknowledge the Vestal Virgins (on the south side), then stop at the emperor's box (supposedly marked today by the cross that stands at the "50-yard line" on the north side—although no one knows for sure where it was). They would then raise their weapons, shout, and salute—and begin fighting. The fights pitted men against men, men against beasts, and beasts against beasts. Picture 50,000 screaming people around you (did gladiators get stage fright?), and imagine that they want to see you die.

Some gladiators wielded swords, protected only with a shield and a heavy helmet. Others represented fighting fishermen, with a net to snare opponents and a trident to spear them. The gladiators were usually slaves, criminals, or poor people who got their chance for freedom, wealth, and fame in the ring. They learned to fight in training schools, then battled their way up the ranks. The best were rewarded like our modern sports stars, with fan clubs, great wealth, and, yes, product endorsements.

The animals came from all over the world: lions, tigers, and bears (oh my!), crocodiles, elephants, and hippos (not to mention exotic human "animals" from the "barbarian" lands). They were kept in cages beneath the

Cross marking the emperor's box

The arena with underground passageways

arena floor, then lifted up in the elevators. Released at floor level, animals would pop out from behind blinds into the arena—the gladiator didn't know where, when, or by what he'd be attacked. Many a hapless warrior met his death here, and never knew what hit him. (This brought howls of laughter from the hardened fans in the cheap upper seats who had a better view of the action.)

Nets ringed the arena to protect the crowd. The stadium was inaugurated with a 100-day festival in which 2,000 men and 9,000 animals were killed. Colosseum employees squirted perfumes around the stadium to mask the stench of blood.

If a gladiator fell helpless to the ground, his opponent would approach the emperor's box and ask: Should he live or die? Sometimes the emperor left the decision to the crowd, who would judge based on how valiantly the man had fought. They would make their decision—thumbs-up or thumbs-down.

Did they throw Christians to the lions like in the movies? Christians were definitely thrown to the lions, made to fight gladiators, crucified, and burned alive...but probably not here in this particular stadium. Maybe, but probably not.

Why were the Romans so blood-thirsty? Consider the value of these games in placating and controlling the huge Roman populace. Seeing Germanic barbarians or African lions slain by a gladiator reminded the citizens of civilized Rome's conquest of distant lands. And having the thumbs-up or thumbs-down authority over another person's life gave the downtrodden masses a sense of power. Once a nation of warriors, Rome became a nation of bureaucrats, who got vicarious thrills by watching brutes battle to the death. The contests were always free, sponsored by rich rulers to bribe the people's favor or to keep Rome's growing masses of unemployed rabble off the streets.

▶ With these scenes in mind, wander around, then check out the upper level. There are stairs on both the east and the west sides, as well as an elevator at the east end. The upper deck offers more colossal views of the arena, plus a bookstore and temporary exhibits. Wherever you may Rome, find a spot at the west end of the upper deck, where you can look out over some of the sights nearby. Start with the big, white, triumphal Arch of Constantine.

Views from the Upper Level

Arch of Constantine

If you are a Christian, were raised a Christian, or simply belong to a so-called "Christian nation," ponder this arch. It marks one of the great turning points in history—the military coup that made Christianity mainstream.

In A.D. 312, Emperor Constantine defeated his rival Maxentius in the crucial Battle of the Milvian Bridge. The night before, he had seen a vision of a cross in the sky. Constantine—whose mother and sister were Christians—became sole emperor and legalized Christianity. With this one battle, a once-obscure Jewish sect with a handful of followers was now the state religion of the entire Western world. In A.D. 300, you could be killed for being a Christian; a century later, you could be killed for not being one. Church enrollment boomed.

The arch trumpets the legitimacy of Constantine's rule by including

Arch of Constantine—Christianity triumphs

glorious emperors that came before. Hadrian is in the round reliefs, Marcus Aurelius in the square reliefs, and statues of Trajan and Augustus adorn the top. Originally, Augustus drove a chariot. Fourth-century Rome may have been in decline, but Constantine clung to its glorious past.

Surrounding Hills

The Colosseum stands in a valley between three of Rome's legendary seven hills. Palatine Hill rises to the southwest, beyond the Arch of Constantine, dotted with umbrella pines. The Caelian is to the south and the Esquiline is to the north. Next to the Arch of Constantine is the road called the Via Sacra, or Sacred Way, once Rome's main street, that leads uphill from the Colosseum to the Forum.

▶ *Looking west, in the direction of the Forum, you'll see some ruins sitting atop a raised, rectangular-shaped hill. The ruins—consisting of an arched alcove made of brick and backed by a church bell tower—are all that remain of the once great Temple of Venus and Rome.*

The Temple of Venus and Rome

Rome's biggest temple could be seen from almost everywhere in the city. The size of a football field, it covered the entire hill, surrounded by white columns, six feet thick.

The tall brick arch in the center was once the temple's *cella,* or sacred chamber. Here sat two monumental statues, back to back—Venus the goddess of Love (Amor, in Latin) and the city's patron (Roma). Roma and Amor—a perfectly symmetrical palindrome—showing how love and the city were meant to go together. In ancient times, newlyweds ascended the staircase from the Colosseum (some parts are still visible) to the temple, to ask the twin goddesses to bring them good luck. These days, Roman couples get married at the church with the bell tower to ensure themselves love and happiness for eternity.

The Colosseum's Legacy: A.D. 500 to the Present

With the coming of Christianity to Rome, the Colosseum and its deadly games gradually became politically incorrect. The stadium was neglected as the Roman Empire dwindled and the infrastructure crumbled. Around A.D. 523—after nearly 500 years of games—the last animal was slaughtered, and the Colosseum shut its doors.

For the next thousand years, the structure was used by various squatters, as a make-shift church, and as a refuge during invasions and riots. Over time, the Colosseum was eroded by wind, rain, and the strain of gravity. Earthquakes weakened it, and a powerful quake in 1349 toppled the south side.

More than anything, the Colosseum was dismantled by the Roman citizens themselves, who carted off pre-cut stones to be re-used for palaces and churches, including St. Peter's. The marble facing was pulverized into mortar, and 300 tons of iron brackets were pried out and melted down, resulting in the pock-marking you see today.

After centuries of neglect, a series of 16th-century popes took pity on the pagan structure. In memory of the Christians who may (or may not) have been martyred here, they shored up the south and west sides with bricks and placed the big cross on the north side of the arena.

Today, the Colosseum links Rome's glorious past with its vital present. Major political demonstrations begin or end here, providing protestors with an iconic backdrop for the TV cameras. On Good Fridays, the pope comes here to lead pilgrims as they follow the Stations of the Cross.

The legend goes that so long as the Colosseum shall stand, the city of Rome shall also stand. For nearly 2,000 years, the Colosseum has been the enduring symbol of the Eternal City.

Temple of Venus and Rome

Roman Forum Tour

Foro Romano

For nearly a thousand years, the Forum was the vital heart of Rome. Nestled in Rome's famous seven hills, this is the Eternal City's birthplace. While only broken columns and arches remain today, this tour helps resurrect the rubble.

Stroll down main street, where shoppers in togas once came to browse and gawk at towering temples and triumphal arches. See where senators passed laws and where orators mounted a rostrum to address their friends, Romans, and countrymen. Visit the temple where Vestal Virgins tended a sacred flame and the spot where Julius Caesar's body was burned. In the middle of it all, you'll still find the main square where ancient citizens once passed the time, just as Romans do in piazzas today.

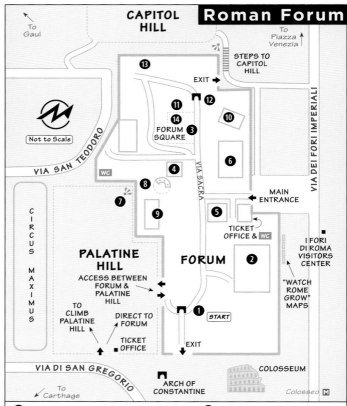

Roman Forum

CAPITOL HILL

To Gaul

To Piazza Venezia

STEPS TO CAPITOL HILL

EXIT

Not to Scale

VIA SAN TEODORO

FORUM SQUARE

WC

VIA SACRA

MAIN ENTRANCE

TICKET OFFICE & WC

CIRCUS MAXIMUS

PALATINE HILL

FORUM

ACCESS BETWEEN FORUM & PALATINE HILL

TO CLIMB PALATINE HILL

DIRECT TO FORUM

TICKET OFFICE

START

EXIT

VIA DI SAN GREGORIO

To Carthage

ARCH OF CONSTANTINE

COLOSSEUM

Colosseo M

I FORI DI ROMA VISITORS CENTER

"WATCH ROME GROW" MAPS

VIA DEI FORI IMPERIALI

1. Arch of Titus
2. Basilica of Constantine
3. The Forum's Main Square
4. Temple of Julius Caesar
5. Temple of Antoninus Pius & Faustina
6. Basilica Aemilia
7. Caligula's Palace
8. Temple of Vesta
9. House of the Vestal Virgins
10. The Curia
11. Rostrum
12. Arch of Septimius Severus
13. Temple of Saturn
14. Column of Phocas

ORIENTATION

Cost: €12 combo-ticket also includes Colosseum and Palatine Hill; ticket valid two consecutive days—one entry per sight; also covered by Roma Pass. To avoid standing in a long ticket-buying line, ✪ see tips on "Avoiding Lines" on page 14 of the Colosseum Tour.

Hours: The Roman Forum, Colosseum, and Palatine Hill are all open daily 8:30 until one hour before sunset: April–Sept until 19:15, Oct until 18:30, off-season closes as early as 16:30; last entry one hour before closing.

Getting There: The main entrance is on Via dei Fori Imperiali, a quarter-mile west of the Colosseo Metro stop. The less-crowded Palatine Hill entrance (150 yards south of the Colosseum on Via di San Gregorio) admits you to the Forum, near the Arch of Titus.

Information: Tel. 06-3996-7700. A free visitors center (I Fori di Roma) is 100 yards east of the entrance on Via dei Fori Imperiali (daily 9:30-18:30).

Tours: Official guided tours in English run Monday through Friday at around 13:00 (€4, 45 minutes, confirm time at ticket office). The unexciting yet informative audioguide is €5. My free Roman Forum audio tour is available from iTunes, Google Play, or at www.ricksteves.com.

Length of This Tour: Allow 1.5 hours.

Services: For information on food and WCs in the area, ✪ see page 16.

THE TOUR BEGINS

▶ *Start at the Arch of Titus (Arco di Tito). It's the white triumphal arch that rises above the rubble on the east end of the Forum (closest to the Colosseum). Stand at the viewpoint alongside the arch and gaze over the valley known as the Forum.*

Overview

The Forum is a rectangular valley running roughly east (the Colosseum end) to west (Capitol Hill, with its bell tower). The rocky path at your feet is the Via Sacra. It leads from the Arch of Titus, through the trees, past the large brick Senate building, through the triumphal arch at the far end, and up Capitol Hill. The hill to your left (with all the trees) is Palatine Hill.

Picture being here when a conquering general returned to Rome with crates of booty. The valley was full of gleaming white buildings topped with bronze roofs. The Via Sacra—Main Street of the Forum—would be lined with citizens waving branches and carrying torches. The trumpets would sound as the parade began.

First came porters, carrying chests full of gold and jewels. Then a parade of exotic animals from the conquered lands—elephants, giraffes, hippopotamuses—for the crowd to "ooh" and "ahh" at. Next came the prisoners in chains, with the captive king on a wheeled platform so the people could jeer and spit at him. Finally, the conquering hero himself would drive down in his four-horse chariot, with rose petals strewn in his path.

The whole procession would run the length of the Forum and up the face of Capitol Hill to the Temple of Saturn (the eight big columns midway up the hill—#13 on the map), where they'd place the booty in Rome's

Forum overview

Arch of Titus relief—looting the temple

Arch of Titus—built by Jewish slaves

coffers. Then they'd continue up to the summit to the Temple of Jupiter (only ruins of its foundation remain today) to dedicate the victory to the King of the Gods.

❶ Arch of Titus (Arco di Tito)

The Arch of Titus commemorated the Roman victory over the province of Judaea (Israel) in A.D. 70. The Romans had a reputation as benevolent conquerors who tolerated the local customs and rulers. All they required was allegiance to the empire, shown by worshipping the emperor as a god. No problem for most conquered people, who already had half a dozen gods on their prayer lists anyway. But Israelites believed in only one god, and it wasn't the emperor. Israel revolted. After a short but bitter war, the Romans defeated the rebels, took Jerusalem, destroyed their temple (leaving only the foundation wall—today's revered "Wailing Wall"), and brought

Rome: Republic and Empire (500 B.C.–A.D. 500)

Ancient Rome spanned about a thousand years, from 500 B.C. to A.D. 500. During that time, Rome expanded from a small tribe of barbarians to a vast empire, then dwindled slowly to city size again. For the first 500 years, when Rome's armies made her ruler of the Italian peninsula and beyond, Rome was a republic governed by elected senators. Over the next 500 years, a time of world conquest and eventual decline, Rome was an empire ruled by a military-backed dictator.

Julius Caesar bridged the gap between republic and empire. This ambitious general and politician, popular with the people because of his military victories and charisma, suspended the Roman constitution and assumed dictatorial powers in about 50 B.C. A few years later, he was assassinated by a conspiracy of senators. His adopted son, Augustus, succeeded him, and soon "Caesar" was not just a name but a title.

Emperor Augustus ushered in the Pax Romana, or Roman peace (A.D. 1–200), a time when Rome reached her peak and controlled an empire that stretched even beyond Eurail—from England to Egypt, Turkey to Morocco.

home 50,000 Jewish slaves...who were forced to build the Colosseum and this arch.

Roman propaganda decorates the inside of the arch. A relief shows the emperor Titus in a chariot being crowned by the goddess Victory. (Thanks to modern pollution, they both look like they've been through the wars.) The other side shows booty from the sacking of the temple in Jerusalem—soldiers carrying a Jewish menorah and other plunder. The two (unfinished) plaques on poles were to have listed the conquered cities. Look at the top of the ceiling. Carved after Titus' death, the relief shows him riding an eagle to heaven, where he'll become one of the gods.

The brutal crushing of the A.D. 70 rebellion (and another one 60 years later) devastated the nation of Israel. With no temple as a center for their faith, the Jews scattered throughout the world (the Diaspora). There would be no Jewish political entity again for almost two thousand years, until modern Israel was created after World War II.

▶ *Walk down the Via Sacra into the Forum. After about 50 yards, turn right and follow a path uphill to the three huge arches of the...*

❷ Basilica of Constantine (a.k.a. Basilica Maxentius)

Yes, these are big arches. But they represent only one-third of the original Basilica of Constantine, a mammoth hall of justice. The arches were matched by a similar set along the Via Sacra side, where only a few squat brick piers remain. Between them ran the central hall. Overhead was a roof 12 stories tall—about 55 feet higher than the side arches you see. (The stub of brick you see sticking up began an arch that once spanned the central hall.)

The hall itself was as long as a football field, lavishly furnished with colorful inlaid marble, a gilded bronze ceiling, and statues, and filled with strolling Romans. At the far (west) end was an enormous marble statue of Emperor Constantine on a throne. Pieces of this statue, including a hand the size of a man, are on display in Rome's Capitoline Museums.

No doubt about it, the Romans built monuments on a more epic scale than any previous Europeans, wowing their "barbarian" neighbors.

▶ *Now stroll deeper into the Forum, downhill along Via Sacra, through the trees. Many of the large basalt stones under your feet were walked on by Caesar Augustus 2,000 years ago. Pass by the only original bronze door still swinging on its ancient hinges (the green door at the Tempio di Romolo, on the right) and continue between ruined buildings until the Via Sacra opens up to a flat, grassy area.*

These arches are all that remain of the once-grand Basilica of Constantine

Today's field of rubble...

...was once a gleaming canyon of marble

❸ The Forum's Main Square

The original Forum, or main square, was this flat patch about the size of a football field, stretching to the foot of Capitol Hill. Surrounding it were temples, law courts, government buildings, and triumphal arches.

Rome was born right here. According to legend, twin brothers Romulus (Rome) and Remus were orphaned in infancy and raised by a she-wolf on top of Palatine Hill. Growing up, they found it hard to get dates. So they and their cohorts attacked the nearby Sabine tribe and kidnapped their women. After they made peace, this marshy valley became the meeting place and then the trading center for the scattered tribes on the surrounding hillsides.

The square was the busiest and most crowded—and often the seediest—section of town. Besides the senators, politicians, and currency exchangers, there were even sleazier types—souvenir hawkers, pickpockets, fortune-tellers, gamblers, slave marketers, drunks, hookers, lawyers, and tour guides.

The Forum is now rubble, but imagine it in its prime: blinding white marble buildings with 40-foot-high columns and shining bronze roofs; rows of statues painted in realistic colors; processional chariots rattling down Via Sacra. Mentally replace tourists in T-shirts with tribunes in togas. Imagine the buildings towering and the people buzzing around you while an orator gives a rabble-rousing speech from the Rostrum. If things still look like just a pile of rocks, at least tell yourself, "But Julius Caesar once leaned against these rocks."

▶ *At the near (east) end of the main square (the Colosseum is to the east) are the foundations of a temple now capped with a peaked wood-and-metal roof.*

❹ Temple of Julius Caesar
(Tempio del Divo Giulio, or Ara di Cesare)

Julius Caesar's body was burned on this spot (under the metal roof) after his assassination. Peek behind the wall into the small apse area, where a mound of dirt usually has fresh flowers—given to remember the man who, more than any other, personified the greatness of Rome.

Caesar (100–44 B.C.) changed Rome—and the Forum—dramatically. He cleared out many of the wooden market stalls and began to ring the square with even grander buildings. Caesar's house was located behind the temple, near that clump of trees. He walked right by here on the day he was assassinated. Along the way, a street-corner Etruscan preacher warned him, "Beware the Ides of March!"

Though he was popular with the masses, not everyone liked Caesar's urban design or his politics. When he assumed dictatorial powers, he was ambushed and stabbed to death by a conspiracy of senators, including his adopted son, Brutus *("Et tu, Brute?")*.

The funeral was held here, facing the main square. The citizens gathered, and speeches were made. Mark Antony stood up to say (in Shakespeare's words), "Friends, Romans, countrymen, lend me your ears. I come to bury Caesar, not to praise him." When Caesar's body was burned, the citizens who still loved him threw anything at hand on the fire, requiring the fire department to come put it out. Later, Emperor Augustus dedicated this temple in his name, making Caesar the first Roman to become a god.

▶ *Behind and to the left of the Temple of Julius Caesar are the 10 tall columns of the...*

❺ Temple of Antoninus Pius and Faustina

The Senate built this temple to honor Emperor Antoninus Pius (A.D. 138–161) and his deified wife, Faustina. The 50-foot-tall Corinthian (leafy) columns must have been awe-inspiring to out-of-towners who grew up in thatched huts. Although the temple has been inhabited by a church, you can still see the basic layout—a staircase led to a shaded porch (the columns), which admitted you to the main building (now a church), where the statue of the god sat. Originally, these columns supported a triangular pediment decorated with sculptures.

Picture these columns, with gilded capitals, supporting brightly painted statues in the pediment, and the whole building capped with a gleaming

Temple of Antoninus Pius and Faustina

Religion in Ancient Rome

The superstitious Romans had a god for every moment of their day—from king Jupiter who ruled over all, to Fornax who controlled the family oven, to Cunina who protected baby's cradle, to the sewer goddess Venus Cloacina. Romans appeased the fickle gods with elaborate rituals at temples and shrines. Priests interpreted the will of the gods by studying the internal organs of sacrificed animals, the flight of birds, and prophetic books. A clap of thunder was enough to postpone a battle.

Roman life was permeated with astrology, magic rites, the cult of deified emperors, house gods, and the near-deification

of ancestors. But all these practices were gradually replaced when Emperor Constantine embraced Christianity in A.D. 312. By 390, the Christian God was the only legal god in Rome.

bronze roof. The stately gray rubble of today's Forum is a faded black-and-white photograph of a 3-D Technicolor era.

▶ *There's a ramp next to the Temple of A. and F. Walk halfway up it and look to the left to view the...*

❻ Basilica Aemilia

A basilica was a Roman hall of justice. In a society that was as legal-minded as America is today, you needed a lot of lawyers—and a big place to put them. Citizens came here to work out matters such as inheritances and building permits, or to sue somebody.

Notice the layout. It was a long, rectangular building. The stubby columns all in a row form one long, central hall flanked by two side aisles. Medieval Christians used basilicas like this as the model for their churches, because their worship services required a larger meeting hall than Roman temples provided. Cathedrals from France to Spain to England, from Romanesque to Gothic to Renaissance, all have the same basic floor plan as a Roman basilica.

► *Return again to the Temple of Julius Caesar. To the right of the temple are the three tall Corinthian columns of the Temple of Castor and Pollux. Beyond that is Palatine Hill—the corner of which may have been...*

❼ Caligula's Palace (a.k.a. the Palace of Tiberius)

Emperor Caligula (ruled A.D. 37–41) had a huge palace on Palatine Hill overlooking the Forum. It actually sprawled down the hillside (where a few supporting arches remain) into the Forum.

Caligula was not a nice person. He tortured enemies, stole senators' wives, and parked his chariot in handicap spaces. But Rome's luxury-loving emperors only added to the glory of the Forum, with each one trying to make his mark on history.

► *To the left of the Temple of Castor and Pollux, find the remains of a small white circular temple.*

❽ Temple of Vesta

This is perhaps Rome's most sacred spot. Rome considered itself one big family, and this temple represented a circular hut, like the kind that Rome's first families lived in. Inside, a fire burned, just as in a Roman home. And back in the days before lighters and butane, you never wanted your fire to

Temple of Castor and Pollux

Temple of Vesta

go out. As long as the sacred flame burned, Rome would stand. The flame was tended by priestesses known as Vestal Virgins.

▶ *Around the back of the Temple of Vesta, you'll find two rectangular brick pools. These stood in the courtyard of the...*

❾ House of the Vestal Virgins

The Vestal Virgins lived in a two-story building surrounding a long central courtyard with these two pools at one end. Rows of statues depicting leading Vestal Virgins flanked the courtyard. This place was the model—both architecturally and sexually—for medieval convents and monasteries.

Chosen from noble families before they reached the age of 10, the six Vestal Virgins served a 30-year term. Honored and revered by the Romans, the Vestals even had their own box opposite the emperor in the Colosseum.

As the name implies, a Vestal took a vow of chastity. If she served her term faithfully—abstaining for 30 years—she was given a huge dowry, and allowed to marry. But if they found any Virgin who wasn't, she was strapped to a funeral car, paraded through the streets of the Forum, taken to a crypt, given a loaf of bread and a lamp...and buried alive. Many women suffered the latter fate.

▶ *Return to the Temple of Julius Caesar and head to the Forum's west end (opposite from the Colosseum). As you pass alongside the big open space of the Forum's main square, consider how the piazza is still a standard part of any Italian town. It has reflected and accommodated the gregarious and outgoing nature of the Italian people since Roman times.*

Stop at the big, well-preserved brick building (on right) with the triangular roof. (Note that ongoing archaeological work may restrict access to the Curia and surrounding structures.) Look in at...

❿ The Curia (Senate House)

The Curia was the most important political building in the Forum. While the present building dates from A.D. 283, this was the site of Rome's official center of government since the birth of the republic. Three-hundred senators, elected by the citizens of Rome, met here to debate and create the laws of the land. Their wooden seats once circled the building in three tiers; the Senate president's podium sat at the far end. The marble floor is from ancient times. Listen to the echoes in this vast room—the acoustics are great.

Rome prided itself on being a republic. Early in the city's history, its people threw out the king and established rule by elected representatives. Each Roman citizen was free to speak his mind and have a say in public policy. Even when emperors became the supreme authority, the Senate was a power to be reckoned with. The Curia building is well-preserved, having been used as a church since early Christian times. Note: Although Julius Caesar was assassinated in "the Senate," it wasn't here—the Senate was temporarily meeting across town.

▶ *Go back down the Senate steps and find the 10-foot-high wall just to the left of the big arch, marked...*

⑪ Rostrum (Rostri)

Nowhere was Roman freedom more apparent than at this "Speaker's Corner." The Rostrum was a raised platform, 10 feet high and 80 feet long, decorated with statues, columns, and the prows of ships (rostra).

On a stage like this, Rome's orators, great and small, tried to draw a crowd and sway public opinion. Mark Antony rose to offer Caesar the laurel-leaf crown of kingship, which Caesar publicly (and hypocritically) refused while privately becoming a dictator. Cicero railed against the corruption and decadence that came with the city's newfound wealth. In later years, daring citizens even spoke out against the emperors, reminding them that Rome was once free. Picture the backdrop these speakers would have had—a mountain of marble buildings piling up on Capitol Hill.

In front of the Rostrum are trees bearing fruits that were sacred to the ancient Romans: olives (provided food, light, and preservatives), figs (tasty), and wine grapes (for a popular export product).

▶ *The big arch to the right of the Rostrum is the...*

Slaves on the Arch of Septimius Severus

Column of Phocas amid rubble

Arch of Septimius Severus

⑫ Arch of Septimius Severus

In imperial times, the Rostrum's voices of democracy would have been dwarfed by images of the empire, such as the huge six-story-high Arch of Septimius Severus (A.D. 203). The reliefs commemorate the African-born emperor's battles in Mesopotamia. Near ground level, see soldiers marching captured barbarians back to Rome for the victory parade. Despite Severus' efficient rule, Rome's empire was crumbling.

▶ *Pass underneath the Arch of Septimius Severus and turn left. On the slope of Capitol Hill are the eight remaining columns of the...*

⑬ Temple of Saturn

These columns framed the entrance to the Forum's oldest temple (497 B.C.). Inside was a humble, very old wooden statue of the god Saturn. But the statue's pedestal held the gold bars, coins, and jewels of Rome's state treasury, the booty collected by conquering generals.

▶ *Standing here, at one of the Forum's first buildings, look east at the lone, tall...*

⑭ Column of Phocas—Rome's Fall

This is the Forum's last monument (A.D. 608), a gift from the powerful Byzantine Empire to a fallen empire—Rome. Given to commemorate the pagan Pantheon's becoming a Christian church, it's like a symbolic last nail in ancient Rome's coffin.

After Rome's 1,000-year reign, the city was looted by Vandals, the population of a million-plus shrank to about 10,000, and the once-grand city center—the Forum—was abandoned, slowly covered up by centuries

Rome Falls

Remember that Rome lasted 1,000 years—500 years of growth, 200 years of peak power, and 300 years of gradual decay. The fall had many causes—corruption, plagues, crumbling infrastructure, and a false economy based on spoils of war. On the borders, barbarian tribes poured in, pushing the Roman legions back. The Europe-wide empire gradually shrank to little more than the city of Rome. In A.D. 410, barbarians even looted Rome itself, leveling many of the buildings in the Forum. In 476, the last emperor checked out, switched off the lights, and plunged Europe into centuries of poverty, ignorance, superstition, and hand-me-down leotards—the Dark Ages.

But Rome lived on in the Catholic Church. Christianity was the state religion of Rome's last generations. Emperors became popes (both called themselves "Pontifex Maximus"), senators became bishops, orators became priests, and basilicas became churches. The glory of Rome remains eternal.

of silt and dirt. In the 1700s, an English historian named Edward Gibbon overlooked this spot from Capitol Hill. Hearing Christian monks singing at these pagan ruins, he looked out at the few columns poking up from the ground, pondered the "Decline and Fall of the Roman Empire," and thought, "Hmm, that's a catchy title...."

▶ *There are several ways to exit the Forum:*

1. Near the Arch of Septimius Severus are stairs that lead up to Capitol Hill.

2. The Forum's main entrance spills you back out onto Via dei Fori Imperiali.

3. From the Arch of Titus, you can climb and tour Palatine Hill (for details, ✪ see page 135).

4. Exiting past the Arch of Titus lands you at the Colosseum.

Night Walk Across Rome

From Campo de' Fiori to the Spanish Steps

A stroll in the cool of the evening brings out all the romance of the Eternal City. Sit so close to a bubbling fountain that traffic noise evaporates. Jostle with kids to see the gelato flavors. Watch lovers straddling more than the bench. Jaywalk past *polizia* in flak-proof vests. And marvel at the ramshackle elegance that softens this brutal city for those who were born here and can imagine living nowhere else. These are the flavors of Rome best tasted after dark.

Even by day, this walk shows off Rome's most colorful lanes, piazzas, markets, and boutiques. But when the sun sets, magic happens.

THE WALK BEGINS

▶ *Start this mile-long walk at the Campo de' Fiori. This walk is equally pleasant in reverse order: You could ride the Metro to the Spanish Steps and finish at Campo de' Fiori, my favorite outdoor dining room after dark—for recommendations,* ✪ *see page 192 in the Eating chapter.*

Campo de' Fiori

One of Rome's most colorful spots, this bohemian piazza hosts a fruit and vegetable market in the morning, cafés in the evening, and pub-crawlers at night. In ancient times, the "Field of Flowers" was an open meadow. Later, Christian pilgrims passed through on their way to the Vatican, and a thriving market developed.

The square is watched over by a brooding statue of Giordano Bruno, an intellectual heretic who was burned on this spot in 1600. The pedestal shows scenes from Bruno's trial and execution, and reads, "And the flames rose up." When this statue honoring a heretic was erected in 1889, the Vatican protested, but they were overruled by angry Campo locals. The neighborhood is still known for its free spirit and anti-authoritarian demonstrations.

The Campo de' Fiori is the product of centuries of unplanned urban development. At the east end of the square (behind Bruno), the ramshackle apartments are built right into the old outer wall of ancient Rome's mammoth Theater of Pompey. Julius Caesar was assassinated in the Theater, where the Senate was renting space.

The square is surrounded by fun eateries, great for people-watching. Bruno faces the bustling Forno (in the left corner of the square, closed

Campo de' Fiori's morning market

Giordano Bruno (1548–1600)

Lauded as a martyr to free thought and reviled as an intellectual con-man and heretic, the philosopher-priest Bruno has a legacy only a Roman could love.

As a young man, Bruno had to flee Italy to avoid a charge of heresy. In Geneva, he joined the Calvinists. In London, he met with Queen Elizabeth. In Germany, the Lutherans excommunicated him.

Bruno's writings reflect his vast-ranging mind. He claimed to have discovered the "Clavis Magna" (Great Key) to training the human memory. His satirical plays tweaked Church morals.

He advanced the heretical notion that the earth revolved around the sun, and speculated about life on other planets.

In 1593, Bruno was arrested by the Inquisition and locked up for six years. When he was finally condemned, he replied: "Perhaps you who pronounce this sentence are more fearful than I who receive it." On February 17, 1600, they led him to the stake on Campo de' Fiori. As they lit the fire, he was offered a crucifix to hold. He pushed it away.

Sun), where take-out *pizza bianco* is sold hot out of the oven. On weekend nights, when the Campo is packed with beer-drinking kids, the medieval square is transformed into one vast Roman street party.

► *If Bruno did a hop, step, and jump forward, then turned right on Via dei Baullari and marched 200 yards, he'd cross the busy Corso Vittorio Emanuele; then, continuing another 150 yards on Via Cuccagna, he'd find...*

Piazza Navona

Rome's most interesting night scene features street music, artists, fire-eaters, local Casanovas, ice cream, fountains by Bernini, and outdoor cafés that are worthy of a splurge if you've got time to sit and enjoy Italy's human river.

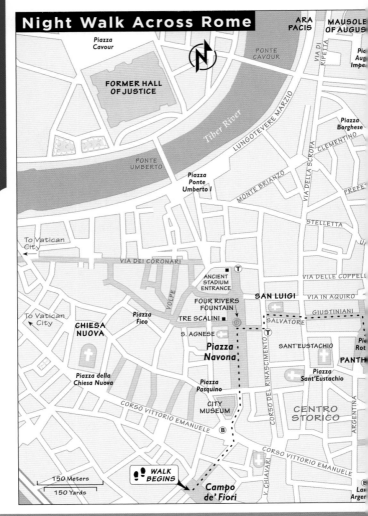

Night Walk Across Rome

ARA PACIS

MAUSOLE OF AUGUS

Piazza Cavour

FORMER HALL OF JUSTICE

PONTE CAVOUR

VIA DI RIPETTA

Pia Aug Impe

Tiber River

LUNGOTEVERE MARZIO

Piazza Borghese

VIA DELLA SCROFA

CLEMENTINO

PONTE UMBERTO

Piazza Ponte Umberto I

MONTE BRIANZO

PREFE

STELLETTA

To Vatican City

VIA DEI CORONARI

VIA DELLE COPPELL

ANCIENT STADIUM ENTRANCE

T

SAN LUIGI

VIA IN AQUIRO

FOUR RIVERS FOUNTAIN

GIUSTINIANI

To Vatican City

CHIESA NUOVA

Piazza Fico

VOLPE

TRE SCALINI

SALVATORE

T

S. AGNESE

SANT'EUSTACHIO

Pie Rot

Piazza Navona

PANTH

CORSO DEL RINASCIMENTO

Piazza della Chiesa Nuova

Piazza Pasquino

Piazza Sant'Eustachio

CENTRO STORICO

CORSO VITTORIO EMANUELE

CITY MUSEUM

B

ARGENTINA

CORSO VITTORIO EMANUELE

150 Meters

150 Yards

V. CHIAVARI

WALK BEGINS

Campo de' Fiori

E La Arger

Piazza
Popolo

CROCE

**Piazza
di Spagna** Ⓣ Ⓜ Spagna

CAROZZE

**WALK
ENDS**

**SPANISH
STEPS**

VIA SISTINA

VIA CONDOTTI

Ⓣ **Piazza
Mignanelli**

VIA BORGOGNONA

■ McD

PROPAGANDA

VIA FRATTINA

F. BORGHESE

VIA DUE MACELLI

**Piazza
S. Lorenzo**

VIA VITE

POST

V. MERCEDE

To
Barberini
Ⓜ

**Piazza del
Parlamento**

V. CONVERTITE

**Piazza
San Silvestro**

VIA DEL TRITONE

Ⓣ

PARLIAMENT

RIO

STAMPERIA

**Piazza
Monte-
citorio**

**Piazza
Colonna** Ⓣ

SABINI

Ⓣ

**TREVI
FOUNTAIN**

AQUIRO

**Piazza
Pietra**

MURATTE

PALAZZO
DEL
QUIRINALE

STINI

DATARIA

NARIO

VIA DELL'UMILTÀ

Piazza del

Quirinalle ◎

**SAN
IGNAZIO**

VIA DEL CORSO

ANT
E

**Piazza
Collegio Rom.**

MARMO

**SANTA
MARIA
SOPRA
MINERVA**

**GALLERIA
DORIA
PAMPHILJ**

BATTISTI

VIA IV NOV.

To
Termini

PLEBISCITO

Ⓑ

**Piazza
Venezia**

GESÙ

To
Capitol
Hill ↓

VIA IV
NOV.

This long, oval piazza retains the shape of the original racetrack that was built around A.D. 80 by the emperor Domitian. Since ancient times, the square has been a center of Roman life. In the 1800s, the city would flood the square to cool off the neighborhood.

The Four Rivers Fountain in the center is the most famous fountain by the man who remade Rome in Baroque style, Gian Lorenzo Bernini. Four burly river gods—from the four continents that were known in 1650—support an Egyptian obelisk. The water of the world gushes everywhere. The Nile has his head covered, since the headwaters were unknown then. The Ganges holds an oar. The Danube turns to admire the obelisk. And Uruguay's Río de la Plata tumbles backward in shock, wondering how he ever made the top four.

The Plata river god is gazing upward at the church of St. Agnes, worked on by Bernini's former student–turned-rival, Francesco Borromini. Borromini's concave facade helps reveal the dome and epitomizes the curved symmetry of Baroque. Tour guides say that Bernini designed his river god to look horrified at Borromini's work. Or maybe he's shielding his eyes from St. Agnes' nakedness, as she was stripped before being martyred. But either explanation is unlikely, since the fountain was completed two years before Borromini even started work on the church.

▶ *Leave Piazza Navona directly across from Tre Scalini (famous for its rich chocolate ice cream), and go east down Corsia Agonale, past rose peddlers and palm readers. Jog left around the guarded building (where Italy's senate meets), and follow the brown sign to the Pantheon, which is straight down Via del Salvatore.*

Piazza Navona

Bernini's Four Rivers Fountain

Four Rivers Fountain and church of St. Agnes

The Pantheon

Sit for a while under the floodlit and moonlit portico of the Pantheon.

The 40-foot single-piece granite columns of the Pantheon's entrance show the scale the ancient Romans built on. The columns support a triangular Greek-style roof with an inscription that says "M. Agrippa" built it. In fact, it was built *(fecit)* by Emperor Hadrian (A.D. 120), who gave credit to the builder of an earlier structure. This impressive entranceway gives no clue that the greatest wonder of the building is inside—a domed room that inspired later domes, including Brunelleschi's Duomo (in Florence) and Michelangelo's St. Peter's.

For more information, ✪ see the Pantheon Tour on page 55.

▶ *With your back to the Pantheon, veer to the right, uphill toward the yellow sign that reads* Casa del Caffè *at the Tazza d'Oro coffee shop on Via Orfani.*

The Pantheon—temple to all the gods

From the Pantheon to Piazza Colonna

Tazza d'Oro Casa del Caffè, one of Rome's top coffee shops, dates back to the days when this area was licensed to roast coffee beans. Locals come here for its fine *granita di caffè con panna* (coffee slush with cream).

▶ *Continue up Via Orfani to...*

Piazza Capranica is home to the big, plain Florentine Renaissance–style Palazzo Capranica (directly opposite as you enter the square). Big shots, like the Capranica family, built towers on their palaces—not for any military use, but just to show off.

▶ *Leave the piazza to the right of the palace, heading down Via in Aquiro.*

The street Via in Aquiro leads to a sixth-century B.C. **Egyptian obelisk** taken as a trophy by Augustus after his victory in Egypt over Mark Antony and Cleopatra. The obelisk was set up as a sundial. Walk the zodiac markings to the well-guarded front door. This is Italy's **parliament building**, where the lower house meets, and you may see politicians, political demonstrations, and TV cameras.

▶ *To your right is Piazza Colonna, where we're heading next—unless you like gelato...*

A one-block detour to the left (past Albergo Nazionale) brings you to Rome's most famous *gelateria*. **Giolitti's** is cheap for take-out or elegant and splurge-worthy for a sit among classy locals (open daily until past midnight, Via Uffici del Vicario 40); get your gelato in a cone *(cono)* or cup *(coppetta)*.

"Gold Cup Coffee: Best in the World"

An obelisk adorns Italy's parliament building

Piazza Colonna features a huge second-century column. Its reliefs depict the victories of Emperor Marcus Aurelius over the barbarians. When Marcus died in A.D. 180, the barbarians began to get the upper hand, beginning Rome's long three-century fall. The big, important-looking palace houses the headquarters for the deputies (or cabinet) of the prime minister.

Noisy **Via del Corso** is Rome's main north-south boulevard, running ramrod-straight for a mile through the neighborhood's tangled streets. In ancient times, visitors from northern Europe entered along this road, where they got their first glimpse of the grand city. Via del Corso is named for the rider-less horse races *(corse)* that took place here during Carnevale. In 1854, the Via became one of Rome's first gas-lit streets and hosted the classiest boutiques. Nowadays most of Via del Corso is closed to traffic for a few hours every evening and becomes a wonderful parade of Romans out for a stroll (✪ see page 155).

▶ *Cross Via del Corso to enter a big palatial building with columns, which houses the Galleria del Sordi shopping mall. Inside, take the fork to the right and exit out the back. (If you're here after 22:00, when the mall is closed, circle around the right side of the Galleria on Via dei Sabini.) Once out the back, head up Via de Crociferi, to the roar of the water, lights, and people of...*

The Trevi Fountain

The bubbly Baroque fountain is a minor sight to art scholars, but a major nighttime spot for teens on the make and tourists tossing coins.

This watery avalanche celebrates the abundance of pure water, which has been brought into the city since the days of ancient aqueducts. Oceanus rides across the waves in his chariot, pulled by horses and horn-

The Trevi Fountain

Insert coins here

blowing tritons, as he commands the flow of water. The illustrious Bernini sketched out the first designs. Nicola Salvi continued the project (c. 1740), using the palace behind the fountain as a theatrical backdrop.

The scene is always lively, with lucky Romeos clutching dates while unlucky ones clutch beers. Take some time to people-watch and whisper a few breathy *bellos* or *bellas*.

Legend says if you throw a coin in, you'll be sure to return to Rome. Confused and creative types have expanded the legend—two coins brings romance, three means marriage (no coins means divorced and paying alimony), coins must be thrown with the right hand over the left shoulder, etc. Hey, it's Rome by night and the world is yours—make your own wish.

How do you make a Roman laugh? Tell him that the coins tourists deposit daily are collected to feed Rome's poor.

▶ *From the Trevi Fountain, we're 10 minutes from our next stop, the Spanish Steps. Just use a map to get there, or follow these directions: Facing the Trevi Fountain, go forward, walking along the right side of the fountain on Via della Stamperia. Cross the busy Via del Tritone. Continue 100 yards and veer right at Via delle Fratte, a street that changes its name to Via Propaganda before ending at...*

The Spanish Steps

The wide, curving staircase is one of Rome's iconic sights. Its 138 steps lead sharply up from Piazza di Spagna, forming a butterfly shape as they fan out around a central terrace. The design culminates at the top in an obelisk framed between two Baroque church towers.

Built in the 1720s by a little-known architect (Francesco de Sanctis), the steps are called "Spanish" because of the Spanish Embassy to the Vatican located here. In springtime, the already-picturesque staircase is often colored with flowers.

At the base of the steps is the playful "Sinking Boat" *Barcaccia* Fountain (1627-29), by Pietro Bernini and/or his famous son Gian Lorenzo. The half-submerged boat brims with water, recalling the urban legend of a fishing boat—supposedly lost during a 1598 flood of the Tiber—that ended up beached on this spot.

The Spanish Steps have been the hangout of many Romantics over the years (Keats, Wagner, Openshaw, Goethe, and others). The British poet John Keats pondered his mortality, then died of tuberculosis (1821) at age 25 in the pink building on the right side of the steps. Fellow Romantic Lord Byron lived across the square at #66.

It's clear that the main sight here is not the steps but the people who gather around them. By day, shoppers swarm the high-fashion boutiques at the base of the steps, along Via Condotti. On warm evenings, the area is alive with young people in love with the city.

► *Our walk is finished. The Spagna Metro stop (usually open until 22:00) is to the left of the steps. Just outside the Metro is a free elevator to the top of the steps (closes at 21:00). A huge McDonald's (with a WC) is a block to the right of the steps. When you're ready to leave, zip home on the Metro or grab a taxi at either end of the piazza.*

The Spanish Steps

Pantheon Tour

The Roman Temple

If your imagination is fried from trying to reconstruct ancient buildings out of today's rubble, visit the Pantheon, Rome's best-preserved monument. Engineers still admire how the Romans built such a mathematically precise structure without computers, fossil-fuel–run machinery, or electricity. (Having unlimited slave power didn't hurt.)

We'll examine the classic exterior, step inside past 40-foot columns, and see several important tombs. Most of all, we'll stand beneath the Pantheon's solemn dome to gain a new appreciation for the sophistication of these ancient people.

ORIENTATION

Cost and Hours: Free, Mon–Sat 8:30–19:30, Sun 9:00–18:00, holidays 9:00–13:00, closed for Mass Sat at 17:00 and Sun at 10:30.

Information: Tel. 06-6830-0230.

Audioguides: €5 for a 25-minute tour. My free Pantheon audio tour is available from iTunes, Google Play, or at www.ricksteves.com.

Getting There: The Pantheon is a few blocks north of a major transportation hub, the chaotic square called Largo Argentina. Taxis and buses #64 and #40 stop here. The most dramatic approach is on foot coming from Piazza Navona along Via Giustiniani—✪ see page 45 in the Night Walk Across Rome chapter.

Length of This Tour: Allow a half-hour.

Photography: It's allowed—even with flash.

WCs: The nearest WCs are at bars and downstairs in the McDonald's on the Pantheon's square.

Cuisine Art: Restaurants and gelaterias abound. For recommendations, ✪ see page 188. Two of Rome's most venerable coffee shops are just steps away. Tazza d'Oro Casa del Caffè, at Via degli Orfani 84, serves an icy *granita di caffè* that's heaven on a hot day. Tiny Bar Sant'Eustachio is nearly always jammed with regulars and coffee pilgrims, at Piazza di Sant'Eustachio 82.

The Pantheon exterior...

...and view from the interior

THE TOUR BEGINS

▶ *Start the tour at the top of the square called Piazza della Rotunda, with cafés and restaurants around the edges and an obelisk-topped fountain in the center.*

The Pantheon's Exterior

The Pantheon was a Roman temple dedicated to all *(pan)* of the gods *(theos)*. The original temple was built in 27 B.C. by Augustus' son-in-law, Marcus Agrippa. In fact, the inscription below the triangular **pediment** proclaims in Latin, "Marcus Agrippa, son of Lucio, three times consul made this." But after a couple of fires, the structure we see today was completely rebuilt by the emperor Hadrian around A.D. 120. Some say that Hadrian, an amateur architect (and voracious traveler), helped design it.

The Pantheon looks like a pretty typical temple from the outside, but

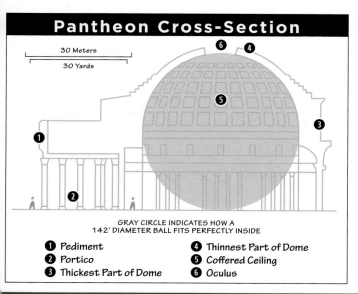

Pantheon Cross-Section

30 Meters

30 Yards

GRAY CIRCLE INDICATES HOW A
142' DIAMETER BALL FITS PERFECTLY INSIDE

1 Pediment
2 Portico
3 Thickest Part of Dome
4 Thinnest Part of Dome
5 Coffered Ceiling
6 Oculus

this is perhaps the most influential building in art history. Its dome was the model for the Florence cathedral dome, which launched the Renaissance, and for Michelangelo's dome of St. Peter's, which capped it all off. Even Washington, D.C.'s capitol building was inspired by this dome.

The 40-foot-high columns of the **portico** (entrance porch) are made from single pieces of red-gray granite (not the standard stacks of cylindrical pieces). They were taken from an Egyptian temple. The holes in the triangular pediment once held a huge bronze Roman eagle. Back up or step to one side to look above the pediment to the building itself. You'll see a roofline that was abandoned mid-construction. The pediment was originally intended to be higher, but when the support columns arrived, they were shorter than expected. Even the most enlightened can forget to "measure twice, cut once."

▶ *Pass through the portico, with its forest of enormous columns. Look up at the porch roof, and imagine the ceiling covered in its original bronze plating. It was removed in the 17th century by a scavenging pope from the Barberini family, inspiring the well-known quip, "What the barbarians didn't do, the Barberini did." Melted down, some of the bronze was used to build the huge bronze canopy over the altar at St. Peter's Basilica. Now pass through the giant **bronze door**—a copy of the original. Take a seat and take it all in.*

Interior

The dome, which was the largest made until the Renaissance, is set on a circular base. The mathematical perfection of this dome-on-a-base design is a testament to Roman engineering. The dome is as high as it is wide—142 feet from floor to rooftop and from side to side. To picture it, imagine a basketball set inside a wastebasket so that it just touches bottom.

The dome—recently cleaned and feeling loftier than ever—is made from concrete (a Roman invention) that gets lighter and thinner as it reaches the top. The base of the dome is 23 feet thick and made from heavy concrete mixed with travertine, while near the top, it's less than five feet thick and made with a lighter volcanic rock (pumice) mixed in. Note the square indentations in the surface of the dome. This **coffered ceiling** reduces the weight of the dome without compromising strength. The walls are strengthened by blind arches built into the wall (visible outside).

Both Brunelleschi and Michelangelo studied this dome before

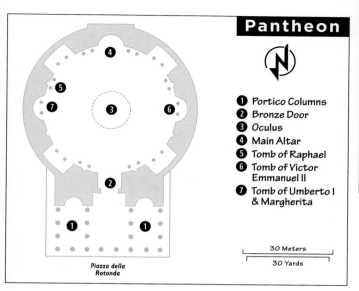

Pantheon

1. Portico Columns
2. Bronze Door
3. Oculus
4. Main Altar
5. Tomb of Raphael
6. Tomb of Victor Emmanuel II
7. Tomb of Umberto I & Margherita

30 Meters

30 Yards

Piazza della Rotonda

building their own (in Florence and the Vatican, respectively). Remember, St. Peter's Basilica is really only the dome of the Pantheon atop the Forum's Basilica of Constantine.

At the top, the **oculus**, or eye-in-the-sky, is the building's only light source and is almost 30 feet across. The 1,800-year-old floor has holes in it and slants toward the edges to let the rainwater drain. Though some of the floor's marble has been replaced over the years, the design—alternating circles and squares—is original.

In ancient times, this was a one-stop-shopping temple where you could worship any of the gods whose statues decorated the niches. Entering the temple, Romans came face-to-face with a larger-than-life statue of Jupiter, the King of the Gods, where the **altar** stands today. Early in the Middle Ages, the Pantheon became a Christian church (from "all the gods" to "all the martyrs"), which saved it from architectural cannibalism and ensured its upkeep through the Dark Ages. The year 2009 marked the building's 1,400th anniversary as a church. In the seventh century, a

The Pantheon interior

Byzantine emperor stripped the dome's interior of its original golden-tile ceiling. The twin, grilled windows just right of the altar (at 2 o'clock) are original and, along with the inlaid marble floor, give you a sense of the ancient decor.

Tombs

The only new things in the interior are the decorative statues and the tombs of famous people. The artist Raphael lies to the left of the main altar, in a lighted glass niche. Above him is a statue of the Madonna and Child that Raphael himself commissioned for his tomb. The Latin inscription on his tomb reads, "In life, Nature feared to be outdone by him. In death, she feared she too would die."

You'll also see the tombs of modern Italy's first two kings. To the right

The Italian Royal Family...in Switzerland

From Italy's unification in 1870 to the end of World War II, the country had four kings, all members of the Savoy family. One of Europe's oldest royal families (from the 10th century), the Savoia had long ruled the kingdom of Piedmont in northern Italy. When they were chosen to preside over the whole country in 1870, they brought prestige and stability to Italy's fledgling democracy.

However, the once-popular Savoia lost favor in the 1920s when they got too cozy with Italy's fascists. It was the Savoy king who invited dictator Benito Mussolini to form a government, and then signed off on Mussolini's anti-Semitic laws. And in 1943, instead of standing by his people, the king abandoned Rome to the Germans and fled. After the War, the Italians voted for a republic and sent the Savoia into exile.

The former ruling family is still controversial. Recently, the Savoia heir said that the racist laws signed by his grandfather weren't really all that bad. And while the family lives in stunning wealth in Switzerland, they insist that Italy owes them €260 million for damages incurred as a result of their exile.

Until 2002, a law proclaimed that no male Savoia could set foot on Italian soil. That's why only the first two kings are buried in the Pantheon. The last two died in exile, where they remain.

is Victor Emmanuel II (*"Padre della Patria,"* father of the fatherland). As king of the region of Piedmont, Victor Emmanuel II became a rallying point for Italians as they threw out foreign rulers and unified the country. In 1870, they chose him (and his distinguished family, the Savoy) to head the first government.

To the left (as you face the altar) is Umberto I (son of the father). These tombs are a hit with royalists. In fact, there is often a guard standing by a guestbook, where visitors can register their support for these two kings'

The dome and oculus

now-controversial family, the Savoys. And finally, under Umberto, lies his queen, who's most famous for the dish named in her honor (in 1889)—the classic combination of mozzarella, tomato sauce, and basil, called Pizza "Margherita."

The Pantheon is the only ancient building in Rome continuously used since its construction. When you leave, notice that the building is sunken below current street level, showing how the rest of the city has risen on 20 centuries of rubble.

The Pantheon also contains the world's greatest Roman column. There it is, spanning the entire 142 feet from heaven to earth—the pillar of light from the oculus.

Vatican Museum Tour

Musei Vaticani

The glories of the ancient world are on display in this lavish papal palace. Start with ancient Egyptian mummies and some of the best Greek and Roman statues in captivity. Then traverse long halls lined with old maps, tapestries, fig leaves, and broken penises. Pass through the popes' former home, where the painter Raphael boldly celebrated pagan philosophers in the heart of Christendom. Our visit culminates with Michelangelo's glorious Sistine Chapel, whose centerpiece shows God reaching out to pass the divine spark of life to man.

It's inspiring...and exhausting. But with this chapter as your guide, you'll easily sweep through 5,000 years of human history.

ORIENTATION

Cost: €16 plus optional €4 reservation fee. Free on the last Sun of each month (when it's very crowded).

Hours: Mon–Sat 9:00–18:00, last entry at 16:00. Closed Sun, except last Sun of the month 9:00–14:00, last entry at 12:30. May be open Fri nights May-July and Sept-Oct 19:00–23:00 (last entry at 21:30) by online reservation only—check the website. Those with reservations can enter as early as 8:00, before the ticket-buying crowds. The Sistine Chapel closes 1.5 hours before the museum does, and guards start ushering people out of the museum 30 minutes before the official closing time. The museum is closed about a dozen days a year for religious holidays. Check the calendar and the latest hours for your exact visit at http://www.vatican.va.

When to Go: The museum is generally hot and crowded, with waits of up to two hours to buy tickets and shoulder-to-shoulder crowds in the most popular rooms. The worst times are Saturdays, free Sundays, Mondays, rainy days, any day before or after a holiday closure, and mornings in general.

Avoiding Lines: You can reserve an entry time and buy a ticket online at http://mv.vatican.va (pay with credit card). You choose your day and time and they email you a confirmation voucher immediately. At the Vatican Museum entrance, bypass the ticket-buying line and enter at the "Entrance with Reservations" (to the right). Once inside the museum, go to a ticket window, present your voucher (and ID), and they'll issue your ticket. You can also skip the ticket-buying line by buying a ticket from the TI or the "Roma Cristiana" office in St. Peter's Square or by booking a guided tour (see below). If you don't have a reservation, try arriving after 14:00.

Dress Code: Modest dress is required (no short shorts or bare shoulders).

Getting There: Taxis take you right to the entrance—hop in and say, "moo-ZAY-ee vah-tee-KAH-nee." Metro stops Cipro and Ottaviano are both a 10-minute walk from the entrance (see map on page 97). Bus #64 stops on the other side of St. Peter's Square, a 15-minute walk away. On foot from St. Peter's Square, face the church, take a right through the colonnade, and follow the Vatican Wall.

Information: Tel. 06-6988-3860 or 06-6988-1662; http://mv.vatican.va.

Tours: English tours are easy to book online (€31, includes admission, http://mv.vatican.va) and allow you to skip the ticket line.

Audioguides: €7 plus ID. My free audio tour of the Sistine Chapel (but not of the entire museum) is available from iTunes, Google Play, or at www.ricksteves.com.

Length of This Tour: Until you expire, the museum closes, or 2.5 hours, whichever comes first.

Security and Baggage Check: To enter the museum, you pass through a metal detector (no pocket knives allowed). The baggage check (upstairs from the lobby) takes only big bags; you'll need to carry your day bag with you.

Museum Strategies: If you're planning on visiting St. Peter's Basilica right after the Vatican Museum, there's a shortcut that leads directly from the Sistine Chapel to St. Peter's Basilica (spilling out alongside the church; ✪ see map on page 100). This route saves you a 30-minute walk—15 minutes back to the Vatican Museum entry/exit, then 15 minutes to St. Peter's. It also lets you avoid the often-long security line at the basilica's main entrance. To take this shortcut, you'll need to: adhere to St. Peter's stricter dress code, forgo a Vatican Museum audioguide (which must be returned), tour the Pinacoteca before the Sistine, and be prepared for the odd chance that the shortcut is simply closed (which sometimes happens). To see the Sistine Chapel with fewer crowds, visit at the end of the day (but remember, the chapel closes 1.5 hours before the rest of the museum).

Photography: No photos are allowed in the Sistine Chapel. Elsewhere in the museum, photos without a flash are permitted.

Cuisine Art: A self-service cafeteria is inside, near the Pinacoteca, and a smaller café is near the Sistine Chapel. Outside the museum, there's cheap pizza by the slice along Viale Giulio Cesare. Picnickers can browse the colorful Via Andrea Doria produce market three blocks north of the entrance along Via Tunisi (head across the street, down the stairs, and continue straight). For restaurant recommendations, ✪ see page 190.

Starring: World history, from Egyptian mummies to Greek and Roman statues to the Renaissance masters Raphael and Michelangelo.

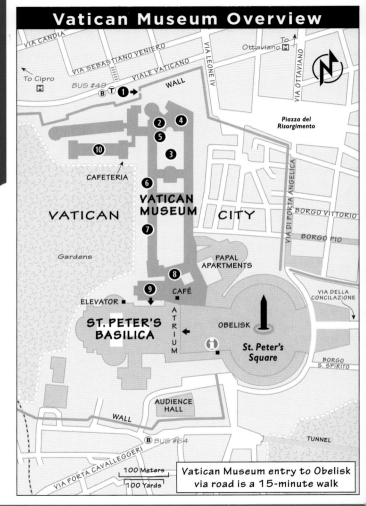

Vatican Museum Overview

Vatican Museum entry to Obelisk via road is a 15-minute walk

THE TOUR BEGINS

This heavyweight museum is shaped like a barbell—two buildings connected by a long hall. The entrance building covers the ancient world (Egypt, Greece, Rome). The one at the far end covers its "rebirth" in the Renaissance (including the Sistine Chapel). The halls there and back are a mix of old and new. Move quickly—don't burn out before the Sistine Chapel at the end— and see how each civilization borrows from and builds on the previous one.

▶ *Leave Italy by entering the doors.*

Once you clear the security checkpoint, exchange your printed voucher for a ticket (on the ground floor) or buy your ticket (upstairs). Punch the ticket in the turnstiles, then take the long escalator or spiral stairs up, up, up to a covered courtyard with a view of the St. Peter's dome. Pause at the courtyard: To your right is the cafeteria and the Pinacoteca painting gallery.

To start our tour, go left, then take another left up a flight of stairs to reach the first-floor Egyptian Rooms (Museo Egizio) on your right. Don't stop until you find your mummy.

Note: If the stairs up to Egypt are temporarily closed off, just keep following the masses through the spacious Cortile della Pigna courtyard until you reach the *Apollo Belvedere* and *Laocoön* figures. Tour the museum from there to the "Sarcophagi," where you'll find the entrance to the Egyptian rooms.

❶ Main Entrance & Exit
❷ Egyptian Rooms
❸ Cortile della Pigna
❹ Octagonal Courtyard
❺ Etruscan Wing
❻ Tapestries
❼ Map Gallery & View of Vatican City
❽ Raphael Rooms
❾ Sistine Chapel & Exit to St. Peter's
❿ Pinacoteca

EGYPT (3000–1000 B.C.)

Egyptian art was for religion, not decoration. A statue or painting preserved the likeness of someone, giving him a form of eternal life. Most of the art was for tombs, where they put the mummies.

▶ *Pass beyond the imitation Egyptian pillars to the left of the case in the center of the room, and you'll find...*

Mummies

This woman died three millennia ago. Her corpse was disemboweled, and her organs were placed in a jar like those you see nearby. Then the body was refilled with pitch, dried with natron (a natural sodium carbonate), wrapped in linen, and placed in a wood coffin, which went inside a stone coffin, which was placed in a tomb. (Remember that the pyramids were just big tombs.) Notice the henna job on her hair—in the next life, your spirit needed a body to be rooted to...and you wanted to look your best.

Painted inside the coffin lid is a list of what the deceased "packed" for the journey to eternity. The coffins were decorated with magical spells to protect the body from evil and to act as crib notes for the confused soul in the netherworld.

▶ *In the next room are...*

Egyptian Statues

Egyptian statues walk awkwardly, as if they're carrying heavy buckets, with arms straight down at their sides. Even these Roman reproductions (made for Hadrian's Villa) are stiff, two-dimensional, and schematic—the art is only realistic enough to get the job done. In Egyptian belief, a statue like

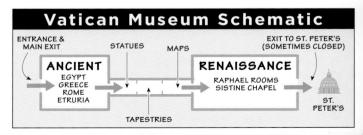

Anubis—a jackal in a toga

Sumerian writing on clay tablets

this could be a stable refuge for the wandering soul of a dead man. Each was made according to an established set of proportions.

 ▶ *Walk through the next small room and into the curved hallway, and look for...*

Various Egyptian Gods as Animals

Before technology made humans top dogs on earth, Egyptians saw the superiority of animals and worshipped them as incarnations of the gods. Wander through a pet store of Egyptian animal gods. Find Anubis, a jackal in a toga. In the curved room, find the lioness, the fierce goddess Sekhmet. The clever baboon is the god of wisdom, Thot. At the end of the curved hall on your right is Bes (the small white marble statue), the patron of pregnant women (and beer-bellied men).

▶ *Continue to Room VIII (the third room), pausing at the glass case, which contains brown clay tablets.*

Sumerian Writing

Even before Egypt, civilizations flourished in the Middle East. The Sumerian culture in Mesopotamia (the ancestors of the ancient Babylonians and of Saddam Hussein) invented writing in about 3000 B.C. People wrote on clay tablets by pressing into the wet clay with a wedge-shaped (cuneiform) pen. The Sumerians also rolled cylinder seals into soft clay to make an impression used to seal documents and mark property.

▶ *Pass through the next room, and then turn left, to a balcony with a view of Rome through the window. Then enter the octagonal courtyard.*

SCULPTURE—GREECE AND ROME (500 B.C.–A.D. 500)

This palace wouldn't be here, this sculpture wouldn't be here, and our lives would likely be quite different if it weren't for a few thousand Greeks in a small city about 450 years before Christ. Athens set the tone for the rest of the West. Democracy, theater, economics, literature, and art all flourished in Athens during a 50-year "Golden Age." Greek culture was then appropriated by Rome, and revived again 1,500 years later, during the Renaissance. The Renaissance popes built and decorated these papal palaces, re-creating the glory of the classical world.

Apollo Belvedere

Apollo, the god of the sun and of music, is hunting. He's been running through the woods, and now he spots his prey. Keeping his eye on the animal, he slows down and prepares to put a (missing) arrow into his (missing) bow. The optimistic Greeks conceived of their gods in human form... and buck naked.

The Greek sculptor Leochares, following the style of the greater Greek sculptor Praxiteles, has fully captured the beauty of the human form. The anatomy is perfect, his pose is natural. Instead of standing at attention, face-forward with his arms at his sides (Egyptian-style), Apollo is on the move, coming to rest, with his weight on one leg.

The Greeks loved balance. A well-rounded man was both a thinker and an athlete, a poet and a warrior. In art, the *Apollo Belvedere* balances several opposites. He's moving, but not out of control. Apollo eyes his target, but

Apollo Belvedere—a god in human form

"Snakes! Why did it have to be snakes?"

The Ancient World

↖ BALCONY
WITH VIEW
OF ROME

To
"New Wing" →

WC

OCTAGONAL
COURTYARD

ROMAN
PINE
CONE

Cortile
della
Pigna
(Grass)

HALL OF ANIMALS

ANIMALS

❶ MUMMIES
START

❷

❸

EGYPTIAN
ROOMS

❺

❻

❼

❽

❾

❿

END

UP

To "The
Long March" →

FROM
ENTRANCE

ROUND
ROOM

To
Cafeteria
& Pinacoteca ↓

❶ Mummies
❷ Egyptian Statues
❸ Gods as Animals
❹ Sumerian Writing
❺ Apollo Belvedere

❻ Laocoön
❼ Belvedere Torso
❽ Hercules
❾ Porphyry Basin
❿ Sarcophagi

hasn't attacked yet. He's realistic, but with idealized, godlike features. The only sour note: his left hand, added in modern times. Could we try a size smaller?

▶ *In the neighboring niche to the right, a bearded old Roman river god lounges in the shade. This pose inspired Michelangelo's* Adam, *in the Sistine Chapel (coming soon).*

Laocoön

Laocoön (lay-AWK-oh-wahn), the high priest of Troy, warned his fellow Trojans: "Beware of Greeks bearing gifts." The attacking Greeks had brought the Trojan Horse to the gates as a ploy to get inside the city walls, and Laocoön tried to warn his people not to bring it inside. But the gods wanted the Greeks to win, so they sent huge snakes to crush Laocoön and his two sons to death. We see them at the height of their terror, when they realize that, no matter how hard they struggle, they—and their entire race—are doomed.

The figures (carved from four blocks of marble pieced together seamlessly) are powerful, not light and graceful. The poses are as twisted as possible, accentuating every rippling muscle and bulging vein. Follow the line of motion from Laocoön's left foot, up his leg, through his body, and out his right arm (which some historians used to think extended straight out—until the elbow was dug up early in the 1900s). Goethe would stand here and blink his eyes rapidly, watching the statue flicker to life.

Laocoön was sculpted four centuries after the Golden Age, after the scales of "balance" had been tipped. Whereas *Apollo* is poised, graceful, and godlike, Laocoön is restless, emotional, and gritty.

Laocoön—the most famous Greek statue in ancient Rome—was lost for more than a thousand years. Then, in 1506, it was unexpectedly unearthed near the Colosseum. They cleaned it off and paraded it through the streets before an awestruck populace. Young Michelangelo saw the statue; its unbridled motion influenced his work in the Sistine Chapel, which itself influenced generations of artists.

▶ *Leave the courtyard to the right of* Laocoön *and swing around the Hall of Animals, a jungle of beasts real and surreal. Then continue to the limbless torso in the middle of the next large hall.*

Belvedere Torso—ugly beauty

Hercules—Roman grandeur

Belvedere Torso

This rough hunk of shaped rock makes you appreciate the sheer physical labor involved in chipping a figure out of solid stone. It takes great strength, but at the same time, great delicacy.

This is all that remains of an ancient statue of Hercules seated on a lion skin. Michelangelo loved this old rock. As the best sculptor of his day, his only peers were the ancients. He'd caress this statue lovingly and say, "I am the pupil of the Torso." To him, it contained all the beauty of classical sculpture, though compared with the pure grace of the *Apollo,* it's downright ugly.

Michelangelo, an ugly man himself, wasn't looking for the beauty of idealized gods, but the innate beauty of every person, even so-called ugly ones. With its knotty lumps of muscle, the Torso has a brute power and a distinct personality despite—or because of—its rough edges.

▶ *Enter the next, domed room.*

Round Room

This room, modeled on the Pantheon interior, gives some idea of Roman grandeur. Romans took Greek ideas and made them bigger, like the big bronze statue of Hercules with his club. The mosaic floor once decorated the bottom of a pool in an ancient Roman bath. The enormous Roman basin/hot tub/birdbath/vase, which once decorated Nero's palace, is made of a single block of purple porphyry marble stone imported from Egypt. Purple was the color of emperors, and—since porphyry doesn't occur naturally in Italy—it was also rare and expensive.

▶ *Enter the next room.*

Sarcophagus of porphyry

Minerva

Sarcophagi

These two large porphyry marble coffins were made (though not used) for the Roman emperor Constantine's mother and daughter. They were Christians—and therefore outlaws—until Constantine made Christianity legal in A.D. 312, and they became saints.

▶ *See how we've come full circle in this building—the Egyptian Rooms are ahead on your left. Go upstairs and prepare for the Long March down the hall lined with statues (the Gallery of the Candelabra) leading to the Sistine Chapel and Raphael Rooms.*

THE LONG MARCH— SCULPTURE, TAPESTRIES, MAPS, AND VIEWS

This quarter-mile walk gives you a sense of the grandeur of the former papal palaces, once decorated with statues, urns, marble floors, friezes, tapestries, and stuccoed ceilings. As heirs of imperial Rome, the popes of the Renaissance felt they deserved such luxury. It was their extravagant spending on palaces like this that inspired Martin Luther to rebel, starting the Protestant Reformation.

Gallery of the Candelabra: Classical Sculpture

In the second "room" of the long hall, stop at the statue (on the left) of

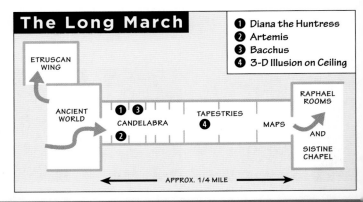

The Long March
1 Diana the Huntress
2 Artemis
3 Bacchus
4 3-D Illusion on Ceiling

ETRUSCAN WING

ANCIENT WORLD

CANDELABRA

TAPESTRIES

MAPS

RAPHAEL ROOMS

AND

SISTINE CHAPEL

APPROX. 1/4 MILE

Fig leaf

Tapestry that "moves" as you pass

Diana, the virgin goddess of the hunt. Roman hunters would pray and give offerings to statues like this to get divine help in their search for food.

Farmers might pray to another version of the same goddess, Artemis, on the opposite wall. "Boobs or bulls' balls?" Some historians say this billion-breasted beauty stood for fertility. Others contend that bulls were sacrificed and castrated, with the testicles draped over the statues as symbols of fertility.

▶ *Shuffle along to the next "room." On the left is Bacchus, with a baby on his shoulders.*

Fig Leaves

Why do the statues have fig leaves? Like Bacchus, many of these statues originally looked much different than they do now. Most were painted, often in gaudy colors. Bacchus may have had brown hair, rosy cheeks, purple grapes, and a leopard-skin sidekick at his feet. Also, many statues had glass eyes like Bacchus.

And the fig leaves? Those came from the years 1550 to 1800, when the Church decided that certain parts of the human anatomy were obscene. (Why not the feet?) Perhaps Church leaders associated these full-frontal statues with the outbreak of Renaissance humanism that reduced their power in Europe. Whatever the cause, they reacted by covering classical crotches with plaster fig leaves, the same leaves Adam and Eve had used when the concept of "privates" was invented.

▶ *Cover your eyes in case they forgot a fig leaf or two, and continue to the tapestries.*

Tapestries

Along the left wall are tapestries designed by Raphael's workshop and made in Brussels. They show scenes from the life of Christ: baby Jesus in the manger, being adored by shepherds, and presented in the temple. *The Supper at Emmaus* tapestry (with Jesus sitting at a table) is curiously interactive. As you walk, the end of the table seems to follow you.

On the ceiling, admire the workmanship of the sculpted reliefs, then realize that it's not a relief at all—it's painted on a flat surface.

Map Gallery and View of Vatican City

This gallery—crusted with a ceiling of colorful stucco and lined with colorful maps—still feels like a pope's palace. The maps (16th-century) let popes take visitors on a virtual tour of Italy's regions, from the toe (entrance end) to the Alps (far end). The scenes on the ceiling portray exciting moments in Church history in each of those regions.

Glance out the windows at the tiny country of Vatican City, formed in 1929. It has its own radio station, as you see from the tower on the hill. What you see here is pretty much all there is—these gardens, the palaces you're in, and St. Peter's (lean out and look left for a good view of Michelangelo's dome).

At the room's far end, you'll find a map of a city you'll surely recognize—Venice.

▶ *Exit the map room and take a breather. When you're ready, rejoin the flow and turn left, on the route leading to the Raphael Rooms.*

The Map Gallery—papal luxury

Sobieski liberating Vienna

RENAISSANCE ART

Raphael Rooms: Papal Wallpaper

We've seen art from the ancient world; now we'll see its rebirth in the Renaissance. We're entering the living quarters of the great Renaissance popes—where they slept, worked, and worshipped. They hired the best artists—mostly from Florence—to paint the walls and ceilings, combining classical and Christian motifs.

Entering, you'll immediately see a huge (non-Raphael) painting that depicts the Polish King Jan III Sobieski liberating Vienna from the Ottomans in 1683, finally tipping the tide in favor of a Christian Europe.

The second room's (non-Raphael) paintings celebrate the doctrine of the Immaculate Conception, establishing that Mary herself was conceived free from original sin. The largest fresco shows how the inspiration came straight from heaven (upper left) in a thin ray of light directly to the pope.

► *Next, you'll pass along an outside walkway that overlooks a courtyard (is that the pope's Fiat?), finally ending up in the first of the Raphael Rooms, the...*

Constantine Room

The frescoes (which were finished by Raphael's assistants, notably Giulio Romano) celebrate the passing of the baton from pagan Rome to Christian Rome. On the night of October 27, A.D. 312 (left wall), as General Constantine (in gold, with crown) was preparing his troops for a coup d'état, he looked up. He saw a cross in the sky with the words, "You will conquer in this sign."

The next day (long wall), his troops raged into battle with the Christian cross atop their Roman eagle banners. There's Constantine in the center with a smile on his face, slashing through the enemy, while God's warrior angels ride shotgun overhead.

Victorious, Constantine stripped (right wall) and knelt before the pope to be baptized a Christian (some say). As emperor, he legalized Christianity and worked hand in hand with the pope (window wall). When Rome fell, its glory lived on through the Dark Ages in the pomp, pageantry, and learning of the Catholic Church.

Look at the ceiling painting. A classical statue is knocked backward, crumbling before the overpowering force of the cross. Whoa! Christianity triumphs over pagan Rome. (This was painted, I believe, by Raphael's surrealist colleague, Salvadorus Dalio.)

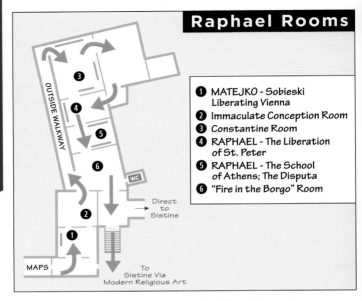

Raphael Rooms

1. MATEJKO - Sobieski Liberating Vienna
2. Immaculate Conception Room
3. Constantine Room
4. RAPHAEL - The Liberation of St. Peter
5. RAPHAEL - The School of Athens; The Disputa
6. "Fire in the Borgo" Room

OUTSIDE WALKWAY

WC

Direct to Sistine

MAPS

To Sistine Via Modern Religious Art

▶ *While viewing these frescoes, ponder the life and times of...*

Raphael

Raphael was only 25 when Pope Julius II—the same man who hired Michelangelo to paint the Sistine Ceiling—invited him to paint the walls of his personal living quarters.

Raphael lived a charmed life. He was handsome and sophisticated, and painted masterpieces effortlessly. In a different decade, he might have been thrown out of the Church as a great sinner, but his love affairs and devil-may-care personality seemed to epitomize the optimistic pagan spirit of the Renaissance. His works are graceful but never lightweight or frilly—they're realistic, balanced, and harmonious. When he died young in 1520, the High Renaissance died with him.

▶ *Continue on. In a room or two (depending on the current route), you'll reach a room with frescoes arching over the windows. Block the sunlight with your hand to see...*

The Liberation of St. Peter

Peter, Jesus' right-hand man, was thrown into prison in Jerusalem for his beliefs. In the middle of the night, an angel appeared and rescued him from the sleeping guards (Acts 12). The chains miraculously fell away (and were later brought to the St. Peter-in-Chains Church in Rome), and the angel led him to safety (right), while the guards took hell from their captain (left). This little "play" is neatly divided into three separate acts that make a balanced composition.

▶ *Enter the next room. Here in the pope's private study, Raphael painted...*

The School of Athens

In both style and subject matter, this fresco sums up the spirit of the Renaissance—the rebirth of classical art, literature, and science, and the optimistic spirit that man is a rational creature. Raphael pays respect to the great thinkers of ancient Greece, gathering them together at one time in a mythical school setting.

In the center are Plato and Aristotle, the two greatest Greeks. Plato points up, indicating his philosophy that mathematics and pure ideas are the source of truth, while Aristotle points down, showing preference for hands-on study of the material world. There's their master, Socrates (midway to the left, in green), ticking off arguments on his fingers. And in the foreground at right, bald Euclid bends over a slate to demonstrate a geometrical formula.

Raphael shows that Renaissance thinkers were as good as the ancients. There's Leonardo da Vinci, whom Raphael worshipped, in the role of Plato. Euclid is the architect Donato Bramante, who designed St. Peter's. Raphael himself (next to last on the far right, with the black beret) looks out

The School of Athens, by Raphael

Raphael's colleague, Michelangelo

at us. And the "school" building is actually an early version of Bramante's St. Peter's Basilica, under construction at the time.

Raphael balances everything symmetrically—thinkers to the left, scientists to the right, with Plato and Aristotle dead center—showing the geometrical order found in the world. Look at the square floor tiles in the foreground. If you laid a ruler over them and extended the line upward, it would run right to the center of the picture. Similarly, the tops of the columns all point down to the middle. All the lines of sight draw our attention to Plato and Aristotle, and to the small arch over their heads—a halo over these two secular saints in the divine pursuit of knowledge.

When Raphael was putting the finishing touches on this room, Michelangelo was at work down the hall in the Sistine Chapel. Raphael got a peek at Michelangelo's powerful work, and was astonished. He returned to *The School of Athens* and added one more figure to the scene—Michelangelo, the brooding, melancholy figure in front, leaning on a block of marble.

▶ *On the opposite wall is...*

The Disputa

As if to show how pre-Christian and Church philosophies could coexist, Raphael painted this "School of Heaven" facing the *School of Athens.* Christ and the saints are overseeing a discussion of the Eucharist by deep-thinking Christians below.

Raphael connects heaven and earth with descending circles: Jesus in a halo; down to the dove of the Holy Spirit in a circle; which enters the communion wafer in its holder. Balance and symmetry reign, from the angel trios in the upper corners to the books littering the floor.

Moving along, the last Raphael Room (called the "Fire in the Borgo" Room) shows work done mostly by Raphael's students, who were influenced by the bulging muscles and bodybuilder poses of Michelangelo.

▶ *Pause here and plan. (WCs are nearby, but sometimes closed.) Leaving this final Raphael Room, you can turn left to go directly to the Sistine. Or...*

Bearing right (a five-minute walk and a few staircases longer) gets you to the Sistine by way of the impressive Modern Religious Art collection. Though longer, this route leads to quiet rooms at the foot of the stairs, with benches where you can sit in peace and read ahead before entering the hectic Sistine Chapel. Your call.

THE SISTINE CHAPEL

The Sistine Chapel contains Michelangelo's ceiling and his huge *The Last Judgment*. The Sistine is the personal chapel of the pope and the place where new popes are elected.

When Pope Julius II asked Michelangelo to take on this important project, he said, "No, *grazie.*" Michelangelo insisted he was a sculptor, not a painter. The Sistine ceiling was a vast undertaking, and he didn't want to do a half-vast job. But the pope pleaded, bribed, and threatened until Michelangelo finally consented, on the condition that he be able to do it all his own way.

Julius had asked for only 12 apostles along the sides of the ceiling, but Michelangelo had a grander vision—the entire history of the world until Jesus. He spent the next four years (1508–1512) craning his neck on scaffolding six stories up, covering the ceiling with frescoes of biblical scenes.

In sheer physical terms, it's an astonishing achievement: 5,900 square feet, with the vast majority done by his own hand. (Raphael only designed most of his rooms, letting assistants do the grunt work.)

First, he had to design and erect the scaffolding. Any materials had to be hauled up on pulleys. Then, a section of ceiling would be plastered. With fresco—painting on wet plaster—if you don't get it right the first time, you have to scrape the whole thing off and start over. And if you've ever struggled with a ceiling light fixture or worked underneath a car for even five minutes, you know how heavy your arms get. The physical effort, the

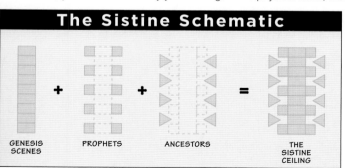

The Sistine Schematic

GENESIS SCENES   +   PROPHETS   +   ANCESTORS   =   THE SISTINE CEILING

The Sistine Ceiling

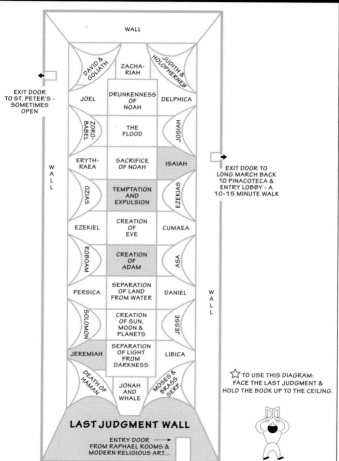

WALL

DAVID & GOLIATH

ZACHA-RIAH

JUDITH & HOLOPHERNES

EXIT DOOR TO ST. PETER'S - SOMETIMES OPEN

JOEL

DRUNKENNESS OF NOAH

DELPHICA

WALL

ZORO-BABEL

THE FLOOD

JOSIAH

ERYTH-RAEA

SACRIFICE OF NOAH

ISAIAH

EXIT DOOR TO LONG MARCH BACK TO PINACOTECA & ENTRY LOBBY - A 10-15 MINUTE WALK

OZIAS

TEMPTATION AND EXPULSION

EZEKIAS

EZEKIEL

CREATION OF EVE

CUMAEA

ROBOAM

CREATION OF ADAM

ASA

PERSICA

SEPARATION OF LAND FROM WATER

DANIEL

WALL

SOLOMON

CREATION OF SUN, MOON & PLANETS

JESSE

JEREMIAH

SEPARATION OF LIGHT FROM DARKNESS

LIBICA

DEATH OF HAMAN

JONAH AND WHALE

MOSES & BRASS SERP.

☆ TO USE THIS DIAGRAM: FACE THE LAST JUDGMENT & HOLD THE BOOK UP TO THE CEILING.

LAST JUDGMENT WALL

ENTRY DOOR → FROM RAPHAEL ROOMS & MODERN RELIGIOUS ART...

paint dripping in his eyes, the creative drain, and the mental stress from a pushy pope combined to almost kill Michelangelo.

But when the ceiling was finished and revealed to the public, it simply blew 'em away. Like the *Laocoön* statue discovered six years earlier, it was unlike anything seen before. It both caps the Renaissance and turns it in a new direction. In perfect Renaissance spirit, it mixes Old Testament prophets with classical figures. But the style is more dramatic, shocking, and emotional than the balanced Renaissance works before it. This is a very personal work—the Gospel according to Michelangelo—but its themes and subject matter are universal. Many art scholars contend that the Sistine ceiling is the single greatest work of art by any one human being.

The Sistine Ceiling: Understanding What You're Standing Under

The ceiling shows the history of the world before the birth of Jesus. We see God creating the world, creating man and woman, destroying the earth by flood, and so on. God himself, in his purple robe, actually appears in the first five scenes. Along the sides (where the ceiling starts to curve), we see the Old Testament prophets and pagan Greek prophetesses who foretold the coming of Christ. Dividing these scenes and figures are fake niches (a painted 3-D illusion) decorated with nude statue-like figures with symbolic meaning.

The key is to see three simple divisions in the tangle of bodies:

1. The central spine of nine rectangular biblical scenes;
2. The line of prophets on either side; and
3. The triangles between the prophets showing the ancestors of Christ.

▶ *Within the chapel, grab a seat along the side (if there's room). Face the altar with the big The Last Judgment on the wall (more on that later). Now look up to the ceiling and find the central panel of...*

The Creation of Adam

God and man take center stage in this Renaissance version of creation. Adam, newly formed in the image of God, lounges dreamily in perfect naked innocence. God, with his entourage, swoops in with a swirl of activity (which—with a little imagination—looks like a cross-section of a human brain...quite a strong humanist statement). Their reaching hands are the center of this work. Adam's is limp and passive; God's is strong and forceful, his finger twitching upward with energy. Here is the very moment of

The Creation of Adam

creation, as God passes the spark of life to man, the crowning work of his creation.

This is the spirit of the Renaissance. God is not a terrifying giant reaching down to puny and helpless man from way on high. Here they are on an equal plane, divided only by the diagonal patch of sky. God's billowing robe and the patch of green upon which Adam is lying balance each other. They are like two pieces of a jigsaw puzzle, or two long-separated continents, or like the yin and yang symbols finally coming together—uniting, complementing each other, creating wholeness. God and man work together in the divine process of creation.

▶ *This celebration of man permeates the ceiling. Notice the Adonises-come-to-life on the pedestals that divide the central panels. And then came woman.*

The Garden of Eden: Temptation and Expulsion

In one panel, we see two scenes from the Garden of Eden. On the left is the leafy garden of paradise where Adam and Eve lie around blissfully. But the devil comes along—a serpent with a woman's torso—and winds around the forbidden Tree of Knowledge. The temptation to gain new knowledge is too great for these Renaissance people. They eat the forbidden fruit.

At right, the sword-wielding angel drives them from Paradise into the barren plains. They're grieving, but they're far from helpless. Adam's body is thick and sturdy, and we know they'll survive in the cruel world. Adam firmly gestures to the angel, like he's saying, "All right, already! We're going!"

The Nine Scenes from Genesis

Take some time with these central scenes to understand the story that the ceiling tells. They run in sequence, starting at the front:

1. God, in purple, divides the light from darkness.
2. God creates the sun (burning orange) and the moon (pale white, to the right). Oops, I guess there's another moon.
3. God bursts toward us to separate the land and water.
4. *The Creation of Adam.*
5. God creates Eve, who dives into existence out of Adam's side.
6. *The Garden of Eden: Temptation and Expulsion.*
7. Noah kills a ram and stokes the altar fires to make a sacrifice to God.
8. The great flood, sent by God, destroys the wicked, who desperately head for higher ground. In the distance, the Ark carries Noah's family to safety. (The blank spot dates to 1793, when a nearby gunpowder depot exploded, shaking the building.)
9. Noah's sons see their drunken father. (Perhaps Michelangelo chose to end it with this scene as a reminder that even the best of men are fallible.)

Prophets

You'll notice that the figures at the far end of the chapel are a bit smaller than those over *The Last Judgment*.

Michelangelo started at the far end, with the Noah scenes. By 1510, he'd finished the first half of the ceiling. When they took the scaffolding down and could finally see what he'd been working on for two years, everyone was awestruck—except Michelangelo. As powerful as his figures

Prophet Isaiah—stately

Prophet Jeremiah—brooding

are, from the floor they didn't look dramatic enough for Michelangelo. For the other half, he pulled out all the stops.

Compare the Noah scenes (far end) with their many small figures to the huge images of God at the other end. Similarly, Isaiah (near the lattice screen, marked "Esaias") is stately and balanced, while Jeremiah ("Hieremias," in the corner by *The Last Judgment*) is a dark, brooding figure. This prophet who witnessed the destruction of Israel slumps his chin in his hand and ponders the fate of his people. Like the difference between the stately *Apollo Belvedere* and the excited *Laocoön,* Michelangelo added a new emotional dimension to Renaissance painting.

The Last Judgment

When Michelangelo returned to paint the altar wall 23 years later (1535), the mood of Europe—and of Michelangelo—was completely different. The Protestant Reformation had forced the Catholic Church to clamp down on free thought, and religious wars raged. Rome had recently been pillaged by roving bands of mercenaries. The Renaissance spirit of optimism was fading. Michelangelo himself had begun to question the innate goodness of mankind.

It's Judgment Day, and Christ—the powerful figure in the center, raising his arm to spank the wicked—has come to find out who's naughty and who's nice. Beneath him, a band of angels blows its trumpets Dizzy Gillespie–style, giving a wake-up call to the sleeping dead. The dead at lower left leave their graves and prepare to be judged. The righteous, on Christ's right hand (the left side of the picture), are carried up to the glories of heaven. The wicked on the other side are hurled down to hell, where demons wait to torture them. Charon, from the underworld of Greek mythology, waits below to ferry the souls of the damned to hell.

The Last Judgment

The Last Judgment

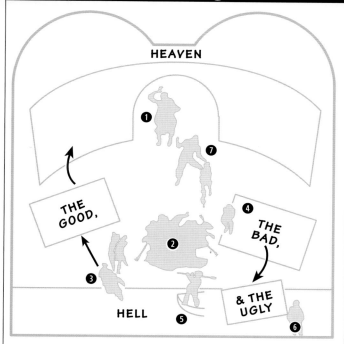

HEAVEN

THE GOOD,

THE BAD,

& THE UGLY

HELL

ENTRY DOOR TO SISTINE →

1 Christ with Mary
2 Trumpeting Angels
3 Righteous Dead Ascending
4 Damned Man

5 Charon the Ferryman
6 Demon/Critic Wrapped in Snake
7 St. Bartholomew Holding Flayed Skin (Michelangelo's Face)

It's a grim picture. No one, but no one, is smiling. Even many of the righteous being resurrected (lower left) are either skeletons or cadavers with ghastly skin. The angels have to play tug-of-war with subterranean monsters to drag them from their graves.

Over in hell, the wicked are tortured by gleeful demons. One of the damned (to the right of the trumpeting angels) has an utterly lost expression, as if saying, "Why did I cheat on my wife?!" Two demons grab him around the ankles to pull him down to the bowels of hell, condemned to an eternity of constipation.

But it's the terrifying figure of Christ that dominates this scene. He raises his arm to smite the wicked, sending a ripple of fear through everyone. Even Mary beneath his arm (whose interceding days are clearly over) shrinks back in terror at loving Jesus' uncharacteristic outburst. His expression is completely closed, and he turns his head, refusing to even listen to the whining alibis of the damned. Look at Christ's bicep. If this muscular figure looks familiar to you, it's because you've seen it before—the Belvedere Torso.

When *The Last Judgment* was unveiled to the public in 1541, it caused a sensation. The pope is said to have dropped to his knees and cried, "Lord, charge me not with my sins when thou shalt come on the Day of Judgment."

And it changed the course of art. The complex composition, with more than 300 figures swirling around the figure of Christ, was far beyond traditional Renaissance balance. The twisted figures shown from every imaginable angle challenged other painters to try and top this master of 3-D illusion. And the sheer terror and drama of the scene was a striking contrast to the placid optimism of, say, Raphael's *School of Athens*. Michelangelo had Baroque-en all the rules of the Renaissance, signaling a new era of art.

With the Renaissance fading, the fleshy figures in *The Last Judgment* aroused murmurs of discontent from Church authorities. (After Michelangelo's death, prudish Church authorities painted many of the wisps of clothing that we see today.) Michelangelo rebelled by painting his chief critic into the scene—in hell. He's the jackassed demon in the bottom right corner, wrapped in a snake. Look at how Michelangelo covered his privates. Sweet revenge.

If *The Creation of Adam* was the epitome of the optimistic Renaissance, *The Last Judgment* marks its end. Michelangelo himself must have wondered how he would be judged—had he used his God-given talents wisely? Look at St. Bartholomew, the bald, bearded guy at Christ's left foot (our right). In the flayed skin he's holding is a barely recognizable face—the twisted self-portrait of a self-questioning Michelangelo.

▶ *There are two exits from the Sistine Chapel. To return to the main entrance/exit and the Pinacoteca (a 15-minute walk away), leave the Sistine through the side door next to the screen.*

Or, if you're planning to take the shortcut directly to St. Peter's Basilica (✪ see map on page 100), exit out the far-right corner of the Sistine Chapel (with your back to the altar). Though this corner door is likely labeled "Exit for private tour groups only," you can usually just slide through with the crowds (or protest that your group has left you behind). If for some reason this exit is closed, hang out in the Sistine Chapel for a few more minutes—it'll likely reopen shortly.

The Long March Back

Along this corridor (located one floor below the long corridor that you walked to get here), you'll see some of the wealth amassed by the popes, mostly gifts from royalty. Find your hometown on the 1529 map of the world—look in the land labeled "Terra Incognita." The elaborately decorated library that branches off to the right contains rare manuscripts.

▶ *The corridor eventually spills out back outside. Follow signs to the...*

PINACOTECA

Like Lou Gehrig batting behind Babe Ruth, the Pinacoteca (Painting Gallery) has to follow the mighty Sistine & Co. See this gallery as you'd view a time-lapse blossoming of a flower, walking through the evolution of painting from medieval to Baroque with just a few stops.

Melozzo da Forli—*Musician Angels* (Room IV)

Salvaged from a condemned church, this playful series of frescoes shows the delicate grace and nobility of Italy during the time known fondly as the Quattrocento (1400s). Notice the detail in the serene faces; the soothing primary colors; the bright and even light; and the classical purity given these religious figures. Rock on.

Raphael—*The Transfiguration* (Room VIII)

Christ floats above a stumpy mountaintop, visited in a vision by the prophets Moses and Elijah. Peter, James, and John cower in awe under their savior, "transfigured before them, his face shining as the sun, his raiment

Musician Angels, by Melozzo

The Transfiguration, by Raphael

white as light" (as described by the evangelist Matthew—who can be seen taking notes in the painting's lower left).

Raphael composes the scene in three descending tiers: Christ, the holiest, is on top, then Peter-James-John, and finally, the nine remaining apostles surround a boy possessed by demons.

Before Raphael died in 1520 (at age 37), the last thing he painted was the beatific face of Jesus, perhaps the most beautiful Christ in existence. When Raphael was buried in the Pantheon, this work accompanied the funeral.

Leonardo da Vinci—*St. Jerome* (c. 1482) (Room IX)

Jerome squats in the rocky desert. He's spent too much time alone, fasting and meditating on his sins. His soulful face is echoed by his friend, the roaring lion.

This unfinished work gives us a glimpse behind the scenes at Leonardo's technique. Even in the brown undercoating, we see the psychological power of Leonardo's genius. Jerome's emaciated body on the rocks expresses his intense penitence, while his pleading eyes hold a glimmer of hope for divine forgiveness. Leonardo wrote that a good painter must paint two things: "man and the movements of his spirit."

Caravaggio—*Deposition* (1604) (Room XII)

Christ is being buried. In the dark tomb, the faces of his followers emerge, lit by a harsh light. Christ's body has a deathlike color. We see Christ's dirty toes and Nicodemus' wrinkled, sunburned face.

A tangle of grief looms out of the darkness as Christ's heavy, dead body nearly pulls the whole group with him from the cross into the tomb. After this museum, I know how he feels.

▶ *Go in peace.*

St. Peter's Basilica Tour

Basilica San Pietro

St. Peter's is the greatest church in Christendom. Its vast expanse could swallow up other churches whole. The basilica represents the power and splendor of Rome's 2,000-year domination of the Western world. Built on the memory and grave of the first pope, St. Peter, this is where the grandeur of ancient Rome became the grandeur of Christianity.

Besides sheer size, St. Peter's houses Michelangelo's dreamy Pietà and Bernini's towering bronze canopy. It's the place where the pope presides, and we'll catch a glimpse of his apartment house nearby. We'll finish our visit with a sweaty climb up Michelangelo's dome for one-of-a-kind view of Rome.

ORIENTATION

Cost: Free entry to basilica and Crypt. Dome climb—€5 to climb stairs up, €7 to take an elevator for part of the climb. Museum-Treasury—€7.

Dress Code: No shorts, bare shoulders, or miniskirts. This dress code is strictly enforced.

Hours of Church: Daily April–Sept 7:00–19:00, Oct–March 7:00–18:00. The church closes on Wednesday mornings during papal audiences. Mass is held almost hourly every day, generally in the south (left) transept. Confirm the schedule on-site or at www.vatican.va. The **Museum-Treasury** is open daily (April–Sept 9:00–18:15, Oct–March 9:00–17:15) and so is the **Crypt** (9:00–16:00).

Dome Climb (Cupola): Daily April–Sept 8:00–18:00, Oct–March 8:00–16:45. You can take the elevator or stairs to roof level (231 steps up, with good views), then climb another 323 steps to the top of the dome (stunning views). The entrance (follow signs to the "cupola") is just outside the basilica on the north side of St. Peter's (though the line often backs up to the church's front steps).

Getting There: A taxi from Termini train station to St. Peter's costs about €10. From Metro stop Ottaviano, it's a 10-minute walk. The #40 express bus drops off at Piazza Pio, next to Castel Sant'Angelo—a 10-minute walk. Bus #64 stops just south of St. Peter's Square. (After crossing the Tiber, get off at the first stop past the tunnel; backtrack toward the tunnel and turn left when you see the columns of St. Peter's Square.)

Avoiding the Line: To bypass the long security-checkpoint line, consider visiting the Vatican Museum first, then taking the shortcut from the Sistine Chapel directly to St. Peter's (✪ see map on page 100).

Avoiding Crowds: The best time to visit the church is before 10:00 or after 16:00; the 17:00 service is ideal, when sunbeams work their magic and the late-afternoon Mass fills the place with music. The church is especially crowded on days when the pope makes appearances.

Information: The TI on the left (south) side of the square is excellent (Mon–Sat 8:30–18:30). Tel. 06-6988-1662, www.saintpetersbasilica.org.

Services: WCs are to the right and left on St. Peter's Square, near the baggage checkroom, and on the roof. The Vatican City post office, next to the TI (Mon–Sat 8:30–18:30, closed Sun), is famous for its stamps. Buy stamps and postcards and drop them into a postbox home.

Tours: Free 1.5-hour tours depart from the TI, generally Mon–Fri at 14:15 and Tue and Thu at 9:45 (confirm schedule at TI, tel. 06-6988-1662).

Audioguides: €5 plus ID. My free St. Peter's Basilica audio tour is available from iTunes, Google Play, or at www.ricksteves.com.

Seeing the Pope: Your best bets are on Sundays and Wednesdays. To find out the pope's schedule, call 06-6982-3114. On Sunday, the pope often gives a blessing at noon (except in July and August) from his apartment overlooking St. Peter's Square. No tickets are required—just show up in the square. On Wednesday at 10:30, the pope greets and blesses large crowds in St. Peter's Square (except in winter, when it's held in a huge auditorium next to the church). While you can look on from the distant fringes of the square, to get closer and have a seat, you'll need to get a (free) ticket in advance. Book free tickets online through www.santasusanna.org, and pick them up at the English-friendly Santa Susanna Church (Via XX Settembre 15, Metro: Repubblica, tel. 06-4201-4554). Alternatively, get a ticket from the usually crowded Vatican guard station on St. Peter's Square (✪ at #6 on the map on page 100), open Tuesday 12:00–19:30 and on Wednesday morning if there are any remaining tickets.

Other Vatican City Tours: To see the Vatican Gardens, you must book a tour (€31) at http://biglietteriamusei.vatican.va. To see St. Peter's actual tomb beneath the church, you must book a Scavi/Excavations tour (€12) at least two months in advance; get info at www.vatican.va.

Length of This Tour: Allow one hour, plus another hour if you climb the dome (or a half-hour to the roof).

Checkroom: Free and mandatory for bags larger than a purse or daypack.

Starring: Michelangelo, Bernini, St. Peter, a heavenly host...and, occasionally, the pope.

THE TOUR BEGINS

▶ *Find a shady spot where you like the view under the columns around St. Peter's oval-shaped "square." If the pigeons left a clean spot, sit on it.*

Background

Nearly 2,000 years ago, this area was the site of Nero's Circus—a huge cigar-shaped Roman chariot racecourse. The tall obelisk you see in the middle of the square once stood about 100 yards from its current location, in the center of the circus course (to the left of where St. Peter's is today). The Romans had no marching bands, so for halftime entertainment they killed Christians. This persecuted minority was forced to fight wild animals and gladiators, or they were simply crucified. Some were tarred up, tied to posts, and burned—human torches to light up the evening races.

One of those killed here, in about A.D. 65, was Peter, Jesus' right-hand man, who had come to Rome to spread the message of love. At his own request, Peter was crucified upside-down, because he felt unworthy to die as his master had. His remains were buried in a nearby cemetery located where the main altar in St. Peter's is today. For 250 years, these relics were quietly and secretly revered.

When Christianity was finally legalized in 313, the Christian emperor Constantine built a church on the site of Peter's martyrdom. "Old St. Peter's" lasted 1,200 years (A.D. 329–1500).

By the time of the Renaissance, Old St. Peter's was falling apart and was considered unfit to be the center of the Western Church. The new, larger church we see today was begun in 1506 by the architect Bramante. He was succeeded by a number of different architects, including Michelangelo, who designed the magnificent dome. The church was finally finished in 1626.

▶ *More on the church later—for now, let's talk about the square.*

St. Peter's Square

St. Peter's Square, with its ring of columns, symbolizes the arms of the church welcoming everyone—believers and non-believers—with its motherly embrace. It was designed a century after Michelangelo by the Baroque architect Gian Lorenzo Bernini, who did much of the work that we'll see inside.

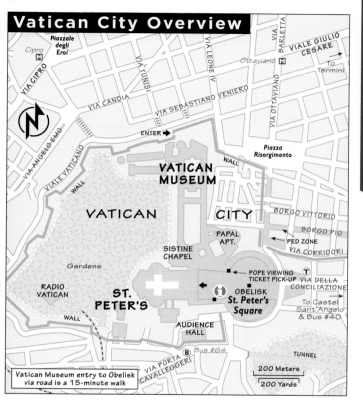

Vatican City Overview

Piazzale degli Eroi

Cipro Ⓜ

VIA CIPRO

VIA TUNIS

VIA LEONE IV

VIA BARLETTA

VIALE GIULIO CESARE

Ottaviano Ⓜ

To Termini

VIA CANDIA

VIA SEBASTIANO VENIERO

VIA OTTAVIANO

VIA ANGELO EMO

VIALE VATICANO

ENTER ➡

Piazza Risorgimento

WALL

VATICAN MUSEUM

VATICAN

CITY

BORGO VITTORIO

BORGO PIO

PAPAL APT.

PED ZONE

VIA CORRIDORI

SISTINE CHAPEL

Gardens

POPE VIEWING TICKET PICK-UP Ⓣ

VIA DELLA CONCILIAZIONE

RADIO VATICAN

ST. PETER'S

◀ ⓘ ◼ OBELISK
St. Peter's Square

To Castel Sant'Angelo & Bus #40

WALL

AUDIENCE HALL

TUNNEL

Ⓑ Bus #64

VIA PORTA CAVALLEGGERI

200 Meters

200 Yards

Vatican Museum entry to Obelisk via road is a 15-minute walk

Numbers first: 284 columns, 56 feet high, in stern Doric style. Topping them are Bernini's 140 favorite saints, each 10 feet tall. The "square" itself is actually elliptical, 660 by 500 feet. It's a little higher around the edges so that even when full of crowds, those on the periphery can see above the throngs.

The obelisk in the center is 90 feet of solid granite weighing more than 300 tons. Think of how much history this monument has seen. Originally erected in Egypt more than 2,000 years ago, it witnessed the fall of the

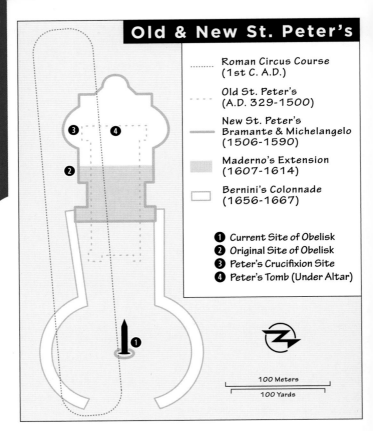

Old & New St. Peter's

.... Roman Circus Course
(1st C. A.D.)

- - - - - Old St. Peter's
(A.D. 329-1500)

——— New St. Peter's
Bramante & Michelangelo
(1506-1590)

Maderno's Extension
(1607-1614)

Bernini's Colonnade
(1656-1667)

❶ Current Site of Obelisk
❷ Original Site of Obelisk
❸ Peter's Crucifixion Site
❹ Peter's Tomb (Under Altar)

100 Meters
100 Yards

pharaohs to the Greeks and then to the Romans. Then the emperor Caligula moved it to imperial Rome, where it stood impassively watching the slaughter of Christians. As Rome fell and Christians triumphed, the obelisk was moved to this spot (in 1586) and topped with a cross. Today, it watches over the church, a reminder that each civilization builds on the previous ones.

St. Peter's Basilica

▶ *Venture out across the burning desert to the obelisk, which provides a narrow sliver of shade.*

As you face the church, the gray building to the right at two o'clock, rising up behind Bernini's colonnade, is where the pope lives. The last window on the right of the top floor is his bedroom. To the left of that window is his study window, where he appears occasionally to greet the masses. If you come to the square at night as a Poping Tom, you might see the light on—the pope burns much midnight oil.

On more formal occasions (which you may have seen on TV), the pope appears from the church itself, on the small balcony above the central door.

The Sistine Chapel is just to the right of the facade—the small gray-brown building with the triangular roof, topped by an antenna. The tiny chimney (the pimple along the roofline midway up the left side) is where the famous smoke signals announce the election of each new pope. If the smoke is black, a two-thirds majority hasn't been reached. White smoke means a new pope has been selected.

Walk to the right, five pavement plaques from the obelisk, to one marked *Centro del Colonnato*. From here, all of Bernini's columns on the right side line up.

St. Peter's Square

❶ Obelisk
❷ Papal Apartments (Top Story, Right)
❸ Sistine Chapel (in Vatican Museum)
❹ "Centro del Colonnato" Plaque
❺ Swiss Guard at Vatican City Entrance
❻ Papal Ticket Pick-up at Bronze Doors
❼ Tourist Info, Vatican Post Office, Bookstore & WC
❽ Baggage Checkroom, Audioguides & WC
❾ Exit from Sistine Chapel
❿ Elevator to Dome & Crypt Entrance
⓫ To Ottaviano Metro (10 min), Cipro Metro (20 min) & Vatican Museum (15 min)

ST. PETER'S BASILICA
DOME
B
Bus #64
SISTINE CHAPEL
WALL
BERNINI'S COLONNADE
ST. PETER'S SQUARE
VATICAN WALL
VIA DI PTA. ANGELICA
VIA DELLA CONCILIAZIONE

▶ Climb the gradually sloping pavement past crowd barriers, the security checkpoint, and the huge statues of St. Paul (with his two-edged sword) and St. Peter (with his bushy hair and keys).

On the square are two entrances to Vatican City: one to the left of the facade, and one to the right in the crook of Bernini's "arm." Guarding this small but powerful country's border crossing are the mercenary guards from Switzerland. You have to wonder if they really know how to use those pikes. Their colorful uniforms are said to have been designed by Michelangelo, though he was not known for his sense of humor.

▶ Enter the atrium (entrance hall) of the church.

THE BASILICA

The Atrium

The atrium is itself bigger than most churches. The huge white columns on the portico date from Old St. Peter's (fourth century). Five famous bronze doors lead into the church.

The central door, made from the melted-down bronze of the original door of Old St. Peter's, is only opened on special occasions.

The far-right entrance is the Holy Door, opened only every 25 years, at the dawn of each Holy Year. For Holy Year 2000 (see the Roman numerals "MM" in the plaque above the door), Pope John Paul II opened the door on Christmas Eve, 1999. In the ceremony, the pope knocks three times with a silver hammer and the door opens, welcoming pilgrims to pass through. At the end of the year, the pope bricks it up again with a ceremonial trowel to wait another 24 years. On the door, note crucified Jesus' shiny knees, polished by pious pilgrims who touch them for a blessing.

▶ *Now for one of Europe's great "wow" experiences. Enter the church. Gape for a while. But don't gape at Michelangelo's famous* Pietà *(on the right). That's this tour's finale. I'll wait for you at the round maroon pavement stone on the floor near the central doorway.*

The Church

This church is appropriately huge. Size before beauty: The golden window at the far end is two football fields away. The bronze canopy over the main altar is the size of a seven-story building. The babies at the base of the pillars along the main hall (the nave) are adult-size. The lettering in the gold band along the

Sistine Chapel with chimney and antenna

The Vatican's Swiss Guard

St. Peter's Basilica

Not to Scale

8

7

9   **14**   **4**   **5**   **6**   **13**
DOME ENTRANCE

10

3   **15**

12   EXIT FROM
SISTINE
CHAPEL

2

11

ATRIUM

1

SWISS
GUARDS

STEPS   ↑
↓   ENTER

AUDIOGUIDES,
WC &
BAGGAGE
STORAGE

ST. PETER'S SQUARE

top of the pillars is seven feet high. Really. The church covers six acres, and can accommodate 60,000 standing worshippers (or 1,200 tour groups).

The church is huge, but everything is designed to make it seem smaller and more intimate than it really is. For example, the statue of St. Teresa near the bottom of the first pillar on the right is 15 feet tall. The statue above her near the top looks the same size, but is actually six feet taller, giving the impression that it's not so far away.

The nave gives a sense of the splendor of ancient Rome that was

1. **Holy Door**
2. **Charlemagne's Coronation Site**
3. **Extent of Original "Greek Cross" Plan**
4. **St. Andrew Statue; View of Dome; Crypt Entrance**
5. **St. Peter Statue (with Kissable Toe)**
6. **Pope John XXIII**
7. **Main Altar (over Peter's Tomb)**
8. **BERNINI—Dove Window & Throne of St. Peter**
9. **St. Peter's Crucifixion Site**
10. **RAPHAEL – Mosaic Copy of The Transfiguration**
11. **MICHELANGELO–Pietà**
12. **Tomb of Pope John Paul II**
13. **Dome Entrance**
14. **Museum-Treasury**
15. **Blessed Sacrament Chapel**

carried on by the Catholic Church. The floor plan is based on the ancient Roman basilica, or law-court building, with a central aisle (nave) flanked by two side aisles. In fact, many of the stones used to build St. Peter's were scavenged from the ruined law courts of ancient Rome.

On the floor near the central doorway is a round slab of porphyry stone in the maroon color of ancient Roman officials. This is the spot where, on Christmas night in A.D. 800, the French king Charlemagne was crowned Holy Roman Emperor. Even in the Dark Ages—when Rome was virtually abandoned and visitors reported that the city had more thieves and wolves than decent people—St. Peter's was the symbolic center of Europe.

St. Peter's was very expensive to build. The popes financed it by selling "indulgences," allowing the rich to buy forgiveness for their sins. This kind of corruption inspired an obscure German monk named Martin Luther to rebel and start the Protestant Reformation.

The ornate, Baroque-style interior decoration—a riot of marble, gold, stucco, mosaics, columns of stone, and pillars of light—was part of the Church's "Counter-" Reformation. Baroque served as cheery propaganda, impressing followers with the authority of the Church, and giving them a glimpse of the heaven that awaited the faithful.

▶ *Now, walk straight up the center of the nave toward the altar.*

"Michelangelo's Church"—The Greek Cross

The plaques on the floor show where other, smaller churches of the world would end if they were placed inside St. Peter's: St. Paul's Cathedral in London (Londinense), Florence's Duomo, and so on.

The nave

You'll also walk over circular golden grates. Stop at the second one (at the third pillar from the entrance). Look back at the entrance and realize that if Michelangelo had had his way, this whole long section of the church wouldn't exist. The nave was extended after his death.

Michelangelo was 71 years old when the pope persuaded him to take over the church project and cap it with a dome. He put the dome over Donato Bramante's original "Greek Cross" floor plan, with four equal arms, symbolic of the orderliness of the created world and the perfection of man. But after Michelangelo's death, the Church—struggling against Protestants and its own corruption—opted for a Latin cross plan, designed to impress the world with its grandeur.

▶ Continue toward the altar, entering "Michelangelo's Church." Park yourself in front of the statue of St. Andrew to the left of the altar. The Crypt entrance is down the stairs beside the statue, but you can save it for later (see end of this tour).

From Pope to Pope

When a pope dies—or retires—the tiny, peaceful Vatican stirs from its timeless slumber and becomes headline news. Millions of people converge on Vatican City, and hundreds of millions around the world watch anxiously on TV.

A deceased pope's body is displayed in state in front of the main altar in St. Peter's Basilica. Thousands of pilgrims line up down Via della Conciliazione, waiting for one last look at their pope. On the day of the funeral, hundreds of thousands of mourners, dignitaries, and security personnel gather in St. Peter's Square. The pope's coffin is carried out to the square, where a eulogy is given.

Most popes are laid to rest in the crypt below St. Peter's Basilica, near the tomb of St. Peter and among shrines to many other popes. Especially popular popes—such as John Paul II or John XXIII—may eventually find a place upstairs, inside St. Peter's itself.

While the previous pope is being laid to rest, cardinals representing Catholics around the globe descend on Rome to elect a new pope. Once they've assembled, the 100-plus cardinals, dressed in crimson, are stripped of their mobile phones, given a vow of secrecy, and locked inside the Sistine Chapel. This begins the "conclave" (from Latin *cum clave*, with key). As they cast votes with paper ballots, the used ballots are burned in a stove temporarily set up inside the Sistine Chapel. The smoke rises up and out the tiny chimney, visible from St. Peter's Square. Black smoke means they haven't yet agreed on a new pope. Finally, the anxious crowd in St. Peter's Square looks up to see a puff of white smoke emerging from the Sistine Chapel. The bells in St. Peter's clock towers ring out gloriously (a new tradition) confirming that, indeed, a pope has been elected. The crowd erupts in cheers, and Romans watching on their TVs hail taxis to hurry to the square.

On the balcony of St. Peter's facade, the newly-elected pope steps up and raises his hands, as thousands chant *"Viva il Papa."* A cardinal introduces him to the crowd, announcing his newly-chosen name. "Brothers and sisters," the cardinal says in several languages, *"Habemus Papam."* "We have a pope."

The Dome

The dome soars higher than a football field on end, 448 feet from the floor of the cathedral to the top of the lantern. It glows with light from its windows, the blue and gold mosaics creating a cool, solemn atmosphere. In this majestic vision of heaven (not painted by Michelangelo), we see (above the windows) Jesus, Mary, and a ring of saints, more rings of angels above them, and, way up in the ozone, God the Father (a blur of blue and red without binoculars).

When Michelangelo died (1564), he'd completed only the drum of the dome—the base up to the windows flanked by half-columns—but the next architects were guided by his designs.

Listen to the hum of visitors echoing through St. Peter's and reflect on our place in the cosmos: half animal, half angel, stretched between heaven and earth, born to live only a short while, a bubble of foam on a great cresting wave of humanity.

▶ *But I digress.*

Michelangelo's dome—448 feet tall

Peter

The base of the dome is ringed with a gold banner telling us in massive blue letters why this church is so important. The banner in Latin quotes every one of Jesus' recorded words to Peter, including, "You are Peter *(Tu es Petrus)* and upon this rock I will build my church, and to you I will give the keys of the kingdom of heaven" (Matthew 16:18).

According to Catholics, Peter was selected by Jesus to head the church. He became the first bishop of Rome. His prestige and that of the city itself made this bishopric more illustrious than all others, and Peter's authority has supposedly passed in an unbroken chain to each succeeding bishop of Rome—that is, the 250-odd popes that followed.

Under the dome, under the bronze canopy, under the altar, some 23

Peter

According to the Bible, Peter was a fisherman who was chosen by Christ to catch sinners instead. This "fisher of men" had human weaknesses that have endeared him to Christians. He was the disciple who tried to walk on water— but failed. In another incident, he impetuously cut off a man's ear when soldiers came to arrest Jesus. And he even denied

Venerated statue of Peter

knowing Christ, to save his own skin. But Jesus chose him anyway, and gave him his nickname—Rock (in Latin: *Petrus*).

Legends say that Peter came to the wicked city of Rome after Jesus' death to spread the gospel of love. He may have been imprisoned in the Mamertine Prison near the Roman Forum (❁ see page 137), and other stories claim he had a vision of Christ along the Appian Way (❁ see page 165). Eventually, Peter's preaching offended Emperor Nero. Christ's fisherman was arrested, crucified upside-down, and buried here, where St. Peter's now stands.

St. Andrew gazes up at the dome

"Tu es Petrus"—You are Peter...

feet under the marble floor, rest the bones of St. Peter, the "rock" upon which this particular church was built. You can't see the tomb, but go to the railing and look down into the small, lighted niche below the altar with a box containing bishops' shawls—a symbol of how Peter's authority spread to the other churches. Peter's tomb (not visible) is just below this box.

Are they really the bones of Jesus' apostle? According to a papal pronouncement: definitely maybe. The traditional site of his tomb was sealed up when Old St. Peter's was built on it in A.D. 326. In 1940, the tomb was opened for archaeological study. Bones were found, dated from the first century, of a robust man who died in old age. His body was wrapped in expensive cloth. Various inscriptions and graffiti in the tomb indicate that second- and third-century visitors thought this was Peter's tomb. Does that mean it's really Peter? Who am I to disagree with the pope? Definitely maybe.

If you line up the cross on the altar with the dove in the window, you'll notice that the niche below the cross is just off-center compared with the rest of the church. Why? Because Michelangelo built the church around the traditional location of the tomb, not the actual location—about two feet away—discovered by modern archaeology.

Back in the nave sits a bronze statue of Peter under a canopy that dates from Old St. Peter's. In one hand he holds the keys, the symbol of the authority given him by Christ, while with the other hand he blesses us. He's wearing the toga of a Roman senator. It may be that the original statue was of a senator and that the bushy head and keys were added later to make it Peter. His big right toe has been worn smooth by the lips of pilgrims and foot-fetishists. Stand in line and kiss it, or, to avoid foot-and-mouth disease, touch your hand to your lips, then rub the toe. This is simply an

Pope Francis I

In 2013, Jorge Bergoglio of Argentina became Francis I, the church's 266th pope. Francis (b. 1936) grew up in Buenos Aires in a family of working-class Italian immigrants. He spent his twenties in various jobs (chemist, high-school teacher) before entering the priesthood and eventually becoming Archbishop of Buenos Aires.

Pope Francis represents three "firsts" that signal a new direction for the Church. As the first pope from the Americas, Francis personifies the 80 percent of Catholics who now live outside Europe. As the first Jesuit pope—from the religious order known for education—he stands for spreading the faith through teaching, not aggression. And as the first Francis—named after St. Francis of Assisi—he calls to mind that medieval friar's efforts to return a corrupt church to simple Christian values of poverty and humility. In addition to these firsts, Francis is in the unusual position of taking the helm after the previous pope had retired (not died). He shares the world stage with "pope emeritus" Benedict.

Like his namesake Francis, the pope lives simply. He resides in a Vatican guest house rather than the official Papal Apartments overlooking St. Peter's Square. He reportedly eats leftovers.

When people talk about Francis, the word that comes up time and again is… "dialogue." He's known for listening to every point of view, whether it's mediating between dictators and union leaders, sitting down with the Orthodox Patriarch, celebrating Rosh Hashanah with Jews, visiting a mosque, or praising atheists. He speaks a number of languages, including fluent Italian—the language of his parents and of the Vatican.

But Francis is not a liberal. No one expects major changes in the church's positions on abortion, gay marriage, contraception, or the celibate, male-only priesthood. Francis has made it clear he wants the church to focus less on money and power, and more on the poor and the outcast. As Francis himself has pointed out, the original Latin word for pope—"*pontifex*"—literally means "bridge-builder."

act of reverence with no legend attached, though you can make one up if you like.

▶ *Circle to the right around the statue of Peter to find another popular stop among pilgrims: the lighted glass niche with the red-robed body of...*

Pope John XXIII

Pope John XXIII, who reigned 1958–1963, is nicknamed "the good pope." He is best known for initiating the landmark Vatican II Council (1962–1965) that instituted major reforms, bringing the Church into the modern age. The Council allowed Mass to be conducted in the vernacular rather than in Latin. Lay people were invited to participate more in services, Church leadership underwent some healthy self-criticism, and a spirit of ecumenism flourished. In 2000, during the beatification process (a stop on the way to sainthood), Church authorities checked John's body, and it was surprisingly fresh. So they moved it upstairs and put it behind glass, where old Catholics pass by and remember him fondly.

The Main Altar

The main altar beneath the dome and canopy (the white marble slab with cross and candlesticks) is used only when the pope himself says Mass. He sometimes conducts the Sunday morning service when he's in town, a sight worth seeing. I must admit, though, it's a little strange being frisked at the door for weapons at the holiest place in Christendom.

The tiny altar would be lost in this enormous church if it weren't for Gian Lorenzo Bernini's seven-story bronze canopy (God's "four-poster bed"), which "extends" the altar upward and reduces the perceived distance between floor and ceiling. The corkscrew columns echo the marble ones that surrounded the altar/tomb in Old St. Peter's. Some of the bronze used here was taken and melted down from the ancient Pantheon.

Bernini (1598–1680), the Michelangelo of the Baroque era, is the man most responsible for the interior decoration of the church. The altar area was his masterpiece, a "theater" for holy spectacles. Besides the bronze canopy, Bernini did the statue of lance-bearing St. Longinus ("The hills are alive..."), the balconies above the four statues, and much of the marble floor decoration. Bernini gave an impressive unity to a diverse variety of pillars, windows, statues, aisles, and chapels.

▶ *Approach the apse, the front area with the golden dove window.*

Bernini's bronze canopy over the altar

Bernini Blitz

Nowhere is there such a conglomeration of works by the flamboyant genius who remade the church—and the city—in the Baroque style. Here's your scavenger-hunt list. You have 20 minutes. Go!

1. St. Peter's Square: design and statues
2. Constantine equestrian relief (right end of atrium)
3. Decoration (stucco, gold leaf, marble, etc.) of side aisles (flanking the nave)
4. Tabernacle (the temple-like altarpiece) inside Blessed Sacrament Chapel
5. Much of the marble floor throughout the church
6. Bronze canopy over the altar
7. St. Longinus statue (holding a lance) near the altar
8. Balconies (above each of the four statues) with corkscrew, Solomonic columns from Old St. Peter's.
9. Dove window, bronze sunburst, angels, "Throne," and Church Fathers (in the apse)
10. Tomb of Pope Urban VIII (far end of the apse, right side)
11. Tomb of Pope Alexander VII (between the apse and the left transept, over a doorway, with the gold skeleton smothered in jasper poured like maple syrup)

Bizarre...Baroque...Bernini.

The Apse

Bernini's dove window shines above the smaller front altar used for everyday services. The Holy Spirit, in the form of a six-foot-high dove, pours sunlight onto the faithful through the alabaster windows, turning into artificial rays of gold and reflecting off swirling gold clouds, angels, and winged babies. During a service, real sunlight passes through real clouds of incense, mingling with Bernini's sculpture. This is the epitome of Baroque—an ornate, mixed-media work designed to overwhelm the viewer.

Beneath the dove is the centerpiece of this structure, the so-called "Throne of Peter," an oak chair built in medieval times for a king. Subsequently, it was encrusted with tradition and encased in bronze by

The dove window designed by Bernini

Bernini as a symbol of papal authority. Statues of four early Church Fathers support the chair, a symbol of how bishops should support the pope in troubled times—times like the Counter-Reformation.

Remember that St. Peter's is a church, not a museum. In the apse, Mass is said for pilgrims, tourists, and Roman citizens alike (Thu at 9:00, Sun at 10:30, 12:15, 16:00, and 17:45—after vespers at 17:00). Wooden confessional booths are available for Catholics to tell their sins to a listening ear and receive forgiveness and peace of mind. The faithful renew their faith, and the faithless gain inspiration. Look at the light streaming through the windows, turn and gaze up into the dome, and quietly contemplate your deity (or lack thereof).

► *To the left of the main altar is the south transept. At the far end, left side, find the dark "painting" of St. Peter crucified upside-down.*

South Transept—Peter's Crucifixion Site

Because smoke and humidity would damage real paintings, this and all the other "paintings" in the church are actually mosaic copies made from thousands of colored chips the size of your little fingernail.

This work marks the exact spot (according to tradition) where Peter was killed 1,900 years ago. Peter had come to the world's greatest city to preach Jesus' message of love to the pagan, often hostile Romans. During the reign of Nero, he was arrested and brought to Nero's Circus so all Rome could witness his execution. When the authorities told Peter he was to be crucified just like his Lord, Peter said "I'm not worthy" and insisted they nail him on the cross upside-down.

The Romans were actually quite tolerant of other religions, but monotheistic Christians refused to worship the Roman emperor even when burned alive, thrown to the lions, or crucified. Their bravery, optimism in suffering, and message of love struck a chord with slaves and the lower classes. The religion started by a poor carpenter grew, despite persecution by fanatical emperors. In three short centuries, Christianity went from a small Jewish sect in Jerusalem to the official religion of the world's greatest empire.

▸ *Back near the entrance to the church, in the far corner, behind bullet-proof glass, is the...*

Pietà

Michelangelo was 24 years old when he completed this *Pietà* (pee-ay-TAH) of Mary mourning the dead body of Christ taken from the cross. It was Michelangelo's first major commission (by the French ambassador to the Vatican), done for Holy Year 1500.

Pietà means "pity." Michelangelo, with his total mastery of the real

The *Pietà*, by 24-year-old Michelangelo

Vatican City

This tiny independent country of little more than 100 acres, contained entirely within Rome, has its own postal system, armed guards, helipad, mini–train station, radio station (KPOP), and euro coin (featuring the pope). Politically powerful, the Vatican is the religious capital of 1.1 billion Roman Catholics. If you're not a Catholic, become one for your visit.

The pope is both the religious and secular leader of Vatican City. The city is the last remnant of the once-powerful Papal States of central Italy ruled by popes since the fall of Rome. When modern Italy was created in 1870, the Papal States became part of the nation of Italy, and the Italian government tried to gain control of Vatican City. It wasn't until 1929's Lateran Pact that Italy and the pope officially recognized each other's government, assuring Vatican City's independence.

world, captures the sadness of the moment. Mary cradles her crucified son in her lap. Christ's lifeless right arm drooping down lets us know how heavy this corpse is. His smooth skin is accented by the rough folds of Mary's robe. Mary tilts her head down, looking at her dead son with melancholy tenderness. Her left hand turns upward, asking, "How could they do this to you?"

Michelangelo didn't think of sculpting as creating a figure, but as simply freeing the God-made figure from the prison of marble around it. He'd attack a project like this with an inspired passion, chipping away to find what God put inside.

The bunched-up shoulder and rigor-mortis legs show that Michelangelo learned well from his studies of cadavers. But realistic as this work is, its true power lies in the subtle "unreal" features. Life-size Christ looks childlike compared with larger-than-life Mary. Unnoticed at first, this accentuates the subconscious impression of Mary enfolding Jesus in her maternal love. Mary—the mother of a 33-year-old man—looks like a teenager, emphasizing how Mary was the eternally youthful "handmaiden" of the Lord, always serving God's will, even if it meant giving up her son.

The statue is a solid pyramid of maternal tenderness. Yet within this, Christ's body tilts diagonally down to the right and Mary's hem flows with it. Subconsciously, we feel the weight of this dead God sliding from her lap to the ground.

At 11:30 on May 23, 1972, a madman with a hammer entered St. Peter's and began hacking away at the *Pietà*. The damage was repaired, but that's why there's now a shield of bulletproof glass.

This is Michelangelo's only signed work. The story goes that he overheard some pilgrims praising his finished *Pietà,* but attributing it to a second-rate sculptor from a lesser city. He was so enraged that he grabbed his chisel and chipped "Michelangelo Buonarroti of Florence did this" in the ribbon running down Mary's chest.

On your right (covered in gray concrete with a gold cross) is the inside of the Holy Door. If there's a prayer inside you, ask that—when this door is next opened on Christmas Eve, 2024—St. Peter's will no longer need security checks or bulletproof glass, and pilgrims will enter in peace.

The Rest of the Church

Tomb of Pope John Paul II (Chapel of San Sebastian): The tomb of Pope John Paul II (1920-2005) was moved to the chapel of San Sebastian in 2011, after he was beatified by Pope Benedict XVI (a step on the road to sainthood). John Paul lies beneath a painting of his favorite saint, the steadfast St. Sebastian.

The Crypt (a.k.a. Grottoes, or Tombe): The entrance to the church's "basement" is usually beside the statue of St. Andrew, to the left of the main altar.

Once inside, a ramp leads you down to the floor level of Old St. Peter's, with a few of the earlier church's column fragments. Next come tombs of popes, including Paul VI (1963-1978), who suffered through the church's modernization. Nearby is the chapel where Pope John Paul II was buried before being moved upstairs in 2011. The finale is the unimpressive "sepulcher of Peter," a ceremonial chapel and niche honoring Peter's tomb, which is located behind the niche (and which you can't see). The walk through the Crypt is free and quick (15 minutes), and you end up outside the basilica, usually near the cloakroom.

Museum-Treasury (Museo-Tesoro): The museum (€6), located on the left side of the nave near the altar, contains an original corkscrew column from Old St. Peter's, the room-size tomb of Sixtus IV by Antonio Pollaiuolo, a big pair of Roman pincers used to torture Christians, and assorted jewels, papal robes, and golden reliquaries—a marked contrast to the poverty of early Christians.

Blessed Sacrament Chapel: You're welcome to step through the metalwork gates into this oasis of peace reserved for prayer and meditation. It's located on the right-hand side of the church, about midway to the altar.

Up to the Dome (Cupola)

A good way to finish a visit to St. Peter's is to go up to the dome for the best view of Rome anywhere (open daily April–Sept 8:00–18:00, Oct–March 8:00–16:45). The entrance to the dome is along the right side of the church, but the line begins to form on the church's front steps, near the right door of the main facade (follow signs to *cupola*).

First, you take the elevator (€7) or climb 231 stairs (€5) to the church roof, just above the facade. From the roof, you have a commanding view of St. Peter's Square, the statues on the colonnade, Rome across the Tiber in

View from atop the dome

front of you, and the dome itself—almost terrifying in its nearness—looming behind you.

From here, you can also go inside, to the gallery ringing the interior of the dome, where you can look down inside the church. Study the mosaics up close—and those huge letters! Survey the top of Bernini's seven-story-tall canopy, and wonder how (or if) they ever dust it. It's worth the elevator ride for this view alone.

From roof level, if you're energetic, continue all the way up to the top of the dome. The staircase actually winds between the outer shell and the inner one. It's a sweaty, crowded, claustrophobic 15-minute, 323-step climb, but worth it.

The view from the summit is great, the fresh air even better. Admire the arms of Bernini's colonnade encircling St. Peter's Square. Find the big, white Victor Emmanuel Monument, with the two statues on top. Nearby is the Pantheon, with its large, light, shallow dome. The large rectangular building to the left of the obelisk is the Vatican Museum, stuffed with art. Survey the Vatican grounds, with its mini–train system and lush gardens. Look down into the square on the tiny pilgrims buzzing like electrons around the nucleus of Catholicism.

Borghese Gallery Tour

Galleria e Museo Borghese

More than just a great museum, the Borghese Gallery is a beautiful villa set in the greenery of surrounding gardens. You get to see art commissioned by the luxury-loving Borghese family displayed in the very rooms for which it was created.

There's a superb collection of works by Bernini, including his intricately carved *Apollo and Daphne,* a statue that's more air than stone. Among the many Caravaggio paintings is the artist's portrait of himself—as a severed head. Frescoes, marble, stucco, and interior design enhance the masterpieces.

This is a place where—regardless of whether you learn a darn thing— you can sit back and enjoy the sheer beauty of the palace and its art.

ORIENTATION

Cost: €9, or €13 during special exhibits; both prices include basic €2 reservation fee (see "Reservations" below).

Hours: Tue–Sun 9:00–19:00, last entry one hour earlier, closed Mon.

Reservations: Reservations are mandatory and easy to get in English. Choose your day and an entry time at 9:00, 11:00, 13:00, 15:00, or 17:00. Booking online is easiest (www.galleriaborghese.it, €2 extra booking fee). Calling 06-32810 is also user-friendly, but it can be difficult to reach an operator (press 2 for English; office hours: Mon–Fri 9:00–18:00, Sat 9:00–13:00, closed Sat in Aug). Once you've reserved, simply present your claim number at the Borghese entrance to pick up your ticket. Plan to get there at least 30 minutes before your appointed entry time (or risk forfeiting your reservation). During peak season (May-Sept), reserve a minimum of several days in advance for a weekday visit, at least a week ahead for weekends. Off-season, same-day reservations are possible in person on weekdays but not weekends. The Roma Pass is accepted here, but you still need to make a reservation (by telephone only) and pay the €2 fee. If you don't have a reservation, try arriving before an entry time to see if there are any no-shows; 9:00 is your best bet. Good luck.

Getting There: The museum is set idyllically but inconveniently in the vast Villa Borghese Gardens. A taxi drops you 100 yards from the museum—tell the cabbie "Galleria Borghese," not "Villa" Borghese, which is the park. Bus #910 goes from Termini train station to the Via Pinciana stop, 100 yards from the villa. By Metro, use the Barberini stop, walk up Via Veneto, enter the park, and turn right, following signs (a 20-minute walk).

Information: Tel. 06-32810 or 06-841-3979, www.galleriaborghese.it.

Tours: €6.50 guided English tours are offered at 9:10 and 11:10 (and sometimes at 13:10 and 15:10). You can't book a tour when you make your museum reservation—sign up as soon as you arrive. The excellent 1.5-hour audioguide is €5.

Museum Strategy: Visits are strictly limited to two hours. Budget most of your time for the more interesting ground floor, but set aside 30 minutes for the paintings of the Pinacoteca upstairs. Avoid the crowds by seeing the Pinacoteca first.

Checkroom: Baggage check is free, mandatory, and strictly enforced. Even small purses must be checked. The checkroom does not take coats.

Photography: No photos allowed; you must check your camera.

Cuisine Art: A café is on-site. A picnic-friendly park with benches is just in front of the museum. You can check your picnic with your bags, and feast after your visit.

Starring: Sculptures by Bernini; Canova's *Venus;* paintings by Caravaggio, Raphael, and Titian; and the elegant villa itself.

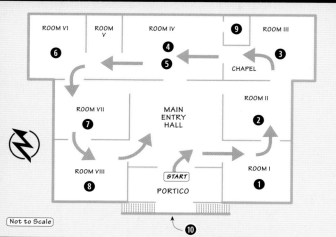

Borghese Gallery-Ground Floor

❶ CANOVA -
   Pauline Bonaparte as Venus
❷ BERNINI - David
❸ BERNINI - Apollo and Daphne
❹ BERNINI - The Rape of
   Proserpine
❺ UNKNOWN - Diana the Hunter;
   Other Marbles

❻ BERNINI - Aeneas
❼ "Theater of the Universe"
❽ CARAVAGGIO - Various
❾ Stairs to Pinacoteca
❿ To Basement (Tickets,
   Info, Shop, WC)

THE TOUR BEGINS

Exterior

As you visit this palace-in-a-garden, consider its purpose. Cardinal Scipione Borghese (1576-1633) landscaped the sprawling Villa Borghese Gardens, built the villa, hired the best artists of his day to decorate it, and filled it with his collection of ancient works—all so he could wine and dine Rome's VIPs and show off his fine art. In pursuing the optimistic spirit of the Renaissance, they invented Baroque.

Main Entry Hall

Guests would enter and be wowed by a multimedia extravaganza of art. Baroque frescoes on the ceiling, Greek statues along the walls, and ancient Roman mosaics on the floor capture the essence of the collection—a gathering of beautiful objects from every age and culture.

Five mosaics from a private Roman villa (second- and third-century A.D.) adorn the floor with colorful, festive scenes of slaughter. Gladiators—as famous in their day as the sports heroes of our age—fight animals and each other with swords, whips, and tridents. The Greek letter Θ marks the dead. Notice some of the gladiators' pro-wrestler nicknames: "Cupid(-o)," "Serpent (-ius)," "Licentious(-us)." On the far left a scene shows how "Alumnusvic" killed "Mazicinus" and left him lying upside down in a pool of blood.

High up on the wall is a thrilling first-century Greek sculpture of a horse falling. The Renaissance-era rider was added by Pietro Bernini, father of the famous Gian Lorenzo Bernini.

Room I

Antonio Canova—*Pauline Bonaparte as Venus* (Paolina Borghese Bonaparte, 1808)

Napoleon's sister went the full monty for the sculptor Canova, scandalizing Europe. ("How could you have done such a thing?!" she was asked. She replied, "The room wasn't cold.") With the famous nose of her conqueror brother, she strikes the pose of Venus as conqueror of men's hearts. Her relaxed afterglow and slight smirk say she's already had her man. The light dent she puts in the mattress makes this goddess human.

Notice the contrasting textures that Canova (1757–1822) gets out of the pure white marble: the rumpled sheet versus her smooth skin, the satiny-smooth pillows and mattress versus the creases in them, her porcelain skin versus the hint of a love handle. Canova polished and waxed the marble until it looked as soft and pliable as cloth.

The mythological pose, the Roman couch, the ancient hairdo, and the calm harmony make Pauline the epitome of the Neoclassical style.

Room II

Gian Lorenzo Bernini—*David* (1624)

Duck! David twists around to put a big rock in his sling. He purses his lips, knits his brow, and winds his body like a spring as his eyes lock onto the target—Goliath, who's somewhere behind us, putting us right in the line of fire.

In this self-portrait, 25-year-old Bernini (1598–1680) is ready to take on the world. He's charged with the same fighting energy that fueled the missionaries and conquistadors of the Counter-Reformation.

David, by Bernini

Compared with Michelangelo's *David,* this is unvarnished realism—an unbalanced pose, bulging veins, unflattering face, and armpit hair. Michelangelo's *David* thinks, whereas Bernini's acts—with lips pursed, eyes concentrating, and sling stretched. Bernini slays the pretty-boy *David*s of the Renaissance and prepares to invent Baroque.

Room III

Bernini—*Apollo and Daphne (Apollo e Dafne,* 1625)

Apollo—made stupid by Cupid's arrow of love—chases after Daphne, who has been turned off by the "arrow of disgust." Just as he's about to catch her, she calls to her father to save her. Magically, her fingers begin to sprout leaves, her toes become roots, her skin turns to bark, and she transforms into a tree. Frustrated Apollo will end up with a handful of leaves.

Stand behind the statue to experience it as Bernini originally intended. It's only when you circle around to the front that he reveals the story's surprise ending.

Walk slowly around the statue. Apollo's back leg defies gravity. Bernini has chipped away more than half of the block of marble, leaving airy, open spaces. The statue spent two years in restoration (described to me as similar to dental work). The marble leaves at the top ring like crystal when struck. Notice the same scene, colorized, painted on the ceiling above.

Bernini carves out some of the chief features of Baroque art. He makes a supernatural event seem realistic. He freezes it at the most dramatic, emotional moment. The figures move and twist in unusual poses. He turns the wind machine on, sending Apollo's cape billowing behind him. It's a sculpture group of two, forming a scene, rather than a stand-alone

Apollo and Daphne

The Rape of Proserpine

portrait. And the subject is classical. Even in strict Counter-Reformation times, there was always a place for groping, if the subject matter had a moral—this one taught you not to pursue fleeting earthly pleasures. And, besides, Bernini tends to show a lot of skin, but no genitals.

▶ *Pass through the cardinal's private chapel and into...*

Room IV

Bernini—*The Rape of Proserpine (Il Ratto di Proserpina,* 1622)

Pluto, King of the Underworld, strides into his realm and shows off his catch—the beautiful daughter of the earth goddess. His three-headed guard dog Cerberus (who guards the gates of hell), barks triumphantly. Pluto is squat, thick, and uncouth, with knotted muscles and untrimmed beard. He's trying not to hurt her, but she pushes her divine molester away and twists to call out for help. Tears roll down her cheeks. She wishes she could turn into a tree.

Even at the tender age of 24, Bernini was the master of marble. Look how Pluto's fingers dig into her frantic body as if it was real flesh. Bernini picked out this Carrara marble, knowing that its relative suppleness and ivory hue would lend itself to a fleshy statue. While Renaissance works were designed to be seen from the front, Bernini creates theater-in-the-round—full of action, designed to be experienced as you walk around it.

▶ *In a niche over Pluto's right shoulder, find...*

Artist Unknown—*Diana the Hunter (Artemide)*

The goddess has been running through the forest. Now she's spotted her prey, and slows down, preparing to string her (missing) bow with an arrow. Or is she smoking a (missing) cigarette? Scholars debate it. The statue is a second century B.C. Greek original, amazingly intact.

The Marbles in Room IV

As you peruse the statues, emperor busts, and decoration in this room, appreciate the beauty of the different types of marble: Bernini's ivory Carrara, Diana's translucent white, purple porphyry emperors, granite-like columns that support them, wood-grained pilasters on the walls, and the different colors on the floor—green, red, gray, lavender, and yellow, some grainy, some "marbled" like a steak. Some of the world's most beautiful and durable things have been made from the shells of sea creatures

Gian Lorenzo Bernini (1598–1680)

A Renaissance Man in Counter-Reformation times, Bernini almost personally invented the Baroque style, transforming the city of Rome. If you're visiting Rome, you will see Bernini's work, guaranteed.

Bernini was a child prodigy in his father's sculpting studio, growing up among Europe's rich and powerful. His flam-

St. Teresa in Ecstasy

boyant personality endeared him to his cultured employers—the popes in Rome, Louis XIV in France, and Charles I in England. He was extremely prolific, working fast and utilizing an army of assistants.

Despite the fleshiness and sensuality of his works, Bernini was a religious man, seeing his creativity as an extension of God's. In stark contrast to the Protestant world's sobriety, Bernini shamelessly embraced pagan myths and nude goddesses, declaring them all part of the "catholic"—that is, universal—Church.

Bernini, a master of multimedia, was a...

- Sculptor (Borghese Gallery and *St. Teresa in Ecstasy*)
- Architect (St. Peter's Square and more)
- Painter (Borghese Gallery)
- Interior decorator (the *baldacchino* canopy and other works in St. Peter's)
- Civic engineer (fountains in Piazza Navona, Piazza Barberini, Piazza di Spagna, and more).

Even works done by other artists a century later such as the Trevi Fountain can be traced indirectly to Bernini, the man who invented Baroque, the "look" of Rome for the next two centuries.

layered in sediment, fossilized into limestone, then baked and crystallized by the pressure of the earth—marble.

Room VI

Bernini—*Aeneas* (*Enea che fugge,* etc., 1620)

Aeneas' home in Troy is in flames, and he escapes with the three most important things: his family (decrepit father on his shoulder, baby boy), his household gods (the statues in dad's hands), and the Eternal Flame (carried by son). They're all in shock, lost in thought, facing an uncertain future. Eventually (according to legend), Aeneas will arrive in Italy, establish the city of Rome, and house the flame in the Temple of Vesta.

Bernini was just 20 when he started this, his first major work for Cardinal Borghese. Bernini's portrayal of human flesh—from baby fat to middle-aged muscle to sagging decrepitude—is astonishing. Still, the flat-footed statue just stands there—it lacks the Baroque energy of his more mature work. More lively are the reliefs up at the ceiling, with their dancing, light-footed soldiers with do-si-do shields.

Room VII

The "Theater of the Universe"

The room's decor sums up the eclectic nature of the villa. There are Greek statues, Roman mosaics, and fake "Egyptian" sphinxes and hieroglyphs. Look out the window past the sculpted gardens at the mesh domes of the aviary, once filled with exotic birds. Cardinal Borghese's vision was to make a place where art, history, music, nature, and science from every place and time would come together..."a theater of the universe."

Room VIII

Caravaggio

This room holds the greatest collection of Caravaggio paintings anywhere. Caravaggio (1571–1610) brought Christian saints down to earth with gritty realism, using ordinary people as his models. His subjects emerge from a dark background, lit by a harsh, unflattering light, which highlights part of the figure, leaving the rest in deep shadows.

Bacchus, by Caravaggio   *Deposition,* by Raphael

Caravaggio's saints are balding and wrinkled. His *Bacchus*—a self-portrait—is pale and puffy-faced. The Madonnas scarcely glow. The boy Jesus is buck naked. The painting of *La Madonna dei Palafrenieri* was removed from St. Peter's because Mary had the face of Rome's most famous prostitute.

In *David with Head of Goliath,* David sticks Goliath's severed head (another self-portrait) right in the viewer's face. The work was painted after Caravaggio had killed a man and was forced to flee Rome. By portraying himself as Goliath, he symbolically gives his head to the pope as a request for forgiveness. The pope accepted, but Caravaggio died of yellow fever on his way home.

▸ *Part one of your visit is done. Remember, you must visit the Pinacoteca (upstairs) within your two-hour window of time.*

To reach the Pinacoteca, head through the main entry hall back to Room IV, find the entry to the staircase in the far right corner, and spiral up. Start in Room XIV.

Pinacoteca (Painting Gallery)

Room XIV

Several objects in this room give a clearer picture of the man who built the villa (Cardinal Scipione), and the man who helped decorate it (Bernini).

▸ *Along the long wall, find the following statues and paintings by Bernini. Start with the two identical white busts set on columns.*

Bernini—*Busts of Cardinal Borghese* (*Ritr. del Card. Scipione Borghese,* 1632)

Say *grazie* to the man who built this villa, assembled the collection, and hired Bernini to sculpt masterpieces. The cardinal is caught turning as if greeting someone at a party. There's a twinkle in his eye, and he opens his mouth to make a witty comment.

This man of the cloth was, in fact, a sophisticated (and not terribly religious) hedonist. But as the pope's nephew, he became cardinal. He used church funds to buy beautiful things, many of which are still on display here in the gallery.

Notice that there are two identical versions of this bust. The first one started cracking along the forehead (visible) just as Bernini was finishing it. *No problema*—Bernini whipped out a replacement in just three days.
▶ *On the left wall above the middle table, find these paintings...*

Two Bernini Self-Portraits (*Autoritratto Giovanile,* 1623, and *Autoritratto in età Matura,* 1630–1635)
Bernini was a master of many media, including painting. The younger Bernini (age 25) looks out a bit hesitantly, as if he's still finding his way in high-class society. The next self-portrait (age 35) has more confidence and facial hair—the dashing, vibrant man who would rebuild Rome in Baroque style.
▶ *On the table below, find the smaller...*

Bust of Pope Paul V
Cardinal Scipione's uncle was a more sober man than his nephew, but he was also a patron of the arts with a good eye for talent who hired Bernini's father. When Pope Paul V saw sketches made by little Gian Lorenzo, he announced, "This boy will be the Michelangelo of his age."
▶ *To the right of the Borghese busts, find a small statue of...*

Two Babies Milking a Goat
Bernini was 11 years old when he did this. That's about the age I was when I mastered how to make a Play-Doh snake.
▶ *Room IX is back near the top of the staircase you ascended to get here.*

Room IX

Raphael (Raffaello Sanzio)—*Deposition (Deposizione di Cristo,* 1507)
Jesus is being taken from the cross. The men support him while the women

support Mary (in purple). The woman who commissioned the painting had recently lost her son. We see two different faces of grief: mother Mary faints at the horror, while Mary Magdalene—rushing up to take Christ's hand—still can't quite believe he's gone.

In true Renaissance style, Raphael (1483–1520) orders the scene with geometrical perfection. The curve of Jesus' body is echoed by the swirl of Mary Magdalene's hair, and then by the curve of Calvary Hill, where Christ met his fate.

Room X

Correggio—*Danaë* (c. 1531)

Cupid strips Danaë as she spreads her legs, most unladylike, to receive a trickle of gold from the smudgy cloud overhead—this was Zeus' idea of intercourse with a human. The sheets are rumpled, and Danaë looks right where the action is with a smile on her face. It's hard to believe that a supposedly religious family would display such an erotic work. But the Borgheses felt that all forms of human expression—including physical passion—glorified God.

▶ *Backtrack through the room with the two cardinal busts, then turn left and travel to the farthest room.*

Room XX

Titian (Tiziano Vecellio)—*Sacred and Profane Love* (*Amor Sacro e Amor Profano, c. 1515*)

The sacred woman and the profane—which is which?

The naked woman on the right actually embodies sacred love. She

Danaë, by Correggio

Sacred and Profane Love, by Titian

has nothing to hide and enjoys open spaces filled with light, life, a church in the distance, and even a couple of lovers in the field.

The material girl who represents profane love is dressed in fine clothes, with her box of treasures, fortified castle, and dark, claustrophobic landscape. She is recently married, and she cradles a vase filled with jewels representing the riches of earthly love. Her naked twin on the right holds the burning flame of eternal, heavenly love. Baby Cupid, between them, playfully stirs the waters.

Symbolically, the steeple on the right points up to the love of heaven, while on the left, soldiers prepare to "storm the castle" of the new bride. Miss Heavenly Love looks jealous.

This exquisite painting expresses the spirit of the Renaissance—that earth and heaven are two sides of the same coin. And here in the Borghese Gallery, that love of earthly beauty can be spiritually uplifting—as long as you feel it within two hours.

Sights

Rome itself is its own best sight. Watching Romans go about their everyday business is endlessly fascinating, whether you ever visit a museum or not. Take time to observe how past and present co-exist in the Eternal City.

I've clustered Rome's sights into 10 walkable neighborhoods for more efficient sightseeing. In the Ancient Rome neighborhood, for example, you could string together a number of great sights, from the Colosseum to Capitol Hill, in one sweaty day of sightseeing. You'll find a full day's worth of sights in the Pantheon neighborhood, near Vatican City, and more. For nearby restaurants, ✪ see the maps on pages 196–199.

Note that some of Rome's biggest sights (marked with a ✪) are described in the individual walks and tours chapters.

ANCIENT ROME

The core of the ancient city, where the grandest monuments were built, stretches from the Colosseum to Capitol Hill. In Caesar's day, this was "downtown Rome"—citizens shopped at the bustling malls of the Forum, razzed gladiators at the Colosseum, or climbed Capitol Hill to sacrifice a goat to Jupiter.

Today, the area is a rather barren tourist zone in the middle of the modern city. You'll find acres and acres of the planet's most famous ruins, but relatively few shops, restaurants, or everyday Romans. Fortunately, the modern world is just a few minutes' walk away. Metro stop Colosseo puts you right in the thick of the action. For recommendations on eateries in the area, ✪ see page 194.

▲▲▲Colosseum (Colosseo)
✪ *See the Colosseum Tour on page 13.*

▲▲▲Roman Forum (Foro Romano)
✪ *See the Roman Forum Tour on page 27.*

Key to Symbols

Sights are rated:
    ▲▲▲   Don't miss
    ▲▲   Try hard to see
    ▲   Worthwhile if you can make it
No rating   Worth knowing about

For opening times, if a sight is listed as "May-Oct daily 9:00-16:00," it's open from 9 A.M. until 4 P.M. from the first day of May until the last day of October.

Ancient Rome

▲▲Palatine Hill (Monte Palatino)

The hill overlooking the Forum is jam-packed with history, but there's only the barest skeleton of rubble left to tell the story.

We get our word "palace" from this hill where the emperors lived in a sprawling 150,000-square-foot palace. You'll wander among vague outlines of rooms, courtyards, fountains, a banquet hall with a heated floor, and a sunken stadium. The throne room was the center of power for an empire of 50 million that stretched from England to Africa. The Palatine museum's statues and frescoes help you imagine the former luxury of this now-desolate hilltop.

In one direction are expansive views over the dusty Circus Maximus chariot course. In the other are photogenic views of the Forum.

Supposedly, Romulus and Remus were suckled by a she-wolf on Palatine Hill, raised by shepherds, and grew to found the city in 753 B.C. Quaint legend? Well, archaeologists claim to have found a revered wolf's cave (not open to tourists), and you can see the remains of shepherds' huts, dated around 800 B.C. The legend enters into history.

▶ *€12 combo-ticket also includes the Roman Forum and Colosseum. Open daily 8:30 until one hour before sunset: April–Sept until 19:15, Oct until 18:30, off-season closes as early as 16:30; last entry one hour before closing.*

The main entrance is 150 yards south of the Colosseum on Via di San Gregorio. Consider buying your combo-ticket or Roma Pass here, where there's rarely a line. You can also enter the Palatine from within the Roman Forum, near the Arch of Titus. WCs are at the main entrance, in the museum, and hiding among the orange trees of the gardens—some of the best in the Colosseum/Forum/Palatine area. Metro: Colosseo. Tel. 06-3996-7700.

▲Circus Maximus

Ancient Rome's most popular chariot-racing stadium was 2,100 feet long and could seat a quarter of a million spectators. Ben Hur-types raced around the central spine for seven thrilling laps while thousands cheered and placed bets on the outcome. Today, only a scant outline remains, but the sunken cigar-shaped track has provided a natural amphitheater for concerts and public spectacles.

▶ *The Circus Maximus is always open and free.*

▲Arch of Constantine
✪ *See page 24 in the Colosseum Tour chapter.*

▲St. Peter-in-Chains Church (San Pietro in Vincoli)
Built in the fifth century to house the chains that held St. Peter (now under the altar), this church is most famous for a monument by Michelangelo featuring his statue of *Moses*.

In 1505, the egomaniacal Pope Julius II asked Michelangelo to build a massive tomb—a free-standing pyramid, with 40 statues, to stand in the center of St. Peter's Basilica. Michelangelo labored on it for four decades, but got distracted by other gigs such as the Sistine Chapel. In 1542, Michelangelo and his assistants half-heartedly pieced together a few remnants in St. Peter-in-Chains.

What we see today is not a full-blown 3-D pyramid but a 2-D wall monument framing a handful of statues. The statue of Pope Julius (probably by Michelangelo's own hand) reclines on his fake coffin midway up the wall and looks down at the monument's centerpiece—*Moses*.

Moses, just returned from meeting face-to-face with God, senses trouble. Slowly he turns to see his followers worshipping a golden calf. As his anger builds, he glares and cradles the Ten Commandments, about to spring out of his chair and spank the naughty Children of Israel.

Why does Moses have horns? Centuries ago, the Hebrew word for "rays" was mistranslated as "horns." But it also captures an air of *terribilità,* a kind of scary charisma possessed by Moses, Pope Julius...and Michelangelo.

▶ *Free. Open April-Sept 8:00-12:30 & 15:30-19:00, Oct-March 8:00-12:30 & 15:00-18:00, modest dress required. The church is a 15-minute uphill, zigzag walk from the Colosseum. Or, from the Cavour Metro station, walk downhill on Via Cavour a half-block, then climb the pedestrian staircase called Via di San Francesco di Paola, which leads right to the church.*

Mamertine Prison

This 2,500-year-old cistern-like prison is where, according to Christian tradition, the Romans imprisoned Saints Peter and Paul. Though it was long a charming and historic sight, its artifacts have been removed, and today it's run by a commercial tour-bus company charging €10 for a cheesy "multimedia" walk-through. Don't go in. Instead, stand outside and imagine how this dank cistern once housed prisoners of the emperor. Amid fat rats and rotting corpses, unfortunate humans awaited slow deaths. It's said that a miraculous fountain sprang up inside so Peter could convert and baptize his jailers, who were also subsequently martyred. Before the commercial ruination of this sacred and ancient site, on the walls you could read lists of notable prisoners (Christian and non-Christian) and the ways they were executed: strangolati, decapitato, morto per fame (died of hunger). The sign by the Christian names read, "Here suffered, victorious for the triumph of Christ, these martyr saints." Today this sight itself has been martyred by a city apparently desperate to monetize its heritage.

Bocca della Verità

The "Mouth of Truth" at the Church of Santa Maria in Cosmedin draws a playful crowd. Stick your hand in the mouth of the gaping stone face in the porch wall. As the legend goes (and was popularized by the 1953 film *Roman Holiday*, starring Gregory Peck and Audrey Hepburn), if you're a liar, your hand will be gobbled up.

▶ *€0.50. Open daily 9:30–17:50, closes earlier off-season. Located on Piazza Bocca della Verità, near the northwest end of Circus Maximus.*

▲Trajan's Column, Market, and Imperial Forums

Trajan's 140-foot column—the grandest from antiquity—was the centerpiece of a complex of buildings built by the Emperor Trajan (who ruled A.D. 98-117). After Trajan conquered and looted central Europe, he returned to Rome with his booty and shook it all over the city. He built a forum of markets, civic buildings, and temples to rival that of the nearby Roman Forum.

Trajan's Column is carved with a spiral relief trumpeting Trajan's exploits. It winds upward—more than 200 yards long with 2,500 figures—from the assembling of the army to the victory sacrifice at the top. A gleaming bronze statue of Trajan once capped the column, where St. Peter stands today.

The rest of Trajan's Forum is now ruined and unimpressive, except for one grand structure—Trajan's Market, a semi-circular brick building nestled into the cutaway curve of Quirinal Hill. Part shopping mall, part warehouse, part office building, this was where Romans could browse through goods from every corner of their vast empire—exotic fruits from Africa, spices from Asia, and fish-and-chips from Londinium. The 13 arches of the lower level may have held produce; the 26 windows above lit a covered arcade; and the roofline housed more stalls—150 shops in all.

The nearby **Museum of the Imperial Forums** has statue fragments and exhibits from both Trajan's Forum and other nearby forums. The museum also gives you access to parts of Trajan's Market and Forum.

Appreciate Trajan's ambition. To build all this, he removed a natural ridgeline that once connected Capitol Hill and Quirinal Hill. Trajan's Column marks the ridge's original height—140 feet.

▶ *Trajan's Column, Forum, and Market (always free and viewable) are just a few steps off Piazza Venezia, near the Victor Emmanuel Monument.*

The Museum of the Imperial Forums is at Via IV Novembre 94, up the staircase from Trajan's Column. €11. Open Tue–Sun 9:00–19:00, closed Mon, last entry 30 minutes before closing. Tel. 06-0608, www.mercati ditraiano.it.

Capitol Hill and Piazza Venezia

The geographical (if not spiritual) center of Rome, this area straddles both the ancient and modern worlds. Capitol Hill was ancient Rome's political center, and today is home to several distinguished sights. At the foot of the hill is modern Piazza Venezia, a traffic-filled square where four major boulevards meet. Between the Hill and the Piazza squats the massive white Victor Emmanuel Monument, 20 stories tall.

▲Capitol (or Capitoline) Hill

Of Rome's famous seven hills, this is the smallest, tallest, and most famous. As home of the ancient Temple of Jupiter—the king of the gods—the hill was the seat of government, giving us our word "capitol." Some 2,500 years later, Rome is still ruled from here.

There are several routes to the top: From the Forum, take the steep staircase near the Arch of Septimius Severus. From Via dei Fori Imperiali, take the winding road. The grandest ascent is up the Michelangelo-built staircase from Piazza Venezia, to the right of the Victor Emmanuel Monument.

The square atop the hill, called the Campidoglio (kahm-pi-DOHL-yoh), resonates with history. In the 1530s, Michelangelo was asked to restore the square to its ancient glory. He placed the ancient equestrian statue of Marcus Aurelius as the square's focal point. Behind the statue he put the mayoral palace. The twin buildings on either side (now the Capitoline Museums) were situated at an angle, drawing the focus inward. Michelangelo gave the buildings the "giant order"—tall pilasters that span two stories—making these big buildings feel more intimate. Michelangelo's design welcomes and draws you in.

Next to the mayor's palace is a copy of the famous statue of the She-Wolf suckling Romulus and Remus, which became the symbol of Rome. The terrace just downhill offers a grand view of the Forum. Near the viewpoint is *il nasone* ("the big nose"), a refreshing water fountain. Block the spout with your fingers, and water spurts up for drinking. A Roman joke goes: Where does a cheap Roman boy take his girl on a date? To the *nasone* for a drink.

Capitol Hill & Piazza Venezia

S. APOSTOLI

VIA DEL CORSO

TIME ELEVATOR ROMA

Villa Colonna

GALLERIA DORIA PAMPHILJ

VIA 4 NOVEMBRE

VIA BATTISTI

(B) #64,40

VIA PLEBISCITO

Piazza Venezia

PALAZZO VENEZIA

8 (T)

(B)

To Gesù & Pantheon

S. MARCO

(B) #64

TRAJAN'S COLUMN

MUSEUM OF IMPERIAL FORUMS & TRAJAN'S MARKET

VIA D'ARACOELI

#110 (B)

VICTOR EMMANUEL MONUMENT

TRAJAN'S FORUM

VIA ALESSANDRINA

(T)

CAFÉ 10

STA. MARIA ARACOELI

VIA DEI FORI IMPERIALI

GRAND STAIRCASE

9

6

7

PALAZZO NUOVO

1

STATUE

2

3

4

5

To Colosseum & M

Piazza Caffarelli

PUBLIC CAFÉ ENTRANCE

TABULARIUM

CAPITOLINE MUSEUMS

PALAZZO SENATORIO

EXIT

VIA TEATRO MARCELLO

5

CAFÉ

ARCH OF SEPTIMIUS SEVERUS

PALAZZO DEI CONSERVATORI

SAN TEODORO

ROMAN FORUM

Piazza d. Consolazione

100 Meters

100 Yards

1 Capitol Hill Square
2 Capitoline Museums Entrance
3 Copy of She-Wolf Statue
4 "Il Nasone" Water Fountain
5 Views of Forum (2)
6 Shortcut to Santa Maria in Aracoeli Church
7 Shortcut to Victor Emmanuel Monument
8 Mussolini's Balcony
9 Michelangelo's Grand Staircase
10 Rome from the Sky

▲▲Capitoline Museums (Musei Capitolini)

Some of ancient Rome's best-known statues are housed in the two palaces that flank the equestrian statue on Capitol Hill. You'll see the original She-Wolf statue and the original equestrian statue of Marcus Aurelius (the ones in the Campidoglio are replicas). The statue of Marcus, a pagan emperor, was not destroyed by Dark Age Christians, perhaps because they mistook it for the Christian-friendly emperor Constantine.

There are other statues you'll likely recognize, such as the *Boy Extracting a Thorn* and the *Dying Gaul*. Don't miss the narcissistic bust of *Emperor Commodus as Hercules*.

The museum displays the scant remains of Capitol Hill's once-massive, renowned Temple of Jupiter. You'll also visit the Tabularium, the ancient Roman archive. While it's pretty vacant now, it offers a superb head-on view of the Forum.

▶ *€7.50–12, depending on the cost of temporary exhibits. Open Tue–Sun 9:00–20:00, closed Mon, last entry one hour before closing. The café has great city views and is open to even non-museum-goers through its entrance off Piazza Caffarelli, through door #4. Tel. 06-8205-9127, www.museicapitolini.org.*

Santa Maria in Aracoeli

This venerable church atop Capitol Hill is built on the site where Emperor Augustus (supposedly) had a vision of Mary and Christ standing on an "altar in the sky" *(ara coeli)*. The church is Roman history in a nutshell—a marble floor from ancient times, Renaissance frescoes by Pinturicchio (first chapel on the right), and side chapels from Gothic to Baroque. A famous wooden statue of the baby Jesus (Santo Bambino) was stolen in 1994, but a copy is still venerated at Christmastime, a Roman tradition. The daunting 125-step staircase up Capitol Hill to the entrance

"Back Door" Entrances to the Victor Emmanuel Monument and Aracoeli Church

A clever shortcut lets you go directly from the Campidoglio atop Capitol Hill to the Victor Emmanuel Monument and Santa Maria in Aracoeli church, avoiding long flights of stairs.

Facing the Campidoglio's mayoral palace, head to the left, climbing the wide set of stairs near the She-Wolf statue. Midway up the stairs (at the column), turn left to reach the back entrance to the Aracoeli church. To reach the Victor Emmanuel Monument, pass by the column and continue to the top of the steps, pass through the iron gate, and enter the small unmarked door at #13 on the right. You'll soon emerge on a café terrace that leads to the monument and Rome from the Sky elevator.

was once climbed—on their knees—by Roman women who wished for a child. Today, they don't...and Italy has Europe's lowest birthrate.

▶ *Open daily April–Oct 9:00–12:30 & 15:00–18:30, shorter hours off-season. To avoid some of those stairs, see the sidebar above.*

▲Victor Emmanuel Monument

This huge, white monument to Italy's first king was built to celebrate the 50th anniversary of the country's unification in 1870. Remember, after the fall of ancient Rome (A.D. 476), there was no Italian nation for over a thousand years. The Italian peninsula was a patchwork of bickering principalities and dukedoms dominated by foreigners. When Italy finally unified, this "Altar of the Nation" was a way to forge a new national identity through symbolism. Near the base, soldiers guard Italy's Tomb of the Unknown Soldier as Italian flags fly and the eternal flame flickers.

The monument's scale is over-the-top—200 feet high and 500 feet wide. The king-on-his-high-horse statue is 43 feet long, the biggest equestrian statue in the world. The king's moustache is five feet wide, and a person could fit into the horse's hoof. Atop the structure stand glorious chariots like on an ancient triumphal arch.

Locals love to hate the monument. They call it "the wedding cake," "the typewriter," or "the dentures." (Less derisively, they refer to it as "the Vittoriano.") It wouldn't be so bad if it wasn't sitting on a priceless acre of ancient Rome.

You can climb the 242 punishing steps to a middle level with great views of the Eternal City. (You can also get there by the "Back Door" short-cut from Capitol Hill.) From the middle level, you can catch the **Rome from the Sky** elevator up to the tippy-top for a truly spectacular, 360-degree view—perhaps even better than from St. Peter's dome. Go in late afternoon, when it's beginning to cool off and Rome glows.

▶ *Free admission to middle level, daily 9:30–18:30. The Rome from the Sky elevator costs €7 and runs Mon-Thu 9:30–18:30, Fri-Sun 9:30-19:30, ticket office closes 45 minutes earlier, tel. 06-6920-2049. Catch it near the top, by the outdoor café, following signs to* ascensori panoramici.

Piazza Venezia

The vast square, dominated by the Victor Emmanuel Monument, is a major transportation hub in the center of the modern city. Stand with your back to the monument to get oriented. Look down Via del Corso, the city's main north-south axis, surrounded by Rome's classiest shopping district. In the 1930s, Benito Mussolini whipped up Italy's fascist fervor from the balcony on the left (the less-grand one). Mussolini created boulevard Via dei Fori Imperiali (to your right) to open up views of the Colosseum to impress his visiting friend Adolf Hitler.

PANTHEON NEIGHBORHOOD

The area around the Pantheon is the heart of Rome. This neighborhood stretches from the Tiber River through Campo de' Fiori and Piazza Navona, past the Pantheon to the Trevi Fountain. To get there by taxi or bus (#64 or 40), aim for the large square called Largo Argentina, a few blocks south of the Pantheon.

Besides being home to ancient sights and historic churches, the Pantheon neighborhood is the place that gives Rome its urban-village feel. Wander narrow streets, sample the many shops and eateries, and gather with the locals in squares marked by bubbling fountains. It's especially enjoyable in the evening, with a gelato in hand. The restaurants bustle and streets are jammed with foot traffic.

For restaurants in the area, ✪ see page 188. For more on nocturnal sightseeing, ✪ see the Night Walk Across Rome chapter on page 43.

Pantheon Neighborhood

▲▲▲Pantheon

⭐ *See the Pantheon Tour on page 55.*

▲▲Campo de' Fiori

⭐ *See page 44 in the Night Walk Across Rome chapter.*

▲▲Piazza Navona
✪ *See page 45 in the Night Walk Across Rome chapter.*

▲▲Church of San Luigi dei Francesi
The French national church in Rome has one truly *magnifique* sight—the chapel in the far left corner, decorated by the ground-breaking Baroque painter Caravaggio (1571-1610).

In *The Calling of St. Matthew* (left wall), Jesus walks into a dingy bar, raises his arm, and points to a sheepish Matthew, calling him to discipleship. The other two paintings show where Matthew's call led him—writing a Gospel of Jesus' life (center wall), and eventually giving up his own life for the Christian cause (*Martyrdom,* right).

Caravaggio shocked the religious world by showing holy scenes with gritty, ultra-realistic details—a balding saint, an angel that doesn't glow, a truly scary executioner—all lit by a harsh third-degree spotlight that pierces the gloom. In the *Martyrdom,* the bearded face in the background (to the left of the executioner's shoulder) is a self-portrait of a dispassionate Caravaggio.

▶ *Free, daily 10:30–12:30 & 15:00–19:00 except closed Thu afternoon, good €3 booklet, www.saintlouis-rome.net. Bring coins to light the Caravaggios.*

▲▲Gesù Church
The center of the Jesuit order and the best symbol of the Catholic Counter-Reformation, the Gesù (jay-zoo) is packed with overblown art and under-appreciated history.

The facade's scroll-like shoulders became the model for hundreds of similar Catholic churches across the globe, signaling the coming of Baroque.

Inside, the huge ceiling fresco (by Il Baciccio) shows a glowing cross with the Jesuit seal ("I.H.S."). The cross astounds the faithful and sends infidels plunging downward. The damned spill over the edge of the painting's frame, becoming 3-D stucco sculptures, on their way to hell. As Catholics fought Protestants for the hearts and minds of the world's Christians, this propaganda art had a clear message—pervert the true faith, and this is your fate.

The founder of the Jesuit order, St. Ignatius of Loyola (1491-1556), lies buried in the left transept beneath a towering altarpiece. Ignatius, a war veteran wounded in battle, rallied Jesuit monks to be ideological warriors, fighting heretics such as Martin Luther. To the right of the altarpiece, a statue shows the Church as an angry nun hauling back with a whip and just spanking a bunch of miserable Protestants. Not too subtle.

▶ *Free, daily 7:00–12:30 & 16:00–19:45, www.chiesadelgesu.org.*

▲▲Church of Santa Maria sopra Minerva

This church is a mish-mosh of minor sights:

From the outside, see an Egyptian obelisk atop a Baroque elephant (by Bernini) in front of a Gothic church built over (sopra) a pagan Temple of Minerva. Inside Rome's only Gothic church, you'll see crisscross arches, a starry ceiling, and stained-glass windows. Under the main altar lies the body of St. Catherine of Siena (her head is in Siena). In the 1300s, this Italian nun was renowned for having visions of her mystical marriage with Jesus.

Left of the altar stands Michelangelo's statue of *Christ Bearing the Cross* (1519–1520). His athletic body, bulging biceps, awkwardly-posed legs—and the fact that the statue was completed by a mediocre assistant—made this one of the master's less-renowned works. Originally, Christ was buck naked, but later censors gave him his bronze girdle. The bronze shoe protects the right toe from the kisses of the faithful.

The tomb of Fra Angelico ("Beato Angelico 1387–1455"), the great early Renaissance painter and Dominican monk, is near the statue, just up the three stairs.

▶ *Free, Mon–Fri 7:00–19:00, Sat-Sun 8:00–12:30 & 15:30-19:00.*

Church of San Ignazio

This church is a riot of Baroque illusions. The colorful ceiling fresco shows St. Ignatius (a small figure perched on a cloud in the center) having a vision of Christ with the Cross. The cross beams heavenly light to the four corners of the earth—including America (to the left), depicted as a bare-breasted Native American maiden spearing naked men. Note how the actual columns of the church are extended into the painting. Now fix your eyes on the arch at the far end of the painting. Walk up the nave, and watch the arch grow and tower over you.

Before you reach the center of the church, stop at the small yellow disk on the floor and look up into the central (black) dome. Keeping your eye on the dome, walk under and past it. Building project runs out of money? Hire a painter to paint a fake, flat dome.

Back outside, the church stands on a square with several converging streets that has been compared to a stage set. Sit on the church steps, admire the theatrical yellow backdrop of the building across the way, and watch the "actors" enter one way and exit another, in the human opera that is modern Rome.

▶ *Free, Mon–Sat 7:30–19:00, Sun 9:00–19:00.*

▲Galleria Doria Pamphilj

This underappreciated gallery, tucked away in the heart of the old city, lets you wander through a lavish palace crammed with paintings by Caravaggio, Titian, Raphael, and Velázquez. The audioguide (included) is lovingly narrated by the current Prince Pamphilj (pam-FEEL-yee).

▶ *€10.50. Open daily 10:00–17:00, last entry 45 minutes before closing, café. Located two blocks north of Piazza Venezia at Via del Corso 305. Tel. 06-679-7323, www.dopart.it/roma.*

▲Trevi Fountain

✪ *See page 52 in the Night Walk Across Rome chapter.*

NEAR TERMINI TRAIN STATION

While the train station neighborhood is not atmospheric, it contains some high-powered sights. These sights are within a 10-minute walk from the station, near Metro stops Termini and Repubblica.

▲▲▲National Museum of Rome
(Museo Nazionale Romano Palazzo Massimo alle Terme)

Ancient Rome lasted a thousand years... and so do most Roman history courses. But if you want a breezy overview of this fascinating society, there's no better place than the National Museum of Rome. The National Museum's main branch, at Palazzo Massimo, is a historic yearbook of Roman marble statues and rare Greek originals.

On the ground floor, gaze eye-to-eye with the busts of famous Romans. There's Julius Caesar, who conquered Gaul, impregnated Cleopatra, and created one-man rule. His adopted son Augustus, shown wearing the hooded robes of a priest, became the first emperor. The rest of the Julio-Claudian family is a parade of shady characters—Augustus'

Sights

Near Termini Train Station

Map labels:

To Villa Borghese Gardens
Piazza Sallustio
U.S. EMBASSY
VIA SALLUSTIANA
VIA FLAVIA
VIA XX SETTEMBRE
VIALE DEL CASTRO PRETORIO
To Spanish Steps
VIA VENETO
V. BISO
SANTA MARIA VITTORIA
VIA CERNAIA
MONTEBELLO
VIA GAETA
S. M. BATT
VIA PALESTRO
CAPPUCCIN CRYPT
VIA BARBERINI
SANTA SUSANNA
PARIGI
BATHS OF DIOCLETIAN
Piazza Indipendenza
VIA VICENZA
VIA MARGHERA
Barb
Piazza Barberini
VIA SISTINA
VIA DEL TRITONE
AVIG.
VIA D. QUATTRO FONTANE
V. D. RAS.
Republica
STA. MARIA DEGLI ANGELI
MAGENTA
Castro Pretorio
VIA MILAZZO
Piazza Republica
EINAUDI
Piazza dei Cinquecento
PALAZZO DEL QUIRINALE
SAN CARLINO
VIA NAZIONALE
VIA FIRENZE
VIA VIMINALE
VIA NICOLA
V. LE ENRICO DE NICOLA
NATIONAL MUSEUM
Terminia
TERMINI STATION
VIA MARSALA
QUIRINALE
VIA NAPOLI
VIA TORINO
MANIN
Piazza del Quirinale
To Trevi & Pantheon
VIA DEPRETIS
VIA DEI SERPENTI
VIA MILANO
VIA PANISPERNA
VIA URBANA
SANTA MARIA MAGGIORE
GIOBERTI
VIA GIO. GIOLITTI
VIA FILIPPO TURATI
Largo Magnanapoli
VIA CAVOUR
NAPOLEONE III
VIA C. ALBERTO
VIA MERULANA
MONTI
SANTA PRASSEDE
Piazza Vittorio Emanuele II
250 Meters
250 Yards
Cavour
VIA G. LANZA
VIA CAVOUR
MUSEUM OF ASIAN ART
Vittorio Emanuele
To Colosseum & Forum

---

wily wife Livia, her moody son Tiberius, and crazy Caligula, who ordered men to kneel before him as a god.

On the first floor is the best-preserved Roman copy of the Greek *Discus Thrower*. Caught in mid-motion, his perfect balance summed up the order the ancients saw in nature. Statues of athletes like this commonly stood in the baths, where Romans cultivated healthy bodies, minds, and social skills, hoping to lead well-rounded lives. Other statues originally stood in the pleasure gardens of the Roman rich—surrounded by greenery, with the splashing sound of fountains, the statues all painted in bright, lifelike colors. Though executed by Romans, the themes are mostly Greek, depicting godlike humans and human-looking gods.

The second floor focuses on frescoes and mosaics that once decorated the walls and floors of Roman villas. They're remarkably realistic and unstuffy, featuring everyday people, animals, leafy gardens, and geometrical designs.

Finally, descend into the basement to see the best coin collection in Europe. It follows the money trail from the ancient Roman *denar* to a monetary unit that is now history—the Italian lira.

▸ €10. Open Tue–Sun 9:00–19:45, closed Mon, last entry 45 minutes before closing. Located 100 yards from the train station entrance; it's the sandstone-brick building at Largo di Villa Peretti. Metro: Termini, tel. 06-3996-7700.

▲Baths of Diocletian (Terme di Diocleziano) at Santa Maria degli Angeli

Around A.D. 300, Emperor Diocletian built the largest baths in Rome—a sprawling complex of pools, gyms, and schmoozing spaces that could accommodate 3,000 bathers at a time. While most of it is ruined, a few sections have been incorporated into the Church of Santa Maria degli Angeli.

Start outside the church entrance on noisy Piazza della Repubblica. Here the baths' *caldarium* once stood, the steam room where Romans worked up a sweat. Next, they'd step into the cooler *tepidarium* (now the domed entry hall of the church), where masseuses rubbed them down.

Continue into what was once the baths' huge central hall—a football field long and seven stories high. The eight red granite columns and crisscross arches on the ceiling are original. Beyond today's church altar was the *frigidarium*, with a 32,000-square-foot swimming pool.

Mentally undress your fellow tourists and imagine hundreds of ancient Romans milling about, wrestling, doing jumping jacks, singing in the baths, and networking. Shops, bars, and fast-food vendors once catered to every Roman need.

The church we see today (from 1561) was partly designed by Michelangelo, who used the baths' main hall as the church's nave. A later architect added the entrance on Piazza della Repubblica, turning Michelangelo's nave into a long transept.

On the floor is a meridian (from 1702), a line that points north and acts as a sundial and calendar. A ray of light enters the church through a tiny hole 65 feet up the wall of the right transept. The light sweeps across the meridian at exactly noon. Where the ray crosses the line tells you the date.

The Baths of Diocletian functioned until A.D. 537, when barbarians cut the city's aqueducts, plunging Rome into a thousand years of poverty, darkness, and B.O.

▶ *Free. Open Mon–Sat 7:00–18:30, Sun 7:00–19:30, closed to sightseers during Mass. Located on Piazza della Repubblica, Metro: Repubblica. Note that the nearby Museum of the Bath, despite its name, has nothing on the baths, just so-so statuary.*

▲Santa Maria della Vittoria

This small church houses Gian Lorenzo Bernini's statue, the theatrical *St. Teresa in Ecstasy* (1652).

Teresa has just been stabbed with God's arrow of fire. Now, the angel pulls it out and watches her reaction. Teresa swoons, her eyes roll up, her hand goes limp, she parts her lips...and moans. The smiling, cherubic angel understands just how she feels. Teresa, a 16th-century Spanish nun, later talked of the "sweetness" of "this intense pain," describing her oneness with God in ecstatic, even erotic, terms.

Bernini (1598-1680), the master of multimedia, pulls out all the stops to make this mystical vision real. Actual sunlight pours through the alabaster windows, and bronze sunbeams shine on a marble angel holding a golden arrow. Teresa leans back on a cloud and her robe ripples from within, charged with her spiritual arousal. Bernini has created a little stage-setting of heaven. And watching from the "theater boxes" on either side are members of the family that commissioned the work.

▶ *Free, but bring €0.50 for coin-op light. Open Mon–Sat 8:30–12:00 & 15:30–18:00, Sun 15:30–18:00. Located 5 blocks northwest of Termini train station on Largo Susanna, Metro: Repubblica.*

NORTH ROME

The Villa Borghese Gardens form the northern border of tourists' Rome. Several sights lie inside the landscaped park, while others ring its southern perimeter, clustered around the Spanish Steps, Via Veneto, and Piazza del Popolo. The area has some of Rome's classiest fashion boutiques. Metro stops Spagna, Barberini, and Flaminio serve the neighborhood. For a list of recommended restaurants in the area, ✪ see page 190.

North Rome

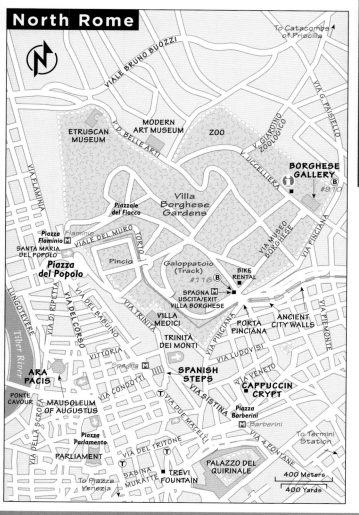

To Catacombs
of Priscilla

VIALE BRUNO BUOZZI

VIA G. PAISIELLO

ETRUSCAN
MUSEUM

V.D. BELLE ARTI

MODERN
ART MUSEUM

ZOO

V. Giardino
Zoologico

V. Uccelliera

BORGHESE
GALLERY

#910

Villa
Borghese
Gardens

VIA MUSEO BORGHESE

VIA PINCIANA

Piazzale
del Fiocco

VIA FLAMINIA

Piazza
Flaminio
Flaminio

VIALE DEL MURO

TORTO

SANTA MARIA
DEL POPOLO

Piazza
del Popolo

Pincio

Galoppatoio
(Track)
#116

BIKE
RENTAL

SPAGNA M
USCITA/EXIT
VILLA BORGHESE

Tiber River

LUNGOTEVERE

VIA DI RIPETTA

VIA DEL CORSO

VIA DEL BABUINO

VIA TRINITA

VILLA
MEDICI

VIA PINCIANA

PORTA
PINCIANA

ANCIENT
CITY WALLS

VIA PIEMONTE

TRINITÀ
DEI MONTI

VITTORIA

Spagna M

SPANISH
STEPS

VIA LUDOVISI

VIA VENETO

CAPPUCCIN
CRYPT

ARA
PACIS

PONTE
CAVOUR

VIA DELLA SCROFA

VIA CONDOTTI

VIA SISTINA

Piazza
Barberini

M Barberini

To Termini
Station

MAUSOLEUM
OF AUGUSTUS

VIA DUE MACELLI

Piazza
Parlamento

PARLIAMENT

VIA DEL TRITONE

SABINA
MURATTE

TREVI
FOUNTAIN

PALAZZO DEL
QUIRINALE

VIA 4 FONTANE

To Piazza
Venezia

400 Meters

400 Yards

▲▲▲Borghese Gallery (Galleria Borghese)
⭐ *See the Borghese Gallery Tour on page 119.*

▲Villa Borghese Gardens
Rome's scruffy three-square-mile "Central Park" is great for its shade and for people-watching the city's modern-day Romeos and Juliets. The best entrance is at the head of Via Veneto (Metro: Barberini, then a 10-minute walk up Via Veneto and through the old Roman wall at Porta Pinciana). There you'll find a cluster of buildings with a café, a kiddie arcade, and bike rental (€4/hour). Rent a bike (or, for romantics, a pedaled rickshaw—*riscio*) and follow signs to discover the park's cafés, fountains, statues, lake, viewpoint over Piazza del Popolo, and prime picnic spots.

Etruscan Museum (Villa Giulia Museo Nazionale Etrusco)
The fascinating Etruscan civilization thrived in central Italy around 600 B.C., back when Rome was just another Etruscan town. The museum's high-light is the famous "husband and wife sarcophagus." The elegant couple reclines atop their tomb (sixth century B.C., from Cerveteri) seeming to en-joy an everlasting banquet. The life-size, clay statue of *Apollo from Veii* strides forward, smiling. There's also an impressive room of gold sheets of Etruscan printing and temple statuary from the Sanctuary of Pyrgi.

▶ *€4. Open Tue–Sun 8:30–19:30, closed Mon, last entry one hour before closing, scant English information. It's in the Villa Borghese Gardens, a 20-minute walk from the Borghese Gallery at Piazzale di Villa Giulia 9, tel. 06-322-6571.*

▲Cappuccin Crypt
If you want to see artistically arranged bones, this is the place. While there's a new museum here, the morbid attraction remains the crypt. The skulls, femurs, and tibias of 4,000 friars who died between 1528 and 1870 line the walls and ceilings in intricate patterns, to the delight—or disgust—of the always-wide-eyed visitor. As you enter, a monastic message on the wall reminds you: "We were what you are...you will become what we are now."

The Crypt of the Resurrection (Room #1) sets the theme of your visit: a painting shows Jesus bringing Lazarus back to life, representing how Christ saves the faithful from the clutches of death. In the Crypt of the Skulls (#2), the central scene is an hourglass with wings. Yes, time on Earth flies. Between crypts #3 and #4, look up to see the jaunty skull with a shoulder-blade bowtie. The Crypt of the Hips (#4) features a canopy of hipbones with vertebrae bangles over its central altar.

In the Crypt of the Tibia and Fibia (#5), niches are inhabited by Capuchin friars, whose robes gave the name to the brown coffee with the frothy white cowl. We see the monks' Franciscan symbol: the robed arm of a Franciscan friar and the bare arm of Christ embracing the faithful. Above that is a bony crown. And below, in dirt brought from Jerusalem 400 years ago, are 18 graves with simple crosses.

Finally, in the Crypt of the Three Skeletons (#6), you reach the Day of Judgment. The ceiling has a skeleton with a grim-reaper scythe and a set of scales weighing the "good deeds and the bad deeds so God can judge the soul." The chapel's bony chandelier and the stars and floral motifs made by ribs and vertebrae are particularly inspired. On the ceiling above the aisle is a clock with no hands, suggesting that—once you've passed to the other side—life goes on forever. As you leave, pick up a few of Rome's most interesting postcards.

▶ *€6. Open daily 9:00–19:00. Modest dress is required, no photos, turn off mobile phones. The crypt is located below the Church of Santa Maria della Immacolata Concezione on Via Veneto, just up from Piazza Barberini, Metro: Barberini. Tel. 06-487-1185.*

▲Spanish Steps

⊕ *See page 53 in the Night Walk Across Rome chapter.*

▲▲Ara Pacis (Altar of Peace)

On January 30, 9 B.C., soon-to-be-emperor Augustus led a procession of priests up the steps and into this newly built "Altar of Peace." They sacrificed an animal on the altar and poured an offering of wine, thanking the gods for helping Augustus pacify barbarians abroad and rivals at home. This marked the dawn of the Pax Romana (C. A.D. 1–200), a Golden Age of good living, stability, dominance, and peace (pax). For the next five centuries, the Ara Pacis (AH-rah PAH-chees) hosted annual sacrifices by the emperor until the area was flooded by the Tiber River, and the monument was forgotten. In 2006, the Altar of Peace reopened to the public in a striking modern (and controversial) building.

Though simple, the Ara Pacis has all the essentials of a Roman temple: an altar for sacrifices surrounded by cubicle-like walls that enclose a consecrated space. At the base of the walls, you can still see the drain holes for washing the blood out.

The reliefs on the north side depict the parade of dignitaries who consecrated the altar. Augustus stands near the head (his body sliced in two vertically by missing stone), honored with a crown of laurel leaves. He's followed by a half-dozen bigwigs and priests (with spiked hats) and the man shouldering the sacrificial axe. Reliefs on the west side (near the altar's back door) celebrate Augustus' major accomplishments: peace (goddess Roma as a conquering amazon, right side) and prosperity (fertility goddess). Imagine the altar as it once was, standing in an open field, painted in bright colors—a mingling of myth, man, and nature.

▶ *€7.50; tightwads can look in through huge windows for free. Open Tue–Sun 9:00–19:00, closed Mon, last entry one hour before closing. The Ara Pacis is located on the east bank of the Tiber near Ponte Cavour, one long block west of Via del Corso on Via di Ara Pacis. From the Spanish Steps (Metro: Spagna) it's a 10-minute walk down Via dei Condotti. Tel. 06-0608, www.arapacis.it.*

Piazza del Popolo and the Church of Santa Maria del Popolo

This vast oval square marks the traditional north entrance to Rome. In medieval times, northern Europeans got their first look at the city from this gate in the wall. Today, three roads head south from the piazza, forming the shape of a trident (the Tridente), and leading to the city center. The piazza is known for its symmetrical design (an obelisk and two large fountains), its art-filled churches, and as the starting point for the city's evening *passeggiata* along Via del Corso.

The Church of Santa Maria del Popolo has two chapels with top-notch art. The Chigi Chapel (second on the left) was designed by Raphael and inspired—as Raphael was—by the Pantheon. Notice the Pantheon-like dome, pilasters, and capitals. Above in the oculus, God looks in, aided by angels who power the eight known planets. Raphael built the chapel for his wealthy banker friend Agostino Chigi, who lies buried in the pyramid-shaped wall tomb to the right of the altar.

In the Cerasi Chapel (left of altar), Caravaggio's *The Conversion on the Way to Damascus* shows Paul sprawled on his back beside his horse while his servant looks on. The startled future saint is blinded by the harsh light as Jesus' voice asks him, "Why do you persecute me?" Paul receives his new faith with open arms. Caravaggio's *Crucifixion of St. Peter* is shown as a banal chore; the workers toil like faceless animals. The light and dark are in high contrast. Caravaggio liked to say, "Where light falls, I will paint it."

▶ *The Church of Santa Maria del Popolo is free. Open Mon–Sat 7:00–12:00 & 16:00–19:00, Sun 8:00–13:30 & 16:30–19:30. Metro: Flaminio.*

Via del Corso *Passeggiata*

Every evening, Rome's main north-south street closes to car traffic for a few hours (roughly 17:00-19:00), and Romans flood the streets for a classic ritual—the *passeggiata,* or evening stroll. Shoppers, people-watchers, and dressed-up older folks mingle with young flirts on the prowl. It's a time to get out of the house after the heat of the afternoon, greet neighbors, show off your latest outfit, and check out your gender of choice. This neighborhood has some of Rome's most fashionable stores (generally open until 19:30), and many bars host happy hours. Saturdays and Sundays bring out the most festive crowds.

Though there's a *passeggiata* in most Italian towns, in Rome it's given a cruder, big-city nickname: the *struscio*—to "rub." Instead of genteel whispers of *"bella"* and *"bello"* ("pretty" and "handsome"), in Rome the admiration runs stronger, oriented toward consumption—they say *"buona"* and *"buono,"* meaning roughly "tasty."

To do a full *passeggiata*, walk from Piazza del Popolo (Metro: Flaminio) down Via del Corso, then turn left up Via Condotti to the Spanish Steps. While the once-classy shops along Via del Corso are a little run down these days, elegance survives in the grid of streets nearby, especially Via Borgognona and Frattini. End your walk either at the Spanish Steps (Metro: Spagna), or continue down Via del Corso to Piazza Venezia for great sunset views from atop Capitol Hill.

▲▲Catacombs of Priscilla (Catacombe di Priscilla)

While most tourists flock to the more famous catacombs on the ancient Appian Way, these are less commercialized and crowded, and feel more intimate. The catacombs are underground tombs for early Christians who once worshipped in a home on this spot. When they died—too poor to afford a plot in a cemetery—the wealthy homeowner let them be buried here.

You enter from a convent and explore a honeycomb of tunnels dug between the second and fifth centuries. You'll see some of the 40,000 burial niches carved into the volcanic tuff stone, along with a few beautiful frescoes, including what is considered the first depiction of Mary nursing the baby Jesus.

▶ €8. Open Tue–Sun 8:30–12:00 & 14:30–17:00, closed Mon, last entry 30 minutes before closing, closed one random month a year—check website or call first. Tel. 06-8620-6272, www.catacombepriscilla.com.

Visits are by 30-minute guided tour only (English-language tours generally available every 20 minutes or so).

The catacombs are far from the center—1.5 miles north of the Villa Borghese Gardens—and best reached by taxi. By bus, it's 30 minutes on bus #92 or #86 from Termini train station, or bus #63 from Piazza Venezia or Via del Corso. Located at Via Salaria 430.

VATICAN CITY

Vatican City contains the Vatican Museum (with Michelangelo's Sistine Chapel) and St. Peter's Basilica (with Michelangelo's exquisite *Pietà*). It sits on the west bank of the Tiber in an otherwise nondescript neighborhood. Nearby are a few lesser sights. Metro stops Ottaviano and Cipro are handy, and buses #64 and 40 stop in the area. For restaurant recommendations, ✪ see page 190.

Vatican City
▲▲▲Vatican Museum (Musei Vaticani)
✪ See the Vatican Museum Tour on page 63.

▲▲▲St. Peter's Basilica (Basilica San Pietro)
✪ See the St. Peter's Basilica Tour on page 93.

▲Castel Sant'Angelo
Built as a tomb for a Roman emperor, used through the Middle Ages as a castle, prison, and papal palace, and today a museum, this giant pile of ancient bricks is packed with history.

Emperor Hadrian designed his own tomb (c. A.D. 139) as a towering cylinder, 210 feet by 70 feet, topped by a cypress grove and crowned with a huge statue of Hadrian himself riding a chariot.

As Rome fell, the mausoleum became a fortress and prison. When the archangel Michael appeared miraculously above the structure (A.D.

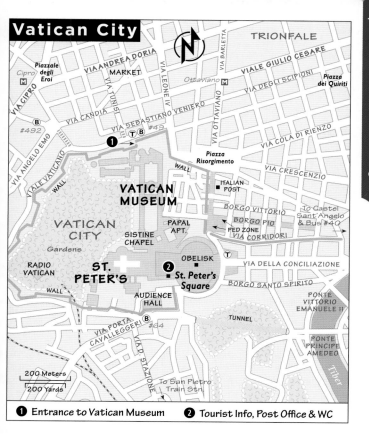

Vatican City

1 Entrance to Vatican Museum   **2** Tourist Info, Post Office & WC

590), the "castle" was renamed for this "holy angel." Through the centuries, it was expanded upward and connected to the Vatican via an elevated corridor (1277), making it a handy place of last refuge for threatened popes.

Touring the place is a stair-step workout. You circle the entire base, tracing the same route as Hadrian's funeral procession. Once inside, imagine the empty niche in the wall filled with a towering "welcome to my tomb" statue of Hadrian. Next, you trudge 400 feet up a spiral ramp to where Hadrian's ashes were placed.

From here, you continue up a staircase into the medieval addition, decorated with papal splendor, including paintings by Andrea Mantegna, Carlo Crivelli, and Luca Signorelli. Don't miss the Sala del Tesoro (Treasury), where the wealth of the Vatican was locked up in a huge chest. (*Do miss the 58 rooms of the lackluster military museum.*) Finally you emerge at the castle's highlight—the rooftop viewpoint—where you can survey the city like a pope or emperor.

▶ *€8, more for special exhibits. Open Tue–Sun 9:00–19:30, closed Mon, last entry one hour before closing. Located along the Tiber, near Vatican City, Metro: Lepanto or bus #40 or #64. Tel. 06-681-9111.*

PILGRIM'S ROME

In eastern Rome lie several venerable churches that Catholic pilgrims make a point of visiting. The main sights are found within a triangle formed by Termini station, the Colosseum, and the San Giovanni Metro stop.

Rome is the "capital" of the world's 1.1 billion Catholics. Since ancient days, pilgrims have flocked to this city where Peter and Paul preached, where Christians were martyred, Constantine legalized the religion, miraculous relics were kept, and where the pope still reigns. It was the flood of pilgrims that shaped Rome's tourist industry. In your visit today, you'll rub elbows with Nigerian nuns, Bulgarian theology students, extended Mexican families, and everyday Catholics returning to their religious roots.

Church of San Giovanni in Laterano

When this church opened its doors in A.D. 318, it became the first place in Rome where once-persecuted Christians could finally "come out" and worship openly. Through medieval times, San Giovanni was home of the popes and the center of Catholicism until the new St. Peter's opened at the Vatican during the Renaissance.

Despite its history, the church is rather barren, having been redone in the 1600s. The spacious nave—a central hall flanked by side aisles— was the model for all basilicas to follow. The 2,000-year-old bronze doors

Pilgrim's Rome

originally hung at the ancient Senate House in the Forum. You'll see (supposed) relics of Peter and Paul and (supposed) bronze columns from the Temple of Jupiter.

The bishop's chair, or "cathedra," reminds visitors that this (not St. Peter's) is the city's cathedral, presided over by the bishop of Rome—the pope.

▶ *Free. Open daily 7:00–18:30. The cloister (€2) has a Cosmati-designed mosaic floor. Metro: San Giovanni, or bus #85 or #87. Tel. 06-6988-6409.*

▲Holy Stairs (Scala Santa)

A building near the Church of San Giovanni in Laterano houses a staircase said to have been touched by Jesus. The 28 marble steps once stood in Pontius Pilate's residence in Jerusalem. Jesus climbed these steps on the day he was sentenced to death. In 326, Emperor Constantine's mother (Sta. Helena) brought them to Rome, where they were subsequently protected with a covering of walnut wood.

Each day, hundreds of faithful penitents climb these steps on their knees, reciting prayers. They look down through glass-covered sections to see stains from Jesus' blood. Visitors can join in or observe from the side. The steps lead to the "Holy of Holies" (Sancta Sanctorum), a chapel which in medieval times held important relics (now gone), and was once considered the holiest place on earth.

▶ Free. Open daily April–Sept 6:15–12:00 & 15:30–18:30, Oct–March 6:15–12:00 & 15:00–18:00. Metro: San Giovanni.

Church of Santa Maria Maggiore

One of Rome's oldest (A.D. 432), simplest, and best-preserved churches, Santa Maria Maggiore was a rare oasis of order in the days when Rome was falling around it. The church is dedicated to Holy Mary, the mother of Christ, and pilgrims come to kneel before an urn containing pieces of wood from Jesus' manger (in a lighted niche under the altar). Some of Rome's best-surviving mosaics line the nave; unfortunately, they're small and poorly-lit—bring binoculars.

The church has a glorious altar of precious stones (left transept) as well as the humble floor tomb of the artist Bernini (right of the altar). In the right transept is a monument to the man who rebuilt Rome in the 16th century, the energetic Pope Sixtus V. Or was it Fiftus VI?

▶ Free. Open daily 7:00–19:00. Metro: Termini or Vittorio Emanuele. Tel. 06-6988-6802.

Church of Santa Prassede

This hidden gem sparkles with ninth-century mosaics, a glimmer of light during Rome's Dark Ages. The apse mosaic shows Christ (on a rainbow river) commanding Peter (white hair and beard) to leave Jerusalem (below Christ) and convert the hostile city of Rome. Peter was given refuge in a house where the church now stands, owned by St. Prassede (to the left of Christ). In the side chapel of St. Zeno, the gold ceiling represents heaven, with Christ supported by four angels in white.

▶ *Free, but bring €0.50 and €1 coins to light this dim church. Open daily 7:00–12:00 & 16:00–18:30. Located 100 yards from Santa Maria Maggiore on Via S. Giovanni Gualberto.*

▲Church of San Clemente

Here, like nowhere else, you'll enjoy the layers of Rome. A 12th-century basilica sits atop a fourth-century Christian basilica, which sits atop a second-century Mithraic Temple and some even earlier Roman buildings.

On street level, you enter the 12th-century church, featuring original mosaics (in the apse) of Christ on the Cross, surrounded by doves, animals, and a Tree of Life. The message: all life springs from Jesus.

Next, descend to a fourth-century church. A faded fresco shows St. Clement holding a secret Mass for persecuted Christians, when he's suddenly arrested. As they try to drag him away (the Latin inscription reads), a man yells, *"Fili dele pute!*... You sons of bitches!"

Finally, descend one more floor, to the dark, dank remains of the pagan cult of Mithras. Worshippers—men only—huddled on the benches of this low-ceilinged room. The room was a microcosm of the universe—the ceiling was once covered with stars, and the small shafts let priests follow the movements of the heavens. A carved altar shows the god Mithras, in a billowing cape, running his sword through a sacred bull. The blood spills out, bringing life to the world. Mithras' fans gathered here to eat a ritual meal celebrating the triumph of light and life over darkness and death.

▶ *Free to visit the upper church, €5 for the lower levels. Open Mon–Sat 9:00–12:30 & 15:00–18:00, Sun 12:00–18:00, last entry for lower church 20 minutes earlier. Located on Via di San Giovanni in Laterano, Metro: Colosseo. Tel. 06-774-0021, www.basilicasanclemente.com.*

Sights

Rick Steves' | Pocket Rome

TRASTEVERE

Trastevere is the colorful neighborhood across *(tras)* the Tiber *(Tevere)* River. It's tucked into the bend in the river, near the island in the Tiber, surrounding the church of Santa Maria in Trastevere. There are no must-see tourist sights. But it's a great people scene, especially at night, and a great place for dinner. For restaurant recommendations, ✪ see pages 190–192.

To reach Trastevere by foot from Capitol Hill, cross the Tiber on Ponte Cestio (over Isola Tiberina). You can also take tram #8 from Piazza Venezia, or bus #H from Termini and Via Nazionale (get off at Piazza Belli). From the Vatican (Piazza Risorgimento), it's bus #23 or #271.

Sights

▲Trastevere

Trastevere (trahs-TAY-veh-ray) offers the best look at medieval-village Rome. Streets are narrow and tangled. The action unwinds to the chime of the church bells. This proud neighborhood was long a working-class area. Now that it's becoming trendy, high rents are driving out some of the local color. But it's still as close to the "real Rome" as you can get. Go there and wander. Wonder. Be a poet. This is Rome's Left Bank.

The piazza outside the church of Santa Maria in Trastevere is the neighborhood meeting place, where kids play soccer, layabouts lay across the fountain steps, and people crowd the outdoor restaurants.

▲Santa Maria in Trastevere Church

One of Rome's oldest churches, this was made a basilica in the fourth century, when Christianity was legalized. It was the first church dedicated to the Virgin Mary. Its portico (covered area just outside the door) is decorated with fascinating fragments of stone—many of them lids from catacomb burial niches—and filled with early Christian symbolism.

▶ *Free. Open daily 7:30–21:00.*

▲Villa Farnesina

This sumptuous Renaissance villa decorated with Raphael paintings was built in the early 1500s for the richest man in Renaissance Europe, Sienese banker Agostino Chigi. It was a meeting place of aristocrats, artists, beautiful women, and philosophers, a place where art, nature, and ideas blended in harmony. Both Agostino and Raphael were notorious womanizers, and the decor drips with erotic themes.

The Loggia of Galatea has Raphael's famous painting of the nymph Galatea. She shuns the ungainly one-eyed giant Polyphemus and speeds away on a chariot led by dolphins. She turns back and looks up, amused by the cyclops' crude love song (which, I believe, was "I Only Have Eye for You"). The trigger-happy cupids and lusty, entwined fauns and nymphs announce the pagan spirit revived in Renaissance Rome.

In the Loggia of Psyche, Raphael's ceiling frescoes depict the myth of the lovely mortal woman, Psyche (in topless robe), who fell in love with the winged boy-god Cupid, or Eros.

Upstairs, you reach Agostino's small bedroom. The painting (by Il Sodoma) shows the wedding of Alexander the Great. His bride Roxanne has the features of Agostino's own bride, and the bed is the jewel-encrusted ebony bed that received Agostino and his beloved here on their wedding night.

▶ €5. Open Mon and Sat 9:00–17:00, Tue–Fri 9:00–14:00, closed Sun. Located a short walk from Ponte Sisto on Via della Lungara. Tel. 06-6802-7268.

Gianicolo Hill Viewpoint and the Tempietto

Gianicolo Hill, to the west of Trastevere, offers superb city views, and the walk to the top holds a treat for architecture buffs.

From Trastevere's Piazza di San Cosimato, follow Via Luciano Manara to Via Garibaldi, which winds up the hill. At the church of San Pietro in Montorio, find the Tempietto by Donato Bramante (1502). This tiny church—too small to be of any practical use—looks like a Greek temple but was built to commemorate the martyrdom of St. Peter. Its dome, circular plan, and Doric columns made it an instant classic of Renaissance architecture.

Continuing up, Via Garibaldi connects to Passeggiata del Gianicolo, which leads to a pleasant park with statues and panoramic city views. Ponder the mixed-message statue of baby-carrying, gun-wielding, horse-riding Anita Garibaldi. She was the Brazilian wife of the revolutionary General Giuseppe Garibaldi, who helped forge a united Italy in the late 19th century.

▲Jewish Quarter

From the 16th through the 19th centuries, Rome's Jewish population was forced to live in a cramped ghetto at an often-flooded bend of the Tiber River. While the medieval Jewish ghetto is long gone, this area—just across the river from Trastevere—is still home to Rome's Jewish community and retains fragments of its Jewish heritage.

The synagogue (rebuilt 1904) stands at the heart of the former seven-acre ghetto. Inside, take in the impressive square dome, painted with the colors of the rainbow. An accompanying museum shows off Jewish artifacts from ancient to modern times.

Behind the synagogue is a square called Largo 16 Ottobre 1943, named for the day when Nazi trucks parked here to take Jews to concentration camps. Eventually, 2,000 Jews were carried off, only a few returned, and the ghetto never recovered.

The big ancient gateway is the Portico d'Ottavia, whose ruins were incorporated into a medieval church. This Christian church sat in the middle of the ghetto, where Jews were forced to sit through Saturday sermons.

Via del Portico d'Ottavia is the main drag of today's small Jewish community. Notice a few kosher restaurants, shops selling menorahs and Jewish-themed art, posters for community events, men wearing yarmulkes, political graffiti, a Jewish school (the big yellow building), and security measures to prevent terrorist acts. In the pedestrianized square, the older folks gather to gossip and kvetch.

Finish at the traditional Jewish bakery with some braided challah bread, almond macaroons, or a little fruitcake dubbed a "Jewish Pizza."

▶ *The synagogue and Jewish Museum (Museo Ebraico) are only accessible to tourists by €10 ticket. Open mid-June–mid-Sept Sun–Thu 10:00–19:00, Fri 10:00–16:00, closed Sat; mid-Sept–mid-June Sun–Thu 10:00–17:00, Fri 9:00–14:00, closed Sat; last entry 45 minutes before closing. Modest dress is required. Located on Lungotevere dei Cenci, tel. 06-6840-0661, www.museoebraico.roma.it.*

A free Rick Steves' audio tour of the Jewish Ghetto is available at www.ricksteves.com or from iTunes or Google Play.

center contains some interesting—but widely scat-
ches from the Colosseum to the very outskirts of the
st of the sights are located either right by a Metro stop
y bus or taxi.

e you'll find ancient ruins, including the famous Appian
erground catacombs. There's the gritty-but-trendy neigh-
accio. South of that is a major pilgrimage church, and far-
erie suburb-of-the-future built by Mussolini, called E.U.R.
se sights, ✪ see the foldout color map.

▲Appian Way

The famous ancient Roman road offers three attractions: the old road itself, lined with crumbling tombs and monuments; the underground Christian catacombs; and the peaceful atmosphere of pine and cypress trees. Concentrate on the sight-packed stretch of road between the Tomb of Cecilia Metella and the Domine Quo Vadis Church.

The Appian Way once ran 430 miles from Rome to the Adriatic port of Brindisi, the gateway to Greece. After Spartacus' slave revolt was suppressed (71 B.C.), the road was lined with 6,000 crucified slaves as a warning. Today you can walk (or bike) some stretches of the road, rattling over original paving stones and past mile markers. The ruins of the Tomb of Cecilia Metella (a massive cylindrical burial place for a rich noble woman) and the Circus of Maxentius (a once-grand chariot race track) are the two most impressive pagan sights.

When the Christian faith permeated Rome, Christians were buried along the Appian Way in labyrinthine underground tunnels called catacombs. Legends say that early Christians actually lived in the catacombs to escape persecution, but that's not true.

The two major catacombs—**San Sebastiano** and **San Callisto**—are a few hundred yards apart. At either place, a guide leads you underground to see burial niches (but no bones), faded frescoes, memorial chapels to saints, Christian symbols (doves, fish, anchors), and graffiti by early-Christian tag artists. Both catacombs are quite similar, so pick one to tour.

You eventually reach the tiny Domine Quo Vadis church. It marks the spot where Peter, fleeing the city to escape persecution, saw a vision of Christ headed in the opposite direction. Peter asked Jesus, "Lord, where are you going?" ("*Domine quo vadis?*" in Latin), to which Christ replied, "I am going to Rome to be crucified again." The vision shamed Peter into returning to the wicked city.

▶ *Most Appian Way sights are open Tuesday through Sunday, closed Monday. However...*

The Catacombs of San Callisto (€8) are open Thu–Tue 9:00–12:00 & 14:00–17:00, closed Wed and Feb. 30-minute tours depart about every half-hour. Located at Via Appia Antica 110, tel. 06-5130-1580 or 06-5130-151, www.catacombe.roma.it.

The Catacombs of San Sebastiano (€8) are open Mon–Sat 10:00–17:00, closed Sun and mid-Nov to mid-Dec. Located at Via Appia Antica 136, tel. 06-785-0350, www.catacombe.org.

Getting There: You could take bus #118 from the Piramide Metro stop, bus #218 from San Giovanni in Laterano, or the Archeobus hop-on-hop-off bus from Termini.

I recommend this route: Take a taxi (€20) or bus (#660 from the Colli Albani Metro stop) to the Tomb of Cecilia Metella. Walk the Appian Way to the Catacombs of San Sebastiano. From there, avoid the most-trafficked stretch of road by taking the peaceful pedestrian path (enter through the arch at #126) which leads to the Catacombs of San Callisto and continues to the Domine Quo Vadis church. From there, catch bus #118 to the Piramide Metro stop. You're back in central Rome—"Quo vadis," pilgrim?

Baths of Caracalla (Terme di Caracalla)

Inaugurated by Emperor Caracalla in A.D. 216, this massive bath complex could accommodate 1,600 visitors at a time. Today it's just a shell—a huge shell—with all of its sculptures and most of its mosaics moved to museums. You'll see a two-story roofless brick building surrounded by a garden, bordered by ruined walls. The two large rooms at either end of the building were used for exercise. In between the exercise rooms was a pool flanked by two small mosaic-floored dressing rooms. Niches in the walls once held statues.

In its day, this was a remarkable place to hang out. For ancient Romans, bathing was a social experience. The Baths of Caracalla functioned until Goths severed the aqueducts in the sixth century. In modern times, grand operas are performed here.

▶ *€6. Open Tue–Sun 9:00 until one hour before sunset (19:00 in summer, 16:30 in winter), and Mon 9:00–14:00, last entry one hour before closing. From the Circus Maximus Metro stop, walk five minutes south along*

Via delle Terme di Caracalla, or take bus #714 from Termini Station. Tel. 06-3996-7700.

Testaccio Neighborhood and Market

Working-class since ancient times, the Testaccio neighborhood has recently gone trendy-bohemian. Visitors wander through an awkward mix of yuppie and proletarian worlds. Even if you don't see it, you'll perhaps sense the "Keep Testaccio for the Testaccians" graffiti.

The covered Mercato di Testaccio (across from Monte Testaccio on Via Galvani) dominates the center of the neighborhood. This is hands-down the best, most authentic food market in Rome (Mon–Sat until 13:00). It's where Romans shop while tourists flock to Campo de' Fiori.

▶ *To visit Testaccio, start at Metro stop Piramide, head northwest on Via*

Sights

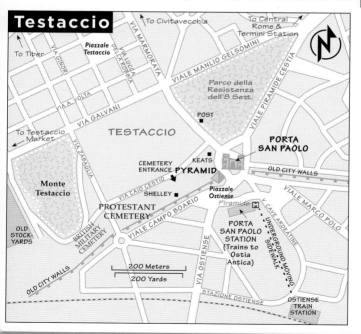

Marmorata, then turn left and start exploring. But first, see four lesser sights that cluster near the Piramide stop...

Pyramid of Gaius Cestius

An Egyptian-style pyramid from ancient Rome stands next to the Piramide Metro stop. When the Roman general Mark Antony wooed the Egyptian queen Cleopatra (c. 30 B.C.), exotic Egyptian styles came into vogue. A rich Roman magistrate, Gaius Cestius, had this pyramid built as his tomb, complete with a burial chamber inside. Made of brick and covered with marble, the 90-foot structure was completed in just 330 days (as stated in its Latin inscription). While smaller than actual Egyptian pyramids, its proportions are correct.

Porta Ostiense and Museo della Via Ostiense

This formidable gate (also next to the Piramide Metro stop) is from the Aurelian Wall, begun in the third century under Emperor Aurelian. The wall, which encircled the city, was 12 miles long and averaged about 26 feet high, with 14 main gates and 380 72-foot-tall towers.

Inside the gate is a tiny museum (find the entrance near the pyramid). The museum offers a free ramble along the ramparts, plus models of Ostia Antica, Rome's ancient port. You'll see Ostia's famed hexagonal harbor and the arrow-straight Ostian Way, the road that paralleled the curvy Tiber for 15 miles from the Porta Ostiense to the sea.

▶ *The museum is free. Open Tue and Thu 9:00–13:30 & 14:30–16:30, Wed and Fri–Sat 9:00–13:30, closed Mon and most Sun.*

Protestant Cemetery

The Cemetery for the Burial of Non-Catholic Foreigners (Cimitero Acattolico per gli Stranieri al Testaccio) is a peaceful tomb-filled park, running along the wall just beyond the pyramid.

Upon entering, head 90 degrees left to find the tomb of English poet John Keats (1795–1821), in the far corner. Keats wanted to be unnamed on a tomb that read, "Young English Poet, 1821. Here lies one whose name was writ in water." The tomb of fellow poet Percy Shelley (1792–1822) is straight ahead from the entrance, up the hill, at the base of the stubby tower. Both Romantic poets came on the Grand Tour and—"captivated by the fatal charms of Rome," as Shelley wrote—never left.

There are cats everywhere. They're cared for as the "Guardians of the Departed" who "provide loyal companionship to these dead."

▶ €2 *suggested donation. Open Mon–Sat 9:00–17:00, Sun 9:00–13:00, last entry 30 minutes before closing. From the Piramide Metro stop, walk between the pyramid and the Roman gate on Via Persichetti, then go left on Caio Cestio to the gate of the cemetery. If it's locked, ring the bell to get inside. www.protestantcemetery.it.*

Monte Testaccio

This small hill is now a popular nightlife spot. The hill, actually a 115-foot-tall ancient trash pile, is made of broken *testae*—earthenware jars used to haul oil 2,000 years ago, when this was a gritty port warehouse district. For 500 years, old jars were discarded here, and slowly, Rome's lowly eighth hill was built.

Because the caves dug into the hill stay cool, trendy bars, clubs, and restaurants compete with gritty car-repair places for a spot. An old military base nearby is now home to Testaccio Village, a site for concerts and techno raves. To do the full monty, arrive after 21:00, when the restaurant-and-club scene is youthful and lively.

▶ *Metro: Piramide. To reach Monte Testaccio, as you leave the Protestant Cemetery, turn left and continue two blocks down Caio Cestio.*

▲Montemartini Museum (Musei Capitolini Centrale Montemartini)

A dreamy collection of 400 ancient statues is set evocatively in a classic 1932 electric power plant, among generators and *Metropolis*-type cast-iron machinery. While the art is not so famous, the effect is fun (kids love it), and you'll encounter absolutely no tourists.

▶ €7.50, €14 *combo-ticket with Capitoline Museums. Open Tue–Sun 9:00–19:00, closed Mon, last entry 30 minutes before closing. Located at Via Ostiense 106, a short walk from Metro: Garbatella. Tel. 06-574-8042, www.centralemontemartini.org.*

▲St. Paul's Outside the Walls (Basilica San Paolo Fuori le Mura)

This was the last major construction project of Imperial Rome and the largest church in Christendom until St. Peter's.

The interior, lit by alabaster windows, is vast. Imagine constructing the roof with those massive wood beams back in A.D. 380. St. Paul's is one of the four great basilicas (along with St. Peter's, San Giovanni in Laterano, and Santa Maria Maggiore) that pilgrims try to visit. St. Paul's feels sterile, but in a good way—like you're already in heaven.

The early apostle Paul supposedly came to Rome to spread Christianity,

Sights

and the church is built upon what was always believed to be his grave. In 2006, archaeologists actually unearthed a sarcophagus here which had early inscriptions identifying it as Paul's. Today, it's visible under the altar.

Ringing the upper part of the church are round mosaic portraits of every pope, from pope #1 (St. Peter) to #265 (Benedict XVI)—plus blank medallions for future popes.

▶ *Free. Open daily 7:00–18:30. Modest dress code enforced. Located at Via Ostiense 186, Metro: San Paolo, exit the Metro station and look for the church's round tower, www.basilicasanpaolo.org.*

E.U.R.

In the late 1930s, Italy's dictator, Benito Mussolini, broke ground on this futuristic office park to show off the wonders of his fascist society. But those wonders brought us World War II, and E.U.R. was only completed in the 1950s to house government offices. Today, E.U.R. (AY-oor) is worth a trip for its Museum of Roman Civilization (for ancient history buffs), its Italian modernism (for architecture buffs), and to see what our world might look like if Hitler and Mussolini had won the war.

E.U.R.'s lone skyscraper and key landmark is understandably nicknamed the "Square Colosseum." With its giant no-questions-asked patriotic statues and black-and-white simplicity, this is the epitome of fascist architecture.

Hike down E.U.R.'s wide, pedestrian-mean boulevards. Patriotic murals, aren't-you-proud-to-be-an-extreme-right-winger pillars, and stern squares decorate the soulless planned grid and stark office blocks. Streets named for Astronomy, Electronics, and Social Security are more exhausting than inspirational.

The vast **Museum of Roman Civilization** displays authentic-looking (but strangely lifeless) plaster casts of actual Roman statues and monuments, such as Trajan's Column. The museum's highlight is an entire room filled with a 1:250-scale model of the city of Rome as it looked circa A.D. 300.

E.U.R. is a 10-minute Metro ride from the Colosseum. Use Metro stop Magliana for the "Square Colosseum" and Metro stop Fermi for the Museum.

▶ *The Museum of Roman Civilization (Museo della Civiltà Romana) costs €6.50. Open Tue–Sat 9:00–14:00, Sun 9:00–13:30, closed Mon, last entry one hour before closing. Located on Piazza G. Agnelli, tel. 06-5422-0919, www.museociviltaromana.it.*

NEAR ROME

An hour or two ride by bus or train can get you out of the big-city bustle to some peaceful sights. Think of these as day trips, as they'll consume most of a sightseeing day.

▲▲Ostia Antica

The ancient Roman port city of Ostia is similar to the famous ruins of Pompeii but a lot closer and less touristed. Wandering around, you'll see ruined warehouses, apartment flats, mansions, shopping arcades, and baths that served a once-thriving port of 60,000 people.

Located at the mouth *(ostium)* of the Tiber, Ostia was Rome's gateway to the open seas. At the peak of the Empire, it was a Europe-wide commercial shipping hub, handling the big business of keeping more than a million Romans fed and in sandals.

Enter through the main city gate (Porta Romana) and walk down the long, straight main drag (Decumanus Maximus), past once-vast warehouses. Pop into the well-preserved Theater, which could seat 4,000 and is still used today. Behind the stage, explore the Square of the Guilds, once lined with more than 60 offices. The sidewalks have mosaics advertising their line of business—grain silos, an elephant for ivory traders, boats for ship-makers, and the symbol of Ostia itself, a lighthouse.

Continuing down main street, detour right down Via dei Molini, and find the Mill (Molino), the tavern (Insula of the Thermopolium), and a typical apartment house (the Insula of the Paintings). Ostia's working class lived in cramped, noisy multi-story buildings, with no plumbing, heat, or kitchens—they survived on take-out food.

The main street spills into the town's main square, or Forum, dominated by the Capitolium temple, dedicated to the trinity of Jupiter, Juno, and Minerva. Now just a brick core, the temple was originally huge, fronted with columns and faced with gleaming white marble.

Near the Forum Baths (Terme del Foro), find the latrine. Yes, those 20 holes are toilets, each with a cutout to hold the sponge-on-a-stick used instead of toilet paper. Rushing water below the seats did the flushing. Privacy? Even today there's no Italian word for it.

Finish your sightseeing with the fine statue museum, then visit the cafeteria and pop something tasty into your *ostium maximus*.

▶ *€8.50. Open Tue–Sun April–Oct 8:30–19:00, Nov–Feb 8:30–17:00,*

March 8:30–18:00, last entry one hour before closing, closed Mon. Tel. 06-5635-8099, www.ostiaantica.info.

A free Rick Steves audio tour of the site is available at www.ricksteves .com or from iTunes or Google Play.

Getting There: From Rome's Piramide Metro stop (which is also a train station), catch any train headed toward Lido—they all stop at Ostia Antica along the way. A single €1.50 Metro ticket covers the one-way train ride. Arriving at Ostia Antica, leave the train station, cross over the blue skybridge, and walk straight down Via della Stazione di Ostia Antica until you reach the parking lot and entrance.

▲Tivoli: The Villa d'Este and Hadrian's Villa

At the edge of the Sabine Hills, 18 miles east of Rome, sits the pleasant medieval hill town of Tivoli. Today, it's famous for two very different villas, or country estates: the Villa d'Este (a 16th-century mansion with playful fountains in the gardens) and Hadrian's Villa (the Roman emperor's large complex of buildings, now in ruins).

The Villa d'Este: Cardinal Ippolito d'Este, a sophisticated lover of luxury, leveled a monastery at Tivoli and replaced it with his personal pleasure palace (1550s). It's a watery wonderland—a mansion with terraced gardens and fountains on a cool hill with breath-catching views. Its design and statuary were inspired by (and looted from) the ancient villa of Hadrian.

The Villa d'Este's star attraction is hundreds of Baroque fountains, most of which are still gravity-powered. The Aniene River, frazzled into countless threads, weaves its way entertainingly through the villa. At the bottom of the garden, the exhausted little streams once again team up to make a sizable river.

Hike through the gardens, then enjoy the terrace restaurant on the highest level of the garden, opportunely placed to catch cool afternoon sea breezes as you gaze across the plain of Rome.

Hadrian's Villa: Emperor Hadrian (ruled A.D. 117–138) built this country residence as an escape from the heat of Rome and the pressures of court life. Hadrian ruled at the peak of the Roman Empire, when it stretched from England to the Euphrates and encompassed countless diverse cultures. The Spanish-born Hadrian—an architect, lover of Greek culture, and great traveler—had personally visited many of the lands he ruled. At Tivoli, he created a microcosm of his empire. In the spirit of Legoland, Epcot, and

Las Vegas, he built modified versions of famous structures from around the world, placed in the largest and richest Roman villa anywhere.

Start your visit at the plastic model of the villa, then explore. The Egyptian Canopus, a canal lined with statues, recreated a sanctuary of the god Serapis. The Greek Pecile, a large open pool surrounded by an arcade, was inspired by the rectangular stoa of ancient Athens. The Teatro Marittimo was Hadrian's retreat within the retreat—a circular palace set on an artifical island surrounded by a moat and a ring of columns. Here Hadrian could sit, at the symbolic center of his vast empire, and ponder what might become of it.

Sights

▶ *Villa d'Este: €6.50. Open Tue–Sun 8:30–18:30, closed Mon, closes earlier off-season, last entry one hour before closing. Upon arrival, check the schedule for the next performance of the cute Water Organ fountain. Expect lots of stairs. Tel. 0774-312-070, www.villadestetivoli.info.*

Hadrian's Villa (Villa Adriana): €10. Open April–Sept daily 9:00–19:00, closes earlier off-season, last entry 1.5 hours before closing. Tel. 0774-382-733, www.pierreci.it (search for "villa adriana").

Getting to Tivoli: From Rome's Metro stop Ponte Mammolo, take the local blue Cotral bus to Tivoli (45 minutes, 3/hour). The Villa d'Este is right in the center of town near the Tivoli bus stop. To continue to Hadrian's Villa (2.5 miles outside Tivoli), catch orange city bus #4X.

Sleeping

I've listed good-value hotels in a few select neighborhoods handy for sight-seeing. I like places that are clean, small, central, quiet at night, traditional, inexpensive, family-run, friendly, and not listed in other guidebooks. A hotel with six out of these nine attributes is a keeper.

Double rooms listed in this book average around €150 (including a private bathroom). They range from a low of roughly €65 (very simple, with toilet and shower down the hall) to €480 (maximum plumbing and more).

A typical €150 double room will have one double bed or two twins. There's probably a bathroom in the room with a toilet, sink, and bathtub or shower. The room has a telephone and TV. Most hotels at this price will have air-conditioning—cheaper places may not. Some rooms have a safe and a small fridge stocked with drinks for sale. Single rooms, triples, and quads will have similar features.

> **$$$** Most rooms are €180 or more.
>
> **$$** Most rooms between €130–180.
>
> **$** Most rooms €130 or less.
>
> These rates are for a standard double room with bath during high season; they don't include the €2/person room tax.

Breakfast is generally included. It's a self-service buffet of cereal, ham, cheese, yogurt, and juice, while a waitress takes your coffee order.

The hotel will likely have some form of pay-as-you-go Internet access, either Wi-Fi in your room (assuming you have your own laptop) or a public terminal in the lobby. The staff speaks at least enough English to get by. Night clerks aren't paid enough to care deeply about problems that arise.

Besides hotels, I also list a few cheaper alternatives. Bed-and-breakfasts (B&Bs) offer a private room in someone's home. At nun-run convents, the beds are twins and English is often in short supply, but the price is right (so reserve early). Hostels offer €20–30 dorm beds and a few inexpensive doubles.

Making Reservations

Reserve at least a few weeks in advance in peak season or for a major holiday. Do it by email (the best way), phone, or through the hotel's website. Your hotelier will want to know:

- the type of room you want (e.g., "one double room with bath")
- how many nights ("three nights")
- dates (using European format: "arriving 22/7/13, departing 25/7/13")
- any special requests ("with twin beds, air-conditioning, quiet, view")

If they require your credit-card number for a deposit, you can send it by email (I do), but it's safer via phone, or the hotel's secure website. Once your room is booked, print out the confirmation, and reconfirm your reservation with a phone call a day or two in advance. If you must cancel your reservation, give the hotel at least three days' notice.

Budget Tips

Some of my listed hotels offer a 5–10 percent discount for readers of this book—it's worth asking when you book your room.

To get the best deals, email several hotels to ask for their best price and check hotel websites for promo deals. You may get a cheaper rate if you offer to pay cash, stay at least three nights, skip breakfast, or simply ask if there are any cheaper rooms. Rates can drop 10–35 percent off-season—roughly November through mid-March, and mid-July through August.

Don't be too cheap when picking a hotel in Rome. Cheaper places can be depressing, and Rome's intensity is easier to handle with a welcoming oasis to call home. Traffic in Rome roars, so light sleepers should ask for a *tranquillo* room in the back. In summer, a room with air-conditioning is a must.

Sleeping

Sleeping

	Price	
NEAR TERMINI TRAIN STATION: VIA FIRENZE		
Residenza Cellini	$$$	Slice of Neoclassical elegance, four-star service, breezy breakfast terrace
Hotel Modigliani	$$$	Bright, minimalist, in-love-with-life style, generous lounge, garden, energetic staff
Hotel Oceania	$$	Peaceful, spacious manor house w/terrace, Stefano continues family tradition of thoughtful service
Hotel Aberdeen	$$	Modern quality plus friendliness from Annamaria and sisters, great deals on website
Hotel Adler	$	Quiet, simple rooms run the old-fashioned way by charming family
Hotel Nardizzi Americana	$	Pleasant rooms and rooftop terrace, excellent value, website-only and cash discounts
Hotel Margaret	$	Welcoming rooms with modern basics: air-con, Wi-Fi, and Impressionist prints
NEAR TERMINI: BETWEEN VIA NAZIONALE AND SANTA MARIA MAGGIORE		
Hotel Opera Roma	$$	Contemporary furnishings and marble accents in spacious but dark rooms
Hotel Sonya	$$	Well-equipped, high-tech rooms, Farhad bakes daily for above-average breakfast
Hotel Selene	$$	Spread over several floors, elegant furnishings and room to breathe, cash discount
Hotel Montreal	$	Bright, secure business-class place in so-so surroundings, run with care
Hotel Italia Roma	$	Bright rooms, quiet street, busy locale, thoughtful staff, decent annex rooms too
Suore di Santa Elisabetta	$	Tranquil convent, tidy twin-bed rooms, 23:00 curfew, book early for super value
Gulliver's Lodge B&B	$	Busy neighborhood but secure and quiet, no lobby, in-room DVDs, Wi-Fi

Address/Phone/Website/Email

Via Modena 5, tel. 06-4782-5204, fax 06-4788-1806, www.residenzacellini.it, residenzacellini@tin.it

Via della Purificazione 42, tel. 06-4281-5226, www.hotelmodigliani.com, info@hotelmodigliani.com

Via Firenze 38, third floor, tel. 06-482-4696, www.hoteloceania.it, info@hoteloceania.it

Via Firenze 48, tel. 06-482-3920, www.hotelaberdeen.it, info@hotelaberdeen.it

Via Modena 5, second floor, tel. 06-484-466, www.hoteladler-roma.com, info@hoteladler-roma.com

Via Firenze 38, fourth floor, tel. 06-488-0035, www.hotelnardizzi.it, info@hotelnardizzi.it

Via Antonio Salandra 6, fourth floor, tel. 06-482-4285, www.hotelmargaret.net, info@hotelmargaret.net

Via Firenze 11, tel. 06-487-1787, www.hoteloperaroma.com, info@hoteloperaroma.com

Via del Viminale 58, Metro: Repubblica or Termini, tel. 06-481-9911, www.hotelsonya.it, info@hotelsonya.it

Via del Viminale 8, tel. 06-474-4781, www.hotelseleneroma.it, reception@hotelseleneroma.it

Via Carlo Alberto 4, 1 block from Metro: Vittorio Emanuele, 3 blocks west of Termini train station, tel. 06-445-7797, www.hotelmontrealroma.com, info@hotelmontrealroma.com, Pasquale

Via Venezia 18, just off Via Nazionale, Metro: Repubblica, tel. 06-482-8355, www.hotelitaliaroma.it, info@hotelitaliaroma.it

Via dell'Olmata 9, Metro: Termini or Vittorio Emanuele, tel. 06-488-8271, www.csse-roma.eu, ist.it.s.elisabetta@libero.it

Via Cavour 101, Metro: Cavour, tel. 06-9727-3789, www.gulliverslodge.com, stay@gulliverslodge.com

Sleeping

	Price	
SLEEPING CHEAPLY, NORTHEAST OF TERMINI TRAIN STATION		
The Beehive	$	Homey American-run all-ages hostel, artsy-mod double rooms and eight-bed dorms
Hotel Select Garden	$	Modern, quiet, welcoming refuge run by cheery family, modern art, lemony garden
Hotel Sileo	$	Shiny chandeliers in dim rooms, friendly owners speak limited English, air-con
Funny Palace Hostel	$	Quiet four-person dorms and stark-but-clean doubles, laundrette next door
Yellow Hostel	$	Ages 18-39 only, 4- to 12-bed coed dorms, hip yet sane, fine facilities, no curfew
Fawlty Towers Hostel	$	Okay four-bed backpacker dorms, games and extras, free Internet, annex okay too
NEAR THE COLOSSEUM		
Hotel Lancelot	$$$	Elegant, quiet refuge with B&B ambience, shady courtyard, restaurant, bar, view terrace
Hotel Paba	$$	Fresh, chocolate-box–tidy rooms, overlooks busy Via Cavour but quiet enough
Nicolas Inn Bed & Breakfast	$$	Delightful, spacious and bright, run by friendly Francois and American Melissa
Hotel Pensione Rosetta	$	Homey and family-run, minimal (no lounge or breakfast) but good location
NEAR PIAZZA VENEZIA		
Hotel Nerva	$$$	Three-star slice of tranquility by Roman Forum, overpriced but rates are soft
Hotel Giardino	$	Great location, tiny lobby and breakfast room, quiet rooms on busy street
Casa Il Rosario	$	Peaceful convent, twin-bed simplicity, good neighborhood, 23:00 curfew, no air-con, book early
NEAR CAMPO DE' FIORI		
Casa di Santa Brigida	$$$	Lavish convent overlooking elegant Piazza Farnese, twin-beds only but a worthwhile splurge
Hotel Smeraldo	$$	Strictly run, clean, air-con, flowery roof terrace, similar annex, great deal

Address/Phone/Website/Email

Via Marghera 8, tel. 06-4470-4553, www.the-beehive.com, info@the-beehive.com

Via V. Bachelet 6, tel. 06-445-6383, www.hotelselectgarden.com, info@hotelselectgarden.com

Via Magenta 39, fourth floor, tel. 06-445-0246, www.hotelsileo.com, info@hotelsileo.com

Via Varese 33/31, tel. 06-4470-3523, www.hostelfunny.com

Via Palestro 44, tel. 06-493-82682, www.yellowhostel.com

Via Magenta 39, tel. 06-445-0374, www.fawltytowers.org, info@fawltytowers.org

Via Capo d'Africa 47, tel. 06-7045-0615, www.lancelothotel.com, info@lancelothotel.com

Via Cavour 266, Metro: Cavour, tel. 06-4782-4902, www.hotelpaba.com, info@hotelpaba.com

Via Cavour 295, tel. 06-976-18483, www.nicolasinn.com, info@nicolasinn.com

Via Cavour 295, tel. 06-478-23069, www.rosettahotel.com, info@rosettahotel.com

Via Tor de' Conti 3, tel. 06-678-1835, www.hotelnerva.com, info@hotelnerva.com

Via XXIV Maggio 51, tel. 06-679-4584, www.hotel-giardino-roma.com, info@hotel-giardino-roma.com

Via Sant'Agata dei Goti 10, bus #40 or #170 from Termini, tel. 06-679-2346, irodopre@tin.it

Monserrato 54, tel. 06-6889-2596, piazzafarnese@brigidine.org

Vicolo dei Chiodaroli 9, tel. 06-687-5929, www.smeraldoroma.com, info@smeraldoroma.com

Sleeping

Sleeping

	Price	
NEAR CAMPO DE' FIORI		
Hotel Arenula	$$	Southeast of Campo de' Fiori in Jewish Ghetto, good value but gym-like ambience
CLOSE TO THE PANTHEON		
Hotel Nazionale	$$$	Big, stuffy four-star hotel, lush public spaces, uniformed staff, worthy splurge
Albergo Santa Chiara	$$$	Big and professional, fine staff, marbled elegance, quiet and spacious rooms
Hotel Due Torri	$$$	Professional and accommodating, big lounge, small rooms, overpriced but great quiet location
Hotel 939 Rome and Hotel Marcus	$	Hotel 939 has renovated rooms, Marcus is more utilitarian, above noisy street
IN TRASTEVERE		
Hotel Santa Maria	$$$	Lazy hacienda amid romantic medieval skyline, small well-equipped rooms, orange-tree patio
Residenza Arco dei Tolomei	$$$	Small, unique, antique-filled rooms in quiet aristocratic setting, book early
Relais le Clarisse	$$$	Tranquil, tastefully furnished rooms around a leafy courtyard, a slice of the countryside
Casa San Giuseppe	$$	Plain, spacious, spotless rooms on laundry-strewn lane, views of Aurelian Walls
Arco del Lauro B&B	$$	White, minimalist rooms in good location, limited public spaces but friendly welcome
NEAR VATICAN CITY		
Hotel Alimandi Vaticano	$$$	Facing the Vatican Museum, spacious rooms with all the modern conveniences
Hotel Alimandi Tunisi	$$	Good value, friendly Alimandi family, modern perfumed rooms, fun public areas
Hotel Gerber	$$	Family-run with well-polished business-like air-con rooms in quiet residential area
NEAR VATICAN CITY		
Casa Valdese	$	Big quiet rooms, efficient but institutional, breezy communal rooftop with views
Casa per Ferie Santa Maria alle Fornaci	$	Convent-esque but user-friendly, stark utilitarian twin-bedded rooms, book early

Address/Phone/Website/Email

Via Santa Maria de' Calderari 47, tel. 06-687-9454,
www.hotelarenula.com, info@hotelarenula.com

Piazza Montecitorio 131, tel. 06-695-001, www.hotelnazionale.it, info@hotelnazionale.it

Via di Santa Chiara 21, tel. 06-687-2979,
www.albergosantachiara.com, info@albergosantachiara.com

Vicolo del Leonetto 23, tel. 06-6880-6956,
www.hotelduetorriroma.com, info@hotelduetorriroma.com

Via del Clementino 94, tel. 06-6830-0312, www.hotel939.com, hotel939@hotmail.it

Vicolo del Piede 2, tel. 06-589-4626, www.hotelsantamaria.info,
info@hotelsantamaria.info

Via dell'Arco de' Tolomei 27, tel. 06-5832-0819, www.bbarcodeitolomei.com,
info@bbarcodeitolomei.com

Via Cardinale Merry del Val 20, tel. 06-5833-4437, www.leclarisse.com,
info@leclarisse.com

Vicolo Moroni 22, tel. 06-5833-3490, www.casasangiuseppe.it,
info@casasangiuseppe.it

Via dell'Arco de' Tolomei 29, tel. 06-9784-0350, www.arcodellauro.it,
info@arcodellauro.it

Viale Vaticano 99, Metro: Cipro, tel. 06-397-45562, www.alimandivaticanohotel.com,
alimandivaticano@alimandi.com

Via Tunisi 8, Metro: Cipro, reserve by phone at tel. 06-3972-3941,
www.alimandtunisi.com, alimandi@tin.it

Via degli Scipioni 241, at intersection with Via Ezio, a block from Metro: Lepanto,
tel. 06-321-6485, www.hotelgerber.it, info@hotelgerber.it

Via Alessandro Farnese 18, tel. 06-321-5362,
www.casavaldeseroma.it, reception@casavaldeseroma.it

Piazza Santa Maria alle Fornaci 27, tel. 06-393-67632,
www.trinitaridematha.it, cffornaci@tin.it

Sleeping

Eating

The Italians are masters of the art of fine eating. Lingering over a multi-course meal at an outdoor table watching a parade of passersby while you sip wine with loved ones...it's one of Rome's great pleasures.

I list a full range of eateries, from budget options for a quick bite to multi-course splurges with maximum ambience. They're located in neighborhoods handy to sightseeing, hotels, and atmosphere— ✪ see the maps on pages 196–199.

When in Rome, I eat on the Roman schedule. For breakfast, I eat at the hotel or grab a pastry and cappuccino at the neighborhood bar. Lunch may be a quick pasta, or a take-out sandwich for an atmospheric picnic. Dinner is the time for slowing down and savoring a restaurant meal.

\$\$\$ Most main dishes €13-20.

\$\$ Most main dishes €10-13.

\$ Most main dishes under €10.

Based on the average price of a meat or seafood dish (a *secondo)* on the menu. Pastas, salads, and appetizers are generally a couple of euros cheaper. So a typical meal at a \$\$ restaurant—including appetizer, main dish, wine, water, and service charge—would cost about €30.

The circled numbers in the restaurant charts refer to the maps on pages 196–199.

Restaurants

Restaurants serve lunch 13:00-15:00 (and rarely open their doors before noon). Dinner is served to Romans from 20:00-22:00 and to tourists at 19:00 (quality restaurants rarely open any earlier).

A full restaurant meal comes in courses: an antipasto, a plate of pasta, the meat course, salad, dessert, coffee, liqueurs, and so on. It can take hours, and the costs can add up quickly, so plan your strategy before sitting down to a restaurant meal.

For light eaters, there's nothing wrong with ordering a single dish as your meal—a plate of pasta, a pizza, an antipasto, or a salad. Couples could each order a dish (or two) and share. If you want a full meal at a predictable price, consider the *menu turistico*—a fixed-price multi-course meal where you can choose from a list of menu items. It includes the service charge, and is usually a good value for non-gourmets.

In Rome, only rude waiters rush you. For speedier service, be prepared with your next request whenever a waiter happens to grace your table. You'll have to ask for the bill—mime-scribble on your raised palm or ask: *"Il conto?"*

Quick Budget Meals

Rome offers many budget options for hungry travelers.

Italian "bars" are not taverns but cafés. These neighborhood hangouts serve coffee, sandwiches (grilled *panini* or cold *tramezzini*), mini-pizzas, pre-made salads, fresh squeezed orange juice (*spremuta),* and drinks from the cooler.

Various cafeteria-style places (called *tavola calda*, *rosticceria*, or "free-flow cafeteria") dish out fast and cheap cooked meals to eat there or take out. You can buy pizza by the slice at little hole-in-the-wall places, sold by weight (100 grams for a small slice). A wine bar (*enoteca*) sells wine by the glass, but they also serve meat-and-cheese-type plates for the business crowd at lunch and happy hour.

At any eating establishment (however humble), be aware that the price of your food and drink may be 20-40 percent more if you consume it while sitting at a table instead of standing at the bar. This two-tier price system will always be clearly posted. Don't sit without first checking out the financial consequences. Also, at many bars, the custom is to first pay the cashier for what you want, then hand the receipt to a barista who serves you.

Picnicking saves euros and time, lets you sample regional specialties, and puts you in contact with everyday Romans in the marketplace. Buy a sandwich or slice of pizza "to go" (*da portar via*), get fruit at the corner grocery store, a bottle of wine, refill your water bottle at a public tap...and dine like an emperor amid atmospheric surroundings. Note that Rome discourages people from picnicking at historic monuments, but it's rarely enforced for discreet adults. Also, when buying produce, it's customary to let the merchant pick it out. If something is a mystery, ask for a small taste—"*un assaggio, per favore.*"

Roman Cuisine

Rome has a few specialties: spaghetti alla carbonara (in egg-bacon sauce), gnocchi alla romana (dumplings), carciofi alla giudia (artichokes), saltimbocca alla romana (veal), pecorino romano cheese (from ewe's milk), and trippa alla romana (tripe—intestines—as good as it sounds).

No meal in Italy is complete without wine. Even the basic house wine (*vino da tavola* or *vino della casa*) is a good choice. The region around Rome produces Frascati (an inexpensive dry white) or Torre Ercolana (an expensive, aged, dense red). You'll also find lots of Chiantis and Montepulcianos from Tuscany(for an upgrade, pay more for a Brunello di Montalcino); well-aged Barbaresco and Barolo from Piedmont; and crisp white Orvieto Classico.

Popular after-dinner liqueurs are amaro (various brands) and anise-flavored Sambuca. For dessert, try Tartufo—a rich dark-chocolate gelato ball. Or pick up a cup or cone of gelato at a gelateria.

Italian coffee is excellent. Even basic bars serve espresso, macchiatos, and cappuccinos. In the summer, Romans like a sugared iced coffee called caffè freddo. Streetside vendors sell grattachecca (grah-tah-KEK-kah): shaved ice with fruit syrup.

Eating

	Price	
NEAR PIAZZA NAVONA (see map on page 197)		
❶ Pizzeria da Baffetto	$	Rustic, energetic local favorite west of Piazza, jammed after 20:00; cash only
❷ Ciccia Bomba	$	Traditional trattoria west of Piazza, serves well-priced homemade pasta, pizza, and more
❸ Cul de Sac	$$	Skinny trattoria packed with wine-loving locals, try salami sampler or full meal
❹ L'Insalata Ricca	$	Popular chain specializing in €8 salads and pastas, two locations in area
❺ Ristorante Pizzeria "da Francesco"	$$	Bustling, unpretentious with hardworking young staff, great seating inside and out
CLOSE TO THE PANTHEON (see map on page 197)		
❻ Ristorante da Fortunato	$$$	Surprisingly reasonable dress-up classics (plan €50 per person); sit indoors; reservations smart
❼ Ristorante Enoteca Corsi	$$	Friendly wine shop serves lunch only; straightforward traditional cuisine at great prices
❽ Miscellanea	$	Much-loved Mikki keeps foreign-study students well-fed with hearty sandwiches, salads, pasta
❾ Osteria da Mario	$$	Mom-and-pop joint with no-stress traditional favorites; fun dining room or picturesque outside tables
❿ Le Coppelle Taverna	$$	Simple basic family-friendly checkered-tablecloth ambience, good-value €9 pizzas
⓫ Antica Salumeria grocery	$	Market on the Pantheon square, convenient for picnic supplies
⓬ Supermercato Despar	$	Supermarket half a block west of the Pantheon, convenient for picnic supplies
⓭ Gelateria Caffè Pasticceria Giolitti	$	Rome's most famous gelato in an Old World setting
⓮ Crèmeria Monteforte	$	Gelato; specializes in super-creamy cremolati sorbets
⓯ Gelateria San Crispino	$	Serves gelato in small portions, made from natural ingredients

Operating Hours and Days	Address/Phone
Wed–Mon 12:00–15:30 & 18:30–24:00, closed Tue	Via del Governo Vecchio 114, tel. 06-686-1617
Mon–Sat 12:00–15:00 & 19:00–24:00; off-season open Sun and closed Wed	Via del Governo Vecchio 76, tel. 06-6880-2108
Daily 12:00–16:00 & 18:00–24:00	A block off Piazza Navona on Piazza Pasquino, tel. 06-6880-1094
Daily 12:00–15:45 & 18:45–24:00	Largo dei Chiavari 85, tel. 06-6880-3656; also on Piazza Pasquino, tel. 06-6830-7881
Open daily	Piazza del Fico 29, tel. 06-686-4009
Mon–Sat 12:30–15:00 & 19:30–23:30	Via del Pantheon 55, tel. 06-679-2788
Mon–Sat 12:00–15:00	Via del Gesù 87, tel. 06-679-0821
Daily 8:00–24:00	Via della Palombella 34, tel. 06-6813-5318
Mon–Sat 13:00–15:30 & 19:00–23:00	Piazza delle Coppelle 51, tel. 06-6880-6349
Daily 12:30–15:00 & 19:30–23:30	Via delle Coppelle 39, tel. 06-6880-6557
Daily 8:00–21:00	On the Pantheon square
Mon–Sat 7:30–13:30 & 16:30–20:30, Sun 8:30–13:30	Via Giustiniani 18
Daily 7:00–2:00 in the morning	Via Uffici del Vicario 40
Tue–Sun 11:00–21:00	Via della Rotonda 22
Mon–Thu 12:00–24:00, Fri–Sat until 1:30 in the morning	Piazza della Maddalena 3

Eating

Eating

	Price	
IN NORTH ROME: NEAR THE ARA PACIS AND SPANISH STEPS (see map on page		
16 Ristorante il Gabriello	$$$	Small, inviting respite; trust waiter's suggestions or €45 "Claudio's Extravaganza"; slightly dressy; reservations smart
17 Osteria Gusto	$$$	Thriving with trendy locals; pricey but fine for wine and appetizers or well-chosen dinner; reservations smart
18 L'EnotecAntica	$$$	Bustling, atmospheric old restaurant and jam-packed wine-bar (€7 wine + €14 appetizer = meal)
19 Trattoria dal Cav. Gino	$$	Tucked-away haunt of VIPs since 1963 (Gino's still there); cash only; reservations essential
NEAR VATICAN CITY (see map on page 196)		
20 Hostaria dei Bastioni	$$	Emilio serves honest food near Vatican Museum; street-side seating or quiet interior
21 La Rustichella	$$	Stellar antipasti buffet (€8) plus pizza and pasta; arrive early; gelateria next door
22 L'Insalata Ricca	$$	The popular chain specializes in healthy salads, plus pasta and secondi
23 Duecento Gradi	$	A good bet for fresh and creative €5 sandwiches
24 Tre Pupazzi	$	Cheap eatery on pedestrian-only street called Borgo Pio—a block NE of Piazza San Pietro—worth a look
25 Vecchio Borgo	$	Cheap eatery across the street from Tre Pupazzi—worth a look
26 Via Andrea Doria outdoor market	$	One of the best outdoor markets in Rome, great for picnic supplies
27 Carrefour Express	$	Supermarket nearby, convenient for picnic supplies
28 Gelateria Old Bridge	$	Scoops up hearty, reasonable portions of gelato for tourists and nuns
IN TRASTEVERE (see map on page 198)		
29 Trattoria da Lucia	$$	Simple, traditional food, good price, quintessential family-run scene since 1950s; cash only

Operating Hours and Days	Address/Phone
Mon–Sat 19:00–23:00	Via Vittoria 51, tel. 06-6994-0810
Daily 12:30–15:30 & 19:00–24:00	Via della Frezza 16, tel. 06-3211-1482
Daily 11:00–24:00	Via della Croce 76b, tel. 06-679-0896
Mon–Sat 13:00–14:45 & 20:00–22:30, closed Sun	Vicolo Rosini 4, tel. 06-687-3434
Mon–Sat 12:00–15:30 & 19:00–23:00	Via Leone IV 29, tel. 06-3972-3034
Tue–Sun 12:30–15:00 & 19:30–24:00	Via Angelo Emo 1, tel. 06-3972-0649
Daily 12:30–15:30 & 18:30–23:45	Piazza Risorgimento 5, tel. 06-3973-0387
Daily 12:00–23:00	Piazza Risorgimento 3, tel. 06-3975-4239
Daily 12:00–14:30 and 19:00–23:00	Via Tre Pupazzi 1
Mon–Sat 9:00–21:00	Borgo Pio 27a
Mon–Sat 7:00–14:00	Three blocks north of Vatican Museum on Via Tunisi
Mon–Sat 8:00–20:00, Sun 9:00–20:00	Via Sebastiano Veniero 16
Daily 10:00–23:00	Via Bastioni 3
Tue–Sun 12:30–15:00 & 19:30–23:00	Vicolo del Mattonato 2, tel. 06-580-3601

Eating

Eating

	Price	
IN TRASTEVERE (see map on page 198)		
❸⓿ Trattoria da Olindo	$	Extreme hominess, like you're part of family—so don't expect smiles; cash only
❸❶ Dar Poeta Pizzeria	$	Informal back alley joint cranks out stellar wood-fired pizza; friendly owners
❸❷ Osteria Ponte Sisto da Oliviero	$$$	Traditional Roman and Neapolitan cuisine, Mediterranean decor, few tourists, fine value
❸❸ Ristorante Checco er Carettiere	$$$	Big Trastevere fixture, white tablecloths, dressy locals, overpriced but good, reservations recommended
❸❹ Pizzeria "Ai Marmi"	$	Bright and noisy festival of assembly-line pizza, jammed after 20:00; cash only
❸❺ Cantina Paradiso Wine and Cocktail Bar	$$	Simple uncrowded romantic charm; happy hour drinks (18:00–21:00) include small buffet
❸❻ Gelateria alla Scala	$	Terrific little ice-cream shop with cinnamon (cannella) and oh-wow pistachio
NEAR CAMPO DE' FIORI (see map on page 198)		
❸❼ Osteria da Giovanni ar Galletto	$$$	Magical outdoor seating (and slow service) on peaceful piazza; reservations smart
❸❽ Osteria Enoteca al Bric	$$$	Mod bistro; Roberto and Barbara love food, wine, and jazz; reservations smart
❸❾ Filetti di Baccalà	$	Cheap, basic, fluorescent-lit classic, where regulars eat deep-fried salt cod; cash only
❹⓿ Trattoria der Pallaro	$$	Fixed-price €25 meal, eccentric staff and forgettable food but fun experience; cash only
❹❶ Pizzeria Baffetto 2	$	Roman-style pizza (thin crust, crispy, and wood-fired), cramped informal interior or outside
❹❷ Sora Margherita	$$	Behind red curtain in Jewish ghetto, local favorite, picturesque commotion; reservations smart

Operating Hours and Days	Address/Phone
Mon–Sat dinner served 20:00–22:30	Via del Mattonato 8, tel. 06-581-8835
Daily 12:00–24:00	Vicolo del Bologna 45, tel. 06-588-0516
Thu–Tue 12:30–15:30 & 19:30–24:00	Via Ponte Sisto 80, tel. 06-588-3411
Daily 12:30–15:00 & 19:30–23:15	Via Benedetta 10, tel. 06-580-0985
Thu–Tue 18:30–24:00	Viale Trastevere 53, tel. 06-580-0919
Daily 12:00–24:00	Via San Francesco a Ripa 73, tel. 06-5899-799
Daily 12:00–24:00	Piazza della Scala 51
Tue–Sun from 19:30 for dinner	Piazza Farnese 102, tel. 06-686-1714
Tue–Sun from 19:30 for dinner	Via del Pellegrino 51, tel. 06-687-9533
Mon–Sat 17:30–23:00	Largo dei Librari 88, tel. 06-686-4018
Tue–Sun 12:00–15:30 & 19:00–24:00	Largo del Pallaro 15, tel. 06-6880-1488
Wed–Mon 12:00–15:30 & 18:30–24:00	Piazza del Teatro di Pompeo 18, tel. 06-6821-0807
Sept–May Mon–Sat 12:30–15:00, dinner seatings on Mon, Wed, Fri, and Sat only at 20:00 and 21:30, closed Sun; June–July same hours except closed Sat, closed in Aug	Piazza delle Cinque Scole 30, tel. 06-687-4216

Eating

Eating

	Price	
NEAR THE TREVI FOUNTAIN (see map on page 199)		
43 L'Antica Birreria Peroni	$$	Rome's answer to a German beer hall: hearty mugs, fun food, giddy locals
44 Ristorante Pizzeria Sacro e Profano	$$	Spicy southern Italian food in old church, €15 antipasti sampler, satisfied tourists
IN ANCIENT ROME, NEAR THE COLOSSEUM (see map on page 199)		
45 Enoteca Cavour 313	$$	Wine bar with quality food, friendly service, mellow ambience for convenient lunch near Forum
46 Caffè dello Studente	$	Student crowds, royal welcome for my readers; good toasted sandwiches, salads, pizzas
47 Hostaria da Nerone	$	Cozy place with homemade pasta, €9 choose-your-own antipasti plate makes quick lunch
48 Ristorante del Giglio	$$$	Elegant old hall; pricey traditional dishes for dressy locals and satisfied tourists
49 Ristorante Da Giovanni	$	Old-school, high-energy diner cranks out standard fare at great prices
50 Ristorante La Pentolaccia	$$	Dressy, tourist-friendly place with tight seating, some romance, and classic Roman cooking
51 Ricci Est Est Est Pizzeria	$	Venerable family-run pizzeria also has dangerously tasty fried cod and zucchini flowers
52 Hostaria Romana	$$	Busy fun-loving bistro; fish and traditional; €10 antipasti a meal in itself
53 Bar Tavola Calda	$	Cafeteria-style workers' favorite; point to what you want, they'll bring it
54 Snack Bar	$	Cafeteria-style quality lunch, loyal customers love caffè con crema whipped with sugar
55 Panificio Firenze	$	Take-out pizza, sandwiches, and an old-fashioned alimentari (grocery)—assemble a picnic
56 Flann O'Brien Irish Pub	$$	Sports bar with grilled meats, giant salads, Guinness, late kitchen, Italian crowd

Operating Hours and Days	Address/Phone
Mon–Sat 12:00–24:00	Via di San Marcello 19, tel. 06-679-5310
Mon–Sat 12:00–15:00 & 18:00–24:00, closed Sun	Via dei Maroniti 29, tel. 06-679-1836
Daily 12:30–14:45 & 19:30–24:00	Via Cavour 313, tel. 06-6785-496
Mon–Sat 7:30–22:30, April–Oct Sun 9:00–22:30, Nov–March closed Sun	Via delle Terme di Tito 95, tel. 06-488-3240
Mon–Sat 12:00–15:00 & 19:00–23:00	Via delle Terme di Tito 95, tel. 06-481-7952
Mon 19:00–23:00, Tue–Sat 12:15–15:00 & 19:00–23:00	Via Torino 137, tel. 06-488-1606
Mon–Sat 12:00–15:00 & 19:00–22:00, closed Aug	Via Antonio Salandra 1, tel. 06-485-950
Mon–Sat 12:00–15:00 & 17:30–23:00, Sun 17:30–23:00	Via Flavia 38, tel. 06-483-477
Tue–Sun 19:00–24:00, closed Aug	Via Genova 32, tel. 06-488-1107
Mon–Sat 12:15–15:00 & 19:15–23:00	Via de Boccaccio 1, tel. 06-474-5284
Mon–Fri 6:00-18:00	Via Torino 40
Daily 6:00–24:00	Via Firenze 33, mobile 339-393-1356
Mon–Fri 7:00–19:00, Sat 7:00–14:00	Via Firenze 51–52, tel. 06-488-5035
Daily 7:00–24:00	Via Nazionale 17, tel. 06-488-0418

Restaurants Near Vatican City

Piazzale degli Eroi

VIA ANDREA DORIA

Ottaviano

Piazza dei Qui

Cipro

VIA CANDIA

V. PISANI

V. VATICANO

VIA LEONE IV

VIA OTTAVIANO

VIA COLA DI RIENZO

VIA CRESCENZIO

㉖ ㉗ ⑳ ㉒ ㉓ ㉘ ㉑

Piazza Risorgimento

VATICAN MUSEUM

VATICAN CITY

BORGO PIO

㉔ ㉕

VIA CONCILIAZIONE

ST. PETER'S

St. Peter's Square

PON VITTO EMANUE

PONTE AMEDEO

VIA PORTA CAVALLEGGERI

TUNNEL

VIA MURA AURELIE

SAN PIETRO STATION

200 Meters
200 Yards

Restaurants Close to the Pantheon and in North Rome

Piazza del Popolo

VIA M. A. COLONNA

VIA COLA DI RIENZO

PONTE REG. MARGHERITA

VIA DI RIPETTA

VIA DEL BABUINO

VILLA MEDICI

PRATI

Piazza Cavour

ARA PACIS

PONTE CAVOUR

MAUSOLEM OF AUGUSTUS

Piazza di Spagna

FORMER HALL OF JUSTICE

River

Spagna M

ASTEL ANT' GELO

VIA DEL CORSO

PONTE UMBERTO I

ONTE ANGELO

Tiber

Piazza Ponte Umberto I

🔟9️⃣

PARLIAMENT

VIA DEL TRITONE

VIA CORONARI

CORSO DEL RINASCIMENTO

🔟 9️⃣

Piazza Colonna

CORSO RIO EMANUELE

5️⃣

CHIESA NUOVA

2️⃣

Piazza Navona

VIA GIUSTINIANI

1️⃣2️⃣ 1️⃣1️⃣

1️⃣5️⃣

6️⃣

1️⃣

Piazza della Chiesa Nuova

3️⃣

1️⃣4️⃣

PANTHEON

SEMINARIO

CENTRO STORICO

8️⃣

VIA D. ARGENTINA

SANTA MARIA SOPRA MINERVA

4️⃣

7️⃣

Piazza Venezia

VIA GIULIA

Campo de' Fiori

Piazza Farnese

Largo Argentina

VICTOR EMMANUEL MONUMENT

ONTE ZINI

LUNGOTEVERE

POTEVERE

PALAZZO FARNESE

Eating

Restaurants in Trastevere & Campo de'Fiori

PONTE MAZZINI

VIA GIULIA

LUNGOTEVERE

38

37

41

Campo de'Fiori

40

VIA GIUBBONARI

VIA CHIAVARI

VIA DEI FARNESE

Piazza Farnese

VIA DEL FARNESE

VIA MONSERRATO

39

Tiber River

LUNGOTEVERE FARNESINA

PALAZZO FARNESE

POLVERONE

VILLA FARNESINA

VIA PETTINARI

GHETTO

VIA DELLA SCALA

PONTE SISTO

LUNGOTEVERE DEI VALLATI

VIA ARENULA

42

VIA BENEDETTA

32

Piazza Trilussa

31

33

36

VIA GARIBALDI

VIA MATTONATO

VIA A. D. BOLOGNA

V. DE CINQUE

LUNGOTEVERE R. SANZIO

PONTE GARIBALDI

30

29

VIA PANIERI

Piazza Belli

VIA PAGLIA

VIA LUNGARETTA

SANTA MARIA

ARCO DI S. CALLISTO

TRASTEVERE

34

VIA LUCIANO MANARA

Piazza Mastai

VIALE TRASTEVERE

100 Meters
100 Yards

35

Restaurants Near Trevi Fountain, Ancient Rome & The Colosseum

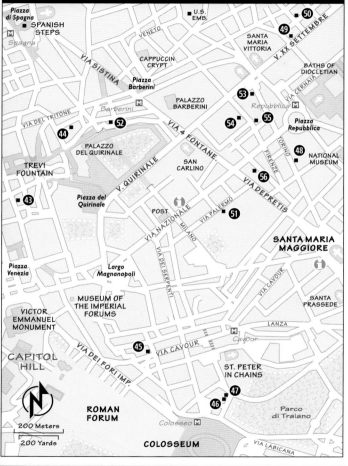

Piazza di Spagna
SPANISH STEPS
Spagna

U.S. EMB.

50
49
V. XX SETTEMBRE

VENETO

SANTA MARIA VITTORIA

VIA SISTINA

CAPPUCCIN CRYPT

BATHS OF DIOCLETIAN

Piazza Barberini

VIA CERNAIA

VIA DEL TRITONE

Barberini

PALAZZO BARBERINI

53

Repubblica

52

54

55

Piazza Repubblica

44

VIA 4 FONTANE

TORINO

48

NATIONAL MUSEUM

PALAZZO DEL QUIRINALE

V. QUIRINALE

SAN CARLINO

FIRENZE

TREVI FOUNTAIN

Piazza del Quirinale

56

VIA DEPRETIS

43

POST

VIA PALERMO

51

MILANO

VIA NAZIONALE

SANTA MARIA MAGGIORE

Piazza Venezia

Largo Magnanapoli

VIA DEI SERENTI

SANTA PRASSEDE

VIA CAVOUR

VICTOR EMMANUEL MONUMENT

MUSEUM OF THE IMPERIAL FORUMS

LANZA

Cavour

CAPITOL HILL

45

VIA CAVOUR

VIA DEI FORI IMP.

ST. PETER IN CHAINS

N

47

46

Parco di Traiano

200 Meters

ROMAN FORUM

200 Yards

Colosseo

VIA LABICANA

COLOSSEUM

Practicalities

PLANNING

When to Go

Rome's best travel months—also the busiest and most expensive—are May, June, September, and October. These months combine the convenience of peak season with pleasant weather. The summer heat in July and August can be brutal. In winter, Rome is cold and crisp, there are fewer crowds, and some sights have shorter hours.

Rome's Climate: First line—average daily high; second line—average daily low; third line—average days without rain.

J	F	M	A	M	J	J	A	S	O	N	D
52°	55°	59°	66°	74°	82°	87°	86°	79°	71°	61°	55°
40°	42°	45°	50°	56°	63°	67°	67°	62°	55°	49°	44°
13	19	23	24	26	26	30	29	25	23	19	21

Before You Go

Consider this checklist: You need a passport, of course (see www.travel.state.gov). Call your debit and credit card companies about your plans (see below). Book hotel rooms in advance during peak season (May-Sept). Research travel insurance, railpasses, and car rentals. Check up-to-date airline carry-on restrictions at www.tsa.gov/travelers. Make reservations for the Borghese Gallery (required) and Vatican Museum (recommended).

MONEY

Italy uses the euro currency: 1 euro (€) = about $1.30. To convert prices in euros to dollars, add about 30 percent: €20 = about $26, €50 = about $65. (Check www.oanda.com for the latest exchange rates.)

The standard way for travelers to get euros is to withdraw money from a cash machine (called a *bancomat* in Italy) using a debit or credit card, ideally with a Visa or MasterCard logo. Before departing, call your bank or credit-card company: Confirm that your card will work overseas, ask about international transaction fees, and alert them that you'll be making withdrawals in Europe. Small Roman businesses prefer cash, and some

Helpful Websites

Rome's Tourist Information: http://en.turismoroma.it
Italian Tourist Information: www.italia.it
Passports and Red Tape: www.travel.state.gov
Travel Insurance Tips: www.ricksteves.com/insurance
Packing List: www.ricksteves.com/packlist
Cheap Flights: www.skyscanner.net
Airplane Carry-on Restrictions: www.tsa.gov/travelers
General Info on Lots of Topics: www.inromenow.com
Current Events and Accommodation Rentals: www.wantedinrome.com
The Vatican: http://mv.vatican.va
European Train Schedules: www.bahn.com
Railpasses: www.ricksteves.com/rail
Updates for This Book: www.ricksteves.com/update

won't take credit cards at all, so withdraw large amounts (€250-300) from the cash machine.

To keep your valuables safe, wear a money belt. But if you do lose your credit or debit card, report the loss immediately with a collect phone call: Visa (303/967-1096), MasterCard (636/722-7111), and American Express (623/492-8427).

For a typical five-day stay in Rome, budget about $900 per person, plus airfare. That covers your hotel (splitting a $200 double), food ($40 a day), transportation ($10 a day), sightseeing ($20 a day), and miscellaneous ($10). Tightwads can save significantly on hotels (figure $35 for a hostel bed) and food.

ARRIVAL IN ROME

Fiumicino (Leonardo da Vinci) Airport

Rome's main airport has ATMs, banks, shops, bars, and a tourist information office (in terminal 3, daily 9:00–18:30). For airport information, call 06-65951, or visit www.adr.it. To inquire about flights, call 06-6595-3640.

To get between the airport and downtown Rome, there are several options:

"Leonardo Express" Train: A direct train connects the airport and Rome's central Termini train station in 30 minutes for €14. Departures are twice hourly from roughly 6:00 to 23:00. From the airport's arrival gate, it's a 10-minute walk to the train, easily do-able with wheeled luggage in tow. Follow signs to *Stazione/Railway Station*. Buy your ticket from a machine, the Biglietteria office, or a newsstand, then validate it in a yellow machine near the track. Make sure the train you board is going to the central "Roma Termini" station, not "Roma Orte" or others.

Going from Termini train station to the airport, trains depart from track 24. Buy the €14 ticket at the platform from self-service machines or a newsstand.

Taxi: A taxi between Fiumicino and any destination in downtown Rome takes 45 minutes in normal traffic and costs an official fixed rate of €48, for up to four people with bags. To get the €48 fare, catch your taxi at the airport's taxi-stand, and only use a Rome city cab (with the "SPQR" shield on the door). Avoid unmarked, unmetered taxis or other cab companies; these guys will try to tempt you away from the taxi-stand lineup by offering an immediate (rip-off) ride. When you're departing Rome, your hotel can arrange a €48 taxi to the airport at any hour.

Rome Airport Shuttle Bus: This works best from your hotel to the airport, since it requires making a reservation (€25/1 person, extra people-€6 each, tel. 06-4201-4507, www.airportshuttle.it).

A useful video on the options for getting into the city from the airport is at www.romewalks.com.

Arrival at Ciampino Airport: Rome's smaller airport (tel. 06-6595-9515) handles budget airlines such as Ryanair and some easyJet flights. To get to downtown Rome, the Terravision Express Shuttle bus connects Ciampino and Termini, leaving every 20 minutes (€4 one-way, €8 round-trip, www.terravision.eu). Rome Airport Shuttle (listed above) also offers service. A taxi should cost about €30.

Termini Train Station

Of Rome's four train stations, by far the most important is the centrally located Termini Station, which has connections to the airport.

Termini is a buffet of tourist services: information desks, cheap eateries, the handy Drugstore Conad (downstairs), late-hours banks, a good bookstore, and 24-hour thievery—avoid anybody selling anything unless they're in a legitimate shop at the station.

Along track 24, about 100 yards down, you'll find the tourist information office (TI, daily 8:00–21:00), a post office, car rental desks, and baggage storage (€5/5 hours). The "Leonardo Express" train to Fiumicino (Leonardo da Vinci) Airport also runs from track 24.

Termini is a major transportation hub. The city's two Metro lines (A and B) intersect at Termini Metro station (downstairs). City buses, taxis, and the hop-on, hop-off bus tours leave from the front of the station.

Tips for Train Travelers: To buy train tickets or make reservations, avoid Termini's long lines by buying from the station's automated ticket machines or from an uncrowded travel agency near your Rome hotel.

Termini offers trains to many major cities, including Florence (departures every hour, 1.5 hour trip, reservations required on most trains); Venice (roughly hourly, 3.5 hours, overnight possible); Milan (hourly, 3.5 hours, overnight possible); Naples (hourly, 1.25-2.5 hours); and Paris (4/day, 12-15 hours, several overnight options).

The best all-Europe train schedule information is online at www.bahn.com. To see if a railpass could save you money, check www.ricksteves.com/rail. For the new high-speed Italo service, see www.italotreno.it.

Tiburtina Bus Station

Buses and some high-speed trains connecting Rome with the rest of Italy arrive and depart from Tiburtina train/bus station, located in the city's northeast corner (Metro: Tiburtina on Line B, direction: Rebibbia). Buses connect Rome to Assisi (2/day, 3 hours—the train makes more sense); Siena (8/day, 3 hours); Sorrento (1–2/day, 4 hours—faster and easier than the train).

Arrival by Car

Approaching Rome, exit the freeway that circles the city (the Grande Raccordo Anulare) at the Settebagni exit. Follow the ancient Via Salaria (and the black-and-white *Centro* signs) past the Villa Borghese Gardens to Via Veneto, right in downtown Rome. Avoid rush hour and drive defensively.

Don't sightsee by car in traffic-choked Rome—rely on public transportation. Park your car (about €25 per day) at a garage that your hotel can assure you is safe.

For more car tips, including car rental and the international driver's license, see www.ricksteves.com/driving.

HELPFUL HINTS

Tourist Information (TI): Rome has major tourist information offices (TIs) at Fiumicino Airport (terminal 3) and Termini train station (open until 20:30, way down track 24, look for signs). There are also smaller kiosks—generally open daily 9:30–19:00—located near tourist sights such as the Forum, Piazza Navona, and the Trevi Fountain. The TIs share a website: http://en.turismoroma.it.

At any TI, get the freebies: a city map (also available from most hotels), a listing of sights and hours, and the *Evento* booklet of cultural events.

For travel and English language books, try Borri Books at Termini train station, or Feltrinelli International at Largo Argentina.

Rome's single best source of up-to-date tourist information is its call center, tel. 06-0608 (open daily 9:00–21:00, press 2 for English).

Time: Italy uses the 24-hour clock. It's the same through 12:00 noon, then keeps going: 13:00, 14:00, and so on. Italy's time zone is six/nine hours ahead of the east/west coasts of the US.

Business Hours: Most businesses are open throughout the day Monday through Saturday, generally 10:00–19:00. Some small businesses close for lunch (roughly 13:00–15:30).

Holidays: Besides major holidays, Rome celebrates local festivals that can strike without warning, shutting down sights and bringing unexpected crowds. Get specifics on your visit at the Rome TI website (http://en.turismoroma.it) or see www.ricksteves.com/festivals.

Watt's Up?: Europe's electrical system is 220 volts, instead of North America's 110 volts. Most newer electronics (such as laptops, hair dryers, and battery chargers) convert automatically, so you won't need a "converter" plug, but you will need a special "adapter" plug with two round prongs, sold inexpensively at travel stores in the US.

Laundry: Your hotelier can direct you to the nearest self-serve launderette. Ondablu is near Termini station at Via Principe Amedeo 70b (about €8 to wash and dry a load, daily 8:00–22:00).

Pedestrian Safety: Use caution crossing Rome's chaotic streets. Follow locals like a shadow when you cross. Don't be a deer in the headlights, especially with oncoming scooters. Find a gap in the traffic and walk with confidence while making eye contact with approaching drivers. They won't hit you if they can tell where you intend to go.

Numbers and Stumblers: What Americans call the second floor

Tipping

Tipping in Italy isn't as generous as it is in the US. As in the US, the proper amount depends on your resources, tipping philosophy, and the circumstances, but some general guidelines apply.

In restaurants, the "service" charge (*servizio*) is usually built into your bill's grand total. If you're pleased with the service, you can round up the bill by a euro or two, though Italians rarely do.

To tip a taxi driver, round up to the next euro on the fare (for a €4.50 fare, give €5). Toss in a little more for long rides (e.g., to the airport) or for hauling your bags. If a tour guide holds out their hand after they give their spiel, tip a euro, but only if they've really impressed you.

At hotels, if you let the porter carry your luggage, give them a euro for each bag. I don't tip the maid, but if you do, you can leave a euro per night at the end of your stay.

of a building is the first floor in Europe. Europeans write dates as day/month/year, so Christmas is 25/12/13. Commas are decimal points and vice versa—a dollar and a half is 1,50, and there are 5.280 feet in a mile.

Italy uses the metric system: A kilogram is 2.2 pounds; a liter is about a quart; and a kilometer is six-tenths of a mile.

Italians measure temperature in Celsius. 0°C = 32°F. For a rough conversion from Celsius to Fahrenheit, double the number and add 30.

GETTING AROUND ROME

The public transportation system, which is cheap and efficient, consists primarily of buses, a few trams, and the two underground subway (Metro) lines. Consider it part of your Roman experience. Use taxis to fill the gaps.

Buying Tickets

All public transportation uses the same ticket. A single ticket costs €1.50 and is valid for one Metro ride (including transfers underground) plus unlimited city buses during a 100-minute period. You can buy a transit pass for one day (€6, good until midnight), three days (€16.50), or one week (€24, about the cost of three taxi rides). The Roma Pass for sightseers includes a three-day transit pass.

You can buy tickets and passes at some newsstands, tobacco shops (*tabacchi*, marked by a black-and-white *T* sign), and major Metro stations and bus stops, but not onboard. It's smart to stock up on tickets early in your visit rather than hunt around for an open vendor when you really need one.

For more information, call 06-57-003, or visit www.atac.roma.it.

The Metro

The Roman subway system (Metropolitana, or "Metro") is simple, with two lines—A and B—that intersect at Termini train station. Line B splits in northern Rome. If you're going to Tiburtina or Ponte Mammolo, take trains going to "Rebibbia." The Metro runs from 5:30 to 23:30 (Fri–Sat until 1:30 in the morning). Beware of pickpockets in crowded trains.

Validate your ticket by sticking it in the Metro turnstile (magnetic strip-side up, arrow-side first), and retrieving it. Watch others and imitate. To get through a Metro turnstile with a transit pass, use it just like a ticket.

While much of Rome is not served by its skimpy subway, these stops are helpful:

- Termini: Train station and recommended hotels
- Colosseo: Colosseum and Roman Forum
- Spagna: Spanish Steps and classy shopping area
- Barberini: Cappuccin Crypt, Trevi Fountain, and Villa Borghese
- Ottaviano and Cipro: St. Peter's and the Vatican Museum
- Piramide: South Rome sights and trains to Ostia Antica

City Buses

Buses are crowded-but-efficient people movers. Bus routes are clearly listed at the bus stops. Read the sign with its list of stops (e.g. "Colosseo" or "Piazza Venezia"), and you can usually figure out if that bus will take you where you want to go. For a good route planner in English, see www.atac .roma.it.

As you board, stamp your ticket in the box (magnetic strip-side down, arrow-side first), and retrieve it. Transit passes or the Roma Pass only need to be validated once, on your first trip. Watch out for pickpockets.

Two bus routes are especially helpful. Bus #64 cuts east-west across the city, from Termini train station to the Vatican, stopping at Piazza della Repubblica (near several sights), Via Nazionale (recommended hotels), Piazza Venezia (near Forum), Largo Argentina (near Pantheon), and St. Peter's Basilica (get off just past the tunnel). It's always jammed with tourists and pickpockets. Bus #40 is an express bus that follows the #64 route but has fewer stops and crowds.

Taxis

I use taxis in Rome more often than in other cities. They're reasonable and efficient in this big, hot metropolis. Three or four companions with more money than time should taxi almost everywhere. Besides, careening through Roman traffic in a speeding taxi is a video-game experience you won't soon forget.

Taxis start at €2.80, then charge about €1.30 per kilometer. Legitimate surcharges are clearly posted in the cab: €1 extra on Sun, €3 after 22:00, one suitcase rides free, and so on. Tip your cabbie about 10 per cent by rounding up to the nearest euro (for a €5.50 fare, pay €6).

Some sample fares: Termini train station to Vatican-€10; Termini to Colosseum-€6; Colosseum to Trastevere-€7; or look up your route at www.worldtaximeter.com.

It's tough to wave down a taxi in Rome, especially at night. Find the nearest taxi stand *(fermata dei taxi)*, have your hotel or restaurant call a taxi for you, or call them yourself (06-4994 or 06-6645). The meter starts when the call is received, generally adding a euro or two to the bill. It's routine for Romans to ask the waiter in a restaurant to call a taxi when they ask for the bill.

Beware of corrupt taxis. Make sure the meter is running and has been reset to around €2.80 (or around €5 if you've phoned for the taxi). If the meter is "broken," tell the driver to stop and let you out. Only use official taxis, with a *taxi* sign and phone number marked on the door. If you think you've been overcharged, point to the price chart and ask the cabbie to explain it to you. Making a show of writing down the taxi number (to file a complaint) can motivate a driver to quickly settle the matter.

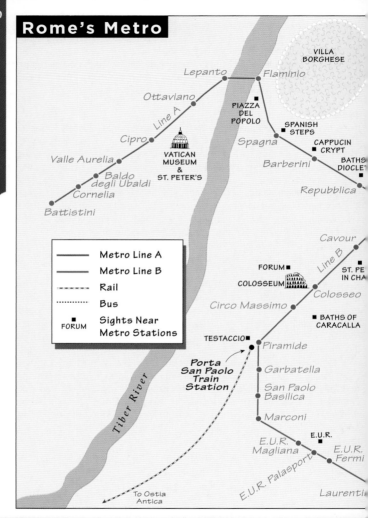

Rome's Metro

VILLA BORGHESE

Lepanto — Flaminio

Ottaviano

PIAZZA DEL POPOLO

Line A

SPANISH STEPS

Cipro

Spagna

CAPPUCIN CRYPT

VATICAN MUSEUM & ST. PETER'S

Valle Aurelia

Barberini

BATHS DIOCLE

Baldo degli Ubaldi

Repubblica

Cornelia

Battistini

Cavour

—— Metro Line A
—— Metro Line B
- - - Rail
· · · · · Bus
■ FORUM   Sights Near Metro Stations

FORUM ■
COLOSSEUM

Line B

ST. PE
IN CHA

Colosseo

Circo Massimo

■ BATHS OF CARACALLA

TESTACCIO ■ Piramide

Porta San Paolo Train Station

Garbatella

San Paolo Basilica

Tiber River

Marconi

E.U.R. ■
E.U.R. Magliana

E.U.R. Fermi

E.U.R. Palasport

To Ostia Antica

Laurenti

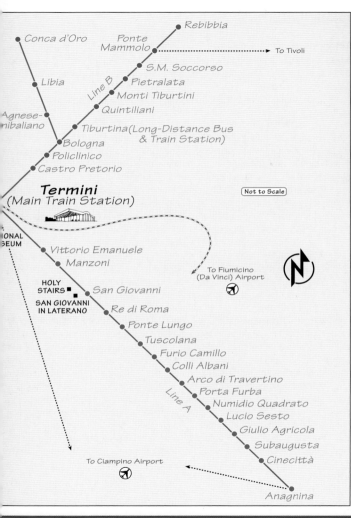

Conca d'Oro

Rebibbia

Ponte
Mammolo

To Tivoli

Libia

Line B

S.M. Soccorso

Pietralata

Monti Tiburtini

Quintiliani

Agnese-
nibaliano

Tiburtina (Long-Distance Bus
& Train Station)

Bologna

Policlinico

Castro Pretorio

Termini
(Main Train Station)

Not to Scale

IONAL
GEUM

Vittorio Emanuele

Manzoni

To Fiumicino
(Da Vinci) Airport

HOLY
STAIRS

San Giovanni

SAN GIOVANNI
IN LATERANO

Re di Roma

Ponte Lungo

Tuscolana

Furio Camillo

Colli Albani

Arco di Travertino

Line A

Porta Furba

Numidio Quadrato

Lucio Sesto

Giulio Agricola

Subaugusta

Cinecittà

To Ciampino Airport

Anagnina

COMMUNICATING

Telephones

Making Calls: To call Italy from the US or Canada: Dial 011-39 and then the local number. (The 011 is our international access code, and 39 is Italy's country code.)

To call Italy from a European country: Dial 00-39 followed by the local number. (The 00 is Europe's international access code.)

To call within Italy: Just dial the local number.

To call from Italy to another country: Dial 00 followed by the country code (for example, 1 for the US or Canada), then the area code and number. If you're calling European countries whose phone numbers begin with 0, you'll usually have to omit that 0 when you dial.

Phoning Inexpensively: Since coin-op pay phones are virtually obsolete, you'll need a phone card. The best option is a €5 international phone card *(carta telefonica internazionale)*, which works with a scratch-to-reveal PIN code. This gives you pennies-per-minute rates on international calls, decent rates for calls within Italy, and can even be used from your hotel phone. Buy them at newsstands and *tabacchi* (tobacco) shops. Tell the vendor where you'll be making the most calls *("per Stati Uniti"*—to America), and he'll select the most economical brand. Calling from your hotel room can be a rip-off for long-distance calls unless you use an international phone card.

Mobile Phones: Mobile phones—whether an American one that works in Italy, or a European one you buy when you arrive—are increasingly affordable. You'll find mobile-phone stores selling cheap phones (for as little as $20 plus minutes) and SIM cards, at Fiumicino airport, Termini train station, and throughout Rome.

Many smartphones, such as the iPhone or Android, work in Europe—but beware of sky-high fees, especially for data downloading (checking email, browsing the Internet, watching videos). Switch off data-roaming entirely until you have free Wi-Fi.

For more on the fast-changing world of telephones, talk to your service provider or see www.ricksteves.com/phoning.

Internet

Many hotels offer some form of free or cheap Internet access—either a computer in the lobby or Wi-Fi in the room (for use with your own mobile

Useful Phone Numbers

Police (English-speaking help): 113

Ambulance: 118

Directory Assistance (In English): 170

US Embassy: 24-hour emergency line—tel. 06-46741, non-emergency—tel. 06-4674-2420 (passport services Mon–Fri 8:30-12:30, closed Sat–Sun, Via Vittorio Veneto 121, www.usembassy.it)

Canadian Embassy: 06-854-441, www.italy.gc.ca

device or laptop). Otherwise, your hotelier can point you to the nearest Internet café. You may be asked to show your passport before going on-line. Wi-Fi hotspots are not as plentiful in Rome as in many other large cities.

If you've got the software, you can make phone calls to other computers and telephones for free or cheap using Skype (www.skype.com), Google Talk (www.google.com/talk), or Facetime (preloaded on many Apple devices).

SIGHTSEEING TIPS

Sightseeing can be hard work. Use these tips to make your visits to Rome's finest sights meaningful, fun, efficient, and painless.

Hours: Opening and closing hours of sights can change unexpectedly; confirm the latest times with a TI, at http://en.turismoroma.it, or the tourist call center (tel. 06-0608). Many sights stop admitting people 30–60 minutes before closing time, and guards start shooing people out before the actual closing time, so don't save the best for last.

Typical Rules: Important sights such as the Colosseum have metal detectors or conduct bag searches that will slow your entry. Others require you to check (for free) daypacks and coats. To avoid checking a small backpack, carry it under your arm like a purse as you enter.

Photos and videos are normally allowed, but flashes or tripods usually are not. Many sights only accept cash, no credit cards. Many offer guided tours and rent audioguides (€4–7). Most have an on-site café. Expect changes—artwork can be on tour, on loan, out sick, or shifted at the whim of the curator.

Churches: Many churches have divine art and free entry. They're generally open 7:30-12:00 and 15:00-19:00. Churches encourage a modest dress code (no shorts, bare shoulders, or miniskirts), and a few major churches enforce it. Bring coins to illuminate art in dim churches.

Sightseeing Passes: The Roma Pass (see below) can be a good deal for sightseeing and transportation. The TI's other passes—Roma and Piu Pass ("Rome and More") and the Archeologia Card—are generally not worth the trouble.

Discounts: Many sights offer reduced admission for children under 18 and students (with International Student Identity Cards, www.isic.org). Senior discounts are generally only for EU residents (but it's worth asking).

Museum Reservations: They're required at the Borghese Gallery and recommended at the always-crowded Vatican Museum.

Pace Yourself: The siesta is a key to survival in summertime Rome—try to schedule in a mid-day break at your air-conditioned hotel. I carry a plastic water bottle and refill it at Rome's many public drinking spouts. Because public restrooms are scarce, use toilets whenever you can at museums, restaurants, and bars.

Guided Tours: Hiring your own personal tour guide can be delightful but pricey (roughly €50/hour, €180/half-day).

Tour companies are cheaper, but the quality can be spotty. A number of companies offer three-hour guided walks for small groups, usually led by American ex-pats, charging about €25–30 per person. Try www.context rome.com, www.enjoyrome.com, or www.romewalks.com.

Free Rick Steves' Audio Tours: I've produced free audio tours of many of Rome's best sights. With an iPod (or other MP3 player) or a smartphone, you can tour the Colosseum, Roman Forum, Pantheon, St. Peter's Basilica, Sistine Chapel, Trastevere, Jewish Ghetto, Ostia Antica, and Pompeii. Download them from iTunes, Google Play, or www.rick steves.com.

The Roma Pass

For many visitors, the Roma Pass is a clear time- and money-saver. The Roma Pass costs €34 and is valid for three consecutive days. You get free admission to your first two sights, where you also get to skip the ticket line. After that, you get a discount of about 30 percent on other sights. The Roma Pass also comes with a three-day transit pass good on the Metro, buses, and trams.

Major sights covered by the pass include the Colosseum/Palatine Hill/Roman Forum, the Capitoline Museums, the National Museum of Rome, and the Borghese Gallery (though you still must make a €2 reservation). It also covers some Appian Way sights, the Castel Sant'Angelo, Ara Pacis, and more. Get a full list from the website.

Add up your sightseeing to see if it's worth it: €12 Colosseum + €12 Capitoline + €13 Borghese + the three-day transit pass (€16.50). Factor in the time saved waiting in ticket lines, and even if you only visit two sights, the pass can pay for itself.

Buy the pass at participating sights, TIs, and even the Colosseum Metro's *tabacchi* shop. Try to buy it at a less crowded TI or sight. Ordering it online saves you no time because you have to physically pick up the pass in Rome.

To get the most from your pass, visit the two most expensive sights first. Definitely use it to bypass the long ticket line at the Colosseum. The Colosseum/Palatine Hill/Roman Forum count as only a single entry against your Roma Pass. Sweet!

For more info, see www.romapass.it.

THEFT AND EMERGENCIES

Theft

While violent crime is rare in the city center, petty theft is rampant. With sweet-talking con artists meeting you at the station, well-dressed pickpockets on buses, and fast-fingered moms with babies at the ancient sites, Rome is a gauntlet of rip-offs and scams—too many to list.

The key is to keep alert to the possibility of theft, even when you're absorbed in the wonder, newness, and chaos of Rome. Don't trust kind strangers. Keep nothing important in your pockets. Assume beggars are pickpockets, and any commotion is simply a distraction by a team of thieves. Be on guard when crowds press together, especially while boarding and leaving buses and subways. I keep my valuables—passport, credit cards, crucial documents, and large amounts of cash—in a money belt that I tuck under my beltline.

Dial 113 for English-speaking police help. Report lost or stolen items to the police at Termini train station (tracks 11 or 20) or at Piazza Venezia. To replace a passport, file the police report, then call your embassy to make an appointment (US embassy: tel. 06-46741, www.usembassy.it).

Medical Help

For emergencies, call 118 to summon an ambulance, or ask your hotelier for help. Anyone is entitled to free emergency treatment at public hospitals (Policlinico Umberto 1 is near Termini at Metro: Policlinico).

For minor ailments, first visit a pharmacy (marked by a green cross), where qualified technicians routinely diagnose and prescribe.

If you need a doctor, embassies can recommend English-speaking doctors. MEDline has English-speaking doctors who make house calls to your hotel for €150-180 (tel. 06-808-0995). The American Hospital, a private hospital on the edge of town, is accustomed to helping Yankees (Via Emilio Longoni 69, tel. 06-22-551).

ACTIVITIES

Shopping

Most shops are open Monday to Saturday 10:00-19:00, though some close for lunch (13:00-16:00). For everyday items, there's a full array at Termini Station, or try a UPIM department store (many branches).

Shopping Neighborhoods: The Spanish Steps is the neighborhood for high fashion boutiques, especially Via Condotti and Via Borgognona for the big-name shops. Via del Babuino is known for trendy design shops, and Via Margutta has classy antiques and art galleries. Via del Corso is a good, midrange shopping area.

Around Piazza Navona and Campo de' Fiori you'll find antiques, especially along Via de Coronari (between Piazza Navona and the river), Via Giulia (between Campo de' Fiori and the river), and Via Giubbonari (funkier items, near Campo de' Fiori).

Flea Markets: The granddaddy of open-air street markets is the Porta Portese *mercato delle pulci* (flea market). This Sunday-morning market (6:30–13:00) is long and spindly. Start at Porta Portese (a gate in the old town wall) and stroll to the Trastevere train station, through a tacky parade of second-hand junk, cheap bras and shoes, con artists with shell games, pickpockets, food vendors, a few antique treasures, and price-less people-watching. (Catch bus #75 from Termini station or tram #8 from Piazza Venezia to Viale Trastevere, and walk toward the noise.)

Open-Air Produce Markets: Rome's outdoor markets are muse-ums for people-watchers. Many neighborhoods open up one street or square every Monday through Saturday from 7:00–13:00.

Campo de' Fiori's market has become quite touristy, but it's still a fun scene. Also try Via della Pace (near Piazza Navona) and Piazza delle Coppelle (near the Pantheon). In the Vatican neighborhood, consider the huge Mercato Trionfale, three blocks in front of the Vatican Museum at Via Andrea Doria. Near the Termini train station is the small market along Via Balbo and the large Mercato Esquilino (on Via Turati, Metro: Vittorio). My favorite is the gritty Mercato di Testaccio, a hit with photographers (Piazza Testaccio, near Metro: Piramide).

Sizes: European clothing sizes are different from the US. For exam-ple, a woman's size 10 dress (US) is a European size 40, and a size 8 shoe (US) is a European size 38½.

Getting a VAT Refund: If you purchase more than €155 worth of goods at a single store, you may be eligible to get a refund of the 21–23 percent Value-Added Tax (VAT). If you're lucky, the merchant will subtract the tax when you make your purchase. Otherwise, you'll need to get an official document from the merchant (a "cheque") and have your cheque stamped by a customs official at your final EU border or airport. You can usually collect your refund right on the spot through a VAT-refund service such as Global Blue (www.global-blue.com) or Premier Tax Free (www.premiertaxfree.com), which have offices at major airports, ports, and border crossings. For more details, see www.ricksteves.com/plan/tips/vat.htm.

Customs for American Shoppers: You are allowed to take home $800 worth of items per person duty-free, once every 30 days. You can also bring in duty-free a liter of alcohol.

As for food, you can take home many processed and packaged foods: vacuum-packed cheeses, dried herbs, jams, chocolate, oil, vinegar, and honey. However, fresh fruits and vegetables and most meats are not allowed. Any liquid-containing foods must be packed in checked luggage, a potential recipe for disaster. To check customs rules and duty rates, visit www.cbp.gov.

Renting a Bike

Roman traffic is too stressful to use a bicycle as your main transportation. But joy-rides are nice on small streets. There's a bike path along the west bank of the Tiber River, stretching from Ponte Regina Margherita to Ponte Sublicio.

Top Bike Rental rents bikes (€15/day), offers four-hour bike tours (€35 and up), and gives good tips on where to ride (located south of Termini station, at Via dei Quattro Cantoni 40, tel. 06-488-2893, www.topbikerental .com). Cool Rent, next to the Colosseo Metro stop, is cheaper (€10/day) but less helpful.

Nightlife

The best after-dark activity is to do what the Romans do: enjoy a leisurely meal, then grab a gelato and stroll the streets, past floodlit squares and fountains. For romantic ambience, head for Piazza Navona, the Pantheon, Campo de' Fiori, Trevi Fountain, Spanish Steps, Via del Corso, or Trastevere.

The entertainment guide *Evento* (free at TIs) lists concerts, operas, dance, and films. Or visit www.inromenow.com, www.wantedinrome.com, or http://rome.angloinfo.com.

Classical Concerts: The Teatro dell'Opera, near Termini, has an active schedule of opera and classical concerts (Via Firenze 72, tel. 06-4816-0255, www.operaroma.it). Also near Termini, the Anglican Church of St. Paul's Inside the Walls hosts classical, opera, and Sunday-night candlelit concerts (Via Nazionale 16a, tel. 06-482-6296, www.imusiciveneziani .com). Trendy Romans flock way north of downtown to make the scene at the ultra-modern Rome Auditorium (a.k.a. Parco della Musica, at Via Vittorio Veneto 96, tel. 06-8024-1281, www.auditorium.com).

Nightclubs: For late-night club-hopping (after 21:00), travel to Monte Testaccio. The small hill has cool caves housing funky restaurants and trendy clubs, surrounded by a rough neighborhood. Take the Metro to Piramide and follow the noise.

Resources from Rick Steves

This Pocket guide is one of more than 30 titles in my series of guidebooks on European travel. I also produce a public television series, *Rick Steves' Europe,* and a public radio show, *Travel with Rick Steves.* My website, www.ricksteves.com, offers free travel information, free vodcasts and podcasts of my shows, free audio tours of Europe's great sights, a Graffiti Wall for travelers' comments, guidebook updates, my travel blog, an on-line travel store, and information on European railpasses and our tours of Europe.

How was your trip? If you'd like to share your tips, concerns, and discoveries after using this book, please fill out the survey at www.ricksteves.com/feedback. It helps us and fellow travelers. Thanks, and *buon viaggio!*

Italian Survival Phrases

English	Italian	Pronunciation
Good day.	**Buon giorno.**	bwohn JOR-noh
Do you speak English?	**Parla inglese?**	PAR-lah een-GLAY-zay
Yes. / No.	**Si. / No.**	see / noh
I (don't) understand.	**(Non) capisco.**	(nohn) kah-PEES-koh
Please.	**Per favore.**	pehr fah-VOH-ray
Thank you.	**Grazie.**	GRAHT-seeay
You're welcome.	**Prego.**	PRAY-go
I'm sorry.	**Mi dispiace.**	mee dee-speeAH-chay
Excuse me.	**Mi scusi.**	mee SKOO-zee
(No) problem.	**(Non) c'è un problema.**	(nohn) cheh con proh-BLAY-mah
Good.	**Va bene.**	vah BEHN-ay
Goodbye.	**Arrivederci.**	ah-ree-vay-DEHR-chee
one / two	**uno / due**	OO-noh / DOO-ay
three / four	**tre / quattro**	tray / KWAH-troh
five / six	**cinque / sei**	CHEENG-kway / SEHee
seven / eight	**sette / otto**	SEHT-tay / OT-toh
nine / ten	**nove / dieci**	NOV-ay / deeAY-chee
How much is it?	**Quanto costa?**	KWAHN-toh KOS-tah
Write it?	**Me lo scrive?**	may loh SKREE-vay
Is it free?	**È gratis?**	eh GRAH-tees
Is it included?	**È incluso?**	eh een-KLOO-zoh
Where can I buy / find...?	**Dove posso comprare / trovare...?**	DOH-vay POS-soh kohm-PRAH-ray / troh-VAH-ray
I'd like / We'd like...	**Vorrei / Vorremmo...**	vor-REHee / vor-RAY-moh
...a room.	**...una camera.**	OO-nah KAH-meh-rah
...a ticket to ___.	**...un biglietto per ___.**	oon beel-YEHT-toh pehr
Is it possible?	**È possibile?**	eh poh-SEE-bee-lay
Where is...?	**Dov'è...?**	DOH-veh
...the train station	**...la stazione**	lah staht-seeOH-nay
...the bus station	**...la stazione degli autobus**	lah staht-seeOH-nay DAYL-yee OW-toh-boos
...tourist information	**...informazioni per turisti**	een-for-maht-seeOH-nee pehr too-REE-stee
...the toilet	**...la toilette**	lah twah-LEHT-tay
men	**uomini, signori**	WOH-mee-nee, seen-YOH-ree
women	**donne, signore**	DON-nay, seen-YOH-ray
left / right	**sinistra / destra**	see-NEE-strah / DEHS-trah
straight	**sempre diritto**	SEHM-pray dee-REE-toh
When do you open / close?	**A che ora aprite / chiudete?**	ah kay OH-rah ah-PREE-tay / keeoo-DAY-tay
At what time?	**A che ora?**	ah kay OH-rah
Just a moment.	**Un momento.**	oon moh-MAYN-toh
now / soon / later	**adesso / presto / tardi**	ah-DEHS-soh / PREHS-toh / TAR-dee
today / tomorrow	**oggi / domani**	OH-jee / doh-MAH-nee

Practicalities

In the Restaurant

English	Italian	Pronunciation
I'd like...	Vorrei...	vor-REHee
We'd like...	Vorremmo...	vor-RAY-moh
...to reserve...	...prenotare...	pray-noh-TAH-ray
...a table for one / two.	...un tavolo per uno / due.	oon TAH-voh-loh pehr OO-noh / DOO-ay
Non-smoking.	Non fumare.	nohn foo-MAH-ray
Is this seat free?	È libero questo posto?	eh LEE-bay-roh KWEHS-toh POH-stoh
The menu (in English), please.	Il menù (in inglese), per favore.	eel may-NOO (een een-GLAY-zay) pehr fah-VOH-ray
service (not) included	servizio (non) incluso	sehr-VEET-seeoh (nohn) een-KLOO-zoh
cover charge	pane e coperto	PAH-nay ay koh-PEHR-toh
to go	da portar via	dah POR-tar VEE-ah
with / without	con / senza	kohn / SEHN-sah
and / or	e / o	ay / oh
menu (of the day)	menù (del giorno)	may-NOO (dayl JOR-noh)
specialty of the house	specialità della casa	spay-chah-lee-TAH DEHL-lah KAH-zah
first course (pasta, soup)	primo piatto	PREE-moh peeAH-toh
main course (meat, fish)	secondo piatto	say-KOHN-doh peeAH-toh
side dishes	contorni	kohn-TOR-nee
bread	pane	PAH-nay
cheese	formaggio	for-MAH-joh
sandwich	panino	pah-NEE-noh
soup	minestra, zuppa	mee-NEHS-trah, TSOO-pah
salad	insalata	een-sah-LAH-tah
dessert	dolci	DOHL-chee
tap water	acqua del rubinetto	AH-kwah dayl roo-bee-NAY-toh
mineral water	acqua minerale	AH-kwah mee-nay-RAH-lay
milk	latte	LAH-tay
(orange) juice	succo (d'arancia)	SOO-koh (dah-RAHN-chah)
coffee / tea	caffè / tè	kah-FEH / teh
wine	vino	VEE-noh
red / white	rosso / bianco	ROH-soh / beeAHN-koh
glass / bottle	bicchiere / bottiglia	bee-keeAY-ray / boh-TEEL-yah
beer	birra	BEE-rah
Cheers!	Cin cin!	cheen cheen
More. / Another.	Ancora un po.' / Un altro.	ahn-KOH-rah oon poh / oon AHL-troh
The same.	Lo stesso.	loh STEHS-soh
The bill, please.	Il conto, per favore.	eel KOHN-toh pehr fah-VOH-ray
tip	mancia	MAHN-chah
Delicious!	Delizioso!	day-leet-seeOH-zoh

For more user-friendly Italian phrases, check out *Rick Steves' Italian Phrase Book & Dictionary* or *Rick Steves' French, Italian, and German Phrase Book*.

Practicalities

INDEX

Index

Index

Index

PHOTO CREDITS

Photo Credits, continued next page

Audio Europe™

Start your trip at

Free information and great gear to

▶ Plan Your Trip

Browse thousands of articles and a wealth of money-saving tips for planning your dream trip. You'll find up-to-date information on Europe's best destinations, packing smart, getting around, finding rooms, staying healthy, avoiding scams and more.

▶ Eurail Passes

Find out, step-by-step, if a railpas makes sense for your trip—and how to avoid buying more than y need. Get a bunch of free extras!

▶ Graffiti Wall & Travelers Helpline

Learn, ask, share—our online community of savvy travelers is a great resource for first-time travel to Europe, as well as seasoned pr

Rick Steves' Europe Through the Back Door, Inc.

Avalon Travel
a member of the Perseus Books Group
1700 Fourth Street
Berkeley, CA 94710, U.S.A.

Printed in China by R.R. Donnelley
Updated for sixth printing April 2013
Seventh printing September 2013

Portions of this book were originally published in Rick Steves' Mona Winks ©
2001, 1998, 1996, 1993, 1988 by Rick Steves and Gene Openshaw, and in Rick
Steves' Italy © 2009, 2008, 2007, 2006, 2005, 2004, 2003, 2002, 2001, 2000,
1999 by Rick Steves.

ISBN 978-1-59880-381-5
ISSN 2158-6152

For the latest on Rick's lectures, guidebooks, tours, public radio show, and public
television series, contact Rick Steves' Europe Through the Back Door, Box 2009,
Edmonds, WA 98020, tel. 425/771-8303, fax 425/771-0833, www.ricksteves.com,
rick@ricksteves.com.

Europe Through the Back Door Managing Editor: Risa Laib
ETBD Reviewing Editor: Jennifer Madison Davis
Avalon Travel Senior Editor and Series Manager: Madhu Prasher
Avalon Travel Project Editor: Kevin McLain
Proofreader: Nikki Ioakimedes
Research Assistance: Ben Cameron
Indexer: Stephen Callahan
Interior Design, Production & Typesetting: Darren Alessi
Cover Design: Kimberly Glyder Design
Cover Photos: Fountain of the Neptune © ROMA-OSLO/istockphoto.com; stair-
case of the Vatican Museum © Allg / dreamstime.com
Graphic Content Director: Laura VanDeventer
Maps & Graphics: David C. Hoerlein, Lauren Mills, Laura VanDeventer, Kat
Bennett, Mike Morgenfeld, Brice Ticen, Barb Geisler

*Although the author and publisher have made every effort to provide accurate,
up-to-date information, they accept no responsibility for loss, injury, overcooked
pasta, or inconvenience sustained by any person using this book.*

ABOUT THE AUTHORS

Rick Steves

Since 1973, Rick Steves has spent 100 days every year exploring Europe. Along with writing and researching a bestselling series of guidebooks, Rick produces a public television series *(Rick Steves' Europe)*, a public radio show *(Travel with Rick Steves)*, and an app and podcast *(Rick Steves Audio Europe)*; writes a nationally syndicated newspaper column; organizes guided tours that take over ten thousand travelers to Europe annually; and offers an information-packed website (www.ricksteves.com). With the help of his hardworking staff of 80 at Europe Through the Back Door—in Edmonds, Washington, just north of Seattle—Rick's mission is to make European travel fun, affordable, and culturally enlightening for Americans.

Connect with Rick:

f facebook.com/RickSteves   twitter: @RickSteves

Gene Openshaw

Gene Openshaw is a writer, composer, tour guide, and lecturer on art and history. Specializing in writing walking tours of Europe's cultural sights, Gene has co-authored ten of Rick's books and contributes to Rick's public television series. As a composer, Gene has written a full-length opera *(Matter)*, a violin sonata, and dozens of songs. He lives near Seattle with his daughter, and roots for the Mariners in good times and bad.

FOLDOUT COLOR MAP

The foldout map on the opposite page includes:
• A map of Rome on one side
• Maps of South Rome, Rome Transportation, and Italy on the other side

Praise for *New York Times* bestselling author Tanya Michaels

"Michaels...gives a familiar plot an interesting and fantastic twist—one that's laden with terrific charm and sexy sparks."
—*RT Book Reviews* on *Mistletoe Cinderella*, 4.5 stars, Top Pick

"*His Valentine Surprise* is a delight and I hope the beginning of another one of [her] series."

—*Dear Author*

"A sweet, heartwarming, fun and steamy story that you will not be able to put down."

—*Harlequin Junkie* on *Her Secret, His Baby*

Praise for Michelle Major

"Ingeniously funny and poignantly heartbreaking page-turner... Major handles her unforgettable characters' issues with compassion and finesse."
—*RT Book Reviews* on *Suddenly a Father*, 4.5 stars, Top Pick

"A fantastic mix of drama and romance, starring a fragile, belligerent heroine and wounded hero. The innuendos, banter and role-perfect nicknames make it exceptional and genuine."

—*RT Book Reviews* on *A Kiss on Crimson Ranch*, 4.5 stars

"Major spins her storytelling web with a visual narrative that enlivens the majestic beauty of Colorado while telling her heartbreaking tale."

—*RT Book Reviews* on
A Second Chance at Crimson Ranch, 4.5 stars

HOME ON THE RANCH:
COLORADO REDEMPTION

———— ✪ ————

New York Times Bestselling Author
TANYA MICHAELS

MICHELLE MAJOR

Previously published as *Her Cowboy Hero*
and *A Kiss on Crimson Ranch*

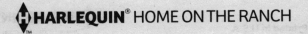

HARLEQUIN® HOME ON THE RANCH

ISBN-13: 978-1-335-50718-1

Home on the Ranch: Colorado Redemption
Copyright © 2018 by Harlequin Books S.A.

First published as Her Cowboy Hero by
Harlequin Books in 2014 and
A Kiss on Crimson Ranch by
Harlequin Books in 2014.

The publisher acknowledges the copyright
holders of the individual works as follows:

Her Cowboy Hero
Copyright © 2014 by Tanya Michna

A Kiss on Crimson Ranch
Copyright © 2014 by Michelle Major

PLEASE RECYCLE
THIS PRODUCT IS RECYCLABLE

Recycling programs
for this product may
not exist in your area.

Printed in U.S.A.

HARLEQUIN®
™ www.Harlequin.com

CONTENTS

Tanya Michaels, a *New York Times* bestselling author and five-time RITA® Award nominee, has been writing love stories since middle-school algebra class (which probably explains her math grades). Her books, praised for their poignancy and humor, have received awards from readers and reviewers alike. Tanya is an active member of Romance Writers of America and a frequent public speaker. She lives outside Atlanta with her very supportive husband, two highly imaginative kids and a bichon frise who thinks she's the center of the universe.

Books by Tanya Michaels

Harlequin Western Romance

Cupid's Bow, Texas

Falling for the Sheriff
Falling for the Rancher
The Christmas Triplets
The Cowboy Upstairs

Harlequin American Romance

Hill Country Heroes

Claimed by a Cowboy
Tamed by a Texan
Rescued by a Ranger

The Colorado Cades

Her Secret, His Baby
Second Chance Christmas
Her Cowboy Hero

Visit the Author Profile page at
Harlequin.com for more titles.

HER COWBOY HERO

TANYA MICHAELS

This is dedicated to everyone who emailed and posted online after reading the first Colorado Cades book to say they couldn't wait for Colin's story!

Chapter 1

For Colin Cade, one of the chief selling points of his motorcycle had been solitude. He preferred being alone, making it a conscious choice rather than a tragic circumstance, but that meant a lot of time in his own head. Unfortunately, not even the Harley could outrun his thoughts. Or his anger.

How the hell had he—a man who'd lived like a monk for the better part of two years—been fired for "sexual misconduct"?

Raising younger siblings had taught him patience the hard way, but right now his temper was providing uncharacteristic daydreams of shaking Delia McCoy's shoulders until her professionally whitened teeth rattled. She'd had no business showing up naked in his bed. The more he thought about it, the more convinced he was that his former employer's wife didn't even want

an affair. There had been plenty of other men working the ranch who would have taken advantage of her
adulterous offer. So why target the guy who'd never
once returned her flirtatious smiles? Was it possible
she only wanted to shock Sean McCoy into paying
more attention to her? Ranches took a lot of work, and
Delia had complained to anyone who would listen that
her husband neglected her.

Maybe she had cause to be bitter, but that sure didn't
give her the right to screw up Colin's life.

He was supposed to have stayed on at the McCoy
place for another month. The McCoys were crossbreed-
ing Angus and Hereford cows, and Colin, the former
owner of a large-animal vet practice, had been hired to
help deliver calves and see them off to a healthy start.
His job would have included routine disease prevention
and facilitating adoption for the expected twin sets and
any heifers that lost their babies. His next contract—
helping move two herds to the high country for summer grazing—was all lined up, but the cattle drive was
nearly six weeks away, after his brother's wedding.

What was he supposed to do in the meantime?

An old trail guide acquaintance had given him a
possible lead, but he had sounded skeptical about it.
"There's a lady in the northwest, not far from where
I hired on, who's been looking for help. The Widow
Shaw. None of the qualified ranch hands will waste
time working for her, because her place is going belly-
up any day now. Everyone knows it 'cept her. Frail little
thing is clearly addled. Bakes the best rum cake I've
ever had in my life, though."

Despite his friend's warning, Colin thought the job

sounded promising enough to head for Bingham Pass and call on the Widow Shaw.

After his last two jobs—which had included the naked Mrs. McCoy and, prior to that, a moony-eyed teenage daughter of a foreman in Routt County— an elderly, absentminded woman who liked to bake sounded perfect. Colin wouldn't stay long, but while he was there, he'd do what he could to get her back on her feet. And if that proved impossible…well, life sucked sometimes.

Who knew that better than him?

Inhaling deeply, Hannah Shaw took stock of her situation. The early evening sky was starting to darken sooner than it should, and she had a flat tire on a stretch of road where cell service was nonexistent. How was it possible that astronauts could tweet from space, but there were still places in modern Colorado where a woman couldn't get bars on her phone?

Bright side, Hannah. Find the bright side. After four years, her mantra was automatic. She tried every day to keep the vow she'd made in that hospital bed, to live with courageous optimism. Of course, that vow was currently being challenged by unyielding loan officers and the countless maintenance issues she'd inherited along with the Shaw family ranch. But she hadn't survived this long by whining or embracing negativity.

The silver lining here was that Evan was spending the night at her friend Annette's house instead of watching with worried eyes from his booster seat. Also, Hannah had successfully changed a flat tire once before, so there was no reason to think she couldn't do it again. If the problem had been, say, her carburetor, she'd really be screwed.

"I got this," she muttered, flipping on her hazard lights. She wished she'd been able to move the truck farther off the road, but there wasn't exactly a reliable shoulder on these winding curves. She shrugged out of the lightweight blazer she'd borrowed from Annette. Beneath it, Hannah wore a white blouse that strained at the buttons down her chest, a premotherhood relic from the back of her closet. It was one of the few items in her wardrobe professional enough for a bank meeting, and the neatly buttoned jacket had camouflaged the imperfect fit.

As she twisted her long black hair up in an elastic band, she tried not to dwell on the banker's condescending expression. She'd once again been told that maybe *after* she made significant improvements on the ranch, demonstrating that it was a solid investment, she could reapply. How was she supposed to make "significant" improvements without funds? She'd planned to rename the spread the Silver Linings Ranch, but it might be more accurate to call it The Catch-22. She'd received money after Michael's death, of course, but a good chunk of that was in savings for Evan. Despite her careful planning—and the money she'd set aside to hire competent help—she had underestimated how much work the ranch would need before she could realize her plans.

One thing at a time. Fix the tire now, save the ranch tomorrow.

She climbed down from the cab and went to the back of the truck, where the tools and spare tire were kept under a cover that could be worth more than the vehicle. *Note to self: maybe you should start keeping spare work clothes in the bed of the truck.* While she wouldn't necessarily mourn the ruination of the tight blouse, getting on the ground to change the tire was going to be murder on her pretty navy skirt.

A rumble of thunder echoed off the surrounding mountains, confirming Hannah's suspicions about the prematurely dark sky. Rain hadn't been in the forecast until tomorrow, but spring storms could move fast. Which meant she had better move fast, too.

Hurrying, she found a couple of good-size rocks on the side of the road to place in front of the tires. She was reluctant to completely trust the pickup's emergency brake. The air seemed to crackle with expectancy, and wind whipped around her, chilling her skin. She'd only ever changed the tire on a car, and there had been a notch where the jack belonged. The truck did not have one. She was feeling around, trying to determine the correct place for the jack so she didn't crack anything on the undercarriage, when the sky opened. Fat drops pelted her with enough force to sting.

But on the bright side, after a couple of years of drought, ranchers like her really needed the rain.

The shower had moved in fast, catching Colin by surprise. He'd anticipated getting into town before the rain started. He was scanning the side of the road for possible shelter when he rounded the curve and saw a stopped truck.

A woman knelt by a tire in the path of traffic. Not that there were any cars in sight, but lives could be taken in an instant. Stifling unwelcome memories— the call from the hospital, the twisted wreckage—

he steered his motorcycle off the road and lifted his helmet.

"Need a hand?" he called over the rain.

The woman stood and he realized that, while she didn't even reach his shoulder, she wasn't tiny everywhere. She looked like the generously endowed winner of a wet T-shirt contest. A blouse that had probably once been white but was now translucent was plastered to an equally see-through lace bra. He abruptly glanced away but not before catching a glimpse of dark, puckered nipples.

In one motion, he ripped off his leather jacket and shoved it toward her. "Here."

"Thanks." Cheeks flushed with color, she accepted the coat, her hazel eyes not quite meeting his.

Watching her put on his clothing felt uncomfortably intimate, and he found himself annoyed with her for being here, in his path. "Don't you have some kind of road service you could call?"

"Even if I did, there's no reception here. But I'm not incapable of—"

"Wait in the cab," he ordered. "No sense in both of us getting drenched."

Her posture went rigid, and she drew herself up to her full—what, five feet? But she didn't argue. "Far be it from me to look a gift Samaritan in the mouth." Once inside, she rolled down the window. Literally. The truck had one of the manual window cranks that had been replaced with electric buttons in most modern vehicles. She seemed to be supervising his work.

"This truck is ancient," he said. "God knows why you're driving it when the kinder thing would be to shoot it and put it out of its misery."

"It's not *that* bad," she retorted. Was that indignation or worry in her tone? "It just needs a little TLC."

He grunted, focusing on getting the tire changed. Stomping on the wrench to loosen the lug nut felt good. He was in the mood to kick something's ass. By the time he had the spare in place, the rain had shifted to a heavy drizzle. Ominous black clouds rolled closer. The storm might be taking a coffee break, but it hadn't quit.

"That spare's not going to get you far," he warned. "It's in lousy shape. Kind of like the rest of this heap." His disdain encompassed the replacement door that was a different color from the body of the truck and a side mirror that looked loose.

She met his contempt with a half smile. "On the bright side, getting the flat gave me a chance to rest the engine and let the radiator cool down. Don't worry, my ranch is only a few miles away. In fact, you should come with me. Wait out the storm. Judging from those clouds, we're in for a lot worse."

Although he recognized the logic in her words, the invitation irked him. "Lady, I could be a serial killer. You don't invite strangers home with you."

"Not normally, no." Her hazel eyes darkened, her expression somber. "If it helps, I was taught self-defense by a marine and I'm a lot tougher than I look."

A sizzle of lightning struck close enough to make both of them start.

"You shouldn't be riding that motorcycle in this," she scolded. For a split second, she reminded him of his sister, Arden. Not all women were so at ease bossing around grown men who towered over them. He wondered if Hazel Eyes had brothers. If they worked on that

ranch she'd mentioned, it could explain why she wasn't
worried about bringing a total stranger home with her.

"Come on," she prompted, impatience creeping into
her tone as more lightning flashed. "I have enough
problems without picking up my morning paper and
seeing that you got fried to the asphalt."

He didn't realize he was going to agree until the
words left his mouth. "Lead the way." He hadn't been
there the day a car accident had shattered his world,
hadn't been able to do a damn thing to help. He found
he couldn't abandon this woman until she and her rattling joke of a truck were out of the rain.

Mounting his bike, he shook his head at the unexpected turn of events. Hazel was not the first woman
who'd invited him back to her place. But it was the first
time in two years that he'd accepted.

Colin was too occupied with the diminishing vis-
ibility and handling his bike on the dirt road to study
his surroundings. He had a general impression of going
through a gated entrance; farther ahead were much
larger structures, likely the main house and a barn or
stable. But the truck stopped at a narrow, one-story
building.

The woman parked in the mud, gesturing out her
window that he should go around and park beneath
the covered carport, where the motorcycle would be
out of the worst of the elements. She joined him under
the carport a moment later, her hand tucked inside the
purse she wore over her shoulder. He wondered if she
had pepper spray or a Taser in there. She'd sounded
serious when she mentioned the self-defense lessons.

"This is the old bunkhouse," she said. "I'm about to

start refurbing it as a guest cabin, but at the moment it's mostly empty."

He supposed that any brothers or a husband lived in the main house with her. Although what caring husband would let his wife drive a disaster on wheels like that truck?

She tossed him a key ring and nodded toward the door. "You can get a hot shower, dry off. There's a microwave and a few cans of soup in the cabinet. Before you tell me I'm naive and that you might be a master burglar, let me assure you there's nothing to steal. I doubt you could get thirty bucks on Craigslist for the twin bed and microwave combined."

He unlocked the door, noting how she kept a casual but unmistakable distance. Once he'd flipped the light switch, he saw that she was right about the lack of luxuries. The "carpet" was the kind of multipurpose indoor/outdoor covering used more in screened patios than homes. There was enough space for three or four beds, but only one was pushed against the wall. At one end of the long, rectangular interior was a minifridge and microwave, at the other a bathroom. Aside from a couple of truly ugly paintings of cows, the place was barren.

He stopped in the center of the room, raising an eyebrow. "The minifridge brings up my Craigslist asking price to thirty-five."

She gave a sharp laugh, abruptly stifled. "Sorry the accommodations aren't classier. The ranch is…in a rebuilding phase."

The note of genuine embarrassment in her voice made him uneasy. "It's plenty classy. I've slept on the ground during cattle drives and in horse stalls on more than one occasion." By *slept,* he meant tossing and turning, trying to avoid nightmares of everything he'd lost.

Those hazel eyes locked on him, her expression inexplicably intense. "You work with livestock!"

Isn't that what he'd just said? "As often as I can." He preferred animals to people. "Sometimes I do other odd jobs, too. I was headed into Bingham Pass to get more information about a local employment opportunity."

"Then you haven't already committed to it?" A smile spread across her face, revealing two dimples. "Because, as it happens, *I'm* hiring." She stepped forward, extending her hand. The oversize jacket parted, revealing a still damp but not entirely transparent blouse. Thank God.

"I'm Hannah."

Hannah, Hazel. He'd been close.

"Hannah Shaw," she elaborated when he said nothing. "Owner of the Silver Linings Ranch."

Foreboding cramped low in his belly. Paralyzed, he neglected to shake her hand. "Not the Widow Shaw?" The one who baked cakes and harbored delusions of being a rancher?

She frowned. "People still call me that?"

Crap. It *was* her. He'd imagined Mrs. Shaw would be a temporary solution to his problems, but now, meeting her earnest gaze, his instincts murmured that she posed far more threat to his safety than any rifle-wielding jealous husband.

Chapter 2

"You know I'm rooting for you, but—"

"No *buts,* Annette." Hannah secured the phone be-tween her ear and shoulder, needing both hands to separate the yolk from the egg white. "This is the an-swer to my prayers! Think about it—I've been scour-ing the county for a halfway-competent ranch hand, and one rides to my rescue on a rainy Wednesday eve-ning? It's destiny."

Or, at least, proof that her positive thinking was finally—*finally!*—paying off. She executed a happy twirl, narrowly missing the antique buffet that served as a kitchen island. Though she'd been too excited to eat dinner after she'd showered off the road grime and changed into dry clothes, she was busy mixing a thank-you batch of devil's food cupcakes for Annette.

Over the past three months, Annette Reed had become like a big sister. Annette and her husband were trying to have kids; meanwhile they doted on Evan, helping create the extended family he'd never had. Annette was a blessing in their lives, even if she was slow to embrace Hannah's "bright side" philosophy. The other woman didn't fully understand that the determined optimism was the only thing that had kept Hannah going during the bleakest period of her life, that Hannah owed it to her son to prove good things *could* happen if you worked hard enough.

"Sweetie, please be careful," Annette entreated. "You wouldn't be the first woman in the world to get in trouble because she confused a hot guy on a motorcycle with destiny."

"Hot guy?" Hannah froze, glancing out the window into the dark, as if making sure Colin Cade couldn't overhear them. Which was insane since he was a quarter of a mile away, and she was locked into her house with a watchdog for company. "I never said he was hot."

"Not in so many words, but it was in your tone. What's he look like?"

Dark, with that shaggy, rich brown hair and unshaven jaw. Chiseled. And she didn't just mean the muscles outlined beneath his T-shirt. His features, though striking, looked as if they'd been carved from stone. Had the man ever smiled in his life? *Not that it matters.* Being charming wasn't a job requirement. She needed someone efficient and unflinching in the face of setbacks.

"He has blue eyes," she said noncommittally. Light blue with a hint of green. "And he's tall."

Her friend guffawed. "Next to you, sweetie, *everyone's* tall."

She ignored the crack about her height. "Annette, this isn't me getting my hopes up for no reason. The guy came here specifically looking for me, looking for this ranch." Granted, Colin had seemed more shell-shocked than enthusiastic when he'd realized he found her. "An old friend of Colin's told him I was hiring and he wanted more information." She'd kept her answers in the bunkhouse brief and cheerful, barely mentioning Henry White, the well-intentioned, semiretired ranch hand who came by at least twice a week.

"Did you tell him the truth?"

"More or less," she said, hearing the defensive note in her tone. "I mean, I didn't volunteer that today was my fifth bank meeting and that I got turned down again. I said that I'd inherited a family ranch, have plans to turn it into a cross between a small dude ranch and bed-and-breakfast but have yet to put together a staff." Unless one counted seventy-year-old Henry and his wife, Kitty. "I invited him to the main house for breakfast so we can discuss details. I'm making my homemade coffee cake."

"Ah. Pulling out the big guns, then."

Hell, yes.

As far back as Hannah could remember, she'd always had a plan. Her first one had been Get Adopted. That one had never worked out, but years later, for one shining moment in time, her marriage had made her part of a family. Eyes stinging, she batted away the memories and focused on the present. Current plan: rehabilitate the ranch that had been in her late husband's family, build it into a legacy for her son. And to do that, she needed Colin Cade.

She was a persistent woman looking to hire help, and he was a man with ranch experience who needed a job. A match made in heaven! How hard could it possibly be to convince him to stay?

"Good morning!"

Colin hesitated on the bottom step of the wrap-around porch, momentarily stunned by Hannah's brilliant smile. And bright yellow peasant blouse. She would be murder on a man with a hangover.

As he'd mulled over the circumstances last night, he'd tried to keep thinking of her as the Widow Shaw, but he couldn't reconcile that moniker with the woman who'd stepped outside of the two-story house to meet him. She looked as fresh as a spring morning with her feet bare, revealing hot-pink toenails, and her inky hair pulled high in a ponytail. If it hadn't been for the jeans she wore and the pair of muddy boots sitting on the porch, he would seriously question whether she actually owned this place.

Behind her, on the other side of the screen door, an unseen dog scrabbled against the metal lower half and barked. Hannah shushed the canine over her shoulder, then flashed another sun-bright beam in Colin's direction. "Don't worry, Scarlett doesn't bite. Come on in—breakfast is ready and waiting."

Even from outside the house, the food smelled too enticing, making his stomach growl in anticipation. He was reminded of the fairy tale he used to read his younger sister. *Hansel and Gretel.* Hannah's house might not be made out of candy, but temptation was present just the same.

Then again, she had a job to offer him. It was imperative that Colin stay busy. He needed physically draining, sunup-to-sundown work.

Resigned, he followed her through the front door. "Holy sh—" He broke off, manners belatedly overcoming his shock. "That's…some dog."

Hannah knelt down, patting the dog's head. "Meet Scarlett."

Yesterday, Colin had thought Hannah's truck an eyesore. Next to the dog, it was a luxury sedan. He'd seen "patchwork" mutts before with traits from different breeds that looked a little mismatched. Scarlett went beyond mixed-breed. She was FrankenDog. It was as if someone had placed a disproportionately large German shepherd head on a squat body—not an attractive head, either. The dog had a comically pronounced underbite and her ears weren't parallel. One black ear stood up atop her head, as was common with shepherds, and the other seemed to stick straight out of the side of her skull. What were the legs, basset hound? Her red-and-white coat couldn't decide whether it was supposed to be curly or straight, and her tail was a brindle-colored whip that didn't match anything else on her. He assumed her neck bolts were hidden beneath the bright blue collar.

"Scarlett," he echoed. He would've gone with "Hellhound," although that did imply a creature weighing more than forty pounds.

Hearing her name, the dog whined and smacked him with her wagging tail.

"She likes you. That's a good sign," Hannah declared as she stood, leading him through a spacious living room with a stone fireplace. He got a glimpse of a back hallway and a set of stairs, but she led him past that and into the kitchen. "I'm not a superstitious person, but everything about our meeting has been so lucky."

He kept his response to a vague grunt she could take either way. It was probably best not to argue with a potential employer, but mountainside storms and mutant dogs didn't strike him as auspicious omens.

"Hope you're hungry. I love to cook. Before I came here, I was a pastry chef."

"Big change."

"True, but I'd been studying ranches for years. Running this place was always the plan. Besides, I couldn't have stayed at my last job much longer." She scowled. "My boss—never mind. We should be eating," she chirped.

He was reluctantly fascinated by her total about-face. It was as though she'd flipped a switch. One moment, she'd clearly been remembering something unpleasant, anger seeping into her tone, then, boom, she was back to beaming like a lottery winner.

Maybe she was schizophrenic.

Aware that he was on the verge of staring, he looked away. In appearance, Hannah's kitchen wasn't much fancier than the bunkhouse. Chairs at the oblong table were mismatched, and the countertops bore stains and scratches. Faded wallpaper covered the spaces between appliances but had been scraped off the main wall, which was bare. However, the bounty on the island more than compensated for the modest surroundings. Crisp bacon; eggs scrambled with cheese, peppers and sausage; a bowl of fruit salad; piping-hot coffee; and a cake so moist it looked like the cover photo of some food magazine. His mind darted back to the *Hansel and Gretel* story and the witch who fattened up her prey.

He slanted Hannah an assessing look. "You got any ulterior motives I should know about?"

"Wh-what? You mean, like the old saw about the way to a man's heart being through his stomach? Because I am not interested in you! Not like that."

She sounded so vehement that he experienced a jolt of surprise. Maybe he was a few weeks—months?—overdue for a haircut, but he wasn't repulsive.

"I just wanted to make a good impression," she said. "I don't cook like this every morning, of course. Too many chores to be done. Although, we do splurge once a week, for Sunday breakfasts."

We? So far, he hadn't seen evidence of another person on this ranch.

Handing him a plate edged in feminine purple flowers, she nodded toward the food. "Dig in while the eggs are still warm. I'd love to discuss your references. Then after breakfast, I can give you a tour—"

She was cut off by Scarlett's frantic barking. The house rattled as the front door swung open with gale force. Hannah turned, an automatic smile blossoming as a child's voice hollered, "Mommy!" Then a little boy with a curly mop of hair nearly as dark as Hannah's skidded around the corner, launching himself at her in an exuberant hug.

Colin's heart clenched. The same delicious aromas that had been making his mouth water now turned his stomach. Nausea and memories boiled up inside him.

Physically, the dark-eyed little boy didn't bear any resemblance to Danny, but he looked about the same age Danny would have—

"I have to get out of here." Addressing his words to no one in particular, he dropped his plate on the counter and strode toward the living room.

Colin's nerves had held steady while working with numerous wild-eyed horses too scared to realize he was trying to help; hell, he'd kept his cool during a stampede. But there were limits to his bravery. He couldn't be around kids.

He'd never taken a job where young children lived, and the Silver Linings Ranch would be no exception.

WHAT JUST HAPPENED? Hannah was so stunned by Colin's announcement that it took her a moment to process his abrupt exit. This wasn't the first time someone had turned down her job offer, but none of the other candidates had actually bolted. She'd hit a new low in the interview process. "Wait!"

Gently disentangling herself from her son's sticky hug—was that jam on his fingers?—Hannah sprinted after Colin. And drew up short to avoid smacking into him. He, in turn, had apparently halted to avoid running over a startled Annette.

The blonde's mouth had fallen open in a perfect *O*, making her look like a comic strip character. "Um, hi?" Her eyes darted to Hannah. "Sorry, I…forgot you had a breakfast meeting."

Fat chance. Given the concern Annette had expressed over a stranger spending the night, Hannah wasn't surprised her friend had come over first thing to check on her. At least Annette hadn't dragged her husband, Todd, along. No doubt Annette had plenty of questions about why the man who should be sitting comfortably at the table listing his credentials had almost mowed her over.

Hannah stepped forward to make introductions—which just so happened to strategically place her between Colin and the front door. "Colin, meet Annette. She's here to drop off Evan and pick up some cupcakes. They're really good, if I do say so myself." Deep down, she hoped that if she kept talking, he couldn't leave. He might be gruff, but surely he wasn't brusque enough to walk out midconversation? "Annette, this is Colin Cade. We were about to eat and discuss Colin's previous ranch experience."

"No, we weren't," he said firmly. He gave a curt nod in Annette's direction. "Ma'am."

Annette raised a pale eyebrow. "Don't let me interrupt."

He shook his head, already moving toward the door again. Something in his demeanor suggested he would pick up Hannah and remove her bodily from his path if necessary. "Nothing to interrupt. I was on my way out." He opened the screen door, letting it clatter shut behind him.

Gesturing toward the kitchen in an all-purpose indication that Annette should help herself to the food and please keep an eye on Evan, Hannah followed. Was it her son's appearance that had sent Colin fleeing, or had she been too manic in her perky approach? One of her favorite high school teachers had always said that enthusiasm was contagious, but that didn't seem to be the case with Colin. Maybe she should dial it back a notch.

His much longer legs gave him the advantage. He was already down in the yard, but she wasn't too proud to jog down the porch steps.

"Wait, Colin, I—" *Crack.*

The board under her gave way, and Hannah gasped as her foot went through the fissure at a wrong angle. Suddenly, he was at her side, his hands warm on her hips as he lifted her. For a big man, he moved surprisingly fast.

"You're hurt." Putting his arms around her, he lifted her vertically so she wouldn't have to navigate the steps and lowered her onto the porch. Tingles of awareness erupted like goose bumps across her skin. It had been eternities since she'd been that close to a man.

"Twisted my ankle," she said breathlessly, "but it's nothing ice and ibuprofen won't fix."

He glowered, those blue eyes stormy. "You seem to have some strange ideas about what's fixable. Your truck's a pile of scrap metal, and you live in a house that's rotting out from under you."

"It is not." Annoyed, she shoved away from him, not even caring that she had to hobble to do so. "I'll admit the steps need replacing—all the rain hasn't helped. Maybe some of the railing is a little loose, too. But I made sure the main house was structurally sound before I moved my son here."

At the mention of Evan, Colin's gaze skittered behind her, as if she'd reminded him that there was a nuclear warhead inside rather than a four-year-old boy.

"Wow. You really don't like kids, do you?"

He blanched, but didn't answer.

Admitting defeat, Hannah shook her head sadly. She was stubborn, not delusional. "Thank you for changing my tire yesterday. Safe journeys wherever you're headed next."

Trying to keep her weight off the throbbing ankle, she pivoted toward the door. With a sound of strangled frustration, Colin clamped his fingers around her upper arm.

"I don't know where I'm going next," he said through gritted teeth. "But I'm replacing those damn steps before I go." He glanced around the spacious wraparound porch. "This entire thing's probably a safety hazard that should be reinforced, if not rebuilt."

Renewed hope surged through her, eclipsing her pain. "I insist on paying for your time as well as the materials." She kept her voice calm, trying not to betray her joy at this small victory.

"You have tools?"

She nodded. "There's a small detached garage behind the house. Pretty well stocked, as far as I can tell. I can show you."

He slanted her an assessing glance. "You should get inside, off that ankle. If you've got a tape measure handy, I'll start taking measurements."

"Sure. I'll send Annette out with it. She can take you to the garage." Hannah made a mental note to instruct her friend not to interrogate Colin or overwhelm him with boisterous conversation. Otherwise, he might follow his original impulse and bolt. As it stood, she had at least a couple of days, a window of opportunity to plead her case. But with more subtlety this time.

He narrowed his eyes. "Just this one repair job. That's not the same as signing on with you, Mrs. Shaw."

She nodded innocently. *We'll see about that.*

Chapter 3

In the parking lot of a Bingham Pass diner, Colin sat inside a truck older than he was, as disoriented as if an Arabian Thoroughbred had kicked him in the skull.

Earlier that morning, he'd been ready to jump on his motorcycle and put Hannah Shaw, her energetic son and her ill-fated ranch all behind him. Yet he'd spent several hours purchasing lumber and paint and getting a new tire for her misbegotten truck. Since he'd never actually gotten around to eating breakfast—and because he was in no hurry to return to the Silver Linings—he'd stayed in town for lunch.

Bingham Pass, like his hometown of Cielo Peak, was rife with local gossip. As soon as Colin had mentioned the Silver Linings Ranch, the waitress had sighed sadly and remarked that Hannah's husband, a marine, had been killed overseas.

I was taught self-defense by a marine, and I'm a lot tougher than I look.

In hindsight, Colin acknowledged that his worry and anger at seeing Hannah fall through that bottom step had been disproportional to her minor injury. She seemed irrepressible. A mild sprain wouldn't keep her down for long. But how could he walk away, knowing a young woman or her kid might be hurt when he could have prevented it?

He couldn't leave with a clear conscience until he replaced the boards. Paradoxically, he still couldn't bring himself to return to the ranch yet—hence the sitting in a parked truck. He needed the few extra moments to brace himself for whatever surprise came at him next.

Ever since spotting Hannah through the rain, he'd felt off-kilter, unbalanced by her identity, her affable hellhound, the discovery that she had a little boy. None of it was what he'd expected. He should phone the so-called buddy who'd given him this lead. Colin had a few choice words for the man who'd led him to believe the "frail Widow Shaw" was a little old lady.

He powered up the cell phone he usually kept turned off. If asked, he would claim he left it off to make the charge last, but, truthfully, he was dodging his sister. A few weeks ago, Arden's husband had undergone major surgery in order to donate one of his kidneys to his biological father. As a concerned older brother, Colin had dutifully answered every one of her calls, wanting to be there for her in case anything had gone wrong.

But she'd abused the privilege. She'd acted as if she were calling with post-op updates on Garrett, but then she inevitably worked the conversation around to how Garrett's family could use the extra help on the Double

F Ranch while he recuperated. Wouldn't Colin love the opportunity to use his skills on behalf of relatives and spend some time with his infant niece?

Colin knew his sister worried about him, that Arden wanted to help him heal. How could he explain that it hurt to be around her, the glowing new mother with a husband who adored her? Their brother, Justin, wasn't much better. He was engaged and disgustingly in love.

As soon as his phone finished booting up, it buzzed with the notification that he had 6 Missed Calls from Arden Frost. That was a lot even for her.

Fighting a stab of uneasiness, he dialed his brother Justin's number. If something were wrong, Justin would know. But if her calls were simply more attempts to recruit him to the Double F so she could keep an eye on him, then he was dodging a bullet by not phoning her directly.

It took a few rings before Justin answered. "Hey, old man. Long time, no hear. To what do I owe the honor?"

His brother's glib tone sent an unexpected stab of nostalgia through Colin. He hadn't seen either of his siblings since Christmas, which suddenly seemed like a long time considering how close they'd once been. Although there'd been an elderly aunt's name on the guardianship papers, Colin had all but raised his siblings after their parents' deaths.

He cleared his throat. "I, ah, wondered if you could tell me what our sister's been up to lately. She filled my voice-mail box. I figured it would be quicker to check in with you than listen to all of the messages. You know Arden. She's not brief."

Justin laughed. "Preaching to the choir. I realize it's a wuss move, but now that I'm engaged, I keep trying to make Elisabeth take her calls so I don't have to. Those two can talk wedding plans for *hours*."

Colin squeezed his eyes closed. Weddings, babies, new beginnings. It was difficult not to feel as if Arden and Justin were both just starting out in life while his had abruptly derailed. "So do you know why she's been calling me?"

Justin's heavy pause was worrisome. He usually had a quip for every occasion. "You should really ask her."

Colin's heart skipped a beat. Decades ago, they'd lost their mom to cancer and their father to heart failure. Had Arden inherited any medical problems? "Justin, you tell me right now, is she okay?"

"Relax, bro, it's *good* news." He sighed. "You didn't hear this from me, but she and Garrett are expecting."

"Again? Those two are like rabbits."

"Dude, it's only their second child."

"Yeah, but the first one's not even a year old! Shouldn't they be pacing themselves?"

"If it's all the same to you, I'd rather not think about our sister's sex life." Justin changed the subject. "How are things going with the McCoys?" His carefully neutral tone made it clear he'd heard something. Justin was no better at lying now than he had been as a kid.

"What do you know?"

"Only some very bizarre gossip about you and Delia McCoy. The ranching community talks. Garrett heard that you and Mrs. McCoy were caught in bed together, and he told Arden, who called me screeching. She didn't know whether to be relieved you're interested in a woman romantically or appalled that you'd be part of an adulterous affair."

Colin smacked his forehead. This was why he always left his phone off.

"Calm yourselves. Delia arranged to be caught in my bed, but I was nowhere near it. And I'm not interested in any woman." A pair of mesmerizing hazel eyes flashed through his mind, but no way in hell was he sharing that with his brother. "Look, I gotta go. I'll call Arden when I have more time to chat. I'll pretend to be surprised when she tells me about the baby."

"Gotta go where?" Justin pressed. "Are you still working at the McCoy place? Rumor has it you got canned, or is that part an exaggeration, too?"

Colin rolled his eyes heavenward, choosing his words carefully. If he admitted he was between jobs, he'd seem churlish and petty for not going home to visit his family. But all the Cades were forthright in nature. He was no more skilled at dishonesty than his brother. "I found a temporary gig on a spread in Bingham Pass." Very temporary.

"Glad you landed on your feet. Word of advice?" Justin asked, mischief lacing his voice. "Be careful not to make any goo-goo eyes at the boss's wife."

"I'm hanging up on you now. Also, the boss isn't married."

"Well, there's a relief."

The polar opposite, actually. Colin couldn't imagine anything less comfortable than working for an attractive single mom. Which was why, the second paint started drying on a newly secured porch, he was getting the hell out of Dodge.

When Scarlett worked herself into a frenzy by the front door, Hannah experienced an irrational burst of relief. *He's back.* It wasn't that she'd honestly believed Colin would steal her truck and never return. But he'd seemed so reluctant to be here that it would be good to see him with her own eyes, to have proof he was serious about staying for another day or two.

She got up from the kitchen table, where she'd been paying bills on her laptop, and went to quiet the dog. As usual, indulgent "Aunt Annette" had let Evan stay up too late, and Hannah had sent her increasingly fussy son to take a nap. He'd been asleep only a few minutes.

But when Hannah saw who was on the other side of the screen door, instead of shushing Scarlett, she wanted to snarl right along with her.

"Afternoon, Hannah." Gideon Loomis tipped his gray felt cowboy hat, giving her a smile that would have been so much more handsome without the permanent smugness etched into his features.

Go away. "Gideon." It was tricky to avoid someone in Bingham Pass, downright impossible when that someone owned the neighboring ranch, but why was he standing on her front porch? After their lone dinner date, she'd tried to make it clear she wasn't interested in seeing him again. She'd stopped shy of blunt rudeness, because only an idiot would antagonize the Loomis family. "This is a surprise."

"A pleasant one, I hope." His self-assured tone made it clear he'd drawn his own erroneous conclusion. "Mama sent me over with an order for another one of her social events."

His mother, Patricia Loomis, was Hannah's biggest customer. There were decent restaurants in town that could cater, but no one in the area could bake or decorate desserts like Hannah. While she was thankful for

Patricia's business, it also held her hostage. She longed for the freedom to tell Gideon he was an arrogant ass who was no doubt rendering himself infertile with his obnoxiously tight jeans.

Tugging on Scarlett's collar, she attempted to make the agitated dog sit. Scarlett had never liked Gideon, which proved the people at the shelter had known what they were talking about when they'd told Hannah the mutt was smart. She opened the door, grudgingly inviting her neighbor inside.

He inhaled deeply. "Always smells so delicious here. I just realized, I worked right through lunch. Don't suppose I could trouble you for a slice of cake and some coffee?" He was already making his way to the kitchen.

She ground her teeth together. "I don't have any coffee brewed." Since there was half a cake sitting in a clear domed container on the counter, she saw no polite way to refuse him that. She got a clean plate from the dishwasher and sliced a much smaller piece than she would have offered Annette. "We have to keep our voices down. Evan is sleeping. I was actually thinking about stealing the opportunity for a quick nap myself," she fibbed.

He ignored the hint that he should hurry on his way. "Sorry I missed the little guy. Be sure to tell him hi for me."

Evan didn't like Gideon any more than the dog did. For starters, the fiercely independent four-year-old, who couldn't wait for kindergarten, hated the "little guy" nickname. He also disliked how Gideon chucked him on the chin as if they were in some cheesy made-for-TV movie. Who did that in real life? One of Hannah's objections to the man was how he always seemed to be performing for an invisible audience.

She also objected to his barely concealed lust for her ranch.

Before she'd moved to Bingham Pass, she'd had ideas—and a budget—for guest-friendly investments. An outdoor hot tub, extra beds, more horses. But the six-bedroom ranch had fallen into disrepair since she'd seen it last, and she quickly realized she needed to prioritize roof improvements, furniture, updated plumbing and possibly even new wiring. Most of the outlets were only two-prong instead of the now-standard three. Alarmed by how inadequate her budget was, she'd let the Loomis family talk her into selling a strip of land that adjoined their property.

She'd regretted the hasty decision afterward, and not just because she'd realized they lowballed her on price. The Silver Linings Ranch was Michael's legacy to their son. She would not sell it off piecemeal like a stolen car stripped for parts. Gideon and his family weren't getting their hands on another acre of her land.

Aware of how easily her anger could grow—of the negative emotions that lurked like an undertow to consume her—she forced a smile. It was strained, but Gideon didn't seem to mind. He grinned back, leaning against the island to eat instead of going to the table as she'd hoped.

She found an excuse to move away from him, stepping toward the refrigerator. "Can I get you some iced tea? Maybe a glass of milk to wash down the chocolate?"

"Tea's fine." He took a bite of cake, and unmistakable bliss lit his brown eyes. "Damn, that's good. It's a crying shame you have to expend so much energy into taking care of the horses, cows and goats."

She didn't have goats. She was the proud owner of horses, cows and one attack donkey.

"If you had a husband to worry about the livestock for you," he continued, "think of all the extra time you could spend puttering in the kitchen and developing your recipes."

She straightened abruptly from the fridge shelf, skewering him with a glare. "Yeah, careless of Michael to get killed in action and screw up my *puttering* schedule."

"All I meant was—a woman like you? Deserves a man who can take care of her."

She wanted to rail that not only was she capable of taking care of herself, she'd been doing a splendid job of taking care of Evan for the past four years. Still... being a good mom and a hard worker didn't automatically translate to being able to maintain one hundred and eighty acres alone. *Not alone, exactly.* She had a four-year-old always looking for ways to "help." She also had Henry, who'd worked this property for decades and refused to acknowledge limitations set by age or reality, and Colorado's most unusual ranch dog.

Okay, she needed a man, but not in the romantic sense. Particularly if her options were limited to Gideon Loomis.

His expression earnest, he set down the plate and came toward her. "At the very least, let me talk to my folks about buying your cows from you. The herd would be one less thing for you to manage."

The "herd" was fewer than two dozen heifers, a bull and the resulting calves. Her predecessor, Michael's great-uncle, hadn't used a formal breeding program. He kept the bull in with the heifers, sometimes separating out the younger cows, and let nature take its course. A vet was called in as necessary, but the cattle were actually the least of her problems—with the exception of hauling hay. Hay was a never-ending chore.

"Isn't that sweet of you," she bit out, "offering to shoulder my burdens? No doubt for some sort of grateful, discounted rate."

His voice rose. "Are you accusing me of trying to cheat you? If you were a man…" He stopped, running a hand over his reddened face. His tone changed, slick with his attempt at charm. "But *you* are all woman."

"Maybe you're right, I do need a man." She jutted her chin up. "Good thing that, as of yesterday, I found one."

There was a shiny red pickup in front of the ranch house when Colin returned from town. When he'd left, Annette's car had been there. This must be someone different. He took the steps two at a time, glad Hannah had company. Maybe he could return the truck keys and get to work on the porch without further conversation. Even though she'd affirmed her understanding that he was sticking around only for this one quick repair job, did he really trust that she wouldn't try to coax him into staying?

More to the point, did he trust himself to resist? Home cooking like hers and the sibling-free solitude of the bunkhouse were appealing. If she didn't have a kid—or those arresting hazel eyes—he would have considered staying until his brother's wedding.

Before he had a chance to knock against the door frame, voices carried through the screen.

"—your sense? You can't just bring strange men home!"

"I told you to keep your voice down," Hannah retorted, her own voice only marginally softer. "And it's *my* ranch. I make the decisions. I think it's time for you to go, Gideon."

"I haven't finished," the man argued.

Not bothering to waste time knocking, Colin let himself inside, even as he called himself a fool. For all he knew, "Gideon" was a relative or a boyfriend and Hannah might resent a third-party interloper witnessing the argument. But Colin had a problem with the man's refusal to leave.

"Hannah?" He wheeled around the corner, distantly recognizing that it had been a long damn time since he'd felt protective of anyone but Justin or Arden.

His would-be boss was between the kitchen counter near the fridge and a beefy guy standing close enough that Colin had the urge to yank him back by his collar.

"You're back." Hannah's face went from tense to one of those dimpled smiles faster than a humming-bird could beat its wings. She raised an arm, pushing Gideon out of her way with the heel of her hand and coming to take the truck keys from Colin. "This is my neighbor, Gideon Loomis. He was just leaving."

The man's blond eyebrows shot toward the brim of his gray hat. "Actually, I—"

"Mommy?"

All three adults turned to see Evan in the wide entryway, his hair sticking up in wayward tufts, a child-size green blanket clutched in his hand.

Gideon gave the kid a hearty smile. "Oops—we wake you, little guy?"

Evan scowled.

"How about I make it up to you with a piece of cake?" Gideon offered.

"I don't think so." Hannah crossed the kitchen to scoop the boy up in a hug. "He had some after lunch. No more sweets until after dinner. And only then if you eat some vegetables," she told her son.

Evan's wrinkled nose and unenthusiastic grunt nearly tugged a sympathetic smile from Colin. He himself was a meat-and-potatoes man. Natalie had always cajoled him to set a good example by eating more green stuff.

"If Danny doesn't see you eating food like broccoli or lima beans, he'll form a preconceived notion that they taste bad."

"That's not a notion—that's scientific fact."

Colin blinked, startled by the memory of teasing his wife. He was normally more vigilant about stifling those recollections. Dwelling on what he'd lost made it harder to move forward. *I need air.*

He cleared his throat. "I'm going to back the truck up to the garage and start unloading lumber. So… I'll be outside if you need me." The words were ostensibly for Hannah, but his gaze swung to Gideon. If Hannah asked her neighbor to leave again, Colin would be close enough to offer his assistance in escorting the man from the premises.

A few minutes later, as Colin stood on the porch double-checking some measurements, the front door opened. Hannah walked Gideon outside. She looked calmer, but her smile wasn't genuine. Her hazel eyes were flat, and no dimples showed.

Shaking his head, Colin rejected the involuntary sense of familiarity. He'd known Hannah for less than twenty-four hours. Who was he to assume he could read her?

"Please tell your mom I said thanks for the order," Hannah was saying. "And she's always welcome to call or email me. I hate for anyone to waste their time with an unnecessary trip."

There was a pause as Gideon digested her pointed words, and though Colin kept his eyes on what he was doing, he could feel the man's hostile gaze prickling the back of his neck like sunburn. "Wasn't any trouble. You've only been in Bingham Pass a few months, but we're neighborly around here. You'll come to realize there are a lot of benefits to that."

In Colin's experience, there were also benefits to being left the hell alone.

All Hannah said was, "Careful going down the stairs." She waited on the porch as Gideon climbed into his truck, expelling a frustrated breath as he pulled away from the house. "I swear, that man…"

When she didn't finish the thought, Colin turned toward her. She stood with her hands on her hips and her jaw tight.

"First my boss back in Colorado Springs didn't want to take no for an answer, and now Gideon with his macho I-know-best act. What is it about me that draws these yahoos? It's because I'm short, isn't it? Makes me look like an easy target."

His gaze slid down her body then back to her face, flushed with spirited indignation that made her hazel eyes sparkle like gemstones. "It's a lot more than your height that attracts men." What the devil was he thinking, saying that out loud? He'd spoken the truth, but there were too many wrong ways she could take his comment. She might lump him in with the inappropriate men she'd already been criticizing. Or, worse, she could take it as flirtation.

Colin didn't flirt. He left that to Justin, the glib charmer who'd set Cielo Peak dating records before asking Elisabeth to marry him.

Hannah looked momentarily startled by his words, but then nodded. "You're right, of course. Gideon's attracted to my ranch. I think his family looks at this property as the opportunity to expand their outfit. But I've got my own plans, which don't include the Loomises."

Right, her idea to remake the ranch as a B and B. In theory, he could picture her as the proprietor of a bed-and-breakfast. She seemed outgoing enough to make guests feel welcome and, though he'd yet to try her food, there was evidence suggesting her meals would keep tourists happy. But a friendly personality and impressive menu wouldn't be enough. For starters, she needed front steps that weren't lawsuits waiting to happen. Also, he was having difficulty imagining that abandoned bunkhouse as a guest cottage people would actually pay money to inhabit.

She grinned suddenly, exposing her dimples. "I can't tell if you're a *really* good listener, or if you're ignoring me in the hopes that I'll go away." She reached for the handle on the screen door. "I'll leave you alone so you can work, but thank you. Two rescues in two days—you're quite the hero."

Her praise slithered unpleasantly over him. The waitress in town had used that same word when talking about Hannah's late husband, a hero to his country. Colin was nobody's hero.

"You exaggerate my usefulness," he objected. "If I hadn't come along yesterday, you could have changed that tire without me. And as for today..." He recalled how close Gideon had been standing to her, looming. How bad was the man's temper? Was he the type to lash out at a woman? "Do you think Gideon's a big enough problem that you needed rescuing?"

"You misunderstand. Today, *he's* the one you rescued." Hannah stepped inside, tossing one last beatific smile over her shoulder. "Another ten minutes with that blowhard crowding me, I might have Tasered his ass."

Chapter 4

Evan sat at the dinner table, rolling peas around his plate with his fork—as if his mom wouldn't notice he wasn't eating them as long as they stayed in motion.

"No peas, no dessert," Hannah reminded him gently. Rising, she carried her own plate to the sink.

Through the kitchen window, she could see Colin still working even though the sun had faded to an orange-gold memory stretched across the darkening horizon. She'd stepped outside nearly an hour ago to ask if he wanted to join them for dinner. It hadn't come as a surprise when he'd declined, asking only for a glass of water and for her to turn on the porch lights for more illumination. Granted, she didn't know him, but he seemed easiest in his own skin when he had a job to perform. So wouldn't it benefit them both if he stayed? Lord knew there was plenty to do around here.

Behind her, Evan heaved a martyrlike sigh. "Is this enough peas gone, Mommy?"

She grinned at his put-upon expression and the four remaining peas he was refusing to eat on principle. "I suppose so."

The town librarian had hired Hannah to bake some apple tarts for a fund-raising party, and she'd made extras to keep at home. She warmed one up and served it to Evan with a dollop of vanilla ice cream. Afterward, she settled him on the couch with Scarlett and "Trainket," his beloved green train blanket. Having been washed hundreds of times, the fleecy material was no longer quite as soft as it had originally been, and the appliqué train was missing a car.

"I have to go down to the stable," she said, handing him a walkie-talkie so they could stay in communication. Its match was clipped to her belt. Evan enjoyed feeling like a secret agent, and she couldn't imagine leaving sight of the house without being able to keep in contact. "You can watch cartoons until I get back. Then, bath time."

The first time she'd gone to the stable without Henry, Kitty or Annette to keep an eye on Evan, she'd been nervous. She didn't even like working in the garden without him, and that was within easy view of the house. They'd made a game of how he was a pirate and the sofa was his ship, and the carpet was shark-infested waters. But, truthfully, she allowed him so little television time that when she did, he was transfixed.

Before leaving the house, she stopped by the kitchen and sliced off a piece of the roast beef they'd had for dinner. She stuck it between two pieces of homemade bread, along with romaine, tomato and a dab of horseradish. Then she wrapped it in a napkin and stepped onto the porch—where Colin was swearing in a creatively mixed string of words that reminded Hannah of a long-ago foster brother. Their foster mother had tried washing his mouth out a number of times, but then stopped, figuring that much soap wasn't good for a kid.

"Problem?" Hannah asked.

He turned to her, shoving a hand through his hair. She tried not to notice how lifting his arm like that tightened the white T-shirt against the muscular contours of his chest.

"I'm replacing some of the top boards on the porch so no one crashes through them like you did that step this morning, but it's not just the surface wood that needs fixing. Some of the supporting joists and piers are starting to give out, too. I'll need to make another supply run tomorrow."

Damn. Her budget was already strained, and porch repairs had not been on her priority list. That was the kind of thing she'd hoped to take care of once the bunkhouse was ready for guests and she'd had a chance to generate some revenue. *Bright side, Hannah.* If the scope of the job was greater than Colin had expected, then he'd be here longer, wouldn't he? That gave her a stronger chance of convincing him to help make her vision a reality.

With that in mind, she conjured a friendly smile and held out the sandwich. "I brought you some food."

He reached for it eagerly, but his eyes were wary. "What, just one course?"

Maybe now wasn't the time to mention the six different dessert options inside if he was still hungry later. "I can do understated," she said. "I told you this morning, the kind of spread I laid out for breakfast is indicative of special occasions. Not a daily occurrence."

He scowled, looking uncomfortable at being classified with "special occasions," but then he took a bite of the sandwich. For a second, his features relaxed into an expression of utter satisfaction, and everything female in her clenched at the sight.

Partly out of self-preservation and partly in strategic retreat, she grabbed the now-empty glass of water and went back inside to get him a refill.

"Mommy?" Evan said as she entered the room. "I've seen this one before."

She changed the channel and found him a different cartoon. "I have to give Mr. Colin some water, then I'm going to feed the horses. For real this time," she said, ruffling his dark hair. Evan had her hair and eye color, but Michael was the one who'd had curls as a child. Plus, Evan had his father's smile.

When she returned to the porch, she found Colin packing away tools for the night.

She sat on the bench, tugging on her boots. "Can I ask you a favor? I mean, besides the obvious one you're already doing, rebuilding my disaster of a porch? I was headed to the stable and wondered if you'd come with me. I know you've had more experience with livestock than me, and I'd really appreciate your expert opinion on the horses. Not that Henry isn't an expert, but…"

He cocked his head in silent question. She was used to the chatter of her inquisitive son and Henry's garrulous tales of bygone days. Colin didn't waste a lot of words.

"Henry White," she said. "He worked this ranch for years, and he knows his stuff. His eyesight isn't what it used to be, though, and he's a little more, um, absent lately. I'm learning as fast as I can, but I can't guarantee that if Henry overlooked something I would catch it."

Colin pressed a finger between his eyes, and she could almost see his thoughts floating in the cool evening air. *This lady doesn't know what she's doing. Can't she see this is a doomed enterprise?* She refused to believe that. No one was born an expert at anything. What message would she be sending her son if she gave up whenever she encountered difficulties?

She thought back to her conversation with Colin in the bunkhouse. "You said you work with animals 'as often as you can.' You must care about their well-being."

He sighed. "Lead the way."

"Thank you." Turning so he wouldn't see her victorious grin, she opened the container beneath the porch bench and pulled out a large flashlight. There was enough light to get to the stable, but it would be darker when they came back. She stepped gingerly down the stairs. "You can use the flashlight for your walk to the bunkhouse tonight. Or I could drive you."

"Walking's fine," he said. "It isn't far to the bunkhouse, and I'm not afraid of the dark."

She almost made a joke about her son and his various coping mechanisms for braving the dark but stopped herself. Colin hadn't warmed to Evan. She wished it didn't bother her—tried to tell herself his aloofness was better than Gideon's phony "let's be best pals" demeanor—but she was a mom. She naturally wanted others to see what a great kid Evan was.

"How's your ankle?" Colin asked as they fell into step in the yard.

"Better. Tender, but—"

"Mommy!" Evan called through the screen a moment before banging the door open. He was wearing his own pair of boots and had his blanket around his shoulders like a superhero cape. "Changed my mind. I wanna visit the horsies, too."

Repressing a groan, she stole a peek at Colin. He looked as if he'd swallowed rusty nails.

It was on the tip of her tongue to tell her son no, but the whole reason she'd been comfortable leaving Evan for a short time was because she'd trusted him to watch TV. That obviously wasn't going to work tonight. Apparently, the combination of horses and a newcomer to their ranch was a lot more mesmerizing than watching Shaggy and Scooby unmask villains.

Colin met her gaze. "Makes no difference to me," he said stiffly. But, in direct contradiction to his words, he lengthened his stride, putting distance between himself and the Shaws.

"Come on," she told her son. She pointed at the broken step. "Be careful, though."

Evan scampered down the stairs with no care for his safety, rushing by Hannah and going straight to Colin. "You're tall." Her son's voice was full of admiration. "You're like a *giant*."

Unsurprisingly, Colin didn't answer. The silence didn't deter Evan.

"Did you get tall from eating healthy food? Mommy sings me a song about—"

"Evan!" She intervened before her son reenacted the "Grow Big and Strong" song she'd made up to coax him into eating vegetables. Colin didn't need to hear it—or see the accompanying dance steps. "Don't bother Mr. Colin, okay? He's been working with a noisy saw and hammering nails all afternoon. I'll bet he'd appreciate some peace and quiet."

Her son scowled. "Quiet is *boring*."

"Don't argue with your mother." Colin's sharp admonishment wasn't loud, but it startled both Evan and Hannah. She hadn't expected him to speak. Having him suddenly participate in the conversation was otherworldly, like being riddled by the sphinx.

Evan's eyes were wide as he craned his head back to regard the "giant." "Yessir." Then he miraculously fell silent.

Hannah was impressed. She'd wanted Colin to stick around because of his experience with livestock, but it turned out he wasn't half-bad with outspoken four-year-olds, either. She caught up with him, turning to give him a smile of thanks. It died on her lips, though, when she got a good look at his profile. Even in the dim light of moonrise, there was no mistaking the pain stamped across his handsome features.

It was an expression that felt familiar, the same kind of agony that had contorted her soul when she'd lost both her husband and, in the same day, her mother-in-law. Ellie Shaw hadn't been well, and news of Michael's death had triggered a massive stroke. After years of foster care and praying for home and family, Hannah had lost her only two relatives in one cruel blow. A week later, Hannah had gone into premature labor, barely caring when she was loaded into the ambulance whether she lived or died.

It wasn't until the next day, when she'd heard Evan's lusty wail, that she'd realized a piece of Michael still lived on, that not all her family was dead. She had a son who needed her, and she was ashamed of her earlier ambivalence about surviving. For his sake, she'd sworn to find the positives in life, to resist the bleak drag of depression that sucked at her. Evan was the bright spot that motivated her to keep moving forward during the most challenging times.

What motivated Colin Cade? And what had he suffered? She'd never seen such light eyes filled with so much darkness.

Colin breathed in the familiar scents of leather and wood, horse and hay. They were soothing, but as ragged as his nerves were after walking to the stable with Hannah and her boy, he would have preferred a slug of whiskey. It was weird how being around kids stirred memories not only of his own lost son, but his father, who'd died when Colin was a teenager. *Don't argue with your mother.* How many times had Colin heard that edict from behind the newspaper at the kitchen table, directed either at himself or Justin, who'd been a rambunctious hellion as a kid? When Dad bothered to lower the newspaper before making the pronouncement, you knew you were *really* on thin ice.

Was it strange to miss his parents after all this time? Colin's mom had been dead now for more years of his life than she'd been alive. But it was easier to miss them than to allow himself to miss Natalie and Danny. That was a more recent wound, one that hadn't healed properly. He could almost envision the jagged scar it had left inside him.

After the cover of darkness outside, being beneath the stable's electric lights made him feel too exposed, as if Hannah would be able to glimpse into his memories. He cleared his throat, shifting focus on the horses that had begun to wander into stalls from the outside paddock.

"Guess they know it's dinnertime," he said. "How many horses are there?" There were a total of eight spacious stalls, and the stable was in better shape than either the main house or his current quarters. Whoever had owned the ranch before, decor hadn't been his or her top priority.

"Four. Mavis here is the oldest," she said, coming forward to stroke the nose of a sorrel mare. "She's been on the ranch for seventeen years. I take her out for exercise, but when this place is up and running, I don't plan to let guests ride her. There's Tilly and Apples, both Tennessee walkers and good with people. Viper's the black gelding. He's a little sneaky, but doesn't challenge confident riders."

She showed Colin where the oats and feed buckets were. They hung them over the stall doors and snapped them into place. He noticed that the wood at Viper's stall had been chewed.

"That may be an indication that he needs more roughage," he commented. "Might want to give him more hay before he fills up on the oats."

Evan was suitably quiet and restrained around the horses. Hannah had obviously taught him stable manners. Or he was intimidated by the thousand-pound beasts. He eyed them with a combination of adoration and apprehension.

"We have a donkey, too," Evan informed Colin. "His name is Ninja."

Hannah took her son's hand and gently led him out of the stall where Colin was running a brush over Apples, getting to know the horse and checking her general condition. "I laughed the first time Michael told me donkeys were used to help protect the cattle against predators." She bit her lip. "Michael was my husband."

"The marine." He met her gaze, understanding the relief he saw there. She was glad he already knew, sparing her any awkward explanations. "I heard about him in town."

According to Colin's waitress, Michael had been killed before his son was born. Hannah's late husband had never seen Evan drag his green blanket across the dusty floor or heard his son ask when he would be big enough to ride a horse all by himself. *At least I had two years with Danny before he was ripped away.* But in some ways, wasn't that worse? There were still nights Colin woke from dreams of the past with the sound of his toddler's surprisingly deep belly laugh echoing in his ears.

"Last month, I watched Ninja circle up the cows with the youngest of the herd in the center," Hannah continued. "I never got a look at what they were reacting to—"

"Coyotes, probably."

She nodded. "The incident gave me a new appreciation for donkeys as unexpected heroes."

There was that word again. She'd called him a hero earlier, and he'd bristled, resenting the implied expectations that came with such lofty praise. But if she was comfortable using the same terminology when describing a donkey, maybe Colin should relax and get over himself.

It was a radical thought.

While Hannah and Evan stepped outside to see if they could find the Big Dipper, Colin tried to recall the last time he'd been relaxed. In the weeks following his brother's engagement Colin had figuratively held his breath, afraid that Justin—notorious for being unable to commit—would somehow screw up the best thing that had ever happened to him. Though Colin didn't spend much time in Cielo Peak these days, the habit of worrying after his siblings was tough to break. He should have been at ease during his last few ranch jobs, doing work he enjoyed, but circumstances such as Delia McCoy's unwanted interest had prevented that from happening.

Well, you won't find contentment here. Not with Evan looking for opportunities to talk his ear off and the losing battle of trying to help Hannah turn the run-down house into a tourist destination. Yet even as Colin reminded himself of the reasons he wasn't staying, he had to admit that right now, in this quiet stable, he was experiencing the closest thing to peace he'd felt in longer than he could remember. And he was in no hurry to give that up.

Chapter 5

"So you're the fella lookin' to replace me?" The grizzled man slammed his truck door, and Scarlett ran down the steps to greet him, woofing happily.

Colin set down the hammer and rose, deciding this must be Henry White. The man wore a battered straw cowboy hat that looked a lot like the one atop Colin's own head. "Not sure what you heard, sir, but I'm not replacing anyone. Are you Henry White?"

"Yup." The man's demeanor was so territorial, Colin was surprised it had taken him until Saturday to come size up the perceived competition. "Been working this ranch since before you were born."

As Colin understood it, that was part of the problem. But he had a lot of respect for what could be learned from previous generations. "I'm Colin Cade. Just passing through Bingham Pass and lending Hannah a hand while I'm here."

The man nudged back the brim of his hat. "Lotta people seem eager to help Hannah. Gideon Loomis, for one."

Was he trying to warn Colin away, let him know Hannah was spoken for? *She deserves better.* "Met Loomis. Wasn't impressed."

Henry's craggy, sun-leathered face split into a grin. "Me, neither. His parents may run a successful operation, but their spoiled only child doesn't have the sense God gave a goose."

So Colin had passed a test of sorts. The approval was oddly satisfying, and he found himself returning the old-timer's smile.

"Oh, good, you're here," Hannah called from inside the house. "I—" She stepped onto the porch, then froze, gaping at Colin. She looked so feminine in the white lacy sundress, a dramatic contrast to her shining black hair, that it wouldn't have been a hardship to stand there staring back at her. Over the past couple of days, he'd gotten used to seeing her in jeans and periodically dotted with flour or melted chocolate.

"Something wrong?" He glanced over his shoulder, trying to see if he'd overlooked a glaring mistake. None of the local stores carried the exact decorative spirals that were part of the porch railing, so after consulting the budget with Hannah yesterday morning, they'd decided to alternate. He'd found reasonably priced, complementary balusters and was installing the new ones in a pattern, salvaging as many of the former ones as possible. He was almost ready to paint.

"N-no. Nothing's wrong. I just… You were *smil-*

ing. I didn't think that was possible," she said under her breath.

The observation left him self-conscious. *I smile.* Occasionally.

"I see you've met Henry," she said. "He's going to watch Evan while Annette and I visit an estate sale I've had on my calendar. I'm really optimistic about finding some furniture for the bunkhouse!"

As far as he could tell, "really optimistic" was her default setting. But today her enthusiasm was contagious.

"Best of luck," he said. He even threw in another smile for good measure.

She blinked, but then collected herself. Her dimples flashed in a mischievous smirk. "Warn me next time you're going to do that so I can put on my sunglasses."

He chuckled at that, the sound rusty even to his ears.

Then they were both distracted by Evan joining them on the porch. Hannah explained that the boy was in the middle of lunch and there was plenty of leftover spaghetti in the pot if Henry or Colin wanted some. Colin was always grateful when she brought him food outside, but so far he'd managed to avoid joining her and Evan for meals. Henry, however, had no such reservations about pulling up a chair at the kitchen table.

"I came hungry," he said. "I know better than to eat before setting foot in your house. God knows I love Kitty, but her cooking can't hold a candle to yours. Don't ever tell her I said that," he added, looking suddenly alarmed.

Hannah mimed crossing her heart. "Your secret's safe with me."

Evan was bored with the discussion of spaghetti.

As he threw his slim arms around Henry's legs in a welcoming hug, he demanded, "Are we going fishing today?"

"That depends on how good you are and whether Henry feels up to it," Hannah said sternly. "Don't pester him about it. And if the two of you do go, you have to exit through the back door. This area will probably be covered with wet paint."

He'd done a few boards in the garage last night so that they'd be dry and people could have a pathway through the front door, but he didn't trust the four-year-old to stick to the path. After blowing his mother a kiss goodbye, Evan led Henry inside, talking a mile a minute about the size of the fish he was going to catch.

Hannah watched them go, laughing softly. "Our pond is stocked with trout, but to hear him talk, you'd think we had marlin in there. Henry is good with him—with any luck, you won't even notice they're here. But if you need anything, my cell number is on the fridge. So is Kitty's. She and Henry live just down the road, so she can be here in a matter of minutes. A lot faster than me."

Especially if Hannah ended up with a flat tire or some other roadside emergency. "You're taking the truck?" he asked.

"It has a lot more cargo space than Annette's car and pulls the trailer better. I figured it was best to plan for a big haul. Power of positive thinking and all that."

He opened his mouth to comment, then thought better, shaking his head.

"What?" Her hazel eyes narrowed. "Were you about to make some snide comment about my truck?"

"About you. Not snide," he backpedaled. "I was just

wondering if this is something you were born with or a learned behavior—your sunny disposition, I mean. Does everyone in your family see the world in such a rose-colored view?"

She jerked her head away abruptly, reaching into her purse and pulling out the sunglasses she'd mentioned. When she turned to face him again, the dark-tinted frames obscured her expression. "I was an orphan, actually."

They'd both lost their parents? The revelation of more common ground threw him for a loop. He and Hannah Shaw were polar opposites. He wouldn't have guessed that their backgrounds shared many similarities.

"Your parents are dead?" he heard himself ask.

"I honestly have no idea. Never met them," she said matter-of-factly. "I was abandoned as a newborn and grew up mostly in foster care. But to answer your question, the 'sunny disposition' was self-taught. I suppose I could moan and sulk my way through life, being bitter about anything that went wrong, but what kind of example would that be for my son?"

Her words had an edge to them. Because the topic was upsetting for her, or because she'd taken his question as criticism?

Or was *she* perhaps criticizing *him?* Colin may not have been flashing smiles left and right for the past three days, but he sure as hell wasn't sulking.

"I should go," she said briskly. "Annette is sacrificing most of her Saturday for me. It would be rude to keep her waiting."

He didn't like watching her go, her posture rigid as she climbed into the cab. He'd wanted to say something else, but nothing came to mind. *Goodbye* would have been insultingly trite after she'd shared something so personal, and *I'm sorry* felt like overkill when he wasn't even sure why he'd be apologizing.

It wasn't until the truck disappeared from sight that words formed in his mind, belatedly shaping the questions he wanted to ask. *How?*

How do you do it? Where do you find the strength?

But the sentiments were difficult to even think. There was no chance he'd be voicing them aloud.

No matter how much he ached for the answers.

"I have to hand it to you." Annette spoke over the hard rock station that was Hannah's guilty pleasure. There were a lot of songs she enjoyed listening to that weren't Evan-friendly. So she indulged in suggestive lyrics and some heavy metal when he wasn't riding with her. Annette paused. "You mind if we turn this down?"

Yes. The angry-sounding electric guitar riff suited her temper. "Of course not." Hannah reached for the volume knob. Annette was a fantastic friend and didn't deserve to bear the brunt of Hannah's dark mood. *Damn cowboy.* She'd stepped out of the house in such an upbeat mood and seeing Colin's smile—as rare and awe-inspiring as a unicorn—had seemed like an omen of good things to come. And then it had all gone down the crapper.

Annette started over, her tone admiring. "As I was saying, I'm impressed. I thought you were crazy, bringing home some stranger off the road to solve your problems—especially when it seemed like he didn't want to be there. But somehow you've kept him there."

"It's not like I took him hostage," Hannah grumbled. "He's free to leave anytime he wants." Hell, he could be packed up and gone when she got back and she wouldn't care. Except, of course, she would because the front deck had never looked better and he was great with the horses. She'd followed up with an acquaintance of an acquaintance, the man who'd sent Colin her direction in the first place, and she'd been surprised to learn he'd once been a veterinarian. Large animal vets made a nice living. What was a guy with experience like that doing fixing her porch? *Besides making me crazy.*

"Han? You okay?"

"Fine."

"Uh-huh. You do realize we're doing fifteen miles over the speed limit?" Annette asked cautiously.

Whoa. Hannah immediately eased off the accelerator, embarrassment washing through her. "Sorry."

"Let's try this again, but with you telling me the truth this time. What's wrong?"

Hannah sniffed, mortified to discover that her eyes stung. What was wrong with her? So Colin thought she was some naive Pollyanna with an unrealistic view of the world. What did that matter? He'd made it clear he wasn't sticking around. In the greater scheme of her life, he was barely a footnote. His opinion didn't count.

Except that part of you wonders if he's right. No one thought she could do this—not smug Gideon, not any of the loan officers she'd talked to, not even her best friend, who was on her side.

"Annette, is there a specific part of my plan that you think will cause me to fail? Or is it just that you believe the entire endeavor is doomed?"

"Oh, sweetie, I've been a terrible friend, haven't I? Whenever I call you in tears over starting my latest period, you're there for me, making me laugh and assuring me Todd and I will become parents eventually. But I haven't supported you."

"You've been there for me in tangible ways—helping with Evan, coming with me today." Annette's husband, Todd, who worked out of a home office at their farm as an accountant, had also offered lots of concrete help, giving Hannah monetary advice and going over all of the ranch's financial information.

"I know your skepticism stems from concern," Hannah added. "But…"

"But you need to feel like someone's in your corner? I am so sorry. I'm a hypocrite. I can't stand the idea of you facing any disappointment, yet being disappointed month after month hasn't stopped *me* from trying to get pregnant. You should follow your dream. I mean, this conversation started with me being impressed. More and more people are coming up to me in town wanting your contact information to order baked goods, and when I swung by yesterday to drop off the eggs, I could tell the porch is going to look great when it's finished. If you and Colin can work that magic on the inside of the house—"

"He still hasn't committed to staying once the project is finished," Hannah admitted. "I was getting the impression that he'd changed his mind, but it's not official."

Annette shrugged. "He clearly doesn't have anywhere he needs to be, or he'd be there already. If the two of you are getting along and you can afford to pay him, why leave?"

Hannah nibbled at her lower lip. Her friend's reasoning was logical, but the "getting along" part might be more complex than Annette realized.

"I snapped at him before I came to pick you up."

"You? Your version of snapping is probably different from most people's. You have the patience of a saint."

"No, I don't. I'm no saint. I'm an extremely stubborn woman who masks her stubborn streak with a smile." *Speaking of which...*

She flipped back to that mental photo she'd captured of Colin's smile. Damn, the man was sexy. She'd known that already, of course. Her kitchen window overlooked the porch. She'd had a front-row view of him flexing muscles beneath thin cotton T-shirts damp with sweat. However, she'd assumed his hotness was limited to that brooding, Heathcliff kind of appeal. Today, he'd blown that hypothesis right out of the water. If he leveled that grin against a woman with intent, there was no telling what he could charm her into—or out of.

"So what caused you to snap at him?" Annette asked. "Is it the way he treats Evan?"

Actually, his tolerance of the boy seemed to have increased. He was never going to hand the kid a toy tool set and ask for his help, but he seemed to have fallen into the habit of letting Evan blather while he worked. He didn't engage, but neither did he cringe anymore whenever her son got within twenty feet of him.

"He insinuated I see the world through rose-colored glasses, and it didn't sound like a compliment. Plus, he asked about my family," she added heavily. She didn't need to elaborate. Annette had heard all about her history over a bottle of wine shortly after Hannah moved to Bingham Pass.

When Michael's father died during their first year of marriage, she'd taken it nearly as hard as her husband. The Shaws were the family she'd always craved. Mrs. Shaw had said later that at least he'd lived to see the wedding. Those words had haunted Hannah when Ellie died before seeing her grandson born. If she'd been able to hold Evan in her arms, would it have helped mitigate the loss of her son enough that she could cope? That she might have survived?

But there was no way to know that, and no way to change the past. All Hannah could do was keep working toward the future. And she would do it with or without Colin Cade's assistance.

Colin realized two things simultaneously—first, he was *starving;* second, he no longer heard any noise from inside the house. Earlier, Henry and Evan had been playing some game that consisted of rolling lots of dice at once. The clang of dice rattling together in a cup had been somewhere between maracas and machine gun fire. But Colin had become so absorbed with the paint job that he hadn't noticed when the din stopped. Apparently, they'd gone out the back for their fishing expedition without his even realizing it.

Since he couldn't tackle a second coat until the first dried, he was at loose ends. And Hannah had invited him to help himself to some food. Though he'd been avoiding entering the house unless absolutely crucial, the thought of microwaving a bowl of spaghetti made his stomach growl. It wasn't as if he'd be disturbing anyone. He crossed quickly through the living room,

passing the high-backed couch and absently register-
ing that the laminate floor looked pretty good. Hannah had replaced the carpet this week. She'd said she
didn't have money for real hardwood, but she wanted
that homey, rural effect.

Her plan was to renovate the bunkhouse and common areas first—kitchen, living room, deck—so that
she could open for limited business, then tackle the
four upstairs guestrooms as incoming funds allowed.
He understood the logic, but he wasn't sure visitors
would be able to enjoy a hearty lunch or read peace-
fully by the fireplace while construction was going
on overhead.

His first sight of the kitchen impressed him even
more than her replacing the floor on her own, minus
his negligible contribution of cutting some pieces for
her in the garage. Last time he'd been in here, she'd
still been in the process of stripping wallpaper. Now
the walls gleamed a pale yellow that looked like sunbeams, dotted with thin ribbons of royal blue. The only
downside was that, against the shiny new wall cover-
ings, the chairs and table looked even shabbier. But
what did he know? She'd probably be home in an hour
or so with a perfect set.

He'd spent the past few days marveling at her faith
that things would always work out, but the interior of
her house was proof that Hannah wasn't operating on
blind faith. She was busting her ass to make things happen. She was juggling orders from townspeople, raising Evan, tending the garden, redecorating… When
did she sleep? How did she replenish her energy so that
she had enough left to deal with her spirited son, an
aged, cantankerous ranch hand and a newcomer who

was so surly that he apparently hadn't smiled a single time in three days?

The oregano-laced aroma of spaghetti sauce drew him from his musings and reminded him of his purpose. He was punching buttons on the microwave when he heard an odd thump. From somewhere above him? Maybe a critter on the roof or in the attic. But when the second thump came, he revised his opinion. That would be an awfully big critter. *Scarlett.* The dog was in the house somewhere, so—

Wait a minute. The dog was in the kitchen with him, sitting patiently next to the counter and watching with expectant brown eyes, drool forming at the corner of her mouth. Living with a kid, she was probably accustomed to plenty of food being dropped for her enjoyment.

"Hello?" Colin called. Maybe Hannah was back from her shopping expedition.

Curious, he retraced his steps to the living room. This time, he rounded the sectional sofa, which sat with its back to the kitchen, to get a better look. Henry was asleep on the couch, a DVD case covered with superheroes in his hand and a mostly empty bowl of popcorn kernels on his chest.

"Henry?" Colin shook the man's arm. The babysitter muttered in his sleep, but didn't wake.

Colin winced in realization. The thumping was Evan unsupervised somewhere in the house—hopefully in his own bedroom, where he was doing nothing more hazardous than circling toy trains over a plastic track. But the noise had sounded as if it came from above. He strode quickly toward the back hallway. What kind of shape were those upstairs rooms in? What items were stored there that might be equal parts fascinating and dangerous to a little boy? Having watched Hannah with her son, he doubted she'd intentionally leave anything like matches or power tools in plain sight or easy access, but—

"What are you doing?" The shout erupted before Colin could contain himself, and he bolted toward the top of the stairs just in time to throw his arms around the kid and keep him safely on the landing.

Evan gave him one wide-eyed look of surprise, then burst into tears.

Okay, that probably hadn't been the best way Colin could have handled the situation. He took a deep breath, making a concerted effort not to raise his voice again or shake the boy by the shoulders. It wasn't unheard of for a child to attempt sliding down a banister, but *headfirst?* That would have been a terrible idea even if the railing weren't rickety and led straight to a sharp-edged newel that looked capable of putting an eye out.

"Evan?" Henry's voice came from below, groggy and filled with concern.

When Colin turned to answer, "He's up here," Evan took the opportunity to scamper around him and dart down the steps. During his escape, the ever-present train blanket fluttered from his shoulders and landed on the staircase. It was evidence of the kid's panic that he didn't return for it.

Colin met a shame-faced Henry at the bottom of the stairs.

"I screwed up," the other man said. "We were watching a movie, and I guess I dozed."

"No harm done." What would be the point in Colin telling the man about how Evan had been about to take a dive down the balustrade? It had scared a year off Colin's life, and Henry needed all the years he had left. "But I think I startled him. I don't know about you, but I could use some coffee. Would you mind starting a pot while I go have a talk with him, man to man? I reckon you know where Hannah keeps all the coffee stuff. She talks about you like you're family."

The man's hunched shoulders rolled back as pride lit his expression. "Happy to brew some. But it'll be good old-fashioned regular coffee. I ain't using that fancy cappuccino thing she brought with her from Colorado Springs."

Henry shuffled off to the kitchen, and Colin walked down the hallway. In the front areas of the house, perhaps because they were still being decorated or maybe because Hannah hadn't wanted to make them too personal, he hadn't seen many family pictures. But hanging on the long wall that ran between the stairs and the downstairs bedrooms were a dozen portraits in different styles and sizes. Most were of Evan, a few showed him with his mother, but the largest was Hannah and Michael's wedding picture.

He didn't *want* to look at it, didn't want to put a face to the hero husband she'd lost. Didn't want to look at the joy she radiated as a bride and think about how devastated she must have been to receive the news of Michael's death. Why was it so hard to glance away? And why couldn't he separate where her imagined pain stopped and his pain began? He'd had his own smiling bride, once, and thoughts of all he'd wanted for Natalie were like acid burning through him. If it had been within his power, he would have given her the world. *I miss you, Nat.* He hardly ever let himself think the words, but the truth of them was always there, beneath the surface.

If she were here, she'd know what to say to a startled four-year-old who'd just been busted. Natalie had been a people person. He could almost hear her in his head. *The kid thinks of you as a giant. Imagine how scary you must look to him.*

At the end of the hall were two bedrooms opposite each other, with a shared bathroom between them. To the left, he glimpsed a neatly made queen-size bed with a pale purple and dusky-blue comforter. He abruptly turned away. On his right, there were sounds of sniffling. He followed them into a room decorated with primary colors that were bright enough for the circus. The sniffling came from inside a red-and-yellow pup tent in the corner of the room.

"Hey." Colin knelt in front of the zipped flaps. "Can I come in?"

There was a pause on the other side of the nylon. "Y-you won't fit. Too big."

"Guess you're probably right about that. Can you come out then? I brought your blanket."

There was a metallic whirr as the zipper teeth parted. A skinny arm shot out. Colin handed over the blanket, and the arm disappeared back inside the tent. Hard to say whether this could be considered progress. *At least he didn't rezip the door.*

Colin peeked through the opening but didn't stick his head inside, giving the kid his space. "What were you doing on the stairs?"

"I wanted to fly." Evan twisted his blanket in his hands. "I know I can't—not for-real flying—but I had on my cape and wanted to go fast."

"You would have gone fast, but you probably would've fractured some bones in the process. That's why I yelled, because I was so worried about you."

"Yelling's mean." The sniffing started again. "You *scared* me."

"If it makes you feel better, I think you scared me more." The fool kid could have broken his neck. Colin's stomach churned. "The thought of telling your mom that something had happened to you... She would be—" Emotion swelled in his throat, making it impossible to speak. But, really, what could he say? There were no adequate words for what parents suffered when they lost a child.

"Mr. Colin?" Evan's voice was hesitant, but close.

Colin jerked his head up, realizing Evan had partially emerged from his sanctuary.

"Are you gonna cry?"

"What?" Surprised by the question, Colin raised a hand to his eyes, realizing his vision was beginning to blur. Dammit. He looked back at the curious little boy, but for a moment, he didn't see Evan Shaw. He saw Danny's face. Danny laughingly demanding to be swung high in the air. Danny, solemn as he nodded his understanding that the oven was hot and that he needed to stay back. Danny worn out after a Christmas carnival, asleep on his stomach with his little butt curved in the air.

That now-familiar suffocating sensation crowded Colin's chest. He shot to his feet, wanting to put as much space as possible between himself and this room filled with all the bright adventure of childhood.

"Wait." Evan followed him, and even though Colin's

goal had been to coax the kid out, now he wished the boy would stay away from him. "Do you need Trainket?"

The innocent, heartfelt gesture sliced through him. His throat felt as if it was on fire, but he managed to say, "Thanks, kid." They stood there for long minutes, Colin clutching a grubby green blanket and Evan staring up at him, probably mystified by what could be so awful that it would make a mean old giant teary.

"Mr. Colin? Are you going to tell Mommy what I did?"

Keeping secrets was a bad idea. On some level, Colin knew that. It forged a bond between them that he wanted no part of, plus it might undermine Hannah as a parent. But he neither wanted to rat the kid out, nor scare Hannah with what could have happened. "How about I make you a deal? I'll build you your own headquarters—all the great superheroes have a special place they can go."

"Like my tent?" Evan interrupted.

"Bigger. And outside."

"A tree house?" Evan was practically vibrating with excitement.

"Uh…no." The risk of Evan being high above the ground was exactly the kind of thing Colin wanted to avoid. "But you'll like it. It will be big enough to invite friends inside if you meet some other superheroes in kindergarten. But in return for me building Super-Evan headquarters and my not telling your mom, you have to promise not to try to use any superpowers until you're at least six. No flying, and definitely *no* climbing on the stair rails, okay? Nothing like that. Deal?"

Evan stuck around for the two seconds it took to shake Colin's hand and retrieve his blanket, then he went running to find Henry and tell him all about the proposed headquarters.

It had been Colin's idea to put on a pot of coffee, but he wondered if Henry would notice if he didn't actually drink any. He felt keyed up already, jittery with too many conflicting and unexpected emotions.

"Mommy!"

Hannah was back. He heard the murmur of her feminine voice, undercut with the gravelly rumble of Henry's. Evan was louder than the other two, but except for that first shriek of greeting, Colin couldn't make out the rest of his words. At first, Colin didn't move—he'd been taking the second alone to regain his composure. But then it occurred to him that he didn't want to run into Hannah at the back of the house, amid her son's cherished belongings and in view of her gold-framed wedding portrait. It felt like crossing a line better kept between them.

They ended up nearly colliding just past the staircase. Hannah's brow was furrowed, and he could practically see little question marks dancing over her head as if she were a comic strip character. How much had Evan told her? He was sure the boy had omitted any mention of his near swan dive, but what had he said about their chat afterward?

"Any success at the estate sale?" he asked, as if his roaming her house while she was gone were a completely normal circumstance.

Nodding, she bit her lip. "Possibly too much success. Now that I have some furniture and accessories in my price range, I've got a better idea of what the finished cabin will look like. I want to get started."

"That's good, right?"

"Well, there's the matter of where you're going to sleep once we begin renovations. If you're sticking around?" she asked tentatively. "Evan said something about a clubhouse?"

Hell. He probably shouldn't have said anything without getting the mom's approval first. "Maybe I spoke out of turn. I was thinking that, if it's okay with you, I could build him a playhouse before I go. Something in view of the garden, so he has a place to safely hang out while you're working?"

Her liquid hazel eyes were pools of gratitude. "That would be *wonderful*. We were in such a cramped space in Colorado Springs that I thought all this fresh, open air would be good for him. I still stand by that, but I think it's overwhelming, too. I'm constantly after him not to get too close to the pond or mess around in the rooms upstairs or go to the stables without supervision. It'll mean a lot to a boy with Evan's independent streak to have a place all his own. But I don't under..." Was she afraid that if she pressed her luck by asking too many questions he might change his mind?

"My brother's getting married in a little over a month," he said. "After that, I have another job lined up, but I can give you that long. If you still want it. Plumbing's not my thing, but I'm decent at carpentry and have helped reshingle a roof or two. I can take over a lot of the stuff with the animals, too, which should free up some of your time."

"A month," she breathed. Her face was radiant, making her look entirely too much like a lottery winner. "That's fantastic! Come on, I'll show you the upstairs rooms." As she jogged up the stairs, she added, "They're not much to look at yet, but you never know. A lot can happen in a month."

Chapter 6

It had never been Colin's intention to grow a beard. Taking the time to shave now was simply a delayed reaction, not evidence that he was stalling or anxious about going to the main house for Sunday brunch. When Hannah had told him the Reeds were coming and asked him to join, there'd been no good reason to refuse. It was true that Colin had been trying to spend as little time as possible in the house, but he'd better get used to it since he was moving in this afternoon.

The thought was jarring enough that the razor slipped in his hand, and he scowled at his reflection. Not "moving in," he corrected. That implied a measure of permanence. His stay would be temporary, like renting a room in a hotel. *Yeah, except you're not paying a landlord. She's paying you.*

As he was leaving the bunkhouse, his cell phone

chimed. He glanced at the display screen and saw his sister's name. Pulling the door shut behind him, he stepped into the spring sunshine and answered. "Hello."

"About flipping time!"

"I'm fine, thanks. You?" Despite the sardonic greeting, he secretly loved Arden's feistiness. It gave him confidence that she'd never take any crap from anyone. And he took a certain selfish comfort in her strength. It helped reassure him that he hadn't screwed up too badly raising her.

"Seriously, do you know how many times I've tried to get in touch with you?" she continued as if he hadn't spoken. "You're like the worst brother in the world."

"Don't I get any credit for trying to call you two nights ago?"

Her *ffff* noise seemed like the verbal equivalent of rolling her eyes. "I can't believe the one time you bother phoning, I didn't hear it ring. Hope's cutting her first teeth, and she's not happy about it. The volume level gets intense."

"You sound awfully perky about a shrieking baby."

"I am!" Her voice was full of maternal pride. "The pediatrician is surprised she's teething this soon. He said he wouldn't have expected it for at least another month. Considering the complications during her birth, I was expecting some developmental delays, but she's been right on track for everything, even occasionally ahead of schedule. Garrett and I are really blessed. In fact…we're expecting another baby."

He took a deep breath, offering up a prayer for her safety and the unborn child's. "Congratulations."

As she chatted about the pregnancy, he got closer

to Hannah's, spotting the Reeds' car parked out front. They were staying to help with the bunkhouse today. The four adults were going to rip up the ugly "all-purpose" carpeting and paint the walls. Hannah had ordered the replacement carpet, which they'd put down later this week. Meanwhile, there was a trailer full of furniture waiting beneath the carport.

"Even though I'm barely to my second trimester, I look about five months along," Arden was saying. "Apparently, when you have back-to-back babies, you start showing a lot sooner with the second one."

He heard a bark, then Scarlett raced toward him at a dead run. When she reached him, she sat in the grass, tail thumping, and cocked her head in canine hello. Her tongue lolled out of her mouth, drawing attention to her crooked underbite. She looked so ecstatic to see him she was damn near cute. He scratched behind the dog's ears, not surprised when Arden worked the conversation around to asking when she'd see him again.

"The wedding's at the end of next month," he pointed out. "That's not long."

"I have a great idea," she said as if he hadn't spoken. "Elisabeth's family is throwing a couples' shower for Elisabeth and Justin in two weeks. Nobody expects you to come to Cielo Peak for that, but what if Hope and I drive down to see you? We can go shopping for gifts together."

"Or I can mail them a card and a check."

She huffed in exasperation. "I know shopping's not your favorite thing in the world, but man up. Justin's worth a little effort. Besides, are you saying you wouldn't welcome a visit from your favorite sister? I'm pregnant," she reminded him. "You should humor me. I'm emotionally fragile."

He bit back a laugh. His little sister was about as fragile and delicate as a charging bull. "Admit it, the shopping's a ruse. You just want to harass me in person and meddle in my life."

"Says the man who once threatened to break Garrett's kneecaps if he hurt me," she said wryly.

That wasn't meddling; that was being a brother. "As long as he keeps you happy, he's in no danger from me."

"I've never been happier," she said softly. "I can't even imagine how that would be possible."

He could hear the truth of it in her voice, and it made him smile. "I'm glad. You deserve it. Look, I have to go, but Elisabeth and Justin have one of those wish lists, right?"

"A registry? Yeah."

"Email me the information, and I promise I'll send them something more personal than a check."

"All right. But start answering your phone more, or I will program my GPS for Bingham Pass."

He tried to appease her without actually making any promises he might not keep, then they said their goodbyes.

Now officially late, Colin took the newly reinforced porch steps two at a time, Scarlett at his heels. He let himself in, calling "Knock, knock" as he approached. The buttery smell of pancakes beckoned.

He walked into the kitchen, where Evan, Annette and her husband sat at the table. Hannah stood at the island, slicing squares of hash brown casserole.

Her welcoming smile brought out her dimples.

"You made it." She did a double take, her hazel eyes avid. "And you shaved. You look... I've never seen you clean-shaven." Her gaze slid over him, warm and sweet.

Colin swallowed. "It seemed like time." Acutely aware of their audience, he turned back to the table, ignoring Annette's raised eyebrows and extending a hand to the man who sat at her side. "Colin Cade, nice to meet you."

"Todd Reed." The man had a good grip.

Hannah had mentioned Annette's husband was an accountant. From the guy's stout build, buzz-cut auburn hair and skin that looked ruddy from time in the sun, Colin wouldn't have necessarily pegged him as having a desk job. But Todd's clear gray eyes radiated sharp intelligence.

Colin turned from greeting the Reeds and bumped fists with the little boy. "Mornin', Super-Ev."

He grinned, his face sticky with syrup. "Mr. Colin, are we going to start building my house today?"

"Not yet. But I did sketch some ideas last night. We can look at them later."

Colin poured himself some coffee and refilled everyone else's mugs. As he and Hannah sat at the table, he apologized for his tardiness. "My sister called with big news as I was leaving the bunkhouse. She's pregnant. Again." He shook his head. "Their first one's not even six months old."

Across the table, Annette's expression crumpled. "Excuse me." Her chair let out a discordant squawk as it scraped across the linoleum.

Todd's gaze was troubled as he watched his wife

hurry from the room. Hannah sighed heavily. Evan kept shoving bites of pancake into his mouth, oblivious.

Colin caught Hannah's eye, keeping his voice to a whisper. "I put my foot in my mouth, didn't I?"

She leaned so close that the rich, feminine scent of her shampoo blocked out the food smells. He briefly imagined closing his eyes and breathing her in, tangling his fingers through the silky jet strands of her hair.

She brought him back to the present with her murmured, "Pregnancy's a sore subject right now."

"Sorry." He glanced to Todd, including him in the apology. The man nodded stiffly in acknowledgment.

When Annette returned to the table, she was composed, once again her smiling self, but Colin was careful not to mention babies or pregnancy again for the rest of the meal. After breakfast, all four adults helped clear the table, but Hannah insisted she had to load the dishwasher by herself.

"I'm obsessive-compulsive about where everything goes," she admitted with a self-deprecating grin.

"How about Annette and I go to the bunkhouse and start pulling up the carpeting?" Todd volunteered. The way he excluded Colin made it sound as if he needed a moment alone with his wife.

Colin nodded. "Sounds good. My stuff is packed up to bring over here, and I put the minifridge out on the carport. Only thing left to move is the bed."

Once the Reeds exited the house, Hannah instructed her son to put some toys and books in his backpack to keep himself entertained on the carport while the adults were painting. With four of them helping, it shouldn't take too long.

Colin stepped closer so that he could be heard over the running water as Hannah rinsed dishes without Evan overhearing. "I'm sorry I upset Annette. Did she…lose a baby?"

Hannah shook her head. "They're trying to get pregnant. No luck yet. Annette was trying some medication that might help, but the drugs make her pretty emotional. She and Todd have an appointment with a specialist coming up to discuss options."

Turning off the faucet, she stared sightlessly out the window, her expression faraway and pensive. "When I first found out I was carrying Evan, I was thrown by the timing. I mean, I was happy, but because of when it happened, I knew Michael wouldn't be with me when the baby was born. I really regretted that. But I see now what a gift it was. If I hadn't conceived before he left…"

"It's amazing how you do that." That first afternoon he'd been here, she'd commented on her diminutive height, speculating that it made others see her as weak. Hannah Shaw was one of the strongest people he'd ever met.

She turned toward him, her forehead puckered in confusion. "Do what?"

"Instead of sounding bitter about losing your husband, who died too young on the other side of the world, you count your blessings."

"Being bitter won't bring him back."

"Do you still miss him?" He regretted the question immediately. It was too personal, too intrusive. Inappropriate, somehow, when he was standing this close to her. "I— Forget I asked. I'll go see if Evan needs any help gathering toys and make sure he isn't trying to dismantle his whole train set and stuff it into his backpack."

Not until he rounded the corner did he realize it was the first time in two years that he'd deliberately sought out a kid's company. But, for the moment, hanging out with Evan seemed a lot less complicated than remaining in the sun-dappled kitchen alone with Hannah.

Although Colin generally preferred walking to and from the bunkhouse, it was logical to take the truck since they were bringing paint supplies, tools and outdoor toys for Evan. The little boy asked if he could ride in the bed of the truck with Scarlett. Since it was for such a short distance on private property, Hannah indulged him but only after dire threats of what would happen if he didn't stay seated and an announcement that she'd drive extra slowly for safety's sake.

As the truck began crawling forward, she gave an embarrassed laugh. "You must think I'm being ridiculous. At this rate, snails will pass us."

"It's never ridiculous to want to protect your child," he said softly. In his head, he heard the bone-chilling crunch of metal and glass, but it was a phantom memory. He hadn't been there that day, yet he'd relived the incident hundreds of times in his nightmares. He forcibly suppressed those thoughts, changing the subject. "I wanted to ask you a favor. Well, two technically."

"After everything you're doing for me and Evan? Anything you want!" Red bloomed in her cheeks as she reconsidered her statement. "I mean… What, um, was the favor?"

The way she stumbled over her words might have been amusing if he weren't suddenly having difficulty marshaling his own thoughts. He worked to think of Hannah in a platonic, she's-my-employer-and-nothing-more light, but she was a beautiful woman. The rosy blush and obvious direction of her thoughts only magnified her appeal.

He cleared his throat. "My sister's emailing me information for a gift registry. I, uh, wanted to borrow your laptop to do some online shopping. And I was hoping to get your opinion. This isn't my area of expertise."

Her face softened. "Baby stuff, huh? I can't wait until Annette does announce she's expecting. Buying clothes for infants is so much fun. And, needless to say, she will have the most awesome baby shower menu ever."

"This is actually for a wedding shower."

"Your brother's? You mentioned he's getting married."

"Justin," he said. It felt unexpectedly important that she know his brother's name. The more pieces of herself she revealed, the pettier it seemed that Colin never shared even casual information. "Arden's my sister, the youngest. After my parents died, it felt like the three of us against the world."

She turned to look at him when he mentioned losing his parents, but didn't ask for specifics. "So Arden's pregnant and Justin's getting married?" They rolled up in front of the bunkhouse, and she shifted the truck into park. "A lot to celebrate."

He nodded as he opened the door. Was it selfish, hiding out here in Bingham Pass instead of being part of the celebrations? Or did it give them room to experience their joy fully, without worrying about being insensitive to the brother who'd lost his entire world in one split second? Arden in particular seemed incapable of being in a room with him without pity haunting her gaze; Natalie's death had been nearly as difficult for her as for Colin. The two women had grown up childhood best friends.

He didn't want to be a black cloud hovering over other people's happiness, a grim reminder of how fleeting that happiness could be.

Hannah opened the tailgate. Evan scampered out of the truck like a monkey, Scarlett right beside him. The boy went straight for Colin's motorcycle.

"Stop right there!" Hannah pulled an old coffee can out of the back of the truck. It was full of large, colorful pieces of chalk. She drew a thick blue line across the concrete of the carport. "You don't go past this, understand?" At his nod, she added, "And when we're all done here, maybe we'll go fishing since you and Henry never got around to that yesterday."

The boy brightened, letting out a gleeful whoop that startled a nearby grackle and some sparrows into the air. He sat down with the chalk and his bag of toys. Hannah and Colin began unloading the paint supplies.

Reaching for a bucket of rollers and brushes, she slid him a curious look. "So you don't have a laptop? It's hard to imagine someone without a computer these days."

"A lot of my stuff is in storage, back in Cielo Peak. I've been on, I guess you could say, sabbatical." He hefted a can of primer. "I can check email and everything on my phone, but I don't like shopping on the small screen. Damn fingers are too clumsy," he admitted.

She laughed. "I watched you do detailed work on the

porch—you're not clumsy. Your hands are just really big." Her gaze dropped as she spoke, and her cheeks flushed with color again.

An answering heat rose within him. He was grateful when the side door opened and Hannah looked away.

Annette stuck her head out. "You two need a hand out there?"

Hannah tried unsuccessfully to muffle a giggle. "Um, no, we're covered as far as hands go."

Colin bit the inside of his cheek to keep from laughing.

Once Annette had disappeared back into the house, Hannah said, "If I didn't say so already, of course you're welcome to use the laptop."

"And you'll give me your opinion on the gift registry? I don't understand why people need half that stuff." He recalled Natalie rolling her eyes when he commented that gravy boats were misnamed; they looked more like genie lamps than any boat he'd ever seen. "You, on the other hand, know your way around a kitchen better than anyone, and you have a flair for domestic details. I can't believe how much you've improved the living room and kitchen in one week."

Her smile was glowing. "That's the best thing anyone's said to me in months. Some days, it feels like such an uphill battle that I…" She shook her head in a visible attempt to dismiss doubts.

Realizing he'd said and done things to contribute to that self-doubt made his stomach turn. "Only way to get uphill is one step at a time," he told her. Wanting to put the smile back on her face, he teased, "This morning, I had a moment where I caught myself thinking Scarlett was cute. If that mutant mutt can look adorable, *anything* is possible."

* * *

The fresh paint on the walls and absence of criminally ugly carpet gave Hannah hope. There was more work to do, but at least now the space more closely resembled a potential guest cottage than an abandoned cabin where teens would get murdered in a low-budget horror film. But the fumes were too intense to stand around admiring their work.

She shooed everyone outside to breathe the fresh air. "Thank you, guys, so much for your help this afternoon. And yours, too," she told her son. While the rest of them were speckled with dabs and splatters of paint, Evan was covered in dirt and multicolored chalk dust. "You helped by being so good." He'd kept his boyish impatience to a minimum. Hannah could count on one hand the number of times he'd whined that the project was taking "forever and ever."

"So we can go fishing now?" he demanded.

"Sure."

Todd sighed. "Not us, unfortunately. I've got paperwork I need to get in order for a client meeting tomorrow. But hook a big one for me, okay, buddy?"

"Okay." Evan nodded confidently, in no doubt whatsoever about his fishing prowess.

Hannah grinned. Sometimes her son's innate belief in himself was nerve-racking because, in a four-year-old boy, that occasionally translated to thinking he was invincible. But mostly his conviction that things would turn out for the best was charming. Growing up with no dad and having moved away from his friends in their former apartment complex, he could have a very different outlook on life. She hoped she was leading by example, showing him that happy endings were within reach of anyone willing to work for them.

Evan hugged the Reeds goodbye. As they were driving off, he tugged on the hem of Colin's T-shirt. "Will you come fishing with us, Mr. Colin?"

Colin hesitated. Even if he was simply stalling until he decided how best to say no without hurting Evan's feelings, she was gratified he hadn't refused automatically. Colin's teasing comment earlier made it sound as if Scarlett was beginning to grow on him. Was the same true of her son? That would certainly make it easier for all of them to share a house.

A zing went through her at the thought of sleeping under the same roof as Colin. It wasn't the first time she'd had a physical reaction today. *Be honest, it didn't just start today.* What about the cake she'd almost let burn yesterday because she'd become entranced by the sight of Colin riding Viper? And she was starting to have Pavlovian responses to the sight of his weathered cowboy hat.

Between grief, long working hours and the demands of being a single mom, she'd had maybe ten dates since Evan was born—and one of those was counting a man who'd bought her a coffee after he bumped her and spilled her first one. With only one unoccupied table left in a crowded café, they'd sat together and chatted for fifteen minutes. There'd been one man in Colorado Springs whom she'd gone out with three times, but when he kissed her, she'd had no response. It left her feeling flat and empty inside, and she'd wondered if her libido had died with her husband.

The only man she'd gone out with since moving was Gideon. She'd agreed to dinner to learn more about ranching, but he'd spent two straight hours talking about himself. She didn't learn anything useful, although she did leave the restaurant with keen insight into how he'd won a high school football game and what he looked for in a woman.

Aside from an occasional flutter when a hot guy delivered a great line in a movie, it had been a long time since she'd experienced much sexual interest. Now she was torn between wishing it was anyone but Colin who'd triggered it and simply being grateful she could still feel something. The key was to stick to *feeling*, not acting. As someone who'd been on the receiving end of sexual harassment, she knew better than to lust after someone who worked for her. Given Colin's customary aloofness, he wouldn't welcome the attention any more than she had. But even if the attraction were mutual—her palms dampened at the thought—she had an impressionable young child in the bedroom across the hall from hers.

She'd become so absorbed in her own prurient daydreams that she nearly jumped when Colin's deep voice broke the silence.

"Not today," he told Evan. He sounded almost regretful. "I've got some shuffling to do to get settled in my new room at your place. And I need to get started on my supply list for Super-Ev HQ. Which reminds me…" He walked to his motorcycle and unzipped a large black bag, pulling out a sketch pad. A charcoal pencil fell to the concrete. After retrieving it, he tore a page out of the pad and handed it to her son. "What do you think?"

"This is gonna be my house? Look, Mommy!"

The sketch was impressive, but given the hero worship in Evan's eyes, Colin could have drawn a lean-to held up with a stick, and Evan would have been delighted. It gave her a twinge to see how much Evan looked up to the man who'd be leaving next month. She found herself thankful Colin wouldn't be joining them at the pond. Evan might start to get the wrong idea.

"Would you mind taking Scarlett to the house with you?" she asked Colin. "I don't want to chance her jumping in the pond. You would think she'd know better when the water's still so cold, but that didn't stop her on a sunny day two weeks ago."

The corner of his mouth lifted. "What, bathing a muddy dog isn't your idea of a good time?"

With the playful light in his aquamarine eyes and that half grin, he went from being ruggedly attractive to one of the sexiest men she'd ever seen. "I can think of better ways to spend an evening," she mumbled. *Get a grip. He was making a joke about a mud-covered dog, not flirting with you.*

Apparently, Evan wasn't the only one in danger of wrong ideas.

Working inside was never going to be as exhilarating as being outside in the fresh air and sunlight, but Colin was proud of his progress while Hannah and Evan fished.

When Hannah had shown him the upstairs, she'd talked about the work she'd need to do to make the second story inhabitable for guests. There were two pairs of rooms, each sharing a small connecting bathroom. She couldn't afford to renovate and furnish four bedrooms at once. He'd cleared space for himself and emptied out the adjoining one to give her a fresh canvas to work with. She was hoping to pick the best pieces of furniture from the combined rooms to set up a guest suite. He'd reinforced some slats in a bed frame, fixed a door on an antique wardrobe and was making plans to refinish a cedar chest.

Still, three pieces of furniture in a room painted the ugliest green he'd ever seen was barely a dent in the work to be done. He didn't think he had the energy to do much more today. Not the emotional energy, anyway. Arranging furniture was stirring up a lot of memories. He remembered the day he and Natalie had moved into their house. It had taken them hours longer than it should have because they kept stopping to make out in the different rooms.

He scrubbed a hand over his face. What was the point in torturing himself with memories of times he'd never get back? He'd survived the past couple of years by squashing those memories into the farthest recesses of his mind, but now they were refusing to stay buried. They seemed to be plaguing him more with each passing day.

Impatient and starting to feel suffocated by his own thoughts, he headed out to the barn. Horses were perfect company. They kept you from being lonely, but they didn't ask questions or expect deep conversation. Repressing the urge to saddle spirited Viper for a breakneck gallop across the property, he instead selected Apples. He and Hannah tried to make sure all four horses stayed in the habit of carrying riders.

After his ride, he found enough at the stable to keep him busy until after eight. It was full dark outside, the moon obscured by clouds, and Hannah's house was a blaze of light on the black landscape. The effect should have been welcoming, but it was also uncomfortable, like having the sun shine too brightly in your eyes.

Scarlett bounded to meet him when he walked through the door, and a freshly scrubbed Evan was close behind. He was wearing green pajamas covered with comical alien faces and his hair was still wet from a bath, the curls just starting to spring up around his shining face.

"You missed dinner," Evan said.

Feeling the truth of that in his empty stomach, Colin went straight for the kitchen. "How was the fishing? Did you catch anything?"

Looking up from a box of recipe cards, Hannah shook her head. "Only fish we saw today were the minnows I pulled out of the bait trap. Can't imagine *what* scared the other ones away. Hmm, what do you think, Evan?"

The boy giggled at the unsubtle accusation. "Mommy says I hafta be more quiet. I like loud."

Behind him, Hannah rolled her eyes affectionately. "Believe me, we know. But it's bedtime now, so you'll have to put the loud on hold until tomorrow."

All his time playing outside must have really worn him out, because he didn't even protest. He nodded to Hannah, then unexpectedly threw his thin arms around Colin's denim-clad legs.

"Night-night, Mr. Colin."

The berry scent of kids' shampoo and the stifled yawn in Evan's sleepy voice hit him hard. It took him two tries before he managed, "Night, Super-Ev."

In spite of being hungry mere moments ago, Colin made a half-articulate comment about needing to clean up and fled. In the upstairs bathroom, he was guaranteed absolute privacy. And if his cheeks happened to get damp, he could tell himself it was only the spray of the shower.

The thunderous groan of the upstairs pipes was alarming. Hannah prayed the noise was due to infrequent use and not impending doom. While she knew how to utilize bargain finds to make a place homey and Colin was way better at carpentry than she had any right to expect from a veterinarian-turned-ranch hand, plumbing and electrical work would require paid professionals. On the bright side, horrifying mental images of a flooded second story kept her too preoccupied to envision Colin in the shower. So…there was that.

But now it was time to focus on baking the desserts Patricia Loomis would be coming to pick up tomorrow. She wanted a trio of tortes for a dinner party, plus a baby shower cake for her niece—technically, several small cakes decorated to look like nursery toys. Hannah stood in the center of her kitchen trying to remember where she'd put the three-dimensional "rubber ducky" pan. She'd purchased it for a special order months ago and hadn't used it since. Which probably meant it was up high.

With a sigh, she dragged a chair over to the kitchen counter so that she could begin inspecting the hard-to-see shelf space above the cabinets. But even standing on the chair didn't give her much of a vantage point. She used the chair to boost herself onto the cabinet itself. *There*. On the very end, naturally. She'd been able to utilize the extra storage space only with a ladder and Todd Reed's help. The cabinets ran longer than the counter itself, and the last thing she wanted was to dig the ladder out of the garage at night, so she stretched as—

Hands clamped around her hips. Just below her hips, actually, more in the vicinity of her butt. Heat flamed through her.

"What are you doing?" Colin demanded, his tone rough. "Sometimes I don't think you or Evan have any survival instincts at all."

That stung. She smacked at his hands. "And yet we've survived the last four years without your help just fine." She needed to remember that. Colin wasn't staying, and it would be a mistake to become overly dependent on him.

"Get down from there." He didn't phrase it as a question, but there was something softening the edge in his voice now. Worry? "Please."

She allowed him to take her hand and help her down, which briefly brought her into contact with his body. He was wearing a pair of checkered drawstring pants and a heather-gray T-shirt—dressed for bed. There was a sudden melting sensation in her midsection. Seeing him like this was a novel experience. Without his boots and jeans and ever-present hat, it was as though he'd been stripped of his customary armor. This was a more vulnerable, approachable Colin. Touchable. *No, he's not. You need to keep your distance.*

To be fair, *she* hadn't been the one cupping *his* ass a moment ago.

"I'm over six feet tall," he told her. "If you need something up there, for pity's sake, ask me."

"I need the ducky pan on the end."

His forehead creased in a disbelieving scowl. "You were risking life and limb for a 'ducky pan'?"

"Risking my life?" *Hello, hyperbole.* She eyed the four-foot drop from countertop to tile floor. "You sound like my son, who claims he's *starving to death* if dinner's the tiniest bit late. Or that anything over fifteen minutes is *forever.*" She drew out the whiny emphasis on the words, trying to cajole a smile.

But Colin just glared. "You hurt your ankle earlier this week, and you've been on your feet all day. I saw how you were favoring your leg earlier. Which means your balance is less steady than usual. Can you imagine how much more difficult it would be to get your B and B up and running with a broken arm? You have to be careful!"

There was too much pain in his voice for him to be talking about sprained ankles and duck cakes. Where was this lecture coming from?

"I'm careful," she promised. "I'm a single parent who grew up in foster care. You don't think I've lost sleep, worried that something would happen to me and Evan would be left without a family? That he'd be alone, like I was?"

His face grew shuttered. With seemingly no effort, he hopped up on the chair and reached the cake pan.

"Thank you." Once she had the pan in her hands, she explained, "This may seem silly to you, but it's a paying gig for me. I was hired to make a complicated shower cake. Speaking of showers! My laptop's on the coffee table in the living room. Feel free to look at your brother's registry or check email or anything else that's inconvenient on your phone. If you bring it in here, I can look over your shoulder while I'm mixing and baking."

What was he thinking behind those blue-green eyes?

She would have been content to keep trying to read them, losing herself in them until she reached some kind of clarity, but he was already walking away.

"Maybe tomorrow. I'm beat."

For a man who was supposedly fatigued, he sure was moving fast. He slapped together a sandwich, poured a glass of milk and then retreated back up the stairs.

She was tired enough to be punchy, making jokes in her head about the stranger who'd shown up just long enough to help a short baker in distress, then disappeared as mysteriously as he came. "Who was that pajama'd man?" she asked Scarlett.

Eventually, though, Hannah put thoughts of Colin aside and lost herself in the controlled chaos of baking. If someone were to walk in while she was in the middle of a project—with splotches of batter on the countertop, utensils and mixing bowls piled in the sink and confectioner's sugar clinging to every surface it could find—they wouldn't see order. But it was the precision that Hannah found soothing. The measurements, the motion of perfectly cracking an egg, knowing the exact amount of vanilla to pour for the flavor she wanted.

While cakes were baking, she cleaned the kitchen. Then she streamed a movie on her laptop while waiting for them to cool. She'd mixed the appropriate colors for frosting and wanted to get a foundation layer on the baby shower cakes before going to bed. She'd do the final decorating touches before Patricia picked everything up in the morning.

It was nearly midnight before Hannah knew it. She groaned at the clock, knowing she was going to hate herself when it was time to crawl out of bed in the morning. She let Scarlett out one last time and was brushing her teeth when she heard noises. A muffled moan, or cry? Was Evan ill or having a bad dream?

But it was a much deeper masculine voice that split the night with a shout. *"Danny!"* Colin's raw pain reverberated through the house, and Hannah found herself hurrying up the stairs. She didn't know whether he'd appreciate her waking him from the bad dream, but even if she weren't worried that a second scream would wake up Evan, she wouldn't have been able to leave Colin alone. No one should be trapped in a nightmare that vivid. His anguished roar had given her chills.

As it turned out, though, she didn't need to wake Colin. When she reached the doorway of his room, she saw him sitting on the side of his bed, feet on the floor. Moonlight spilled through the window, casting a silvery glow across his dark hair and bare shoulders. He didn't look up, but his body tensed at her presence.

She felt like an intruder, yet couldn't bring herself to walk away. "Do you want to talk about it?" she asked softly.

"God, no."

She floundered, about to ask him if he wanted a glass of water before stopping herself, feeling stupid. This was not her four-year-old. Her mission had been to wake Colin, and since that had already been accomplished, she should just go.

"Wait." His voice caught. He still wouldn't look at her. "Don't…don't leave."

After a moment's indecision, Hannah stepped into the room. The bed creaked as she sat on the mattress next to him. She settled her hand over top of his, wishing she could do more but hoping this was comfort enough. There had been plenty of nights after Evan was born when she would have settled for someone simply patting her on the shoulder or giving her hand a reassuring squeeze. It would have been more than enough to know she wasn't alone in the world, with a new baby who was depending on her and no parenting experience.

You are not alone. Though she didn't speak the words, she thought them so loud she hoped Colin felt them anyway.

They sat there like that, in silence, and, after a while, his body began to relax. She stole a glance at his profile and was relieved that his jaw was no longer clenched.

"I'm all right now," he said gruffly. "Thank you."

She nodded, almost adding "any time" before catching herself. With any luck, it wouldn't happen again. And not just for his peace of mind, either, but for hers.

Sitting in the dark of Colin's bedroom and holding his hand, she'd felt a crack inside her, felt herself opening to him in a way she hadn't experienced for a very long time. In a way that—if she weren't careful—would hurt like hell when he walked out of their lives in a few weeks.

Chapter 7

When Hannah stumbled bleary-eyed from bed the next morning, Colin had already left the house. There was a note on the table about his checking the young cows and starting to work with them to get them halter trained. She had to admit, she was a little relieved not to face him yet. Even though there was a lot she didn't know about Colin, for a moment, they'd shared an almost intense intimacy. She was hoping the false sense of connection would dissipate before she encountered him again.

She woke Evan, who was always at his quietest and snuggliest for the first hour of the day. Since moving to the ranch, she'd taken advantage of his not being a morning person, letting him sleep in while she tackled some chores first thing. But summer was just around the corner, then kindergarten would start before she knew it. For both their sakes, she should slowly help him adjust to the idea of rising on a schedule.

At least today she had a trip to town to help motivate him. Henry and Kitty were taking him into town for errands followed by lunch at Evan's favorite pizza place. Hannah, always looking for ways to make Henry feel legitimately useful without overtaxing his strength, had asked him to pick up some supplies, including new salt and mineral blocks for the cows and alfalfa seed.

Before much longer, she'd need seeds to start planting beans and squash. In Colorado Springs, she'd grown some herbs and window box tomatoes in the summer. But she loved having a real garden now. She was learning all she could about what grew best during the different seasons, and when she was working in the soil, her mind often drifted to the menus she wanted to offer her guests. She'd also started trading the first of her fresh produce, like radishes, to Annette in exchange for eggs from the Reeds' farm. Soon, she'd also have lettuce and carrots to show for her hard work.

Hannah had her list and envelope of money ready to go when the Whites arrived. She was glad to see Kitty was driving, because Henry seemed strangely jittery.

"Too much coffee," Kitty said in a whisper. "He's determined never to fall asleep on Evan duty again."

Again? Hannah didn't get a chance to ask because Evan was so excited about getting to help like a big boy—and, of course, the pizza—that he practically dragged the Whites out of the house. Hannah had plenty of peace and quiet to finish decorating her cakes and catch up on some laundry.

It was nearly noon when Patricia arrived. She was visibly surprised by the improved front porch. "Why,

I almost didn't recognize the place," she commented, sliding her sunglasses atop her head. She had the same blond hair as her son, but hers was shot through with distinguished silver. "Gideon mentioned you had some extra help." Her mouth thinned in disapproval. "I can't say I would have hired Mr. Cade, given his reputation, but if this porch is any indication, I can't fault his work ethic."

"His reputation?" Hannah asked as she escorted the other woman inside.

"Did he tell you about the last place he worked? Or how he left after having an affair with the owner's wife?"

"What? That can't be right."

Patricia stiffened, sucking in a breath. "Are you calling me a liar? We've purchased three horses from the ranch next to the McCoy place, where he worked. They told us all about him. He's had a string of jobs." She made this declaration with a sneer. To Patricia, anyone whose family hadn't lived on the same property for six generations was suspect. "He was hired to help the McCoys with calving, but ended up destroying their marriage and leaving them in the lurch."

It was next to impossible to believe he'd abandon an obligation. After all, he'd stayed on Hannah's ranch initially because of faulty steps and his sense of responsibility, fixing something that was neither his doing nor his problem.

"Well," Hannah said, "as infallible as secondhand gossip is, I think I'll judge Colin on what I've seen of him." He was polite to Henry but companionable, too, not talking down to him in a "here, let me get that for you, old man" kind of way. And he was building

Evan a playhouse with scraps from her garage and additional materials he insisted on paying for himself, since the project was his idea. They'd argued for ten minutes before she backed down because her budget was strained already.

"You certainly do make some interesting choices about men," Patricia said with a glint in her eye.

With an inward sigh, Hannah admitted to herself that she'd likely alienated her best client. *On the bright side, once you start booking guests, you'll be too busy to fill all of Patricia's special-order demands anyway.* She'd called twice this week to change her mind about frosting colors for the shower cakes.

Hannah gave her a wide smile, eager to see her on her way. "Need any help getting your cakes to the car?"

It wasn't until Patricia was driving off that Hannah asked herself the obvious question. *Why* had she antagonized Patricia in Colin's defense? She filled a pot with water and placed it on the stove, mulling over the situation as she retrieved a box of assorted tea bags from the pantry. As drawn to Colin as she was, she had no idea what he'd done or hadn't done up until now. Before yesterday, she hadn't even known he had a sister. She didn't know what had happened to his parents. Or who Danny was.

Maybe a woman? Dani could be short for Danielle.

The front door banged open and Colin called into the house, "Whoever just left was driving like a maniac. She almost mowed me down."

"Don't worry, I think she fired me, so it's doubtful she'll be back," Hannah answered. Should she tell him the driving might not have been lunacy so much as purpose? Patricia seemed to dislike him strongly.

His boots clacked against the faux hardwood in the living room, then he appeared in the doorway, his expression pensive beneath the brim of his hat. "We need to talk."

Did he mean about what had happened last night? She clutched the box of tea tight enough to dent the cardboard. "I'm listening."

"You might need to think about selling your bull."

"Huh?" It took her mental gears a minute to make the shift, but even once she refocused on the topic at hand, she was confused. Bulls had to be replaced, on average, every five years to avoid defects in the herd caused by inbreeding, but she should still have another couple of years before she did that.

"Last week, he was warning off Henry and me, showing us his side, pawing the ground, tossing his head. Today, he tried to kick me. Luckily, I've got good reflexes. It's not unheard of for bulls to be a little ornery, but he could be a threat to your and Evan's safety." He said the words fiercely. It called to mind the other times he'd been not only anxious for her safety but seemingly *angry.* His reaction was always disproportionate to the supposed "danger."

Something had happened to someone he loved. More recently than his parents.

"Who's Danny?" The words blurted out with no premeditation, and the blood drained from his face.

He swallowed hard. "My son. Danny was my son. He…died in the same car accident that killed my wife."

Oh, God. Sorrow washed over her. She both understood yet simultaneously couldn't imagine what he'd endured. No wonder he had trouble embracing optimism. If anything ever happened to Evan…

"I am so sorry."

"I was working. I wasn't with them. It was about two years ago." The words were awkward and mechanical, as if he were simply spitting out facts because he didn't know what else to say.

"And you've been on the move ever since?" Patricia had insinuated he couldn't keep a job. More likely, he'd been running from his pain.

"No, I stayed close to family. Arden was so torn up, I didn't feel right about leaving Cielo Peak. Then she got pregnant and I promised to stay until the baby was born. It reached a point when I couldn't take it anymore, though. People say it gets better with time, but being in our hometown… Anyway. Now I'm here."

Not for long. They both knew that. Would he be able to heal drifting from one place to the next, without a support system? The Reeds and the Whites were invaluable to her. Maybe if Colin stayed somewhere long enough, he'd—

But that wasn't for her to decide. Opening the Silver Linings B and B was her dream, *her* fresh start, not his.

The only sound in the tensely silent kitchen was bubbling. "Your water's boiling," he said.

"I was making tea to go with lunch." She turned the dial to shut off the stove burner, then stretched on tiptoe to reach a bottle at the back of a cabinet. *Forget the tea.* In a completely uncharacteristic move, she poured a shot of whiskey into a glass tumbler, then quirked an eyebrow at Colin.

He opened his mouth as if to refuse, but then nodded. She set a second glass on the counter and poured another shot.

"In memory of those no longer with us," she said.

He stepped forward to take his glass and clinked it against hers.

The whiskey seared a hot path straight to her middle. Her eyes watered. "Wow."

"Been here a week, and I've already driven you to day-drinking." Colin set his emptied glass on the island. "That can't be a good sign."

She put the whiskey back in the cabinet. "I don't plan to make a habit of it, so you're off the hook." He seemed quick to take responsibility for things that weren't his fault. Did he blame himself for not being with his wife and child? "Are you hungry?" Food was a time-honored response to grief. She had the sudden urge to make him a giant pan of macaroni and cheese, but it would be a lot quicker to reheat some homemade ham and lentil soup.

"I guess I could eat."

"Colin? I won't pry, but if you ever want to talk... When Evan was born, I tried to put aside all the Michael stuff. I couldn't cope with that and deal with a newborn at the same time. When Annette and I became friends, it all came pouring out, and it was such a relief." It had been like facing a horrible fear and realizing it wasn't nearly as bad as she'd dreaded. She was able to answer Evan's questions about his daddy without bursting into tears, was able to remember good times fondly instead of trying to ignore them as if they'd never existed.

"I appreciate the offer." But he had no intention of taking her up on it, judging from his tone.

She changed the subject. "That woman who was here earlier? Patricia Loomis, Gideon's mother."

He made the same expression she would have made

if she'd stepped in cow manure. It almost made her smile.

"Seems she knows the McCoys," she said neutrally. "Just as a heads-up, Patricia also knows everyone in Bingham Pass, so there's a chance she might mention a dumb rumor about you and Mrs. McCoy."

"Good thing I'm not staying in Bingham Pass, I guess." He leaned against the counter, regarding her curiously. "You said 'dumb rumor.' You don't believe it?"

"Nope."

"Thank you for that. Even my own brother double-checked with me to make sure it wasn't true. You'd think the numbskull would know me better than that," he grumbled.

Conversation turned to cattle while she warmed the soup and chopped veggies for quick side salads. Colin said he'd take care of "worming" the cows before he left next month and again urged her to consider replacing the bull. They talked about the considerations she should make and questions she should ask when buying a bull.

She shook her head, feeling as if she should be taking notes. "And I thought buying a new car was complicated."

He helped her carry bowls of hot soup to the table and, as he always did, removed his hat when he sat at the table. They didn't talk much during lunch, but with eating to distract them, it wasn't an awkward silence. And they both needed to get to other chores. She planned to work in the garden, and he wanted to reinforce some pasture fence.

"If I have time, I'm going to get started on Evan's house this afternoon."

It was a bittersweet thought, now that she knew he should be building a playhouse for his own son. But she kept her tone upbeat. "He'll be thrilled. We're both really grateful for everything you're doing."

"You're paying me," he reminded her wryly. "Even if you weren't, I'd probably be willing to do the work in exchange for just the food." He rose from his chair, plopping his hat back on his head. "Thank you for lunch, Hannah. You're a good…"

"Cook?" she supplied when he trailed off, a bemused look on his face.

"Friend." He sounded mystified by the word, as if he couldn't remember the last time he'd made one. "You're a good friend."

It was a good thing Colin spent so much time doing manual labor, because he couldn't remember having ever eaten as well as he did at Hannah's. At least, not since his mom had died. His father's official cause of death was heart failure, but it had seemed to Colin and Justin that their dad had simply given up on life after losing the woman he loved. Colin could empathize, but his dad's unwillingness to fight harder had ticked him off. What about the three kids who'd needed him? Once Colin had run the household, most of their dinners had come from the microwave.

Tonight, Hannah had served homemade garlic bread and a lasagna she'd called the secret weapon in her "nutrition arsenal." While Evan had been washing his hands before dinner, Hannah bragged about the veggies she snuck in amid the layers of pasta and cheese. Now that the dinner dishes had been cleared, she was reading Evan a bedtime story while Colin sat at the kitchen table with her laptop, finally making time to look at Justin and Elisabeth's gift registry.

There were a few whimsical items on the list that made him wonder if they'd taken Kaylee, Elisabeth's adopted daughter, to the department store with them. It was weird to think of his younger brother, the formerly confessed commitment-phobe, as a father. But there was no question Justin had grown to love Kaylee and would be a great dad and husband.

Colin braced himself, waiting for the dark anger to rise, the bitter rage that he was no longer either. But it was getting easier to separate his loss from his genuine happiness for his brother. Justin and Arden deserved their hard-won happily-ever-afters. At times, Colin had felt he'd been the luckiest of the three of them because he'd had the most years with their parents, the most normal childhood.

"All right, so what are we thinking?" Hannah's cheerful voice came from behind him. "Guest towels? Standing mixer? Pillow shams?"

"You do know it's weird that you sound downright giddy about those things, right?" Did her enthusiasm stem from growing up in other people's houses, dreaming of the day she'd have a home of her own? The way she talked about decorating this place, it was as if she wanted every curtain panel and sofa cushion to be just right, to match a picture she'd been carrying in her head. Would the reality live up to her dreams?

That was the problem with hope; its flipside was disappointment.

She pulled up a chair next to him, and he saw she'd changed clothes after tucking Evan into bed. There was nothing revealing or inherently alluring about the polka-dotted flannel pants she wore or the pale pink sweatshirt. But he couldn't help noticing she was bra-less beneath the soft material. That discovery was more distracting than it should have been.

He abruptly lowered his gaze. "What the..." Her slippers had tails.

She wiggled her feet, showing off the cow slippers. "Aren't they great? They were a going-away present from some neighbors in Colorado Springs. To wish me luck as a cattle baron." Her dimples appeared. "Well, baroness. Lucky for you, all baronesses are born with exquisite taste." She waved her hand as if giving a royal decree. "Scroll away."

They looked through several pages of items, none of which felt quite right to Colin. Arden's mini lecture had obviously hit home. It felt coldly impersonal to send his only brother bath mats or a lamp. Hannah offered a compromise that included gifts Elisabeth and Justin had requested while still doing something that showed more thought than simply clicking an on-screen item.

"You can do a play on picnics," she suggested. "They want eight of those china plates. Buy two of those and that pair of wineglasses." She pointed. "Then you can get the pretty throw blanket that was on the last page and put it all together in a basket. Rather, your sister can, if we have it shipped to her and she doesn't mind. Voilà—elegant living room picnic! A perfect date night when you can't find a sitter and need something romantic at home. In fact, hold on..."

She took the mouse from him and opened a new window, browsing outside the registry. A few minutes later, she'd found a trio of ornamental candles that coordinated with the stuff they'd already selected.

"Nice touch," he said. "You really do have a good eye for this."

"The registry made it easy. It showed us what colors they're using and what their tastes are."

Sure, it wasn't rocket science, but he'd always been terrible at shopping. He prioritized function over form. The females in his life hadn't always appreciated that. "I bet you'd get along with Arden. She's a photographer, all about space and light and color. When Natalie and I got married, Arden was our unofficial interior decorator." He was surprised his wife's name slipped out so naturally. But it felt right. For the past fifteen minutes, they'd been discussing Elisabeth and Justin's upcoming marriage. Mentioning his own was a logical progression.

Tentative but feeling unexpectedly liberated, he elaborated. "Arden and Nat were best friends, practically their entire lives. Whenever the two of them got together on a project, it was best to just stay out of their way. I worried about dating Natalie at first, since she was Arden's friend and younger than me. But once she got it in her mind that we belonged together, she wasn't shy about pursuing me."

She'd been a real dynamo, not intimidated by obstacles or setbacks.

He turned to Hannah. "She would have liked you. You're both very determined women." Natalie had been stubborn in a brassy, unmistakable way. With Hannah's dimples and mouthwatering array of baked goods, she was less obviously mule-headed. One could misread her sweetness as mild-mannered, but that would be a superficial conclusion. Only a relentlessly tenacious woman could accomplish what she was attempting.

"I take that as the highest compliment," she said, sounding pleased.

"Good. That's how I meant it."

He returned his attention to the laptop. They looked at baskets, checking the dimensions to make sure all the proposed gift items would fit inside, and Colin found himself volunteering more information he hadn't expected. He spoke softly at first, as if they were in a library. Or a church. "The only room I ever had much hand in decorating was the nursery. Natalie and I did that together."

"How old was he?"

"Two. He'd be Evan's age now."

She reached atop the table and squeezed his hand, the way she had last night. He stared at their fingers, his so dark and rough against hers, until the worst of the ache eased.

"After the funeral," he continued, "when my siblings finally left and I was alone in the house, I thought that room would be the worst to face. So I didn't. I shut the door and never went in. In the end, it wasn't the nursery that drove me to putting the house up for sale. It was the double vanities in the master bathroom. I had my mirror and sink, Nat had hers. Every damn time I brushed my teeth or shaved, there was her side. Empty. She used to gargle mouthwash really loudly and in odd rhythms to make me laugh. And before we went out to dinner parties, she'd talk to me while she was curling her hair, usually trying to guess what woman my brother would bring as a date. All those stupid little rituals."

"Laundry day." Hannah gave him a sad smile. "Michael and I met at a Laundromat, so that's where he proposed. He hid the ring box under some dryer sheets so that I discovered it, then made a big production of asking me to marry him in front of everybody. When we got married, we didn't buy a washer and dryer. We kept the Laundromat as a silly ritual, and when he was overseas, going to do laundry made me feel closer to him. When I had Evan and moved into an apartment that came with a washer and dryer, I cried every time I did the laundry. Which, when you have a newborn, is a lot."

She took a deep breath. "Eventually, the tears stopped and I no longer think of Michael every time I pour a capful of detergent. But he is still part of me. You asked the other day if I still miss him. I do, but it's different than it was. Whenever Evan reaches a milestone, I hate that Michael couldn't be here to see it. The first day of kindergarten is going to flatten me. But doing something with this ranch, which was in his family for years, is a way to honor Michael. We always knew we'd end up here—he was supposed to inherit it from his great-uncle—but I didn't have the B and B idea until last year. Sometimes I feel like...if I don't pull it off, I'd be, I don't know, letting him down. And I realize that's completely irrational, so don't feel compelled to point it out."

"You're a hell of a woman, and you're raising a good kid. I'm sure Michael would be proud." But her words struck an unpleasant chord within him. Since he spent most of his time trying *not* to think about Natalie or Danny, he rarely considered what his wife would have wanted for him. She knew how hard he'd worked to become a vet, and she'd always been one to speak her mind. What would she say about his current lifestyle?

About his giving up the life they'd shared with no real plan for building a new one?

Maybe she'd call him a coward. And maybe she'd be right.

Chapter 8

The Thursday-afternoon sun hinted at a hot summer to come, and Hannah was glad she wore a hat to work in the garden—and not just because it protected her face. She also hoped the wide, floppy brim helped disguise the number of times she stared in Colin's direction. He was currently atop a ladder fifteen yards away, wearing a pair of jeans that looked custom-made by the devil, hammering shingles onto the roof of Evan's playhouse.

He seemed to enjoy building as much as he did working with the animals; it was difficult to tell given the distance and sound of tools, but she could have sworn he'd been whistling earlier. And he'd been like a big kid last night, brainstorming ideas with Evan. Her son wanted a trapdoor for the playhouse, which Colin had nixed. But he'd appeased the boy with the offer of a periscope.

"You'll be able to spy on everyone in the area. I helped my brother make one when he was little. I think I can make one for your headquarters." After dinner, he'd amended the sketch to reflect some minor tweaks to the original design.

It had been nearly a week since he'd moved in, and it wasn't uncommon to see his sketch pad around the house. He'd shown her not only the blueprint for Super-Ev HQ but a great sketch of Viper that captured all of the gelding's better qualities and made her forget what a pain in the ass the horse could be.

"You're talented," she'd told Colin the other day.

"Mom used to say I got it from her. When Justin was in high school, he begged me to draw a picture of this one girl he liked so he could claim credit for it and increase his chances of her going out with him. I refused, but he still ended up taking her to junior prom the following year. Lord knows what elaborate stunt he pulled to impress her."

From the stories Colin told, Justin sounded unrepentantly outrageous; it was difficult to picture him as the brother of someone so serious. "Does Elisabeth know she's marrying a con man?" she'd asked. The more she heard about these people, the more she wanted to meet them.

"Reformed con man. And don't worry about Elisabeth. She knows how to handle my brother."

Undoubtedly, the woman Hannah should be worried about was *herself.* She was having far too many moments like these—replaying conversations with Colin in her head, letting her gaze stray to him. His smiles were coming more easily, and the anecdotes he shared with her about his family and his past no longer sounded as if he were prying them painfully from himself with a crowbar. But the more he opened up to her, the more appealing he was.

Opening up to friends is what people do, she reminded herself.

And getting too attached to a cowboy with one boot already out the door was what fools did.

If Hannah thought she might actually be ready for another relationship, there were at least a dozen women in Bingham Pass who'd offered to set her up with cousins and grandsons and coworkers. It seemed statistically impossible that any of those potential dates had as much emotional baggage as a man who'd lost both of his parents, his wife and his child. That much despair was staggering.

Her gaze went to Evan, who was blowing bubbles and laughing as Scarlett chased and snapped at them, and she closed her eyes in a brief prayer for his continued safety and health.

Noticing her attention, Evan ran toward the garden fence. He'd picked radishes for her, but harvesting the peas was a bit more difficult. "Mommy, are you sure Mr. Colin doesn't need my help? I'm a good helper."

"Yes, you are. But do you remember our talk about staying back while anyone's on a ladder?"

His face twisted into a scowl. "Okay."

"Tell you what, I'm almost—" She was interrupted by her cell phone, which was trilling her ringtone for Annette. "Hold on, honey. Hello?"

"I may have a lead on a horse! For you, I mean. You need more for guests, right?"

"Um...yes? But, practically speaking, I need guests before they can do any riding."

"I know. Maybe this is lousy timing, but you're the person who's always talking about positive thinking and seizing opportunities. Do you know Darcy Arrendale? She and her husband are divorcing, and she's got an everything-must-go mentality. They have to split the money from selling Ringo, and she said she'd rather sell him cheap to a good home than get top dollar and turn the money over to her husband, who, I quote, 'would just spend it on his trampy mistress.' She's doing this pretty quietly, but I told her you might be interested in coming by to see the horse. Did I overstep?"

"No. It never hurts to look, and I appreciate your thinking of me."

"Oh, good, because she's hoping you can come by this afternoon if you're interested. Apparently, some of her girlfriends are taking her away for the weekend. I've got her number, and if you decide to go over there today, you can leave Evan with me."

After they hung up, Hannah went into the house so that she could take notes while talking to Darcy rather than conduct the conversation from the middle of her garden. She took Evan in with her and settled him at the table with a frozen strawberry bar.

Richard Arrendale was the most successful real estate agent in Bingham Pass. She didn't know him well enough to know if he went by Dick or if that was just the moniker his soon-to-be ex-wife favored. Darcy used it about twelve times in their short conversation. As they were getting off the phone, she said with a sigh, "I just hate the way these men think they can do whatever they want—not just Dick but the whole 'good old boy' lot of them. He plays poker with Gideon Loomis and the bank manager. Between you and me, I think the

Loomises hurt your chances of getting a loan. They've made it clear they plan to make an offer as soon as you 'come to your senses.'"

Cold fury knotted in her stomach. "Well, they'd better get used to disappointment, because I'm not going anywhere." Except to Darcy's to meet Ringo.

Hannah sent Evan to wash his sticky hands and to change into cleaner clothes for visiting Aunt Annette. Then she hurried out to discuss the situation with Colin.

When he saw her, he climbed down from the ladder. He lifted the hem of his T-shirt to wipe sweat from his cheek, and the glimpse of hard abs almost made her forget what she'd come out to tell him.

"What's up?"

"Annette called me with what might be a serendipitous opportunity—she knows someone wanting to sell a horse cheap. But the words 'too good to be true' also come to mind. How much would I be throwing off your schedule if I asked you to go look at the horse with me? I'd appreciate a more experienced eye before I make any decisions I might regret later."

"Well, I have to check with the boss lady," he drawled. "She's a real slave driver. I should probably clean up first."

"We have time. Darcy's not expecting us for an hour and a half. Annette ran into her in town, and Darcy's not finished with her errands. Plus, I didn't know how long it would take you to reach a good stopping point, and we need to drop off Evan."

"Sounds like a plan, but word of advice? Any time you go to see a horse for the first time, it's not a bad idea to arrive earlier than expected. Unscrupulous people have been known to drug troublesome horses prior to the appointment to make them appear more docile."

"That's awful! Why do people suck? Obviously, not all people," she clarified. But definitely Gideon Loomis and his parents. "Life is tough enough without us sabotaging each other."

He hit the brim of his hat, tipping it back on his head so he could get a better look at her. "You okay?"

"Yeah." She got a little moody around this time of year—and a *lot* moody when people tried to screw her over—but none of that was Colin's fault. "I need to get back in the house, make sure Evan hasn't tried to repaint the walls or help himself to any unauthorized cookies." It had occurred to her earlier that maybe she should bake a cake for this weekend—Evan would certainly enjoy decorating it with her—but she hadn't been able to work up much enthusiasm for making her own birthday cake.

Colin joined them in the house a few minutes later, while Hannah was trying to give her son an explanation for why people had to wear shoes from the same pair and shouldn't just mix and match at will. Evan had decided he wanted to wear one red rain boot and one sneaker. She suspected this was because he couldn't find the other sneaker and suggested they look harder.

"The ladder and power tools are all secure in the garage, and I'm headed up to grab a quick shower," Colin told her.

She nodded. "I'm going to hunt through Evan's room for a missing shoe. If I'm not back in half an hour, send a search party." Her son's room was overdue for some spring-cleaning. She'd become so focused on renovating guest areas that she occasionally overlooked the private living spaces.

It took her only a few minutes to locate the sneaker, but while she was waiting for Colin, she took the opportunity to direct her son in some rudimentary tidying. Evan put toy cars into a plastic bin while she shelved all the picture books she found on the floor. She was considering dusting his dresser and the shelves lining his walls when Colin appeared in the doorway, his face puckered into a worried frown.

"What is it?" she asked nervously. No good news in the history of the world had ever been delivered with that expression.

"Maybe nothing, but you'd better call a plumber to double-check. I noticed something on the way downstairs. You have a flashlight?"

Stomach sinking, she grabbed one and followed Colin to the stairs. Even with the staircase light on, the windowless space was dim. Using the beam of the flashlight, he showed her some dark spots along the wall.

"It's possible you have some water leakage back there, maybe a broken pipe fitting or something. If so, it's important to find out where and fix the problem before it gets any worse. Water damage…"

She didn't even want to imagine the possibility of flooding or how costly that would be to repair. "I don't suppose there's a way to find or fix the problem without putting holes in my wall?"

His answer was an apologetic wince.

"Dammit!"

"Mommy?" Evan's voice at the bottom of the steps

was scandalized. "We're not supposed to say that word."

She resisted the urge to bang her skull against the wall—why weaken its structural integrity further? "You're right, honey. Mommy forgot. Thank you for the reminder."

Colin's hand was warm and reassuring on the nape of her neck. "If it helps, you can swear all you want after we drop him off. I promise not to tell on you."

"Thanks." She bit her lip. "I should call Darcy back and cancel our appointment. If I'm about to spend thousands on plumbing repairs, I have no business buying a horse, even one that's unbelievably discounted."

"Don't panic," Colin advised. "At least, not until we know more about the plumbing. And even if you don't buy the horse, the act of inspecting him and thinking about the questions you want to ask is good practice. Come on," he cajoled when she remained tense and silent. "What happened to looking at the bright side?"

"You mean looking at the world through rose-colored glasses?" she asked drily.

He sucked in a breath. "Forget I said that," he ordered. "I was an ass. Just because I have trouble maintaining a positive attitude doesn't mean you should lose yours. Promise?"

He sounded so sincerely distraught by the possibility that she nodded. "I promise."

"Good. Then let's go see a woman about a horse."

After they were finished at Darcy Arrendale's, Hannah called Annette to let her know they were on the way to pick up Evan.

"You sure?" Annette said. "He just ate dinner with

us, and he's welcome to stay the night. You know I keep a spare toothbrush for him, and he had Trainket when you dropped him off, so we've got the basics covered."

Letting Evan spend the night with the Reeds would leave Hannah alone in the house with Colin on a night when she was feeling particularly vulnerable. *Oh, hell no.* "Absolutely not. You and Todd have a two-hour drive in the morning. You don't need my child waking you up at three a.m. for a glass of water."

Tomorrow, the Reeds had a consultation appointment at one of the best fertility clinics in the region.

"Any luck with the horse?" Annette asked.

"Not sure," Hannah said. "Colin suggests I always ask for a short trial period and that anyone who really cares about the horse should agree to that, but Darcy wants to get this over and done with before Richard catches wind of it. She assured me she has the legal right to sell the horse without him approving the sale, but it feels shady. I learned a lot, though." Colin had given her lots of tips that she might not have considered.

He'd said that any time a potential buyer arrived to find the horse already saddled, it was a red flag. A seller might be trying to hide that the horse was difficult to handle. Colin said she should always watch a horse be groomed and saddled. And while she obviously wouldn't buy one she hadn't ridden, he'd stipulated that she shouldn't ride a horse without the owner doing so first.

"Besides," she added, "none of the plumbers I called can come out until Monday. If I get good news, I can call Darcy next week and see if the horse is still for sale." Ringo was sweet. At ten years old, he might not have as many prime years in him as a younger horse, but he had experience. Colin said that horses with some mileage—assuming they'd been appropriately trained and well cared for—were much better with beginning riders. Most of her guests would probably not be equestrian experts.

When they got to the Reed farm, Annette told her there were leftover enchiladas. "Help us finish off this food so I don't have leftovers in the refrigerator. Todd and I were planning to stay out of town tomorrow night, anyway, instead of making the return trip, and now he's talking about staying through the weekend, making a minivacation out of it."

Hannah thought that was smart. The stress over not getting pregnant was taking a toll on the couple. A few days away would do them a world of good.

Evan met them at the door, a wireless video game controller clutched in his hand. "Uncle Todd was going to teach me a racing game. I'm gonna ask Santa to bring me one for Christmas!"

Bringing video games would first require Santa to bring a video game console. Which may not be in Santa's budget. "Um... December's a long way away," she said noncommittally.

Next to her, Colin's blue eyes had brightened with interest. "Which racing game?" He followed Evan, and within moments, all three males in the den were excitedly discussing video games.

"Boys will be boys," Annette said with a laugh. "No matter their ages, huh?"

Both women were amused when it was Colin—not Evan—who asked if they had time for one quick football game, promising to set short quarters. Todd had put away the racing disc and was showing Colin some of his other favorites. Hannah sat in a recliner with her plate, while Annette cheered on her husband and Evan rooted for Colin. Todd didn't score once. Colin decimated him.

He hoisted Evan on his shoulders for an impromptu victory dance. "This is the part where they pour Gatorade on us," he told the boy.

"On cream-colored carpeting?" Annette asked in mock horror. "I don't think so."

Colin was still grinning as he and Hannah herded Evan to the car.

"I wouldn't have guessed you were so good at video games," she said, holding out her hand for the keys. Now that she wasn't making a bunch of phone calls, she didn't mind driving.

"Are you kidding? Justin and I used to play for *hours*." He tilted his head at her. "Why would you assume I was bad at them?"

"Oh, it wasn't that I thought you'd be bad at them. They just weren't part of the picture I'd painted of you in my head." Were her cheeks getting red? "Not that I spend a lot of time thinking about this. But you don't have a computer and you carry charcoal pencils and a sketch pad in your motorcycle bag. I guess I had this vision of you as kind of a…bohemian cowboy."

He snorted, but tried to school his features into a serious expression. "Yes, a bohemian cowboy with many deep and mysterious layers. And a competitive streak a mile wide."

From the backseat, Evan asked, "What's competive?"

"Competitive," Hannah corrected. "It means when someone likes to win."

After a moment's thought, Evan proclaimed, "*Everyone* likes to win."

"Yes, but some people can get overzealous about it," she said.

"I don't know that word, either."

"It means they want it really bad," Colin said. "Some people get bad attitudes. You know that word?"

"Ohhh, yes. Mommy tells me all about attitudes."

Hannah stifled a laugh.

"I try not to get a bad attitude about winning," Colin told the boy, "and just try very, very hard to make it happen. Like your mom, putting so much effort into the ranch. She's a real winner."

"I want to be like her when I grow up," Evan said.

"Yeah." Colin smiled in Hannah's direction. "So do I."

Even before habitual nightmares had made him restless, Colin had been a light sleeper. When he was younger, a sense of responsibility for Justin and Arden—a fear of losing any more family—had jarred him from sleep whenever he heard a noise. It had eased somewhat after he married, when he'd been content with life and had Natalie pressed against his side, but after Danny was born, Colin had quickly resumed old habits.

He woke early Friday morning, before the sun had fully risen, to the sound of voices downstairs. Then he heard the front door open and close. He'd slept in a pair of boxer briefs and a T-shirt. Now he pulled on a pair of faded jeans, washed so many times they'd lost their denim texture and were threadbare at the knees.

When he got downstairs, he found Hannah sitting on the sofa, her knees tucked up beneath her. There were no lights on in the living room, but she appeared to be staring at something on the coffee table. He squinted in the gloom. Was that a muffin?

"Morning," he said, trying to gauge her mood.

She didn't look at him. "Sorry if we woke you. Annette came by to bring me a cupcake on her way out of town."

His vision had adjusted. He realized the cupcake had a candle sticking out of it, and there was writing on the brightly colored wrapper. He couldn't discern any of the words but he could guess what they said. "It's your birthday?"

"Yep."

He sat on the couch with her. "So your friend decided to wake you up by delivering a cupcake at six-thirty in the morning?"

"She knew I wouldn't be asleep." Hannah sighed, pressing her head against the back of the sofa as she turned to look at him. "This is my first birthday since moving to Bingham Pass, but she and I have talked about it. This is the day that's the hardest. That sounds so selfish. You'd think it would be Michael's birthday, or the anniversary of when he was killed. But the first year we were married, he forgot my birthday entirely."

Colin let out a low whistle. Since his sister had also been his wife's best friend, Arden had usually started bugging him about coordinating birthday plans months in advance. But he knew the hell Natalie would have given him if he'd ever overlooked it.

Hannah's lips curved in a wistful smile. "He felt so terrible that every year after, he went all out. I mean, it was crazy. His birthday presents to me were bigger than Christmas. He 'kidnapped' me one year and took me cross-country to see a play on Broadway. We were only in New York one night. I've always wanted to go back when I had more time to sightsee, but it was an amazing night."

She gave herself a shake. "Wow. Pity party, table for one. Sorry—I'm fine. Next week, Evan and I will probably go to Annette and Todd's for a belated birthday dinner. You're welcome to come if you want."

"I may take you up on that invitation, but we're not waiting until next week to celebrate your birthday."

"Colin, seriously, it's okay, I just—"

"Is there a miniature golf course in Bingham Pass?"

Her eyebrows rose and she took a second to answer. "Not in town, exactly, but just on the other side of it. Annette and I took Evan once."

"Perfect." He draped his arm over the back of the couch, leaning in so she could see his resolve. She wasn't talking him out of this. Hannah took care of her son, went out of her way to make Henry feel useful, was building this ranch in part for her late husband and cooked for half the damn county. Today, she was going to let someone do something for her. "How about you meet me on the front porch at two o'clock? That gives me time to knock out some work, including your chores. You are under house arrest."

"But—"

"Take the day off," he said sternly. "Play with your kid, read a book, watch a dumb movie."

A smile lit her face. "And at two o'clock we're going to play minigolf?"

"Affirmative. Then we come back here, and I cook you dinner."

"That is incredibly—" She straightened. "Wait, didn't you tell me you were a lousy cook who microwaved everything you ever made for Arden and Justin?"

"And burned half of it," he said. "The other half was usually still cold in the middle."

"I suddenly remembered I'm on a diet."

He grinned. "Don't worry, Hazel, I got this."

"Hazel?"

"Oh." Before, he'd called her that only in his head. He hadn't intended to say it out loud. "Your eyes. You have beautiful eyes." He tried to say it matter-of-factly, but his voice was too low. Raspy.

Now it was her turn to respond with, "Oh."

Were they really sitting so closely he could feel her breath fan across his cheek, or was that his imagination?

"Colin?"

It was hardly the first time she'd said his name, but this time it did something to him. His body tightened, and he found himself angling even closer. "Yeah?"

"You have nice eyes, too."

One move of his hand—that was all it would take. If he lifted the hand at his side and cupped her face, would she meet him halfway? His gut said she would. And then he'd be kissing her.

He shot to his feet. "Two o'clock then?"

She nodded, her words shuddery and slightly out of breath. "Two o'clock."

In a spectacularly stupid lack of self-control, he reached out anyway, from a safe standing distance, and brushed his hand over her cheek. Her skin was velvety soft, and her long hair teased his fingers. She trembled beneath his touch, and he abruptly dropped his hand.

Thank God they'd have Evan to chaperone them on their trip to play putt-putt golf. Otherwise, it might feel like a date. As out of practice as Colin was with dating, even he knew it was customary to end dates with a good-night kiss.

Chapter 9

Holy crap. The sentiment wasn't particularly eloquent or mature, but it kept repeating in Hannah's head as she listened to Colin's booted steps descend the porch stairs.

That had been hot. All he'd done was touch her face, but it had left her entire body tingling. Her heart was pumping as if she'd just chugged an espresso, and parts of her body she hadn't heard from in years were suddenly checking in to wish her a happy birthday. And to offer suggestions on what she should wish for.

For a second, she'd thought he might kiss her. And even though she didn't technically know what kissing Colin would be like, female intuition told her it would be richer and sweeter and more decadent than the world's best devil's food cupcake. Hell, just the way he'd looked at her made her melt.

She reached for the lamp on the end table, switching it on as if seeing more clearly might help her think clearly. Over the past few days, there had been moments... Sometimes he'd smile at her in a way that made her think she wasn't the only one stealing appreciative glances. He'd been more playful. After his taciturn first few days here, he was becoming quick to shower her with compliments. At first, they'd been about her cooking, no more personal than flattery Henry or Todd might have given her. But last night he'd upped the ante. When he'd told Evan she was a winner, it had been tough to contain her sigh. She'd grinned the entire drive home. Then there was this morning.

You have beautiful eyes.

She hugged a throw pillow to her body. As recently as yesterday, she'd been cautioning herself that it would be foolish to care too much for Colin. But a woman would need a heart of stone to resist a man who treated her like this.

"Mommy?"

Hannah whipped her head around guiltily, the same way she'd felt when she accidentally used the D-word in front of Evan. "Hey, honey. You're up early." No wonder—people had been coming and going all morning. She held her hands out for a hug, and he padded toward her, dragging Trainket behind him.

He snuggled against her, and she thought a day of "house arrest" with her kiddo actually sounded pretty perfect.

Suddenly, he gasped, his voice full of wonder. "Mommy, where did the chocolate come from?"

She started to tease "cupcake fairy," but he might take her seriously. "Aunt Annette brought it over as a present because today is my birthday. I was waiting until you woke up so we could share it. Want half a cupcake for breakfast?"

He nodded, his eyes eager.

"I have a surprise for you. We're going to watch cartoons and play games all morning. And after lunch, we're going to play minigolf with Colin."

Evan leaped from the sofa with an ecstatic shriek. He ran in place for a minute, pumping his arms in a celebratory dance. Then he stopped. "I have a surprise for you, Mommy." He zoomed out of the living room and down the hall.

He returned with a folded piece of yellow construction paper, presenting it proudly. Multicolored glitter on the front formed a shape that was heartlike, and the word *MOM* had been written painstakingly in the center.

Love surged through her, a giddy pressure in her chest. "What's this?"

"I made a card at Aunt Annette's house. She said it was a secret mission. We hid it in Trainket when you came to get me," he boasted. Inside, Annette had written the words *Happy Birthday* and *I love you* in pencil, and Evan had attempted to trace over them in crayons.

"It's fantastic—the best card ever!" And for a day she'd been subconsciously dreading, it was off to a pretty fantastic start.

It was good that none of the cows got in the way of the tractor, because, today, Colin might not have noticed. He was preoccupied with the thoughts racing through his head. When was the last time he'd celebrated a birthday—his or anyone else's?

He honestly couldn't remember.

Then you're long overdue. The voice in his head
sounded like Natalie's. She'd loved parties and social
events. One year, when she'd informed him that she
was throwing him a birthday party, he'd said it wasn't
necessary and she'd teased that he had no say in the
matter, she'd just been looking for an excuse to get a
bunch of their friends together. Their circle of friends
had been other young, married couples, some with
kids, some without. Being around them had become
even more wrenching than enduring the pity-filled
glances of his siblings. As politely as possible, Colin
had cut them all out of his life.

Now he found himself thinking about some of those
former acquaintances, wondering if Peter or Don might
want to grab a beer while he was in town for Justin's
wedding. Or had they written him off as a self-ab-
sorbed jerk, too wrapped up in his own misery to be
civil?

He was struck with an unexpected pang of regret.
There wasn't one damn thing he could have done to
keep from losing Nat and Danny. But what about the
other people he'd deliberately lost?

Even though he'd stayed busy with a string of jobs,
he'd been living in suspended animation. It was time
to engage. Taking Hannah and Evan to celebrate her
birthday was a start.

And nearly kissing her? What was that?

Before Colin had left Cielo Peak, there had been
some dark moments, rare shameful nights when he'd
tried to numb his pain by losing himself in physical
oblivion. He hadn't been with any women he actually knew and he hadn't brought any of them home to

the bed he'd shared with Natalie. They'd been frantic, hollow nights. He couldn't recall if he'd kissed any of those women.

If he kissed Hannah, there'd be no forgetting it.

The temptation was so strong. He hadn't felt that pull in so freaking long. But Hannah was a nice woman.

Yesterday, she'd responded gently to all of Darcy's vitriol about her cheating husband and marriage being a trap she should have never willingly entered. Hannah had advised the woman not to close herself to the possibility of love. As they'd talked, it had become evident that Hannah hoped she herself might eventually remarry. It was easy to envision. As nurturing and generous-hearted as she was, a man would be lucky to call her his wife. And a man would be one lucky SOB to have her in his bed.

Someday, she would find a guy who could love her forever, who would give Evan little brothers or sisters. Colin was a temporary figure in her life, a man with a truckload of abandonment issues and survivor guilt who'd alienated most everyone he knew.

Hannah was special. He hoped she got everything she deserved—and she deserved far better than him.

From the passenger seat, Hannah peered through the windshield and bit her lip to keep from laughing. Or groaning.

"So, as it turns out, there's an inherent flaw with impulsive, last-minute birthday party plans," Colin admitted sheepishly.

"Not checking the weather forecast first?" she asked. It had started to drizzle before they even left the ranch, but now it was pouring. This might be an even heavier rain than the storm that had blown through the day they first met.

At least one person in the truck wasn't amused by the situation. "Does this mean we can't golf?" Evan's voice quivered with disappointment.

"Well, it would be difficult to knock a ball into a hole that's full of water," Hannah said. "It would float right back out."

"No worries, Super-Ev. Do you know what a plan B is?" Colin rolled to a stop at a red light, then turned to flash the boy a reassuring smile. "When your first plan flops, you devise a backup. I promised your mom a fun afternoon, and we're not about to turn around now."

"That's good," Hannah whispered, "because the road behind us may be washed out."

He smirked at her. "Quiet, you. Evan, ever been bowling?"

She was surprised when he nodded eagerly because she couldn't remember having ever taken him to a bowling alley.

"Uncle Todd has a bowling video game."

She had a few choice words for Uncle Todd—this time last year, Evan hadn't even been aware of what video games were. Now they found their way into his daily conversations.

"Great," Colin said. "Imagine that but with real pins and balls."

The bowling alley was down the street from the hardware store, where Colin had been making regular trips. There weren't many cars in the parking lot on a rainy Friday afternoon. But the ones present had taken up the front row. The only empty spaces close to the building were reserved for handicapped parking.

Hannah asked her son not to jump in every puddle between the truck and the front door, one of his favorite pastimes. It was a measure of his excitement for their outing that he didn't even pout.

As they all unbuckled, Hannah reminded him not to open his child-size, superhero umbrella in the backseat. "Wait until right before you step out of the truck, okay?" She also kept a regular umbrella under the front seat of the truck, but she and Colin would have to share it. The thought of standing that closely to him made her pulse flutter.

He got out first, taking the umbrella from her and quickly crossing to her side of the truck, sheltering her and Evan as they climbed down.

Colin had showered after working in the pasture all morning—downstairs, as all the upstairs bathrooms were off-limits until after the plumbing inspection on Monday. He didn't smell like anything more exotic than soap and deodorant and himself, yet she still had to fight the urge to huddle closer and inhale deeply. His simple masculinity was far more enticing than any overpowering, lab-created scent designed to attract women. If cologne companies could bottle him, they'd make millions.

Colin opened the door, and Evan scampered inside first, wrestling with his umbrella to get it closed.

"Here, honey. Need some help?" Hannah offered.

"I'll get us a lane," Colin said. "Should I ask for gutter bumpers?"

"Bumpers?" she echoed. It had been a long time since she'd been bowling. And she'd never been especially good at it. "I remember gutter balls."

He chuckled. "They have something they can lay

down in the gutters so that the ball doesn't consistently end up there. To keep certain bowlers from getting too frustrated and not having any fun," he said with a pointed look at Evan.

After a moment's consideration, she shook her head. "Let's start without the bumpers." Nobody was perfect. The important part was to keep trying, and she thought that was a valuable lesson for her son. Then again, they were here to have fun, so if it looked as if he was becoming traumatized by the experience, she was willing to revisit her decision.

Evan turned out to be completely fascinated by the concept of a place where they took your shoes and made you wear different ones. While he wiggled his toes in a pair of brightly striped, ugly bowling shoes, Hannah searched for the smallest-size ball she could find him.

"I like that one!" Evan pointed at a neon orange ball with green swirls. It was fourteen pounds. She immediately had visions of taking her kid to the E.R. for a broken toe.

"Maybe when you get a little bigger. Here, try this one." It looked as if the lowest weight the alley stocked was six pounds.

Colin was already entering their names into the automated scoreboard system. "You want to go first?" he asked Evan. He typed in Super-Ev. "Lots of great athletes have nicknames. What should your mom's be?"

"Birthday Mommy!" His voice carried.

An elderly man two lanes over called to the manager, "Hey, Bert! You do that singing thing like waiters at restaurants? We got a birthday over here."

Bert grunted. "This look like a restaurant to you?"

"You got nachos and beer. Close enough." The man waved to Hannah. "Many happy returns."

Once Super-Ev, Birthday Mommy and Cowboy Colin were all displayed on the overhead monitor, Colin took Evan to the side, on the carpet instead of the slick floor, and demonstrated the pendulum motion used in bowling. Evan's first attempt on the lane was, unsurprisingly, a gutter ball, but his second one managed to bump the pin on the far left. It wobbled for a full thirty seconds, then finally fell. Evan let out an ear-splitting whoop of triumph. Hannah knocked down the six middle pins and knew she didn't have a prayer of picking up the split.

Apparently, Colin was as good at bowling as video football. He got a strike right away, followed by another on his second turn. "If I get three in a row," he told Evan, "that's called a turkey."

But his third turn yielded only a spare.

"Oh, what a shame!" Hannah said to her son. "He didn't get his goose."

Evan giggled. "Turkey, Mommy."

"No." She pointed at the computer monitor, feigning confusion. "*Birthday* Mommy, remember?"

She half feared Evan would get bored since he got only one turn for each of their two, but he was having a blast. The two of them made silly jokes and laughed at the cartoon "replays" that showed on the monitor after each of Colin's strikes. And Evan was mesmerized with watching the ball return. He regarded it with awe, as though it were a futuristic transporter device.

Music played through overhead speakers, and when a song came on that she hadn't heard in years, she ducked down, taking Evan's hand and spinning him in circles on the carpet.

Colin laughed. "You're up, Evan. Maybe I can cut in?"

Hannah assumed he was kidding. The man had once gone seventy-two hours without smiling. He'd acted as if her standing on her kitchen counter would lead to a full-body cast. He seemed to lack the requisite absurd streak needed for dancing to a 1980s hair-band ballad in a bowling alley populated with retirees. She let out a squeal of combined shock and delight when he grabbed her and dipped her dramatically.

Behind the counter, Bert applauded them.

After they finished and went to return their shoes, Bert offered them a second free game in honor of Hannah's birthday.

"Not like I've got a long line of people needing that lane," he said with a shrug.

"Can we stay, Mommy?"

"It's fine with me. We have plenty of time until dinner." She knew Colin had made a brief run to the store earlier, but he'd shooed her from the kitchen before he put the groceries away. In keeping with his plan-B philosophy, she thought to herself that if whatever he was cooking didn't turn out, there was always peanut butter and jelly.

In the second game, Colin finally got his three-in-a-row strikes and Hannah declared, "Huzzah, a chicken!"

"A turkey," Colin and Evan corrected in unison.

Before they left, Bert made Evan's day—possibly his year—by hoisting him atop the counter and letting him sing into the bowling alley microphone.

"Do you and your dad want to serenade your mom for her birthday?" Bert offered.

"Oh, he's not my dad. He just lives with us."

There were guffaws from the other gentlemen gathered around, and Hannah felt her face go crimson.

"He's a ranch hand," she stammered. "At the Silver Linings." Though technically true, her words felt like a lie. There was no denying that Colin Cade was far more to her than just a cowboy passing through.

When they walked into the house, Colin handed her a brown paper bag. "This is for you. Go enjoy, and Evan can stay and be my sous chef."

Evan nodded. "I'll help make soup."

While Colin explained that he hadn't said "soup chef" and that *sous chef* meant second in charge, she pulled a bottle of raspberry-scented bubble bath from the bag. She grinned. "Just what I always wanted. How did you know?"

Filling the tub made her think about the pipes in the old place, but she squashed her concerns in order to enjoy Colin's thoughtful gesture. When you were a mom—especially a single mom—a few completely solitary minutes to relax without interruption were a rare gift. But she didn't stay in the bath long. She was propelled by curiosity and the desire to protect her kitchen. Colin might be unaware of how quickly her son could destroy a room.

Hannah turned on the blow-dryer. Drying her hair completely took forever, but at least this way she wouldn't be dripping on her shoulders through dinner. She twisted her still-damp hair into a knot and secured it with a clip. She put on a pair of flannel pajama pants and a comfy sweatshirt, then frowned at her reflection, momentarily wishing she'd picked something more flattering.

Evan had apparently been appointed lookout duty because he was sitting against the living room wall. As soon as he saw her, he scrambled to his feet. "She's done with the bath!" he shouted, preceding her into the kitchen.

Hannah laughed at the container on her counter that bore the diner's logo. There was a platter of fried chicken sitting on the kitchen table, and she admitted some relief that Colin and Evan hadn't tried making it from scratch. The potential mess from frying chicken was daunting.

Colin caught her eye. "I heated it in the oven all by myself. And Evan and I worked very hard on the salads."

The salads were plated so that each one had two cucumber slices as eyes and a smile of grape tomatoes. There were also little bowls of mixed berries topped with whipped cream. Judging by the sheer amount of whipped topping leaning like the Tower of Pisa, she had a pretty good idea who'd been allowed to work the spray can. The finishing touches were a loaf of bake-and-serve bread from the market and a bottle of chilled white wine—or, in Evan's case, a carafe of chocolate milk.

Tears pricked her eyes, but they were happy tears. "This all looks incredible. I doubt they dine this well in the best restaurants in Denver."

Colin pulled her chair out for her. Once she was seated, he folded a dish towel over his arm and presented the bottle of wine for her inspection. Extremely elegant, even though the towel was hot-pink and printed with éclairs, bonbons and petit fours. She took a mental snapshot, knowing she would want to cherish this moment for a long time to come.

They took their time over the meal. She was halfway through her second glass of wine when she chased Colin away from trying to load the dishwasher.

"I'm the only one who does that," she reminded him. "I have a system."

He grinned, his eyes twinkling at her. "Control freak."

"Everyone's got their quirks."

She hated for the day to end, but they'd all been up earlier than normal. Evan was visibly drooping. After he put on his pajamas, she tucked him into bed, suspecting he was sound asleep before she even made her way down the hall.

Colin was sitting on the couch. It was where they'd started this unforgettable day, and her body tingled with desire, a sense memory of how he'd made her feel that morning.

He held a large manila envelope. "I have one last thing for you. Consider it my version of a birthday card, although mine doesn't have any cool glitter."

She sat next to him, her hand unsteady as she slid a sheet from his sketch pad out of the envelope. Her breath caught. "This is wonderful."

He'd drawn her ranch, although he'd taken creative liberties with the position of things. The playhouse he was building Evan was out front, and a dark, curly head was visible through one of its windows. In the distance, a group of people rode horses. Scarlett was curled up on the beautifully redone porch, and the main gates were shown much closer to the house than they were in reality. The sign above them read SILVER LININGS. She wanted to frame it and hang it above the fireplace. It was a visual reminder of what she wanted to accomplish, and it had never felt so within her reach as it did right now, as if his drawing predicted the future.

"Thank you." She set the picture on the end table, then wrapped him in a hug. Lord, he felt good. All hard planes and corded muscle.

He stiffened—not, she thought, in rejection but more in surprise. Even though Evan had fallen into the habit of hugging him every night before bed, gestures of affection still seemed to catch Colin off guard, as if he was relearning human contact. But then his arms came around her and he was returning the embrace wholeheartedly.

"Happy birthday, Hannah." He brushed a kiss near the corner of her mouth. It was a quick, friendly peck, completely causal—except for how there was nothing at all casual about his nearness, the way he murmured her name. "I hope your wishes come true, and you get everything you want."

"Do you?" Her voice was husky. She didn't sound like herself.

Which was fitting because what she planned to do wasn't like her, either. But this was her birthday. If she didn't take the chance, she knew she wouldn't be brave enough to do it tomorrow or the next day. He'd opened a door between them when he'd feathered his lips over her skin in that teasing whisper of a kiss.

She wanted more.

Keeping her eyes locked on his, she moved forward slowly. The combination of anticipation and anxiety was causing her heart to pound so loudly he could probably hear it. She was glad they were sitting—with their height differences, if they'd been standing, there was no way she could have done this without active cooperation on his part. When his gaze dropped to her mouth, it was as if he was already touching her.

She fit her mouth to his, and liquid fire roared through her veins. His hand tangled in her hair, bringing her closer, and he nipped at her bottom lip. Their tongues met, tentatively at first, but inhibition combusted into fervent need. They tasted each other, exploring eagerly, and her hands were running up and down his arms now, over the well-defined muscles beneath his sleeves. He was strong and sculpted and so deliciously male she wanted to bite into him.

As if a dam had broken and he couldn't decide where he wanted to kiss her the most, suddenly he was everywhere. He moved from her throat to her jawline to her ear, and she moaned beneath the sensual onslaught. Shoving the baggy sweatshirt so that it slid off her shoulder, he followed the slope of her neck all the way to the strap of her bra. The moments blurred together, indistinct, a shifting kaleidoscope of sensation. She didn't know if he'd tugged her into his lap or if she'd moved there in her escalating need to get closer. He was hot and hard beneath her, and she reflexively rocked her hips against him. He groaned into her mouth, his kiss wild. Encouraged by his response and the sharp pleasure drugging her system, she did it again.

He threw his head back against the couch. "Hannah." It was an oath and a plea and an apology. "We…"

Face burning, she scrambled off his lap.

"That got out of control fast." He shoved his hand through his hair, his breathing choppy. "You told me this morning that today is difficult for you. I don't want to add to that difficulty, be something you regret in the morning. I have a few regrets of my own, and I can't do that to you."

"R-right." She'd be more impressed with his gallantry if every nerve ending in her body wasn't throbbing with fierce sexual need.

"Hannah? I'm not saying I don't want you." His tone was rueful as his eyes cut downward, indicating the physical proof of his reaction to her.

She made the mistake of following his gaze, and her yearning intensified.

"But we can't." He ran the pad of his thumb across her still-tingling lower lip; she hadn't realized how sensitive she was there. Then he added two of the most tantalizing, maddening words she'd ever heard. "Not tonight."

Chapter 10

By the weekend, Colin was experiencing the worst insomnia he'd had in months. Although, maybe *insomnia* wasn't the correct medical term for the punishing physical discomfort of being hard enough to drive nails. He lay awake at two in the morning on Sunday, listening to the rain fall against the roof and windows. It was a gentle patter, almost lulling, except that it made him think of Hannah—how she'd looked in that soaked blouse the first time he'd seen her, how close she'd pressed to him beneath their shared umbrella on her birthday.

Who was he kidding? It wasn't the rain making him think of Hannah. He hadn't *stopped* thinking of Hannah since he'd pushed her away on the couch two nights ago.

He still hadn't decided whether that had been a noble

act or perverse selfishness. She'd started her birth-day with red-rimmed eyes and memories of her hus-band, claiming her birthday was the day she missed him most. Deep in some primal, irrational place in-side, Colin hadn't been willing to share her. Granted, her earlier melancholy had seemed thoroughly van-quished by the time she'd reached for him on the sofa, but still....

He was a hypocrite. Last year, he'd indulged in a handful of faceless encounters meant to make him for-get, to blot out the loneliness for a fraction of an instant, but he'd balked at the slightest possibility of being that for her. He'd already acknowledged that he couldn't be a permanent fixture in her life, wasn't what she de-served, yet he was equally unwilling to be a one-night stand. What *did* he want to be to Hannah? Until he figured that out, he'd been doing his best to avoid her.

Which would probably be a more effective long-term plan if he weren't also living with her.

The finance-induced terror Hannah felt as she signed the check for the plumber Monday was a nice change from the pent-up frustration that had gripped her all weekend. With Colin's assistance, the plumber had sawed through the drywall and located the source of the leak. Colin had promised to refashion that sec-tion of the wall as a removable panel so that if she ever needed to get to the pipes again, it would be a simpler process. Plus, they'd planned to repaint the dingy stair-well a fresh, gleaming white anyway, so that would minimize the cosmetic damage. For the time being, the plumber had used some rubber hose to fix her prob-lem, staving off further damage. But he warned that the best way to ensure she didn't come home to costly flooding someday was to replace the faulty pipe. He put in an order for parts and said he'd be in touch to schedule his return his visit.

She was facedown on the kitchen table when the phone rang. Rising from her chair, she prayed the caller was Annette. Hannah desperately needed to vent about the plumbing crisis, her wildly unexpected birthday celebration and the way Colin was suddenly as skittish as a spooked horse.

His attempts to avoid her were humiliatingly blatant. Was he afraid she'd pounce on him in some hormone-fueled frenzy? But on the bright side, he'd spent every spare second over the weekend working on Evan's playhouse, and it was finished. Her son was ecstatic and had been disappointed she wouldn't let him sleep out there last night.

"Hello?" She answered without bothering to check the number first. If it was an unwanted solicitor, he was about to get an earful.

"Hannah?" Henry's voice was thin and reedy. "I hate to be any trouble, but could you come get me in the truck?"

Her heart jumped in her chest. Because Colin had been assisting the plumber behind the wall, Henry had gone out to the pasture alone. "Oh, my God, Henry, are you all right?"

He took a deep breath, and the way it rattled through the phone had her racing for the truck keys. "No, I don't believe I am."

Hannah wanted to pace the hospital waiting room, but it didn't set a good precedent for Evan, whom she was trying to keep still and out of the way. Plus, she thought signs of nervous energy on her part made Kitty more apprehensive.

It had been a crowded truck ride to the E.R. Colin had offered to take Henry to the hospital so that she could stay home with Evan. She'd snapped at him that she realized he was trying not to share any space with her but that he was a moron if she thought she was going to sit at home twiddling her thumbs after Henry had been hurt on her land. The bull had charged him, knocking him to the ground.

"He's always been touchy," Henry had said in the truck. "Gotta be careful not to set him off, and it's a good idea to have a stick with you. But lately he's turned plumb mean. He didn't give me any warning, just came out of nowhere."

Because none of them had wanted Kitty driving while she was worried, they'd stopped briefly on the way to the hospital, just long enough for her to hop in the truck. When they'd all five unloaded from the cab in the parking garage, it had made Hannah think of a clown car.

Colin had helped Henry into the hospital, but once the nurse had taken him back for examination, Colin turned to Hannah, his face ashen.

"I need air. This isn't me avoiding you, I swear." His jaw clenched. "I hate hospitals. I'll be outside. Text me when you hear something?"

It was twenty minutes later when they were allowed to go back and see him. Henry's official diagnosis was a sprained arm and bruised ribs. The doctor said he should heal fine but added sternly that Henry needed to take it easy.

"No ranch work," Kitty told her husband.

"Seconded!" Hannah agreed. It was an unpleasant revelation seeing him here, under the fluorescent lights, with his arm in a sling. She was so used to seeing him ambling across the yard as if he belonged there.

He grimaced. "This mean I'm out of a job?"

"You are welcome at the Silver Linings whenever you want to visit us—which I hope will be often. You're like family." Hannah squeezed his hand. "But I couldn't live with myself if something happened to you because you were trying to help me. You recover. Colin and I can pick up the slack."

Panic clawed at her. Colin was staying only a few more weeks—unless what had happened the other night drove him to leaving sooner. Whenever he departed, the end result was inevitable.

She would be alone with no help on the ranch, faulty pipes, a drastically reduced bank account and a bull with anger-management issues.

Colin strode toward the house Tuesday afternoon. It was late enough that Hannah and Evan had probably already finished lunch. He didn't want to get in Hannah's way if she was baking, but he was starving. Would she be in the kitchen? He missed watching her flit from the pantry to the sink to the stove, moving with an endearing blend of grace and precision. Like a really purposeful butterfly.

In fact, he'd missed a lot of things about her. Going a few days without any prolonged conversation with her had highlighted how much they'd been talking up until then and how much he enjoyed it. They'd discussed their days of course, comparing notes on the ranch and laying out steps for what needed to be done, but he'd fallen into the habit of confiding more personal things, too. About the hilariously irate texts Arden sent when he didn't answer his phone, about the mentor who'd influenced him to become a veterinarian, about his nightmares.

Since that first night in the house, he hadn't had any other bad dreams. Lately, the only dreams he could remember all featured Hannah.

He'd pushed her away in case she was more emotionally vulnerable than she'd realized, but it wasn't her birthday now. He quickened his pace, motivated by the thought of her in that sunny kitchen, her dimpled smile, the addictive vanilla scent that always clung to her even when she wasn't baking anything. Jogging up the steps, he hoped that the car out front belonged to a customer who would be leaving any minute with a basket of cookies or pie pan of savory quiche.

He drew up short at the sight of Hannah at her kitchen table, so close to the sandy-haired man sitting next to her that they might as well be sharing a chair. They were both staring at her laptop screen, but he knew from experience that it was possible to do that with more space between them. A week ago, it had been Colin sharing the computer with her as she made jokes about her cow slippers and helped him put together a gift basket for his brother.

"Oh, hey." Hannah glanced up, meeting his gaze. "I put away all the leftovers from lunch, but the containers are in the fridge if you want to heat something up. This is Malcolm Kilmartin."

The man glanced up long enough to nod and smile before reverting his attention to the computer.

"Kitty found him for me. Her bridge partner is his grandmother." Hannah's smile was dazzling. It was nice to see her mood had improved. With the exception of a couple of single-word responses to Evan, she'd been silent the entire drive back from the hospital yesterday. "Mal's a computer genius."

The man grinned at her. "*Genius* is a strong word. I just have some experience building websites."

"He's only been here an hour and you should see the ideas he's already come up with," Hannah enthused, doing a happy little shimmy in her chair. "I'll be able to advertise for guests in the bunkhouse and have a whole section on the site called Hannah's Homemade, where people who live locally can place baking and catering orders." She rolled her eyes. "With any luck, that will stop people like Gideon from coming to hand-deliver orders in the future."

Malcolm shrugged. "Hard to blame a guy for finding reasons to come see you."

Colin narrowed his eyes. Although he was glad the guy was helping Hannah, Colin found it difficult to like the other man. He liked him even less half an hour later when, as Hannah walked him to the door, Malcolm asked her if she might like to go with him to the town May Day festival on Saturday.

Colin's fingers tightened around the dish he was rinsing.

"Oh." Hannah sounded surprised by the invitation. "That's... Thank you. Evan and I were already planning to go with some friends. Please come say hi if you see us there."

They stepped out onto the front porch together, and Colin didn't hear the rest of what was said.

Kilmartin was the kind of man who made sense for Hannah. While Colin had been eating lunch—which wasn't the same as eavesdropping—he'd discovered that Malcolm worked part-time in an office IT department, spent the rest of his work week consulting with private clients and volunteered as a kids' basketball coach at the rec center in the neighboring town.

If Colin's sister had brought Malcolm to a family dinner back before she'd met her husband, Colin may have even approved. The man seemed easygoing and intelligent, with a sense of humor. Hannah should be with a good guy, and, so far, Malcolm seemed exactly that.

Yet for the rest of the afternoon, as Colin pounded new fence posts into the ground, he envisioned Malcolm's face every time he swung.

In theory, Annette and Hannah were chopping vegetables for a salad while the men fired up the grill Friday night. In reality, the vegetables sat untouched on the kitchen island while Hannah pulled the glass pitcher out of the freezer to refill her friend's salt-rimmed margarita glass. Ever since Henry's injury, Hannah had been experiencing a vengeful craving for steak. And Annette had been fretting because they still hadn't properly celebrated Hannah's birthday. So they'd planned a cookout for tonight.

When the Reeds arrived, the first order of business had been Evan giving them the grand tour of his HQ. Todd was so impressed he'd asked Colin to help him build a toolshed on his farm. After the adults became busy with dinner preparations, Evan remained holed up in the playhouse. The dog was with him, and he'd declared her his sidekick. Yesterday, she'd been his arch nemesis. Scarlett's response to both roles was largely the same—happily padding after Evan wherever he went and hoping he'd drop food at some point. Evan and Colin had been trying to teach her to "play dead" this week to give her a broader dramatic range.

"Here you go." Hannah poured the margarita, teasing, "But if you suck this one down as quickly as the last, you're cut off."

Annette laughed. "Don't blame me. I *had* to drink something frozen. The looks you and your cowboy were exchanging left me overheated."

"I don't know what you're talking about." She totally knew what Annette was talking about.

Something had shifted this week. Colin had stopped avoiding her, but he hadn't kissed her again, either. He'd resumed his previous schedule of eating lunch and dinner with her and Evan. It was as if he wanted things to go back to a prebirthday normal. Except, he kept watching her with barely banked heat and hunger. The atmosphere in the house felt like a storm building. She was waiting for the storm to break.

Last night, she'd passed him in the hall with a basket of laundry and her body had grazed his. He'd inhaled sharply, his desire for her palpable. It had occurred to her that *she* could act on the powerful attraction simmering between them, as she had when she'd kissed him last week. Hannah wasn't a passive person.

But she was a trained pastry chef.

Cooking was often about patience, letting flavors build and waiting for transformations to take place. One did not rush a soufflé. There was an Amish bread recipe that took ten days to make properly. People didn't prepare Baked Alaska because it was easy; they did so because it was worth the time and effort.

Besides, Colin had shared anecdotes about how Natalie had pursued him, how his sister, Natalie's co-conspirator, helped scheme ways to bring her brother and best friend together. Hannah thought Natalie sounded like a lovely person, and what had happened to her was tragic. But Hannah wasn't looking to repeat history. She wanted Colin because he was sexy and principled and talented and surprisingly funny behind that sometimes-guarded interior—not because there was anything about him that reminded her of Michael.

"I don't think the two of you kissing was a onetime thing," Annette said. "He looks at you like he could throw you down on the nearest horizontal surface at any minute."

Hannah had to admit, the unpredictability was exciting. "Between you and me, I think it helped that Malcolm was here the other day." Had Colin heard the man ask her to tomorrow's May Day festival? "Is it wrong that I like the idea of him being a little jealous? I should be more evolved than that."

"As long as it's 'a little jealous' and not 'possessive stalker,' I don't see the harm in it. When Todd took me to my tenth high school reunion, we ran into one of my old flames. Todd was perfectly polite to him, but I could tell he was battling the green-eyed monster." She grinned over the rim of her glass. "It was pretty hot, actually. And so is your cowboy."

She liked the sound of that—her cowboy. But he was careful not to belong to any person or place. In a couple of weeks, he'd be gone. He'd been very candid about having a job lined up that started after Justin's wedding. He'd made a commitment. She knew he took those seriously.

Slumping into her chair, she asked, "What am I going to do when he leaves?"

"You mean because Henry's hurt and you won't have either of them to help around here?"

"You know that's not what I meant."

Annette's expression was full of sympathy. "Maybe it would be best if the two of you stay away from horizontal surfaces between now and when he goes. Why torment yourself with a taste of something you can't have?"

"Because I think I'd rather have the memory than say goodbye to him without exploring this, without knowing how good we could be together."

She was in the prime of her life, and she hadn't had sex in over four years. It hadn't bothered her much before, because there hadn't been anyone important enough to her that she'd wanted to make love. Colin was important.

The question was, how important was she to him?

"So." Todd Reed flipped over one of the steaks on the flame. "You and Hannah?"

It was such an abrupt topic change from plans for a toolshed that Colin wondered if Todd was purposely trying to catch him off guard with the question. Stalling, Colin sipped his beer, but no simple answer came to him. "Not exactly. She's a hell of a woman, though."

Todd nodded. "If it helps, she likes you. Since she's moved here, there have been a few guys interested. Gideon, of course, but also one or two who aren't buttheads. Mostly, she's been so focused on Evan and this ranch she doesn't seem to notice." He gave Colin a level look. "You, she notices."

He flashed back to those hot kisses they'd exchanged the night of her birthday. Yeah, she noticed him. And it was mutual. All week, the tug between them had been growing stronger. At least, it had on his end. It was difficult to say what she'd been thinking since she'd snapped at him on Monday for avoiding her. He hadn't meant to hurt her feelings. He'd only needed some time and space. Now he had more of both than he knew what to do with.

"How did you and Annette meet?" he asked. He was glad to be rediscovering the art of conversation, of making friends, but he didn't want to stand there dissecting his relationship with Hannah.

"She was dating my cousin. I knew the second I saw her that I wanted to be with her, but obviously the situation was complicated. I couldn't make a move until after they broke up, and even then she thought it would be too awkward. She took some convincing." He smiled at the recollection. "The challenge of wooing her was some of the most fun I've ever had."

Colin paused to consider what wooing Hannah might entail. Making birthday plans for her had been enjoyable, but those plans had included Evan. The idea of doing something specifically for her, something intimate and romantic—

"Unfortunately," Todd continued, "Annette and I have been facing a lot of challenges lately."

"The baby thing?"

"I'm trying to support her in this, but it's starting to take over our lives. We both really want kids, but I feel like, personally, I could be happy with just her. She's enough for me. I guess she doesn't feel the same way."

As a brother with two younger siblings, Colin had dispensed tons of advice over the years. He was a little out of practice, but the stark gloom in Todd's voice motivated him to find the words.

"You may be misreading her. I know she would love to have a baby, but maybe that's not the only reason she's upset. What if she sees this as her fault, worries that she's the reason you won't get to be a father?" No one wanted to stand between the person they loved and their happiness. "Maybe deep down, she feels like you deserve better."

Todd's eyebrows shot up. "Then she'd be crazy. I can't think of anything better than finding the right person to love and knowing they love you back."

It seemed like such a simple, comforting concept. But life took agonizing twists and turns. Colin knew that love alone didn't guarantee happiness. Perhaps that was why he'd been holding back with Hannah. He knew he couldn't offer her any guarantees.

Then again, since no one else could honestly offer them, either, what good did it do to keep his distance?

Chapter 11

It was so late when the Reeds left on Friday night that it was technically Saturday. Hannah flopped back on the sofa with a yawn. She'd had a great time, but now she was bone-tired. Far too exhausted to make it to her bed. *Maybe I'll just crash here.*

She always enjoyed Todd and Annette's company, but they'd been a welcome buffer tonight against the tension between her and Colin. And the longer they stayed, the more she'd gradually relaxed and enjoyed herself. The margaritas hadn't hurt. Todd had declined to try them because he had to drive home, which had made Hannah sigh, thinking of all the empty space upstairs. Lord knew when she would be ready for paying guests.

"Sure you don't want to stay the night?" she'd offered. "I am the proud owner of shiny new pipes that cost a fortune. I feel like more people should be using the second-story bathrooms now."

After dinner, she'd put aside her plumbing woes. They'd played a couple of kid-friendly games with Evan. After he'd been tucked into bed, they'd switched to poker for pretzel sticks and other card games that included a lot of good-natured trash talk. When Hannah had gone to put everything back in the closet, Annette had caught sight of the Clue board game, which led to lots of funny quotes from the movie. Even though it was after ten by then, the women had talked the guys into watching the DVD. A wonderful evening—but since she'd rolled out of bed at 5:00 a.m. to bake and decorate cupcakes, she was now thoroughly fatigued.

"Hannah?"

The voice startled her, and she sprang into a sitting position to find Colin leaning against the wall watching her. Oh dear heaven, he was shirtless. His damp hair was slicked away from his face, and he wore a pair of his usual drawstring pajama pants.

She made a valiant effort to unstick her tongue from the roof of her mouth. "I thought you'd gone to bed."

"Not yet." He grinned lazily. "I went up to shower and put those 'shiny new pipes' to good use. When I came back down, I wasn't sure I should bother you. You looked as if you might be asleep."

"In another three seconds, I would've been." She yawned again, covering her face with her hand.

"Well, since you haven't conked out yet, I wanted to ask you a question. Will you go to the festival with me?"

The request took her by surprise. He'd barely said anything when she and the Reeds discussed the festival earlier tonight, deciding where and when they would meet tomorrow afternoon. It would be Hannah and Evan's first time at the annual event, and Annette had recommended her favorite vendors as well as the best spinning rides to make Evan squeal with glee and make Hannah want to throw up.

"Sure," she stammered, realizing it was taking her far too long to reply. She blamed the contours of his shirtless chest. "If you want to come with me and Evan, we—"

"I don't just want to go with you. I want to take you. As in, a date. Between a man and a woman. And, obviously, her adorable four-year-old son," he added ruefully. "I don't want you to think of this as a friend or employee tagging along. I wish I could pick you up, that I had something to drive other than my motorcycle. So I guess I'm asking if I can take you out *and* if I can borrow your truck."

"A date?" She knew he'd said lots of other words, too, but that one had jumped out at her.

With a nod, he moved toward her. "Yeah. The kind where I tell you that you look nice, then I win you a large, fuzzy stuffed animal at an overpriced game booth and kiss you at the end of the night."

"Yes." Her heart was slamming against her rib cage. "I'd like to go on a date with you."

He gave her a brilliant smile. Then he leaned down, and she forgot to breathe. Had he decided not to wait for that good-night kiss? Because she was very okay with that. He lifted her hand and pressed a kiss above her knuckles. "Good night, Hannah."

How was she going to wait until tomorrow? And how on earth was she supposed to sleep now?

* * *

Vegetable soup might never be Evan's favorite lunch, but Hannah wanted to make sure her son got something resembling vitamins in his system before he started filling up on funnel cake and cotton candy. While he dawdled over his lunch, Hannah went to change. She was donating three freshly baked cakes as prizes for the cakewalk and hadn't wanted to risk getting frosting or batter on her dark sundress. When she returned to the kitchen, Evan scowled at her.

"You're in a dress." He said it like an accusation. "Do I hafta wear fancy clothes?"

She laughed. "No, you're fine the way you are." He was in boots, jeans and a T-shirt with a cowboy character from one of his favorite animated movies. She fought the urge to self-consciously double-check her reflection. Was she too fancy for an outdoor, small-town festival? She'd put on a long black cotton dress printed with small yellow daisies, paired with a light-weight denim jacket and boots. *Are you really going to take fashion criticism from a four-year-old?*

So what if she'd taken some extra time to curl her hair before pulling it into a bouncy ponytail? It wasn't as though she'd applied full makeup, only mascara and cranberry-colored lip gloss. Besides, isn't this what women did on dates, expended a little effort on behalf of a guy they liked?

When it was time to go an hour later, she was gratified to see that Colin had dressed a bit nicer than usual, too. He was wearing his best pair of jeans—what did it say about her that she knew his collection of jeans by heart?—and a button-down blue shirt, rolled up to expose sun-bronzed forearms. He was helping her carefully situate the cake boxes in the truck when Evan gave a small cry of dismay.

"I forgot my hat, Mommy!"

She unlocked the door for him and he raced to his room, returning with a black felt cowboy hat Henry had given him when she and Evan first moved here.

Evan mashed it on his head as he got into the truck. "Now I'm like you, Colin!"

Hannah had noticed that, somewhere around her birthday, Evan's new idol had stopped being "Mr. Colin." The boundaries were definitely shifting.

It was a beautiful day. They rolled down the windows and all three sang along to Hannah's CDs. She'd heard Colin whistle or hum as he worked, but this was the first time she'd really heard his singing voice.

She was impressed. "You're good."

"Mom used to insist I got her voice, like I got her talent for drawing, but we all knew she was kidding." He chuckled fondly. "That woman couldn't carry a tune in a bucket. When she belted out Christmas carols, the neighborhood dogs buried their heads in the snow."

Hannah laughed at that, wondering absently what stories Evan would someday tell about her. Hopefully, he'd be able to say that she'd taught him about perseverance and the value of positive thinking. She wanted Evan to believe in himself and have the courage to follow his dreams.

Since pretty much the entire town turned out for the May Day festival, parking was an ordeal. After dropping off the cakes at the designated delivery area, they circled back block by block until they found a lot with open space. Hannah half expected her son to complain about the long walk, but he was too spellbound by the sight of the giant inflatables and large rides temporarily dotting the familiar landscape. By far the biggest attraction was a looming Ferris wheel at the center of the festival.

Evan craned his head all the way back, looking up with wide eyes. "I am not going on that."

Hannah squeezed his shoulders in a sideways hug. "You wouldn't like it anyway—it doesn't go fast enough for you." She knew from their trip to Heritage Square that he was a speed demon. He loved amusement parks. The only obstacle to his joy was frustration that he wasn't tall enough to ride every attraction.

They stopped at a booth to purchase a thick roll of tickets for the rides and games.

"What first?" Colin asked.

As expected, Evan asked for rides, jumping up and down enthusiastically to make his point. But they had to cross a midway en route to the closest ride, and he got distracted by the noises and sights, sucked in by the barkers' calls to win prizes.

Colin gravitated toward a booth where players threw darts in an attempt to pop colorful balloons spread across a corkboard wall. "My kind of game," he said, grinning. "You're looking at a two-time Peak's Pints dart champion. Our local bar back home," he said in answer to Hannah's quizzical expression. He ruffled Evan's hair. "You want to try?"

Colin exchanged two tickets for three darts and was handing them to Evan when he froze, his gaze contrite. "Sorry," he said to Hannah. "Probably should have asked if it was all right before I gave your kid sharp projectiles."

She laughed. "You have my blessing."

"That's a relief." He nudged Evan with his elbow and said in a stage whisper, "After this, we'll try running with scissors."

"Why?" Evan asked, his tone perplexed.

"Not really," Colin said. "It was a joke."

"Oh. It wasn't very funny. Knock-knock jokes are better."

Evan picked up his first dart, and Colin knelt down, helping him aim. The boy didn't put enough force behind his first throw, and it didn't even make it halfway to the wall. He did better with his second try and, with some assistance from Colin, popped a lime-green balloon on his third, winning a plastic horse.

When Colin offered to win something for Hannah, she suggested they postpone that for later in the day so that they wouldn't be carrying it for hours on end. "The horse fits in my purse," she said. "A giant teddy bear won't."

They navigated through the boisterous crowd and finally made their way to one of those awful "spinny rides of dooms," as she called them. It looked like a giant egg that had been cut in half to allow for passengers. The three of them squeezed onto the bench seat with Evan in the middle, and the attendant secured the small metal gate meant to ensure their safety.

Evan wiggled his body, too excited to sit still. "This is gonna be great!"

Then the buzzer sounded and the whirling began, and Hannah had a brief thought about the things mothers endured for the happiness of their children. Although she had to admit that this particular ride wasn't bad. Oh, it went on forever and Evan was screeching the entire time and the crazed looping, dipping pattern was every bit as nausea-inducing as she remembered. But Colin had his arm around the back of the seat, his fingers sliding over the nape of her neck, and the sensations that caused were so enjoyable she almost gave in to Evan's demand of "Again! Again! Again!" when the ride ended.

Colin laughed. "Pace yourself. We're going to be here until the fireworks tonight, so maybe we should see what else they have that we want to spend our tickets on, okay? We can always come back..." Frowning, he glanced at his phone, then tucked it back in his pocket.

"Everything okay?" Hannah asked as they exited the gated ride area.

He nodded. "My sister. Again. She's a little hyper-committed to staying in touch."

"Sounds nice, speaking as someone who's never had any siblings, hyper or otherwise." Sometimes she felt bad for Evan, an only child with no dad. Was she enough family for him, all by herself? But she brushed away the maudlin thought.

Colin gave her a sheepish look. "Didn't mean to sound ungrateful for having a sister who cares about me so much. I love Arden. I'll call her back when I'm not surrounded by so much background noise."

They passed by a corral where kids were getting pony rides, and Colin offered to stop if Evan wanted to participate.

Evan shot them the kind of disgruntled look Hannah expected to see a lot during his teenage years, along with the single-word caption *lame*. "I don't want to ride tiny horses. I want to ride Viper! I know I'm not big enough to ride him by myself, but can you take me, Colin?"

"We'll see."

Hannah got a text from the Reeds that they were running late, so they killed some time in the funhouse. Evan enjoyed the crooked walkways and trick mirrors. His favorite was one that had a normal reflection from the center of the room, but the closer you got, the taller you appeared. He went back and forth, laughing at his dramatic growth spurt. When he got back to where she and Colin stood in the middle, he linked hands with each of them. Reflected back at her were a good-looking man, a little boy having the time of his life and a woman who was dangerously close to being happy. They looked too much like a family, like a dream too treacherous to pursue.

Seeing so clearly what she wished she could have— what she wished she could give her son—caused a lump in her throat. "Need some air," she told the guys before dashing outside. "Feeling a little claustrophobic in here."

According to loan officers, there was a high probability her plan to turn an old ranch house into a tourist destination would fail. But better to channel her time and energy into something that had a chance than to try to build a future with a man still recovering from his past. She planned to make the most of her time with Colin and would try to view it as a gift. But then she'd have to let him go.

A live band played inside a large tent with tiny white lights strung all around. It had been Annette's suggestion to come in and enjoy the music since none of the adults wanted to brave any zooming, zigzagging rides after eating dinner. They still had another hour until the fireworks display.

Within minutes, they'd found a table, although Evan had to share a seat with his mom. They piled the tabletop with purchases, including the carved wooden eagle Hannah had bought Henry as a get-well present, and prizes. True to his word, Colin had won Hannah a giant stuffed animal. Now she just had to figure out the proper place in the house for a lime-green octopus that was roughly the same size as Evan.

Annette sighed happily. "Nice to get off my feet for a few minutes after covering every square inch of the festival." Yet she was tapping her toes with enough vigor to jostle the table, keeping time with the lively song, and there was a wistful quality to her expression as she watched the couples spinning across the portable dance floor.

Hannah nudged Todd with her shoulder. He gave her a quizzical look, but then comprehension dawned.

He leaned over and kissed his wife on the cheek. "Dance with me, gorgeous?"

When they came back, Annette's cheeks were flushed and her eyes were shining. "I don't know why we don't do that more," she told her husband.

"From now on, we'll make a point of it," he promised.

Annette smiled. "Your turn, Hannah! We can watch Evan if you and Colin want to—" She broke off, interrupting herself. "Do you dance, Colin?"

He responded slowly, as if he wasn't sure of the answer. "I used to, but it's been a long time."

"At the very least, we know you can dip me," Hannah said, thinking of the bowling alley.

He grinned. "Well, that's a start. I'm game if you are." Rising from his chair, he took her hand. His thumb brushed back and forth over the spot he'd kissed last night, and a tremor of anticipation went through her.

She clasped one hand in his and slid the other above his waist, and everything else faded to black. She doubted that her rhythm was right because she could barely hear the music over her own heartbeat. He may have even stepped on her toes, but she couldn't feel anything beyond his hand at the small of her back. She wished it was a slow dance, so that she had a reasonable excuse to press herself against him, even with friends and family watching, but she made the best of the situation. It wasn't difficult to find a bright side when Colin was holding her.

The song was over too quickly, and she tried not to feel despondent as she returned to their table.

"We've been talking," Annette said, "and the three of us want ice cream. What if Todd and I take Evan, and we'll meet the two of you for fireworks?"

Which would give Hannah and Colin at least half an hour alone. Annette really was the best friend ever.

"*Please,* Mommy! Can I have a cone with just one scoop?"

He'd already had plenty of junk food today, but she supposed she could make an exception since the May Day festival came only once a year. She tried very hard not to think about Easter baskets, trick-or-treat bags, Christmas stockings or any of the other year-round opportunities to get cavities.

She took an extra moment to give the illusion of

deliberation, then nodded. Her friends were even thoughtful enough to take all the stuff with them, Todd carrying the octopus atop his shoulders as if it was a young child. But the Reeds were so busy shuffling everything that they didn't realize Todd's wallet had dropped. Luckily, Colin spotted it before he took Hannah for another spin around the dance floor.

"Be back in just a sec," he told her, hurrying after them.

She was watching him walk away—and enjoying the view—when someone tapped her on the shoulder. She turned, half expecting Malcolm Kilmartin. Though she'd told him to look for her at the fair, she hadn't seen him all day. She wasn't looking at him now, either. Instead, she found herself face-to-face with Gideon Loomis.

Her mouth twisted. What did he want? "Hello, Gideon." Every time she saw the man, he wore a different cowboy hat. Tonight's was a black Stetson with a studded band.

"You owe me a dance," he informed her.

"How do you figure?"

"I won a cake of yours today." He put his booted foot on the empty chair beside her and winked. "Since you're responsible for the calories, it's only fair you help me work some of them off. Preemptively, so to speak."

Why did all of the man's attempts at flirting make her want to smack him with a rolling pin? Even though she'd been planning to dance, now she wanted to escape the tent. "I'm pretty beat. Comes with trying to keep up with a four-year-old all day. So—"

He grabbed her hand and tugged. "Hannah, Hannah,

Hannah. When are you going to learn?" He chortled. "Loomises don't take 'no' for an answer."

"Do they take painkillers?" Colin asked mildly. "Because you're going to need one if you put your hands on her again."

Yanking her hand free, Hannah stood, putting herself between the two men. She should probably be appalled by the indirect threat of violence, but mostly she was just glad Colin had returned. "I was explaining to Gideon that I'm getting tired and was thinking about going elsewhere."

"Sounds good to me," Colin agreed. He shot Gideon one last fulminating glare. "It's too crowded in here."

As they emerged into the cool night air, Hannah jabbed him in the ribs. "Not that I'm ungrateful for the timely interruption, but you cannot go around threatening to beat up anyone who annoys me."

He ducked his head. "You're right. But don't you think me popping him one on the nose would be more humane than letting you Taser him?"

She laughed. "Let's just agree to avoid Gideon when possible. Although, I'm sorry we left the tent."

"I'm not," he said cheerfully.

"No?" Maybe he hadn't enjoyed the physical proximity of their dance as much as she had. There was a depressing thought.

"I have something else I want to do with you." Mischief laced his tone. "Without Evan around."

"Um...what did you have in mind?"

"You'll see." He reached for her hand. "Come on, Hazel Eyes, this'll be fun."

Ten minutes later, they were handing their tickets to the attendant at the Ferris wheel. It was all lit up for the night, and the garish lights of the carnival were prettier than they should have been. When she climbed into the suspended bucket, it immediately rocked back and forth. The motion didn't bother her when they were at ground level. Once they were one hundred feet in the air, however, she had a slightly more nervous reaction to the swinging. Wind curled around them, and she clutched Colin's hand.

He grinned, tightening his hold on her. "Maybe I should have taken you into the haunted house. That could have been fun. But this," he said as they rotated to the very top and stopped there, "is perfect."

His playful smile dissolved into something more intent, and he cupped his hand around the nape of her neck. She met him halfway, clashing in a hot, open-mouthed kiss. They were as hungry for each other as lovers who'd been separated for months. Throughout the day, wanting him had been a kind of sweet, heavy ache inside her, but now it sharpened to piercing need. Her fingers were meshed in his hair, her chest pressed to his when the bucket lurched. She realized they were moving backward, but she couldn't bring herself to break away yet. He kissed her all the way down.

They finally broke apart, and if she hadn't been too breathless to speak, she might have invoked her son's festival motto. *Again, again, again!*

He took her hand and helped her to her feet, not bothering to let go once she stood. They walked hand in hand to where they were supposed to meet the Reeds, and Hannah gave him a sidelong smile. After that explosive kiss, though, the glittery flare of fireworks was going to be a little anticlimactic.

* * *

Evan fell asleep in the backseat of the truck before they'd even left the parking lot. Smiling, Hannah studied him from the passenger seat. He looked so serene, it was hard to reconcile him with the noisy little boy who'd thrown a fit when he'd discovered he was an inch too short to ride something called The Toxic Blaster.

She'd helped him pull off his boots while Colin started the truck, and his hat hung crookedly from his head. "He can just sleep in his clothes tonight," she said. Then she scowled, rethinking her decision. "Although I guess I should probably wake him to brush his teeth after all that junk food, huh?"

"It's one night. And you did give him that piece of plaque-fighting gum during the fireworks show."

She laughed at his earnest tone, not sure a stick of gum qualified her for Mother of the Year. "Oh, well. I'll make him brush twice as long tomorrow."

When they got to the ranch, Colin volunteered, "I'll get him. You're the one with the house keys."

She pulled them out of her purse and unlocked the door, pausing to shoo Scarlett outside for the night while Colin carried Evan to his room. When she joined them a few minutes later, he'd tucked Evan beneath the blankets and was standing by his bed with a heart-rending expression on his face. She wasn't sure she'd ever seen joy and sadness comingled so poignantly.

Swallowing back a tide of emotion, she passed him to drop a kiss on Evan's forehead. Then she took Colin's hand. "I know it's been a long day," she whispered, "but is it too late for that second dance?"

He shook his head. "I'd like that."

Her purse was on the end table in the living room,

and she pulled out her phone, scrolling through her playlist until she found something appropriate. The music wasn't very loud, but it was enough for barefoot dancing in her living room, illuminated only by the spill of light from a tabletop lamp. Now that they were free of an audience, she put one hand on his shoulder and fit her body to his. It was closer than they'd been all day, but it still wasn't enough. Heat thrummed through her as they swayed, the friction of his jeans erotic through the soft cotton of her skirt. He was tracing his fingers up and down the length of her spine in a slow, sensuous manner that would have been relaxing if it weren't so arousing. Electric shivers broke out over her skin.

She craved his kiss like a drug, but not even standing on her tiptoes would bridge the gap between them. "Colin." His name was somewhere between a plea and a reprimand. "You did promise me a kiss at the end of the date."

His lips quirked in a wicked half smile. "Are you sure you want this to be the end?"

Chapter 12

Hannah's face was covered in a fiery blush, but she was smiling at his bold question. He found it impossible to look away from her mouth. The memory of how she'd kissed him on the Ferris wheel had him hard all over again.

"I don't want this to be over," she admitted. "I want you."

He cleared this throat. "Then maybe we should move to another room. One with doors." Once he got her out of that dress, he might not notice if a marching band came through the room.

She nodded. "Upstairs?"

His self-control lasted only until they reached the hallway at the top of the stairs. He backed her against the wall, holding her hands on each side of her head, fingers laced together, and devoured her with kisses.

When he nipped at her throat, she arched her neck to give him better access. He released her hands long enough to remove her jacket, which crumpled to the floor with a soft thud. Her dress was long, but loose enough to give her freedom of movement. She hooked a leg behind his thigh, and he was cradled against her. For a second, he lost himself in the mindless bliss, rocking his hips and loving the sexy whimper that escaped her.

They might have made love there against the wall if they hadn't bumped a framed picture, knocking it askew and bringing him to his senses. His bed was around the corner and presented fewer safety hazards. He could wait the extra few seconds to be inside her. Maybe.

He stripped off his shirt on the way. When they reached the side of his bed, he gave her ponytail a light tug. "Take this down?"

She humored him, removing the elastic band with nimble fingers, and her hair spilled over her shoulders, framing her face. God, she was beautiful. He felt for a zipper on the back of her dress, but there wasn't one. She gathered the material at the hem and worked it upward, revealing her curvy body one dizzying millimeter at a time. She wore a satiny black bra and panties. The deceptively simple lingerie was a lot like the woman—not fussy, but feminine and stunning.

He cupped her breasts, running his thumbs over the tight peaks. She trembled so violently he was afraid she might stumble.

She seemed embarrassed by the intensity of her reaction. "Sorry."

"Don't be." It was powerful, knowing how he affected her.

She gave him a slight smile. "It's been so long, I…"

The last thing he wanted to do right now was talk, yet he heard himself ask, "Has there been anyone? Since…" It would be less complicated if she said yes. Four-plus years of celibacy was a lot of pressure.

Yet when she shook her head, he felt a rush of fierce joy. He was irrationally glad she'd waited for him.

He sat on the mattress and reached for her hips, pulling her into his lap. Unfastening the front clasp of her bra, he peeled back the silky fabric. He'd dreamed about Hannah like this, but the reality of her was incomparable.

He trailed his fingers across her bare breasts, then kissed a path from her collarbone to one nipple, sucking hard. She writhed against him. They rolled over on the bed, Colin impatiently shedding his jeans with one hand. Earlier in the week, he'd given in to the impulse to buy condoms, then called himself a fool the entire drive back to the ranch. Now the small foil packets in the nightstand seemed like his most valuable possession.

But first he needed to know that she was ready. Kissing her greedily, he lowered one hand to the slick folds between her thighs. She arched off the bed as he stroked her, her soft cries urging him on. The feel of her, the sound of her, was addictive. She tightened her grip on his shoulders. Her body stiffened and she threw her head back, her expression rapturous.

He sheathed himself in the condom and slid inside her, momentarily overwhelmed by how damn good she felt. She tilted her hips, silently asking for more, which he happily gave. They moved together, faster, more urgently, until the pleasure blotted out everything else. His blood roared in his ears, and he heard his own hoarse shout as if from a distance. Then he collapsed against her, holding her tight as if she were the most precious thing in the world. The way he felt at that moment shook him to the core.

They held each other in silence, and he was more content than he could remember feeling in over a year. But eventually, he was going to need to say something. He rolled away from her, uncertain. Most of the words that came to mind were too trite to encompass what they'd shared.

He simultaneously wanted to gauge her reaction and give her space. If *he* was this dazed, what must she be experiencing? It had been longer for her since she'd been with anyone and, on the whole, women were more emotional than men. What if she—

"That was amazing!" She sat up, unself-conscious in her nudity, and beamed at him. "We should do that again sometime. I feel…" She gave him a quick hug. "Did I mention *amazing?*" Then she climbed out of the bed.

He was surprised by her agility. He felt so wrung out he could barely move. In disbelief, he watched her shimmy into her dress, not bothering with her bra. Her denim jacket was still out in the hall somewhere.

He propped himself up on one elbow. "Where are you going?"

"To bake."

"At this hour?" Shouldn't she be mellow and sleepy? "You seem pretty keyed up. A less secure guy might worry you didn't enjoy yourself enough."

She leaned over and kissed him soundly on the mouth. "Oh, I enjoyed myself. Twice! Good sex is just really invigorating, don't you think?"

"Uh-huh."

"What may look like manic energy to you is actually a huge compliment, I promise." She blew him a kiss, then she was gone.

He blinked at the empty space in the room where she'd been standing a moment ago. Well. That was unexpected. No emotional drama, no need to talk things through, not even any freaking cuddling. He was relieved, of course, thankful she'd kept things so simple and light. It would be best this way for both of them.

He turned on his side and punched his pillow, trying to get comfortable. She'd seemed so unbothered about leaving him mere minutes after making such an intimate connection. It was almost discouraging. Then again…at least he knew for future reference that they were on the same page. They could make love without his worrying that she had the wrong idea about his long-term plans.

Maybe she was right—there was always a bright side.

It took about ten minutes for reason to catch up with the endorphins. Hannah stood at the kitchen island, eyeing ingredients that she shouldn't have pulled out. Once she put something in the oven, she wouldn't be able to go to bed until it was finished baking, and she'd barely had any sleep last night. Since she'd spent most of her day at the fair, she had a lot to catch up on tomorrow. *You need rest.*

But she hadn't been able to help her euphoric reaction. After a release like that, she'd felt as if she could fly.

In the past, Michael had teased that "normal" people didn't get that energized after orgasms. The way she saw it, her reaction was like a runner's high. Except what she and Colin had done was way more fun than running.

Still, now that a little bit of time had passed, she acknowledged that the wiser course of action would be to go to bed. She packed the baking ingredients back into the pantry and took a shower. Although the warm water helped relax her some, her mind was still racing.

She carried her phone into the bedroom and texted Annette You awake? Almost instantly, the cell phone rang. Hannah grinned. "I'll take that as a yes."

"Everything okay?" Annette asked.

"Wonderful." She scooted down beneath the covers. "Maybe that's the problem—it's been such a nice day that, subconsciously, I don't want it to end."

"If you're too restless to sleep, I vote you go upstairs and ask that cowboy of yours to do something about it."

"Um." Heat prickled in her cheeks. "Funny you should say that."

"Are you *kidding* me? Wow. I told Todd the two of you looked awfully cozy during the fireworks display! How do we feel about it finally happening? Excited? Regretful?"

How could she regret something so perfect? "I haven't felt this alive in... Well, it's been a while." Satisfaction had given her a potent buzz. She felt womanly and desirable and centered. "But I'm really rusty at this. I may have handled the afterglow part badly.

I thanked him, then ran off to make cookies. Is that weird?"

"Yes."

"Annette!"

"There was a hot naked guy in the bed, and you voluntarily left? I'm sorry, but that's weird."

Had Colin wanted her to stay? Or had he been glad she didn't stick around, crowding him? It was disconcerting, to have been so physically attuned to someone yet still be left guessing what was going on in his mind.

And perhaps that was the real reason she'd sprinted out of there. Was she afraid to find out what he'd been thinking? If he'd told her he thought it was a mistake, she would have been devastated.

"I've been single a long time," she reminded Annette. "I'm not sure I remember how to do this."

"Colin's coming over to help Todd tomorrow with that shed. Do you want me to ask my husband to subtly—"

"No!" Having Annette ask her husband to do some digging on what Colin had thought of the evening, then report back, was immature, if not downright cowardly. "I will muddle my way through this without turning it into a group project."

"Fair enough." Annette sounded disappointed. "Don't overthink it too much, okay? First times can be awkward. Next time..."

Would there be a next time?

Colin had come so far from the haunted outsider who had changed her tire, but would he retreat after what they'd done? In the wake of their first kiss, he'd barely spoken to her for two days. It was possible he'd once again revert to a withdrawn loner. *I won't let that happen*. He deserved joy and laughter and playfulness in his life.

That rainy Wednesday night when Colin had first come here, she'd told Annette it was destiny, a sign that her positive thinking was working and that she could make the ranch a success. Which was a very self-involved analysis of the situation. Maybe fate had brought him here not because *she* needed help, but because he did.

Colin slept so deeply that waking up was disorienting. He had to think about where he was and what day it was. But his first clear thought, aided by the wafting scent of coffee, was *Hannah*. Today was Sunday, which meant a big sit-down breakfast. After what had happened last night, he didn't know if Evan's presence at the table would make facing Hannah more or less awkward.

There was only one way to find out, though.

After a brief shower, he joined the Shaws downstairs in the kitchen. Hannah glanced up from the waffle iron when she heard his footsteps. She immediately looked away but then, resolutely, met his gaze. He could almost hear her inner pep talk as she told herself she had no reason to be nervous.

Colin wished someone would give *him* a pep talk. He was nervous as hell.

Evan, however, suffered from no anxiety. "Morning!" His greeting was crunchy around a bite of bacon. "Can we ride Viper today, Colin?"

"Sorry, but I won't be here. I have ranch chores all morning, then I'm helping your uncle Todd with a project this afternoon."

"But—"

"Evan, stop talking with your mouth full," Hannah reprimanded, handing Colin a cup of coffee.

Before taking it, he ran his thumb over her wrist, needing some physical contact no matter how slight. "Thank you." He glanced around the kitchen, unable to resist teasing her. "I was expecting piles of cupcakes and brownies."

"I did pull everything out of the pantry." She twisted her lips in a self-mocking scowl. "But then I realized I was behaving like a nutcase, so I took a shower and went to bed. Sorry to be so...me."

He shook his head. "If there's one thing you don't *ever* need to apologize for, it's being you."

Her smile heated through him faster than the coffee, and, if Evan weren't sitting ten feet away, he'd be kissing her already.

The phone buzzing in his pocket helped break the mood, and he retrieved it, expecting Todd's call. But Arden's number showed up on the screen, making Colin wince. He declined the call, knowing she'd leave a message.

Watching him, Hannah opened her mouth to speak, then closed it. Then opened it again.

"It was my sister."

She nodded. "I suspected as much. I just don't— You know what? None of my business." She handed him a plate with a fresh waffle on it. "Although, you did say yesterday you were planning to call her back."

Eventually, he would. Talking to Arden, however, was something that required mental preparation, like the Graduate Record Examination to get into vet school. There were trick questions and awkward fill-in-the-blanks where he struggled to find the words to convince her he was fine and she should stop worrying so much. Most of the time, that required a lot of prevarication on his part.

Truthfully, he *was* doing better now.

But if he told Arden that, she would want details, would want to dissect his life in Bingham Pass. Whatever was developing between him and Hannah was excruciatingly new and raw. He wasn't ready to discuss it with anyone, much less Natalie's best friend.

He and Hannah had shared something important. Keeping it between them, protected from the outside world and isolated in the moment—away from painful pasts or uncertain futures—felt like the only way to safeguard it so they could enjoy it a little longer.

After breakfast, Colin complimented Hannah lavishly on her cooking in place of other things he wanted to say but couldn't in front of her son. However, when he came back to the house to grab a quick lunch a few hours later, Evan was playing in his room.

Hannah looked up from the huge sheet cake she was frosting. "Headed to the Reeds' now?"

"In a minute. There's just one thing I need to do first." Gripping her shoulders, he bent down and kissed her. She melted against him, sighing into his mouth as he deepened the kiss. When he straightened, he said, "Your baking is the best I've ever had, but you are more delicious than anything that comes out of this kitchen."

"Flatterer." Pleasure glinted in her bright eyes, reminding him of the way she'd looked at him last night as they eagerly helped each other undress.

With effort, he reminded himself that Evan could interrupt at any moment and that Todd was waiting.

"I don't know exactly how long I'll be gone, but I should be ho—" A pang hit him. No matter how comfortable he was growing with Hannah and Evan, this wasn't his home. They weren't his family. "I should be back by dinner."

"Okay." Her voice carefully casual, she asked, "What about after dinner? Any special plans for tonight?"

The smile she gave him sent need roaring through him. His mouth went dry, and he had to swallow before answering. "I'm at your disposal. Just tell me what needs to be done."

"Oh, I don't know." She peered up through her lashes. "Last night, you did an excellent job figuring that out with no instruction from me. I'm confident you will again."

As he left the house, Colin spared a quick mental apology to Todd. There was only one thing Colin would be able to concentrate on today, and it was not building a shed that was structurally sound.

A thin sliver of moonlight shone through the window, lighting where her fingers were laced with Colin's. They were both lying on their sides, with his arm around her. Hannah couldn't see his expression, but the teasing note in his voice made it easy to imagine.

"I should probably let you go so you can alphabetize your spice rack or spackle holes in a guest-room wall," he said.

Was he never going to let her live down that first night? They'd been together four times since then, and although sex with him still gave her an incredible rush, she'd never left again with such a frantically awkward goodbye.

"It's uncouth to mock a woman while she's naked," she said primly. "And for the record, my spice rack is already alphabetized."

That made him laugh, a rumble that went through his chest and vibrated against her back. "You're right, I shouldn't mock you," he said, not sounding the least bit sorry. But he made up for it by trailing his fingers through her hair. He toyed with the strands and massaged her neck until she was thoroughly relaxed and drowsy. It would be so easy to close her eyes and drift off for a little while.

It wasn't until she jerked herself awake with a sharp jolt that she realized she'd actually started to doze. She should be in her bed. What if Evan called out for her in the middle of the night, or even came looking for her? And heaven forbid she accidentally stay here until morning. It wasn't just a question of what her son would think, either. She didn't know how Colin would react if she spent the night in his arms. It would alter the pattern they'd developed, their unspoken agreement.

During the day, they went about their work separately and kept their relationship scrupulously platonic. But she lived for that moment when, once Evan was asleep, Colin held out his hand and silently led her up the stairs. She hadn't fully realized how much she'd begun looking forward to that until she'd come up yesterday morning to work on one of the guest rooms. The simple act of walking up the staircase had left her besieged with mental images of them together.

And now it was time to go back down those stairs, to reality. With a sigh, she pulled away from him.

He kissed her shoulder. "Leaving?"

She nodded, half wishing he'd try to talk her out of it, at least for a few more minutes. "I need to go." But it was getting more difficult every time she did it.

When she heard the front door open downstairs Saturday afternoon, Hannah experienced a twinge of vanity, wishing she'd had time to clean up after the past two hours of painting an upstairs bedroom. She knew she had flecks of pale peach on her denim shorts and her arms. With the weather becoming increasingly warm, she was wearing a tank top. Her hair was piled on her head and haphazardly secured with an elastic band. It was not her most glamorous look.

Yet when she reached the bottom step, Colin grinned, looking every bit as pleased to see her as he did when she wore a dress and makeup.

"Just the lady I was looking for. I figured everyone would be in the kitchen." He cocked his head, taking in the quiet. "Did you and Evan eat lunch already?"

Passing by him, she shook her head, relishing her secret too much to share it yet. "Nope." She detoured to the front door and let Scarlett outside to run around the ranch. Hannah might have to bathe a muddy dog later, but making sure the dog didn't interrupt them would be worth it. "Hungry?"

"I could eat." Lowering his voice, he added, "But mostly I just want to be in a room with you for a while."

In the kitchen, she poured herself some water while Colin pulled meat and cheese out of the refrigerator. She downed the water, then shared her news. "It'll just be you and me for lunch today. Evan isn't here. Annette borrowed him as her 'excuse to see an animated movie.' They left for a matinee about fifteen minutes ago."

Colin had gone completely still. "We have the house to ourselves?"

"For at least two hours." She felt as wickedly liberated as a teenager whose parents left her alone for the weekend.

His lips curved in that slow grin she'd come to love so much. "And you were going to let me waste part of it with a sandwich?" He advanced on her, scooping her into his arms. Laughter burbled through her, accompanied by need.

When he reached the bottom of the stairs, she said breathlessly, "My room's closer."

Moments later, he was laying her across her bed. But he didn't immediately join her. Instead, he stood, staring so intently that she squirmed beneath the scrutiny.

"What? Paint smears on my face?"

"No. I'm taking a second to savor the reality. I think about you down here sometimes, after you leave my room. There's just one thing…" He slid his fingers through her hair and carefully removed the elastic band, spreading the dark waves in a cascade across her pillow. "Perfect."

"A sweaty woman in cutoffs and speckled with Apricot Sorbet?" She smirked. "I think you may be confused about the definition of perfection."

He pulled off his boots, then rolled onto the bed with her, smiling into her eyes. "If I am, it's only because you redefine the word every day."

His words were like wine, making her light-headed

with their sweetness. She tilted her face toward his, expecting a kiss, but he was preoccupied with inching up her tank top. It occurred to her that, previously, Colin had seen her body only in the dark. Now midday sun streamed through her windows. She had mixed feelings about that, but she got distracted when his fingers began following the path of his gaze, circling her stomach, dipping over her navel, teasing the underside of her breasts.

Arousal shimmered through her, her body liquid with it. But why should he be the only one who got to explore? This was a new opportunity for her as well as him. She let him raise the tank top over her arms, but then caught his hands when he reached for her bra.

"Your turn." Her voice came out in a husky command. "Lose the shirt, cowboy."

He was quick to oblige. She swallowed at the strong shoulders and chiseled chest he bared. If the man wanted to know the definition of perfection, all he had to do was look in a mirror. *And I have free reign to touch him.* Giddy with sensual power, she pushed against him with both hands, guiding him onto his back. She straddled him, then went up on her knees to slide off her denim shorts and kick them free.

Colin watched, rapt, his desire for her etched on his face. His obvious appreciation emboldened her. Eyes locked on his, she slowly removed her bra. He groaned, pulling her down for a hot kiss. Working together, they unfastened and removed his jeans. With his hands on her hips, he started to navigate her back atop him, but she had other ideas. They had two hours, and she wanted to make them count. She leisurely kissed her way down his chest and over the taut plane of his abdomen until she reached his erection. His hips bucked, her name a strangled cry on his lips.

By the time she finally seated herself on him, he let her set the pace for only a few minutes before rolling them both over and driving into her with desperate longing. Sensation tingled from the tips of her toes to the top of her head, and her climax was so explosive she felt as if she'd been flung from her body.

Once her vision returned to normal and she was no longer seeing bright red starbursts, her usual postorgasmic delirious energy flooded her. She sat, grinning down at the big, strong cowboy who looked completely poleaxed.

"Still want that sandwich?" she asked. She was starving.

"Forget the sandwich." His breathing was ragged. "What I really need is medical attention."

She chuckled. "Should I apologize?"

"Don't you dare." He cupped her face in his hands. "That was…"

"I know." She kissed him, her humor fading into something poignant and a little scary. This was uncharted territory for them. They'd had sex before, but it was more personal, here in her bedroom, in broad daylight.

If they ate lunch quickly, they might have time to share a shower, which would be another first. Unsure where her bra had landed, she simply shrugged into Colin's discarded shirt. It fell nearly to her knees.

"I will be back with food," she promised.

"You're an angel." He had his arm thrown over his forehead, and his eyes were closed. Would he be asleep when she returned? She had some creative ideas on how to wake him.

In the kitchen, she made two sandwiches and put them both on the same plate. She also poured two glasses of ice-cold water, then carefully balanced it all to carry.

Colin was wearing his boxer briefs but nothing else, and the sight of him sitting in her bed felt so natural that she wondered how she'd get used to his *not* being here. He reached for the plate and one of the glasses. She set the other on the nightstand, then moved away from him.

"You're not joining me?" he asked, puzzled.

"I'll be back in a flash." She'd decided that, as a precaution, she should text Annette with a request to call when they were on their way back. It would be easy for Hannah to lose track of time, and the last thing she wanted was to be caught unaware when her son came barreling into the house at his usual Mach 10. But her cell phone was in her purse on the living room coffee table.

She'd just scooped it up when she heard a vehicle outside. Her heart beat a staccato rhythm as she gauged the distance to the hallway. They hadn't bothered to shut the storm door, and she'd be visible through the screen. *Crap.* Unless the projector at the movie theater had malfunctioned, there was no way Annette was back so soon. Hannah wasn't expecting anyone else. Whoever it was, it looked as if she'd be chasing them off dressed only in Colin's shirt. Luckily, it more than covered her. She tried not to think about her disheveled hair.

A closing door was followed by quick footsteps on

the porch. She craned her head around to peek and felt her jaw drop in surprise when she locked gazes with the stranger. He was shorter than Colin and there were crinkles around his eyes, a mobility to his face that made him look as if he laughed easily and frequently. But the handsome features and dark-haired, light-eyed coloring were the same. Although she'd never seen a picture of him, she knew instantly who he was.

"You're Colin's brother," she said through the screen.

He looked every bit as surprised as she was but recovered with a grin. "Yes, ma'am. I'm Justin—the good-looking Cade brother." There was no come-on in his tone, just a surfeit of humor. "And based on your knowing me, this must be the right place. Hannah Shaw?" His gaze swept over her, his eyes dancing. "It's a pleasure to meet you."

Chapter 13

When Colin heard the familiar sound of his brother's voice, his first thought was that he must have fallen asleep while waiting for Hannah to return. *Having a nightmare.* He hadn't been able to stomach the idea of so much as talking to his siblings about Hannah and her son. Actually facing them here at Silver Linings would be infinitely worse.

But then he heard the murmur of Hannah saying something he couldn't make out and Justin's unmistakable laugh in reply. Dear Lord—it wasn't a dream. *What is he doing here?* As Colin shoved his legs into his jeans, he glanced around for his shirt, belatedly remembering that Hannah wore it. Was she wearing anything else? Jealousy pinched at him. Colin loathed the idea of any man seeing Hannah without all of her clothes, even knowing how devoted Justin was to his fiancée.

Then Colin realized that, for all he knew, Elisabeth had come along with his brother. It could be a damn family reunion right in Hannah's living room. A cold sweat broke out on his forehead and he lumbered toward the front of the house, uncharacteristically clumsy and feeling as if he were slogging his way through waist-deep wet cement.

Hannah flashed him a bemused smile over her shoulder. "Look who's here." She didn't seem to mind the intrusion, but he was sure she had questions about why Colin's brother had suddenly appeared out of the blue.

She's not the only one.

"Justin, have you eaten lunch?" she asked. Colin had long since recognized that offering food was her default setting when she wasn't sure how to handle a social situation.

"Yes, ma'am."

"Well, I insist you stay and join us for dinner," she said, pointedly ignoring Colin's scowl. "I don't know what your plans are, but you're welcome to spend the night, too, if you're not picky about the digs. We're in the middle of redecorating. Colin can show you upstairs. Meanwhile, I'll go…" She glanced down as if just remembering her unorthodox wardrobe. Her gaze slid to Colin's bare chest, and her cheeks flooded red. They might as well have been wearing sandwich boards that read We Had Sex. "I'll, um, let you two catch up."

She made tracks for the back of the house, where her bedroom door shut loudly.

Justin's eyebrows shot up, and Colin silently dared

him to say anything about their appearances. But for a change, the Cade who had a quip for every occasion was at a loss for words. So Colin started.

"What the devil are you doing here?"

"A guy can't come visit his big brother?"

Narrowing his eyes, Colin waited for the real answer.

"Could be worse, bro. I could've brought Arden with me."

Colin barely repressed a shudder.

"Hey, if you don't want our sister sending out search parties, you have to learn to answer your phone. She's got a bee in her bonnet. With my wedding fast approaching, she's worried that you…" He looked uncomfortable.

It took a second for Colin to follow the implication. With Justin about to tie the knot, Arden was concerned about the poor widower in the family, afraid the wedding would bring up too many difficult memories for him. Truthfully, her own ceremony *had* been tough for him. But now—

Guilt nailed him with the force of a ricocheting bullet. He realized he hadn't thought about Natalie or Danny a single time in *days*. It was as if they hadn't even existed. What was happening to him? When had he made the shift from enjoying an affair that he and Hannah both recognized couldn't last to playing house with her and Evan?

Justin was talking again, faster now, as if he could patch the gaping awkwardness with words. "Anyway. You know how Arden is. And it's worse with her pregnant. She almost jumped in the car and tracked you down herself, but Garrett talked her out of it. Our compromise was that I'd take the weekend off and come check on you."

Justin's primary job was ski patrol, but during spring and summer months, he worked at the lodge his future in-laws owned, leading hikes and rafting excursions and administering first aid. "I'm sorry I haven't been taking her calls," Colin said gruffly. *Very* sorry, now that he was paying the consequences. "But I needed time alone, space to think." *In other words, get lost.* "Good news, you don't have to sacrifice your weekend babysitting me. Go back and tell our sister I'm...fine." He choked on the word. Ironically, he had been doing fine. But the sudden realization of just how well he'd been doing knocked him for a loop. It was if he'd fallen into an alternate reality.

"Go back? I just got here." An unrepentant half grin tugged at the corner of his mouth as he met Colin's irritated gaze. "Besides, the lady of the house invited me to stay for dinner."

Hannah really liked Colin's brother—Justin Cade was funny and charming and quick to offer his help, both with painting upstairs and peeling potatoes for dinner. Yet as enjoyable as his company was, she kind of wished he'd go away and never come back. Because ever since he'd shown up at her front door, Colin had withdrawn so far that he was a shell of himself.

Dinner was bearable only because Justin and Evan carried the conversation. Her son had been delighted by their surprise guest, and Annette had been so openly curious that Hannah had been afraid she'd have to set an extra place for supper. But she'd finally managed to shove her friend out the door, knowing Annette would be phoning later with questions. *Maybe I just won't answer.*

Then again, from what she'd gleaned, Colin was the recipient of this brotherly visit because his siblings had reached their limit with him not taking their calls. She found the evidence of their concern endearing. Judging by Colin's dark scowls, he did not share this opinion.

Hoping that good old-fashioned comfort food could help defuse the tension that had been building all afternoon, she'd fixed meat loaf, mashed potatoes and some green beans that Annette had canned last year. Justin's eyes had lit with pleasure at the first bite, but Colin was hardly touching his food.

Colin was also not making eye contact with her. He'd kept his distance ever since Justin's arrival. They'd always tried to keep their relationship discreet, but his current behavior leaned more toward outright shunning her. She tried not to be ticked off, knowing he hadn't expected this, but his distance stung. It was as if he were ashamed. No matter how much he avoided speaking to her or touching her, it was too late to hide the facts from his brother. There was no way Justin hadn't already drawn the correct conclusions after finding them half-dressed and tousled in the middle of the afternoon.

If Justin had been shocked to find his widowed brother cavorting with his new boss, he'd handled it with aplomb. But finding out she had a child was a different story. He'd been openly troubled when Annette dropped off Evan, staring from her son to Colin, surprise warring with apprehension on his handsome features. Whatever worries he had about Colin getting involved with a single mom, he'd pushed them aside to entertain Evan with stories of his own childhood.

Most of the stories were about scrapes Justin had gotten into and Colin's attempts at creative punishment. "He's so much *old*er than me," Justin stressed teasingly over a dessert of butterscotch pudding, "that it was almost like he was my dad."

Evan nodded, easily relating to Justin's growing up without a father. "My dad's dead, too." His fleeting moment of seriousness evaporated into boyish curiosity. "So what did Colin do to you when he found out about the car?"

As they cleared dishes from the table, Justin made an effort to include Hannah in the discussion, too. "By the way, thank you for the gift basket. Elisabeth and I both loved it."

She was startled by the unexpected gratitude. "That was from your brother."

"Who, when left to his own devices, usually sticks a check in the most unimaginative card he can find?" Justin guffawed. "I don't think so." Lowering his voice, he reached out to squeeze her shoulder. "You're a good influence on him, Hannah. Whatever else happens, I hope you'll remember that."

Viper had never been more ill-tempered, and Colin wondered if the horse was somehow picking up on *his* mood tonight. Somehow, Hannah and Justin had talked him into an evening ride to show his brother the ranch. Alone, either one of them were difficult to argue with, but both together? Besides, he hadn't put up much of a fight. Being out here was preferable to being inside. Justin's presence seemed to shrink the house. Colin had been battling a punishing sense of claustrophobia all afternoon.

In an act of petty revenge, he'd saddled Apples for his brother. Next to the elderly Mavis, Apples was the slowest horse on the ranch. On a good day, Viper could leave her in the dust. But tonight, Viper wasn't himself. There seemed to be a conspiracy to force Colin into his brother's company. Colin half listened while Justin talked about house hunting and the place he and Elisabeth found. After the wedding, he'd be moving out of his rental home and Elisabeth's twin sister was moving into the loft where Elisabeth and Kaylee currently lived.

Eventually, Justin wound down. There was an expectant pause, and Colin knew it was his turn to talk. He didn't have anything he wanted to say. Instead, he let the silence build around him like a protective wall.

He should have known his brother wouldn't be deterred so easily.

"So." Justin cleared her throat. "She's a beautiful woman, and a damn good cook."

"I am not discussing Hannah with you."

"I suppose the fact she has a kid is also off-limits?" Justin sighed. "When I got here this afternoon, I jumped to the conclusion that Arden had been overreacting. You look good, bro, better than I've seen you in a long time. But, now? I think maybe our sister was right to worry. Giving Hannah the cold shoulder isn't fair. It's not her fault I'm here."

Maybe not, but why had she invited him to stay the night? Because she was Hannah. *She's bighearted and generous and willing to take in strays.* During a conversation about Scarlett, he'd realized she'd adopted the ugly mutt because she'd been afraid no one else would. Given her history as a foster child, it was understandable that she worked so hard to make everyone feel welcome. In fact, it was one of the qualities he lov—

It was one of the qualities he admired about her. At least, he admired it when the person she was welcoming wasn't his annoying younger brother.

"I'm not giving Hannah the cold shoulder," he said. But the guilty note in his tone was unmistakable. He wasn't angry with her. He just...

"You've looked strung out since her kid came home from the movies," Justin said. "Does she know about—"

"Yes!" In deference to the horses, Colin quickly lowered his voice. But it shook with unwanted emotion. "Hannah knows everything. I've talked, I've shared. So get off my back."

Peace and quiet prevailed, but the lack of conversation wasn't as soothing as Colin had hoped. Justin had punctured his cocoon of denial. It was easier to compartmentalize the facets of his life around Todd and Henry, people who knew him only as a ranch hand, not as someone's husband. Meshing who he used to be with the life he had now was more difficult with Justin here to witness it.

His brother had been the best man at Colin's wedding. Now things were coming full circle in a way that left him queasy. Had he been trying to replace the wife and son he'd lost with Hannah and Evan?

"After Mom died," Colin said, "one of my first acts of taking care of you or Arden was this splinter you got in your foot. Really deep. Dad was so submerged in grief that I think we could have accidentally amputated our thumbs and he wouldn't have noticed. But the splinter caused you pain when you walked, and I was determined to help you get it out. Every time I came near it, you wailed like the biggest wimp on earth."

"I have no recollection of this. I think you're making it up."

Colin snorted. They both knew better. "It's like I've had a splinter in my heart," he said haltingly. "It got worse and worse and worse for two years, infected probably. And Hannah somehow drew it to the surface. She has this way of getting me to talk—about the accident, about random stuff like picking out nursery furniture before Danny was born. She's not only extracting the memories but the pain."

"She helped you heal." Justin said it with pride and awe.

"Maybe I'm not ready to give up the pain." Once he did, Natalie and Danny would be *gone*. "That sounded stupid. Of course, I don't want to be miserable. But before I came here, I thought I had a handle on who I was. Hannah's changing me."

"Like that's a bad thing?" Justin muttered. "I loved Natalie and Danny, too, you know. They were family. But she wouldn't have wanted pain for you. It's selfish to want it for yourself."

Colin bit back a retort, knowing his brother meant well.

"I'll leave in the morning," Justin said. "I'll tell Arden you've been holding a steady job for a month and seem to be doing well. But in the name of pointless optimism, let me remind you that you're entitled to bring a plus-one to the wedding. Actually, since you're the best man, I think you might even rate a plus-two.

Kaylee would love having someone close to her own age there. Don't answer now," he added hastily when Colin started to speak. "Just think about it. I would consider it my wedding present from you if you bring Hannah to the ceremony."

"That's not a good enough reason to bring her," Colin said. He wouldn't mislead her about the depth of their relationship, not even as a favor to his brother.

Irked, Justin rode on ahead, but his voice carried when he called back, "Bro, from where I'm sitting, you don't have a worthwhile reason *not* to bring her."

Hannah wasn't surprised when Colin turned in early for the night. With his brother sleeping in the room next to him, there had been no chance he'd invite Hannah into his bed. Still, logic didn't stop her from lying awake long past midnight, on the slim hope that he might knock on her bedroom door. His scent lingered on her sheets and the memories of what they'd done in this very bed earlier in the day tormented her.

It would be easy to blame Justin for his inconvenient timing, but with or without his showing up, the end result was going to be the same. She would lose Colin. He'd never made any secret that he wasn't the kind of guy to stick around in one place. He'd always planned to leave for his brother's wedding and that job afterward on a cattle drive. Although she'd enjoyed hearing Justin's anecdotes about wedding plans, each one reminded her that the big day was rapidly approaching.

Her time with Colin was almost at an end.

She blinked rapidly, trying to catch her tears on her lashes. It didn't count as crying over the cowboy if the tears didn't actually make it to her cheeks.

Find a bright side, her inner voice urged. Like...
the ranch was in far better shape than it had been before Colin came.

But what about me? What shape would her heart
be in once he'd gone? Maybe she should be proactive.
Since she wasn't sleeping anyway, she would work on
the wording for a new "help wanted" ad. Or edit her
to-do list to reflect what she'd accomplished over the
past few days and rank the improvements she wanted
to tackle next, ordering her short-term goals.

To Do: Get over Colin Cade. That was priority number one. No, wait. Technically, it was number two. Step
one was figuring out *how.*

By the time Hannah's alarm clock blared at her in
the morning, she felt as if she'd had only twenty minutes of sleep.

Breakfast was a subdued affair. Justin kept shooting
worried glances at Colin, who barely said two words,
and Hannah yawned her way through every sentence
she said. Even Evan seemed affected by the gloomy
mood. As he had the night before, Justin helped her
clear plates off the table then teased her about not letting him help load the dishwasher.

Then it was time to say goodbye to him. The thought
made her unaccountably sad—probably because she
knew she was unlikely to see him again. She wouldn't
have a chance to meet Elisabeth or Kaylee or Arden. In
bits and pieces over the past month, Colin had told her
so much about his family that she felt as if she knew
them. But that was only a pleasant fantasy.

Justin hugged her on the front porch. "It was wonderful to meet you. You're a special woman, Hannah
Shaw."

She swallowed the lump in her throat. "If you ever find yourself in Bingham Pass again, come say hi. You're always welcome here."

He nodded. "I'll keep that in mind. I don't have any immediate plans to return, but that's the funny thing about life. You just never know, do you?"

Biting her lip, she refrained from answering. It was true that life had thrown plenty of curveballs at her, some devastating, others wonderful. And some, like Colin, were both.

Plenty of people claimed that gardening was therapeutic, and, after Justin had driven away, Hannah tried to immerse herself in caring for the plants and vegetables. She tried not to feel miffed that she barely saw Colin all day, battling back an unwelcome wave of neediness. *He's* supposed *to be tending to the cattle and horses, remember? That's his job.*

When evening rolled around, however, and he was still making himself scarce, she was forced to admit he was deliberately avoiding her. She and Evan were halfway through dinner when Colin entered the house. He didn't stay long enough even to eat with them, only to grab his pillow and a few other supplies.

"I'm worried about Viper," he told her. "He was rolling earlier and wasn't himself last night. It may be colic. I'm going to sleep down at the stable to keep a better eye on him."

She wanted to scream. Was sleeping on the rock-hard, hay-strewn ground really preferable to sharing the same house with her? She wasn't planning on attacking him, for pity's sake. Hannah had her pride.

She met his gaze, not bothering to hide her frustration. "Do what you have to do."

He faltered, looking as if he might say more, but ultimately, he shook his head and walked away. Just as she'd known he would.

Sirens.

The jarring Klaxon cry penetrated Colin's sleep, along with the sound of nervous whinnies. And...the smell of smoke?

Colin sat bolt upright. Tonight was like an encore of the months of nightmares he'd experienced, except this time, instead of waking from one, he was waking *to* it. Smoke and sirens meant a fire.

He ran from the stable and saw fire trucks rolling up in front of the main house—which was ablaze. *Jesus, no.* Hannah and Evan! Heart and legs pumping in wild tandem, he sprinted for the house. *No, no, no, not again.* He hadn't been there to get them out safely. He'd failed them. Terror was like ice in his veins.

When he got close enough to see a tear-stained Hannah talking to a fireman, Evan at her side clasping Trainket in his small hands, the stark relief nearly drove Colin to his knees. They were alive. They were okay. But the adrenaline and fear lingered like a nauseating aftertaste.

When he got closer, Hannah saw him. Despite how aloof he'd been with her for the past two days—*face it, you've been an ass*—she rushed toward him and threw her arms around him. That was Hannah. She met life head-on, with faith and forgiveness. She was far too good for him.

He stroked a shaking hand over her hair, furious that she smelled like smoke instead of vanilla. "Are you okay?" Some of his anger that she couldn't catch a break seeped into his gruff tone.

"We're all right." The brave words contrasted with the tremor in her voice, the clamminess of her skin. "I got Evan and Scarlett out safely, and the firemen are containing the blaze to the left side of the house."

The fire wasn't out yet, but it was already noticeably weaker than when he'd caught his first heart-stopping glimpse of it. Still, it had been a dry year. Colin wouldn't breathe easy again until every last spark had been dampened.

"It started upstairs," she said. "I'm glad you weren't there."

Her soft words triggered a spike of guilt. If he *had* slept in his usual bed, maybe he would have noticed it faster, helped put it out before it engulfed the guest rooms she'd been so diligently renovating.

"Th-they think m-maybe a short in the wiring." Her teeth were chattering, and he pulled her closer. "Until recently, I hadn't been in those rooms much, so I wasn't using the electricity up there. On the br-bright side…" She gulped, and he realized that she was about to lose it completely.

"Hannah, it's okay. You can be strong tomorrow. For now—"

"On the bright side," she continued with almost hysterical determination, "we may not lose many of our personal belongings." Her and Evan's rooms were at the opposite end of the house. "But it looks like those guest rooms won't be open for new business anytime soon, huh?" Then she laughed. Which quickly became a sob.

"Colin?" Evan's voice was scared. "Is Mommy okay?"

That cut through Hannah's mini breakdown better than anything Colin could have said—not that he was full of wise words at the moment. Mostly he wanted to shake his fist at the sky and scream obscenities. He was so damn sick of bad things happening to good people. And even though his fear should have ebbed once he saw that Hannah and Evan were all right, it was still there. In fact, it was crippling, ballooning ever larger. How had he put himself in a position to lose someone else? Anguish over the past, coupled with the tragedy that could have happened here tonight, knifed through him.

Hadn't he learned his lesson by now? He'd told his brother he wasn't sure if he were truly ready to let go of the pain. But he'd been lying to himself. The truth was, he wasn't ready to risk that pain again. Not now, not ever.

"I'm okay," Hannah was assuring her son. "But we're going to have a sleepover at Aunt Annette's tonight once we're done here. Colin, will you drive us? I'm…a little shaky."

She made the admission with a twinge of embarrassment that blew his mind. Her house had almost burned down around her! Of course, she was shaky.

"I'll get you there safely," he promised.

Driving her across town was the perfect task for him—a concrete, unemotional form of assistance. That, he could handle. But he suspected it was one of the last things he'd be able to do for Hannah Shaw. She had too many other needs that required dangerous involvement outside his skill set.

Life was precarious. And his was better lived alone.

* * *

Seeing the fire damage in the harsh light of day made Colin's stomach buckle. Annette was bringing Evan by shortly so that he could see his home was still there, but Hannah had wanted to inspect the aftermath of the fire herself first. Colin almost gagged at the lingering stench of smoke. It would be a long, long time before he ate barbecue or roasted marshmallows again.

Hannah sat at the bottom of the staircase, wringing her hands. Behind her, the wall panel he'd built to give her better pipe access was now a charred black patch. "I am so sorry." It hadn't occurred to them until they'd reached Annette's house that *he'd* lost belongings in the blaze.

"Don't worry about me. I didn't have that much," he reminded her. Many of his belongings were in storage. He'd learned the importance of traveling light. It was a lesson he didn't intend to forget again. "Still got my hat. And my motorcycle helmet."

She flinched at the reference to his motorcycle. Because they both knew he'd be riding away soon?

"You lost your sketch pad, though."

He forced a shrug. "They were just doodles when you come right down to it."

"That's *not* all they were! That picture you did for my birthday? It inspired me, gave me hope. But now... God. Maybe it's time for me to face facts. We've already had our own versions of flood and fire. Instead of locusts, I have the killer bull."

Seeing her so defeated caused an ache inside him. He knelt in front of her, trying to coax a smile. "We've arranged a buyer for Beelzebull, remember? The rest can be dealt with, too. Your conversation with the insurance company seemed to go really well this morning. Don't give up."

"Why not?" She leveled him with her damp hazel eyes. "You are."

He backed away, stricken. "Don't put that on me. You *knew* I was going." He raked a hand through his hair. "I helped with the bull, got the cows wormed over the weekend. Viper's doing better, and I put in a call to my buddy Dwayne to see if he wants some temporary work helping you out. He's a seasoned hand, like Henry, but only in his early forties. He may be a good fit."

"*You* were a good fit," she persisted, rising to her feet. "Not just on this ranch, but in my life. Colin, I—"

"Please don't." He shook his head wildly.

She took a deep breath, clenching and relaxing her fists at her sides, but her tone was no calmer when she spoke. "I know you have the wedding, and I know you're scheduled to help with the drive. But give me one good reason why you couldn't come back after that. Assuming an asteroid hasn't taken out the house by then."

It was the most bitter she'd ever sounded, and he wondered whether the fire was behind the broken note in her voice or if it was his fault. He knew of *two* good reasons he couldn't be here: her and Evan. They were both stealing his heart, and he couldn't protect it from further damage if he allowed that to happen.

"Don't you feel anything for me?" she pressed.

It was the worst thing she could have said.

"Of course I do! But I don't *want* to, Hannah. If you or Evan had been… You could have…" He couldn't voice the words. His brain skittered away from even thinking them. Since last night, some part of him had been curled into a ball, rocking back and forth in a dark corner of his mind, trying to numb itself instead of allowing him to think about the possibilities. He didn't have to impress Hannah; he merely had to cope.

She took his hand. "The worst didn't happen. I don't have so much as a twisted ankle this time. We're *okay*."

I'm not. For the past week, living on optimism he'd borrowed from her, he'd thought maybe he could be. But it was time to return the rose-colored glasses to their rightful owner. Colin had lost both his parents, his wife and his son. He would not voluntarily put himself in a position to lose anyone else.

No matter how much he loved her.

Hannah had been through a lot since the day she and Evan had moved onto the ranch. Plumbing disasters, the guilt of Henry being injured by an animal she owned, a damn *fire* for cripes' sake. But none of it had been as difficult to endure as watching Colin Cade drive away on a sunny Wednesday afternoon.

She'd actually envied Evan his freedom to cry when he'd hugged Colin one final time. Her son had sniffled and whined about the unfairness of it. Hannah, on the other hand, had resigned herself to doing the mature thing—wishing Colin well and thanking him for his help.

"You may not have been here long," she'd said, "but the impact you've made is immeasurable." She wished she could have read his expression better, but it was difficult to see his eyes through his dark sunglasses. Colin was a master at finding ways to shut people out—from not answering phone calls to jumping on his motorcycle and fleeing when a situation became too intimate for him to handle.

Even his kiss goodbye had been detached, a quick brush of his lips over her forehead, nowhere in the vicinity of her mouth, as if he was deliberately avoiding any memory of the passion they'd shared.

"Hey? You doing okay?" Annette stepped onto the porch, giving Hannah a half hug. "I've got Evan settled with some cartoons and chocolate doughnuts, so we have a few minutes for venting. If you'd like to call your former ranch hand some obscene names, I have suggestions."

That offer drew a watery chuckle from Hannah. But she ended up defending him. "Colin's not a bad guy. He's just been through a hell of a lot."

"Yes, but now he's putting you through a lot. As your best friend, I'm entitled to be annoyed with him. You guys were *good* together."

We really were. "I think he knows that. I even think it's part of the problem. He doesn't want a relationship, doesn't want to be vulnerable to anyone."

"Then he's going to be a very lonely man."

Hannah met her friend's eyes. "He already is. I thought I could fix that, but I was being arrogant."

She was a single mom and a struggling ranch owner with ambition and baking skill. She was not a miracle worker.

Chapter 14

Justin's automatic smile of greeting crumpled when he stepped outside and got a better look at Colin's face beneath the porch light. "Oh, hell. You blew it with Hannah, didn't you?"

"Coming here was a mistake," Colin growled. "Cielo Peak's got plenty of hotels."

His brother reached out and grabbed his elbow. "Get inside and tell me all about it, you idiot."

Colin had spent the entire ride to Cielo Peak calling himself far worse names. When he relived Hannah's wounded expression as she told him goodbye, he hated himself for ever kissing her, much less making love to her. He was a selfish SOB. By indulging his own desires, he'd hurt her in the process.

He'd rationalized that as long as he was honest with her about his intentions, he couldn't break her heart, but he'd known better. He'd known from the beginning that Hannah was open and loving and full of hope. If he'd destroyed that hope, like some blindly rampaging beast trampling a beautiful flower garden—

"Yo!" Justin snapped his fingers in front of his face. "You haven't answered anything I've said for the last two minutes. Have you gone catatonic on me?"

"No." But that might be an improvement.

"Well, then get inside," Justin repeated. "We can do this the easy way, which involves you and me sitting at my kitchen table over a couple of beers, or the hard way."

"Which would be...?"

His brother gave him a menacing grin. "Me calling Arden and telling her she's needed for an emotional intervention."

"You are a heartless bastard." Nonetheless, Colin followed him inside.

"Before Elisabeth, I think that was true. I was charming when I wanted to be, but mostly heartless. Beth's made me a better man. I saw glimmers of hope that Hannah was restoring *you* to a better version of yourself." He popped the lids off of two bottles of beer with a magnetized opener he kept on the fridge, then slid a bottle across the table to Colin. "Why are you here instead of with her?"

"I was coming for the wedding anyway."

"Not until next week. Cut the crap, and tell me the truth."

"Her house caught fire." Even after seeing it with his own eyes, the words were surreal.

Justin's eyes widened in alarm. "Is she okay? Is Evan—"

"They're all right." Thank God. "But what you're feeling right now? Magnify that by a million, and you'll start to get an inkling of how I felt." Colin knocked back a quarter of his beer, but it was nowhere near strong enough to dull the edge of panic that had taken up residence inside his chest. It was as if he were trying to breathe around a lungful of razor blades. "Justin, I can't go through that again."

His brother sat back in his chair, looking troubled. "I hear what you're saying, and I understand it. But it's a load of manure. What's your plan, to not give a damn about anyone else for the next fifty or sixty years? What about me and Arden? Or have you already decided you don't care about us? That would explain moving away and never answering your freaking phone."

Colin recoiled. "You know how important the two of you are to me!"

"And if I break my neck skiing, would it make you sorry we were brothers? Would you undo that bond now if you could, to prevent having to mourn me later?"

"After everyone we've buried, how dare you be glib about the idea of something happening to you?"

Remorse flickered across Justin's face, but he didn't back down, merely switched tactics. "Okay, forget that line of argument. Let's see how well you do debating your own words. Or don't you remember that verbal ass-kicking you gave me when I almost let Beth slip away?"

Colin downed more of his beer, telling himself the two situations were different.

"You pointed out that when you lost Natalie, you had no choice in the matter, no opportunity to fight for her, whereas I was just too chicken to fight for Elisabeth.

You could be fighting for Hannah now! You could be building a life with her. I saw the way she looked at you, and that woman is in love."

Colin's throat clenched. He was torn between pure, ecstatic joy and sheer horror that Hannah could love him. "She deserves better."

"Then *be* better. You told me at Christmas that you would have traded anything for one more day, one more hour with Natalie. I'm not saying Hannah's a substitute for her—Natalie and Danny are irreplaceable—but life has given you a second chance! There is a wonderful woman out there with the incredibly bad taste to adore you, and you're letting the hours and days you could have with her slip away."

Although Justin was making a lot of sense, it was difficult for reason to combat panic. "It's not as easy as you're making it sound."

"Of course not." Justin's smile was sympathetic. "Love takes work, and when it's real love, it's damn scary."

Then Colin's feelings for Hannah Shaw must be very, very real. But how could he find the courage to do anything about them?

Colin had barely slept a wink when his brother got up the next morning for work. They exchanged nods while the smell of brewing coffee filled the kitchen, but neither attempted actual conversation until they had caffeine running through their veins.

Once Justin drained his mug, he seemed sufficiently awake to start worrying. "I hate to leave you here by yourself all day."

Colin rolled his eyes. "I'm a grown man, not an unsupervised toddler."

"I know. But if you need me to take the afternoon off or—"

"Quit. The best man isn't supposed to be a burden on the groom-to-be. It's the other way around. Don't you have something useful I can do?"

"Now that you mention it..." Justin glanced around the kitchen. A large cardboard box, marked KITCHEN, was sealed and sitting against one wall. Another box, sitting open, took up a big chunk of counter space. "The Donnellys and a couple of guys from my patrol are coming the day after tomorrow to help move stuff, and I'm not finished packing yet. I ran out of tape and paper to wrap the dishes and glass stuff. You can take that over if you need a distraction."

It was clear from Justin's knowing tone that he meant a distraction from thinking about Hannah. Which Colin was *not* going to do. Except for the thought he'd just had...and the roughly two thousand other thoughts that had plagued him during the night.

Her expression as she'd said goodbye haunted him. He wanted to pick up the phone and make sure she was all right. A clean break seemed less selfish, though.

"Packing," he said. "I'm on it."

Once Justin left, Colin made a quick run to town for supplies, eager to have something to do.

When he returned, wrapping plates and stacking them inside the box gave him a soothing sense of purpose. But it didn't take long for the silence of the house to press in around him. He'd become accustomed to Evan's chatter and the background noise of Hannah's mixer whirring or the metallic slide of a cookie sheet going into the oven. Even when Colin had been busy outdoors, there'd been the nickering of horses or—

A frustrated snarl escaped him. Why couldn't he go five minutes without thinking of Hannah and her ranch? *Give it time.* After all, he'd said goodbye to her only yesterday.

He loaded the packing tape into the sharp-edged dispenser so that he could seal up the box. The abrasive sound of tape being stretched across the seam of cardboard and then ripped away from the roll was distinctive. It filled him with a sense of déjà vu. Not too long ago, he and Justin had helped Arden pack up her belongings as she prepared to move to Garrett's ranch.

You packed up your own boxes, too. Colin had a lot of stuff in storage. It seemed an apt metaphor for his life. His siblings were moving on, moving forward to be with the people they loved. Colin was in stasis, his untouched possessions growing musty in a dark, padlocked unit he never visited.

He used to hear Natalie's voice in his head on a fairly regular basis, imagining what she might say to him, but it had been weeks. Now, in the unnatural stillness of Justin's house, he could hear her exasperated tone loud and clear. *The worst part isn't that our stuff is neglected and forgotten—it's just stuff. No, the worst part is that* you're *moldering away. Life is short. And you're squandering it.*

Colin knew better than most how fleeting life could be, yet he was here while so many others had died too young. He glared at the tape roller in his hand. If he didn't start building a real life instead of drifting from place to place, he might as well box up his heart and shove it in that storage unit alongside the furniture and old photo albums. He owed it to the people he'd lost—owed it to *himself*—to live and be happy. And to love.

The insurance settlement was going to be more generous than Hannah had expected. She tried to use that discovery to buoy her battered optimism as she strolled into the town diner at noon on Saturday. She had a lunch appointment to interview the man Colin had recommended. Dwayne had sounded competent and genuinely interested over the phone. Maybe it would go well, and this man would be a solid replacement for Henry.

Positive thoughts, Hannah!

Ever since Colin had abandoned them, she'd been trying to remain upbeat and cheerful. Evan was in a fragile place right now, with his idol gone and the second story of their house a charred mess. But even as she smiled brightly and kept her tone chipper, Hannah fantasized about crawling into a pair of ratty sweats and hiding under her comforter with a gallon or three of ice cream.

Unfortunately, she doubted that Ben and Jerry, wonderful though they may be, were going to help repair her roof, clean her walls or replace her furniture. So it was up to her to keep moving forward. Stubborn anger helped. She was not going to give up at the first sign of trouble like Colin Cade, the man who—*was sitting at a booth in the Bingham Pass diner?*

Hannah's pulse went into overdrive. For a moment, she was afraid she might hyperventilate. When she froze in her tracks, Colin rose and came to her. Her feet hadn't figured out how to move yet, but her eyes roved over him, avidly taking in every detail. He looked so good, and she'd missed him so much. The four days since she'd seen him felt like a lifetime.

"I—I was supposed to be meeting Dwayne," she stammered. This couldn't be a coincidence, Colin just happening to be at the diner when she walked in.

"About that." He tipped his straw hat back on his head. "He and I were talking, and I suggested to him that you may not have a position available after all."

"You did what?" Annoyance spurted at his heavy-handedness. He'd refused to consider staying on long-term, but he was running off the first man who'd seriously considered it?

"It's all right, though. I got him a paying gig on a cattle drive."

A cattle drive? Such as the one he was scheduled to leave for right after Justin's wedding? "So…the two of you will be working together?" she asked cautiously.

"Nope."

Feeling a little weak in the knees, she slid into the booth. Colin sat across from her, his expression unreadable. It wasn't cold or aloof, though—quite the opposite. So many emotions danced in his blue-green eyes that she couldn't catalogue them all.

She hoped the waitress brought them glasses of water soon. Her mouth had gone bone-dry. "Colin, what are you doing here?"

"Applying for a job."

Her heart wrenched. A month ago, that would have been the answer to her prayers. After everything they'd shared, however, she didn't think she could hire him. Any possibility of a platonic, professional relationship had been shot to hell. "I'm not sure that's a good idea."

He nodded solemnly. "I understand why you would

feel that way. But since I'm here, would you humor me by taking a peek at my résumé? I'd appreciate the feedback." He opened a folder she hadn't noticed until then and handed her a crisp sheet of paper.

She stared at it uncomprehendingly, not really seeing the words but needing the chance to recover her composure. But when her eyes landed on a section halfway down the page that read "Related skills: Thorough lover," her cheeks flamed and any chance of poise disappeared. "Is this some kind of joke?" She lowered her voice to an angry hiss. "I was paying you for the work you did on the ranch, not the...you know, other stuff."

"No joke. Did you start at the top with my mission statement?"

Her gaze flew to the words she'd overlooked, and her heart melted. In the boldfaced statement, he'd proclaimed his objective of "fearlessly loving Hannah Shaw" and earning her love in return, standing beside her and braving whatever life threw their way.

"Oh, Colin." Taking her time, she read over the page, each of the heartfelt bullet points heightening the profound joy unfurling inside her. "You could've just picked up the phone and said all of this to me."

"I'm not sure I could have," he admitted. "I needed time to think it through, to try to put my feelings into words and actions. It's been an enlightening week."

"Really?" she asked drily. "My week's been pure hell."

He reached for her hand atop the table, his thumb stroking over the pulse point at her wrist. "I'm sorry I put you through that. I know you don't have any proof, so these may be empty words, but for what it's worth, I think I was getting there—to a place where I could love you freely, where I could let myself be loved. But then Justin showing up, the fire happening... I panicked."

"I do believe you." She'd always had more faith in him than he'd had in himself. And she'd witnessed firsthand how his smiles had come more easily each day, his growing affection with not only her but others around him. He'd made a place for himself where he belonged—only he hadn't wanted it. "What changed your mind?"

"Other than seeing your face in my head every waking hour, not being able to sleep without dreaming of you and my brother consistently reminding me that I was an idiot for leaving?" He shrugged. "Boxes."

She cocked her head, waiting for him to elaborate.

"Justin's moving. Both my siblings are moving forward, and I've been standing still. Maybe that didn't matter to me before because I didn't have anyplace I wanted to be, anyone I wanted to be *with*—but now there's you. Hannah, I'm sorry. And I don't want to waste one more day being without you."

Tears misting her vision, she bounced out of her seat and rushed to his side of the booth to hug him. "I missed you so much," she whispered.

He captured her mouth in a kiss that told her the feeling was mutual. His tongue delved between her lips, and the kiss became more urgent. Need spiraled through her. She longed for a physical closeness that matched the candid intimacy of his words. When he nipped at her earlobe, she groaned in frustration.

"I love you," she said. "Please don't take this the wrong way, but *why* did you have to pick a public diner for this reunion?"

He pulled back with a grin. "No one's come to take

our order yet. Would it be an inappropriate time to mention that my child-free hotel room is within walking distance?"

She grabbed his hand. "Then what are we still doing here?"

Fingers laced together, they hurried from the diner and into the sunshine, into their future.

Epilogue

The wedding was beautiful, but Hannah felt a little guilty for her wandering attention. Instead of focusing on the bride and groom, her gaze continually strayed to the gorgeous best man. In her opinion, Colin Cade was the sexiest man in all of Colorado. He was gorgeous in his tux, but she was looking forward to the next time she saw him in jeans and that cowboy hat, too.

When the ceremony ended, guests began heading to the reception at the Donnelly Ski Lodge. The wedding party stayed behind for pictures, and Evan and Kaylee—who'd taken to each other instantly—asked for permission to play tag just outside the chapel. Hannah sat in one of the pews, keeping one eye on the kids through the window while listening to the photographer cajole smiles and chuckles from the bridal party.

Arden Cade Frost was every bit as lovely and spirited as Hannah had imagined. The two women had been seated next to each other at Justin and Elisabeth's rehearsal dinner. Colin had groaned at the arrangements, seemingly worried that if Hannah and his sister ever ganged up on him, he was doomed. Today, poor Arden had sobbed through the entire ceremony. As she'd pointed out beforehand, now that she was pregnant, she found herself weeping over just about everything. She loudly instructed the photographer to fix her red nose and watery eyes with digital editing.

When all the pictures were done, members of the wedding party and their escorts headed for the appropriate vehicles. Colin had surprised Hannah on the drive to Cielo Peak by suggesting that if they sold her truck and his motorcycle, they might have enough money for a substantial vehicular upgrade.

"You'd sell your motorcycle?" she'd asked.

His reply had been a cryptic, "I don't need it anymore."

Elisabeth's adopted daughter, Kaylee, was supposed to ride with the bride and groom but, at the last second, asked if she could go "in Evan's car." The newlyweds seemed happy about the prospect of a few minutes alone, provided Colin and Hannah didn't mind.

"It's fine with us," Hannah assured them. Although neither brother had revealed the specifics of the conversation, she knew Justin had said some things to Colin that had really resonated, helping to bring him back to Hannah. She would always be grateful to Justin for that.

During the brief car ride, Kaylee and Evan discussed bowling.

"Maybe you can come with us next time," Evan told his new friend.

"I've never been before," Kaylee said, "but I'm sure I'd be very good at it."

Behind the wheel of the car, Colin laughed. "Looks like someone else is a student of positive thinking."

As he parked in front of the lodge, Hannah's cell phone chimed. She pulled it out of her purse and discovered that Annette had texted her a photo. It took Hannah a moment to identify what she was looking at—a tapered, white stick with two red lines showing in a circle. It was captioned TWO LINES!!!!!!

A smile split her face. "Guess who's going to be an honorary aunt?" she whispered to Colin.

He grinned back at her, and she took a mental snapshot, wanting to hold on to this moment. It had been a beautiful day. She was surrounded by wonderful people, including her son and the man she loved. Her best friend was going to have a baby. She was brimming with happiness.

Thirty minutes later, Colin stirred even more emotion within her when he lifted his glass of champagne and gave his toast as best man.

"As many of you know already, for a long time, Justin, Arden and I only had each other. Some days it felt like the three of us against the world. I believed family was the most important thing in life. I still do—but that family has expanded. Our circle of three has grown to include some magnificent people, like the beautiful Elisabeth Donnelly Cade."

The bride beamed at him.

"There was a time, not that long ago, when I would have wondered if a step like marriage was too drastic. Loving someone else so completely opens up the risk of being hurt." Colin's blue-green eyes sought out Hannah in the crowd. "What I'd forgotten is that loving someone else is also the only way to reap life's most incredible rewards. Justin and Elisabeth, you are an inspiration. Thank you for reminding us all that happily-ever-afters aren't fairy tales. They're real for anyone brave enough to work for them. My suggestion to you for many blissful years together is to treat each other with respect, live each day with a sense of humor and always remember to look on the bright side."

* * * * *

Michelle Major grew up in Ohio but dreamed of living in the mountains. Soon after graduating with a degree in journalism, she pointed her car west and settled in Colorado. Her life and house are filled with one great husband, two beautiful kids, a few furry pets and several well-behaved reptiles. She's grateful to have found her passion writing stories with happy endings. Michelle loves to hear from her readers at michellemajor.com.

Books by Michelle Major

Harlequin Special Edition

Crimson, Colorado

Sleigh Bells in Crimson
Romancing the Wallflower
Christmas on Crimson Mountain
Always the Best Man
A Baby and a Betrothal
A Very Crimson Christmas
Suddenly a Father
A Second Chance on Crimson Ranch
A Kiss on Crimson Ranch

The Fortunes of Texas: The Rulebreakers

Her Soldier of Fortune

The Fortunes of Texas: The Secret Fortunes

A Fortune in Waiting

The Fortunes of Texas: All Fortune's Children

Fortune's Special Delivery

The Fortunes of Texas: Cowboy Country

The Taming of Delaney Fortune

Harlequin Serials

Secrets of the A-List

Visit the Author Profile page at Harlequin.com for more titles.

A KISS ON
CRIMSON RANCH

MICHELLE MAJOR

For Jackson. I love you for your heart, your smile and everything you are. I'm so proud to be your mom.

Chapter 1

Sara Wells gripped the steering wheel of her ancient Toyota and tilted her chin. "Punch me," she said, and squeezed her eyes shut. "Right in the face. Go on, before I lose my nerve."

She heard movement next to her and braced herself, flinching when a soft hand stroked her cheek. "I'd never hit you, Sara, even if I wanted to. Which I don't."

Sara opened her eyes to gaze into the kind, guileless face of her best friend in the world, April Sommers. Her only friend. The friend whose entire life savings Sara had recently lost.

She swatted April's arm. "You should. I deserve it." A bead of sweat slid between her shoulder blades and she rolled down the window a crack. Her lungs stung as she inhaled the crisp alpine air. "How does anyone breathe around here?" she muttered. "I miss the L.A. smog."

"Go see the attorney. Stop avoiding reality."

"Reality Bites." She paused, then lifted a finger. "1994. Starring Ethan Hawke, Winona Ryder and a very green Ben Stiller. Who would have thought that of the three, Ben Stiller would end up the biggest star? Come on. *Little Fockers?* Are you kidding me?"

"You're doing it again."

Ignoring the soft admonishment, Sara leaned forward to gaze out the car's front window at the row of brightly colored Victorian stores lining Main Street. "Look at that. Warner Bros. couldn't have created a better Western set."

"This *is* the West."

Right.

Crimson, Colorado. Population 3,500 if the sign coming over the pass into town was accurate. Altitude 8,900 feet. Sara blamed the lack of air for her inability to catch her breath.

April rummaged in the sack at her feet. "Aren't you curious?" She offered Sara an apple. Sara held up a half-eaten Snickers in response.

"I gave up curious a long time ago." She stuffed the candy bar into her mouth. "Along with cigarettes, savage tans, men and chocolate." She swallowed. "Okay, scratch chocolate."

That resolution had fallen by the interstate about four hours into the thirteen-hour drive from Los Angeles. While Crimson was only thirty minutes down the road from the ritzy ski town of Aspen, it held as much appeal to Sara as a blistered big toe.

Sure, it was beautiful if you were one of those back-to-nature types who appreciated towering pines, glittering blue skies and breathtaking views. Sara was a city girl. A blanket of smog comforted her; horns blaring on the I-5 made her smile. In her world, ski boots were a fashion statement, not a cold-weather necessity.

She was out of her element.

Big-time.

"Go on." April leaned over and opened the driver's-side door. "The sooner you talk to the attorney, the quicker we'll be back on the road to la-la land."

Sara's need to put Rocky Mountain Mayberry in her rearview mirror propelled her out of the car. She couldn't do that until she met with Jason Crenshaw, attorney-at-law, whose cryptic phone call two days earlier had started this unplanned road trip.

If nothing else, she hoped the money Crenshaw had for her would buy gas on the way back. And groceries. Sara could live on ramen noodles and snack cakes for weeks, but April was on a strict organic, vegan diet. Sara didn't understand eating food that looked like cat puke and tasted like sawdust, but she had no right to question April's choices. If it weren't for Sara, April would have plenty of money to spend on whatever she wanted. And rabbit food cost plenty of money.

She pulled her well-worn jeans jacket tight and squinted through a mini dust tornado as a gust of wind whipped along the town's main drag. Mid-May in Southern California and the temperature hovered at a balmy seventy degrees, but Crimson still had a bit of winter's chill to the air. The mountain peaks surrounding the town were covered in snow.

Sara didn't do snow.

She opened the pale turquoise door to the office of

Crenshaw and Associates and stepped in, lifting her knock-off Prada sunglasses to the top of her head.

The desk in the reception area sat vacant, large piles of paper stacked precariously high. "Hello?" she called in the general direction of the office door at the back of the lobby.

A chair creaked and through the door came a younger man who looked like he could have been Andy Griffith's rumpled but very handsome son. He peered at her over a pair of crooked reading glasses, wiping his hands on the paper napkin stuffed into his collared shirt.

Sara caught the whiff of barbecue and her stomach grumbled. No food envy, she reminded herself. Noodles were enough for her.

"Sorry, miss," the man said as he looked her over. "No soliciting. Try a couple doors down at the diner. Carol might have something left over from the lunch rush."

Sara felt her eyes widen a fraction. The guy thought she was a bum. Fantastic. She pulled at her spiky bangs. "I'm looking for Jester Crunchless," she said with a well-timed lip curl.

"I'm Jason Crenshaw." The man bristled. "And who might you be?"

"Sara Wells."

Immediately his posture relaxed. "Ms. Wells, of course." He pulled out the napkin as he studied her, revealing a tie decorated with rows of small snowboards. "You know, we watched *Just the Two of Us* religiously around here. You're different than I expected."

"I get that a lot."

"Right." He chuckled self-consciously. "You're a heck of a lady to track down."

"I'm here now."

"Of course," he repeated. "Why don't you step into my office?"

"Why don't you hand over the check?"

His brows drew together. "Excuse me?"

"On the phone you said *inheritance*." She reached into her purse. "I have ID right here. Let's get this over with."

"Were you close to your grandmother, Ms. Wells?"

"No." She could barely remember her grandmother. Sara's mother had burned a trail out of Crimson as soon as she could and had kept Sara far away from her estranged family.

"The heart attack was a shock. We're told she didn't suffer." He paused. "It's a loss for the whole town. Miss Trudy was the backbone of Crimson."

A sliver of something, a long-buried emotion, slipped across Sara's heart and she clamped it down quickly. Shaking her head, she made her voice flip. "It's tragic that she was your backbone and whatnot. I barely knew the woman. Can we talk about the money?"

Another pause. "There is no money." Crenshaw's tone took on a harsh edge. Harsh was Sara's home turf.

Sara matched his emotion. "Then why in the hell did I just drive all the way from California?"

He cleared his throat. "We discussed an inheritance on the phone, Ms. Wells. Not money, specifically." He turned to a rickety file cabinet and peered into the top drawer. "I have it right here."

Great. She and April had driven almost a thousand miles for an old piece of costume jewelry or something.

She mentally calculated if she could get to Denver on the fumes left in her gas tank.

He turned back to her and held out a set of keys. "There's some paperwork, for sure. We should talk to Josh about how he fits into the mix. He and Trudy had big plans for the place. But you look like you could use a rest. Go check it out. We can meet again tomorrow morning."

Tomorrow morning she'd be halfway to the Pacific Ocean. "What place?"

"Crimson Ranch," he told her. "Miss Trudy's property." He jingled the keys.

Sara's stomach lurched. "She left me a *property?*"

Before Crenshaw could answer, cool air tickled Sara's ponytail. She turned as her mother, Rosemarie Wells, glided in with bottle-blond hair piled high on top of her regal head. A man followed in her wake, indiscriminately middle-aged, slicked-back salt-and-pepper hair, slight paunch and cowboy boots that looked custom-made. Sara assumed he was the latest in her mother's long string of rich, powerful, jerk boyfriends.

Could this day get any worse?

Rose slanted Jason Crenshaw a dismissive glance then snapped her fingers at Sara. "We need to talk, Serena."

Sara's stomach lurched, but she focused on the attorney, snatching the keys out of his still-outstretched palm.

"May I help you?" he asked, his eyes a little dazed. Her mother had had that effect on men since Sara could remember. It had been at least two years since she'd seen her mother last, but Rose looked exactly the same as far as Sara could tell. Maybe with a few less wrinkles thanks to the wonders of modern plastic surgery.

"You can ignore her." Sara bit at a cuticle.

"Serena, stop that obnoxious behavior."

She nibbled harder. "This is kind of a coinkydink, Mom. You showing up now." Sara locked eyes with her mother. Rose knew about the will, she realized in an instant.

Her mother's gaze raked her. "You look like hell, Serena."

"Stop calling me that. My name is Sara." She narrowed her eyes but crossed her arms over her chest, suddenly conscious that she was wearing an ancient and not very supportive sports bra. "Sara Wells. The name you put on my birth certificate."

Her mother's large violet eyes rolled to the ceiling. "The name I had legally *changed* when you were eight."

"I changed it back and you know it." Sara took a step forward. "A monumental pain in the back end, by the way." She cocked her head to one side. "Although it's handy when collections comes calling."

Her mother's nose wrinkled. "I can help you with that, Serena."

"Sara."

Rose ignored her. "Richard wants to buy your grandmother's property." She tilted her head at the aging cowboy, who tipped his hat rim at Sara, Clint Eastwood style.

"I don't understand why Gran left it to me."

"To make things difficult for me, of course," Rose said with an exaggerated sigh. She dabbed at the corner of her eye. "Mothers are supposed to look out for their children, not keep them from their rightful inheritance."

Sara never could cry on cue. She envied her mother that.

"No matter. I know you've gotten yourself into another mess, Serena. A financial nightmare, really. We can fix that right now. Mr. Crenshaw, would you be so good as to draw up the paperwork?" She leveled a steely gaze at Sara. "I'm bailing you out again. Remember that."

Rose had never helped Sara out of anything—contract negotiations, come-ons from slimy casting directors, defamatory tabloid headlines, a career slowly swirling down the drain. The only times in Sara's life her mother had stepped in to *help* were when it benefited Rose at Sara's expense.

"I'm not selling."

"What?"

"Not yet. And not to you, Mother."

"Don't be ridiculous." Rose darted a worried glance toward the cowboy, whose hands fisted in front of his oversize belt buckle. "What choice do you have?"

"I'm not sure." Sara turned to the attorney. "Can you give me directions to the ranch?"

"I'll write them down," he said, and with obvious relief, disappeared into the back office.

"What kind of game are you playing?" Her mother pointed a French-tipped finger at Sara. "We both know you're desperate for money. You don't belong on that ranch." Rose's tone was laced with condescension. "She had no business leaving it to you."

Decades of anger boiled to the surface in Sara. "She did, and maybe if you'd look in the mirror beyond the fake boobs and Botox you'd see why. Maybe she wanted to keep it out of your hot little hands." She leaned closer. "Want to talk about that?"

Her mother recoiled for an instant, then straightened. "You don't have a choice."

"No." Sara's spine stiffened. "I didn't have a choice when I was eight and begged you not to take me on another round of auditions. I didn't have a choice when I was thirteen and I wanted to quit the show after the assistant director came on to me. I didn't have a choice at seventeen when you checked me into rehab for *exhaustion* because the publicity would help the fans see me as an adult."

"If you'd taken my advice, you wouldn't be in the position you are now. I had your best interest at heart. Always."

Sara laughed. Actually laughed out loud in her mother's face. The statement was that absurd. "You tell yourself whatever you need to make it through the day. We both know the truth. Here's the kicker. Right now I do have a choice." She gripped the keys hard in her fist. "Stay away from me, Mother. Stay off of my property or I'll have you hauled off to the local pokey."

"You wouldn't—"

Sara met her angry gaze. "Try me."

She flicked a gaze at Jason Crenshaw, who'd returned to the office's lobby. "I'll be in touch," she said and took the piece of paper he handed her. Without another glance at Rose, she reached for the door, but a large hand on her arm stopped her.

"You're making a big mistake here, missy," the aging Marlboro man told her, his voice a harsh rasp.

She shrugged out of his grasp. She'd been intimidated by far scarier men than this old coot. "What's new?" she asked, and pushed out into the too-clean mountain air.

Josh Travers took a deep breath, letting the fresh air clear his muddled head. He'd been doing trail maintenance on the hiking path behind the main house for over three hours, moving logs to reinforce the bridge across a stream that ran between the two properties. His knee had begun throbbing about forty-five minutes into the job. Now it felt like someone had lit a match to his leg. Josh could tolerate the physical pain. What almost killed him was the way the ache radiated into his brain, making him remember why he was stuck here working himself to the point of exhaustion on a cool spring morning.

What he'd lost and left behind. Voices whispering he'd never get it back. The pain was a constant reminder of his monumental fall—both literal and figurative.

He turned toward the house and, for the first time, noticed a silver sedan parked out front. He didn't recognize the car as any of the locals. He squinted and could just make out California plates.

Damn.

He thought of his daughter, Claire, alone in her bedroom, furiously texting friends from New York.

Double damn.

If his leg could have managed it, he'd have run. Instead, he walked as fast as his knee would allow, trying to hide his limp—just in case someone was watching. It was all he could do not to groan with every step.

By the time he burst through the back door, he was

panting and could feel sweat beading on his forehead. He stopped to catch his breath and heard the unfamiliar sound of laughter in the house. Claire's laughter.

He closed his eyes for a moment and let it wash over him, imagining that she was laughing at one of the lame jokes he regularly told to elicit a reaction. One he never got.

He stopped short in the doorway between the back hall and the kitchen. Claire's dark head bent forward into the refrigerator.

"How about cheese?" she asked. "Or yogurt?"

"Really, we're fine" a voice answered, and Josh's gaze switched like radar to the two women sitting on stools at the large island at the edge of the kitchen. One looked in her late thirties, two thick braids grazing her shoulders. She wore no makeup and might have a decent figure, but who could tell with the enormous tie-dye dress enveloping most of her body. She smiled at Claire and something about her made Josh relax a fraction.

His attention shifted to the other woman, and he sucked in another breath. She tapped painted black fingernails on the counter as her eyes darted around the room. Her long blond hair was pulled back in a high ponytail; streaks of—was that really fire-engine red?—framed her face. The same blazing color coated her mouth, making her lips look as plump as an over-ripe strawberry. He had a sudden urge to smear her perfect pout with his own mouth, as if the most important thing in the world was for him to know if it tasted as delicious as it looked.

His body tightened, and he realized with a start that his knee had company in the throbbing department.

No way.

Her lips parted, and he forced his gaze to her eyes. She stared back at him with an expression that said she knew just what he was thinking.

No how.

Her eyes were pale blue, a color made almost silver by the heavy liner that rimmed them. Her skin was unnaturally pale, and he wondered for a moment if she was into that vampire-zombie junk Claire had told him about. He wouldn't put anything past one of those Hollywood types.

"Josh, look who's here. Can you believe it?" Claire gushed. He studied his daughter, who'd spoken in primarily monotone grunts since she'd arrived at the ranch a month earlier, but now thrummed with excitement.

"Call me Dad. Not Josh," he told her.

"Whatever." She gave him one of her patented eye rolls. "It's Serena Wellens." Claire shot a glance at the women. "I mean Sara Wells. But you know who she is, right? A real-life star here in our kitchen."

"A real-life star?" Josh didn't subscribe to *Entertainment Weekly,* but he was pretty sure Sara Wells hadn't been considered a "real star" for close to a decade now. Josh eyed Sara, who wore a faded Led Zeppelin T-shirt and capri sweatpants that hugged her hips like…nope. That was not where he needed his thoughts to go.

Sara pushed back from the counter. "Your kitchen?" she asked, raising a brow. "That's not what Mr. Crapshoot told me."

"You saw Jason Crenshaw."

"Yep." She jangled a set of keys in front of her. "Looks like you've got a little 'splaining to do, Daddy-O."

Maybe he shouldn't have questioned the "star" bit.

What did he know about Hollywood and celebrities? If a former child actor who hadn't had a decent job in years wanted to consider herself a star, it was no business of his. He knew guys who hadn't gotten onto the back of a bull for decades, but their identity was still wrapped up in being a bull rider.

Not Josh, though.

He'd had his years in the ring. Made a pretty good living at it. Broken some records. Truth be told, it had been his whole life. The only thing he'd ever been a success at was bull riding. But the moment they'd wheeled him out of that last event in Amarillo, his kneecap smashed into a zillion bits, he'd known he was done. His world would never be the same. He walked away and never looked back. Hung up his Stetson and traded the Wranglers for a pair of Carhartts.

People had told him he had options. He could try announcing. Get hired on with a breeding operation. Coach young riders. That last one was the biggest laugh. Just the smell of the arena made Josh's fingers itch to wrap around a piece of leather. He could no sooner have a career on the periphery of riding than a drunk could tend bar night after night. Being that close to the action and not able to participate would kill him.

A couple of times in the hospital and during rehab, he'd almost wished the accident had done the job. His gaze flicked to Claire, who looked between Sara and him with a mix of confusion and worry on her delicate features. She looked like her mother. Both a blessing and a curse, if you asked him.

At the end of the day, she was the reason he'd made it this far after the accident. He wasn't going to let some two-bit tabloid diva mess with his plans.

He forced a smile and turned his attention back to Sara. "About that," he began.

He watched her sense the change in him and stiffen. *Charm, buddy. The groupies thought you had it. Let's see what you've still got.*

He stepped forward and held out a hand. "I'm Josh Travers."

She eyed his outstretched palm like he'd offered her a snake. "Why are you living in my house?"

"Her house?" Claire asked.

Josh turned to his daughter. "Maybe you could head up to your room for a bit?"

"You must be joking." Claire crossed her arms over her chest. "And miss this?"

He made his tone all business. "Now, Claire."

His daughter made a face. "Bite me, Josh. I'm not leaving."

He heard Sara muffle a laugh as he stared down the beautiful, belligerent thirteen-year-old who had every right to hate him as much as she did. He'd been a lousy dad. Almost as bad as his own father, which was quite an accomplishment. He didn't know how to deal with her anger or attitude. Did he play bad cop or go soft? He barely knew his daughter, and in the weeks she'd been living at the ranch, he hadn't made much progress on repairing their relationship. One of the laundry list of things he should feel guilty about.

"Fine." He turned to Sara, who smiled at him. At his expense. "Trudy and I were partners."

"Is that so?" She wiggled her eyebrows. "Very *The Graduate,* although you don't strike me as much of a Dustin Hoffman. And from what I remember, Gran was no Anne Bancroft."

Josh shook his head and glanced at the hippie lady. "What is she talking about?"

She gave him a sympathetic smile. "Sara likes movie analogies. Ignore it."

He wished he could ignore this entire situation.

"Dad, is this our house or what?" Claire asked.

He sighed. "Technically, it belonged to Trudy."

Sara jingled the keys again.

"And now to you," he admitted.

"Oh. My. God." Claire let out a muffled cry. "I have no home. Again." She whirled on Josh. "You told me we were going to stay here. I could paint my room. Are you going to send me off like Mom did? Who else is left to take me?"

"No, honey. We *are* going to stay here. I'll work it out. I'm not sending you anywhere."

She sniffled and Josh turned to Sara. "Your grandmother and I were opening a guest ranch. She owns the house, but I have the twenty-five acres surrounding it. We back up onto the National Forest so it's the perfect location for running tours. I've been here since the fall working on renovations and booking clients. Guests start arriving in a couple of weeks."

Sara looked from Claire to Josh, her gaze almost accusatory. "Does it make money?"

He tried to look confident. "It will. I've sunk everything I have into the place." *Everything I had left after medical bills,* he added silently. "Trudy was going to help for the first season. I planned to buy her out with my half of the profits."

"But now the house is mine."

Josh nodded. "I don't expect you to hang around.

I'll cover the mortgage. At the end of the summer, I can take the whole place off your hands."

"Why can't you buy it from me now?" Her gaze traveled around the large room.

"The bank wants to see that it's a viable business before they'll approve my loan. Trust me, it's a good plan. Trudy and I worked it out."

She looked him up and down. "Trudy isn't here anymore."

"I know," he agreed, feeling the familiar ache in his chest as he thought of the woman who'd been more of a mother to him than his own. He wondered how difficult Sara was going to make this for him. He'd known Trudy's granddaughter had inherited the house. Josh had gone directly from the funeral service to the bank to see if he had any options. He didn't. He needed time and a bang-up summer to make this work. Otherwise, he might as well burn his savings in a bonfire out back. There was no Plan B.

"What if I want to sell now?"

His gut tightened. "Rose got to you already."

"How do you know my mother?"

"She and her land-developer boyfriend have been here a couple of times. The guy wants to tear down the house and build luxury condos on the property. Make Crimson a suburb of Aspen. What an idiot."

Claire took a step forward. "Are you going to let us stay or should I start packing?" She eyed both Sara and Josh as she bit her lip. "Because all my stuff is folded and in drawers where I want it."

He heard the desperation in her voice, knew that despite her smart mouth, his daughter was hanging on by a short thread these days. As much as he didn't want to admit it, they had that much in common. He'd promised to take care of her, make up for his past mistakes. The ones he made with her and those he'd buried deeper than that. He needed this summer to do it.

"Claire, I told you—"

"I know what it's like to want a place to call home," Sara said quietly, her attention focused completely on Claire. Her eyes had gentled in a way that made his heartbeat race. For a moment, he wished she'd look at him with that soft gaze.

Claire blew out a pent-up breath and gave Sara a shy smile, not the sarcastic sneer she typically bestowed on him. His heart melted at both her innocence and how much she reminded him of another girl he'd once tried to protect.

Sara returned the smile and his pulse leaped to a full gallop. *Don't go there,* he reminded himself. Not with that one.

"Can you give your dad and me time to talk?" Sara asked. "To work things out? Maybe you could show April around." She pulled her friend forward. "She's into nature and stuff."

"Come on," April said. "Can we walk to the pond I saw on the way in?"

Claire nodded. "It's quicker to go out the back."

As she passed, Josh moved to give his daughter a hug. She shrugged away from his grasp. One step at a time. He'd seen her smile, even if it wasn't at him.

"Thanks," he said when the back door clicked. "I'm sure we can—"

"Cut the bull."

So much for the soft gaze.

She folded her arms across her chest. Josh forced himself to keep his eyes on her face.

"I don't want to hurt your kid, but I don't have time to play *Swiss Family Robinson* for the summer. I need money and I need it now. If you want to make a deal, what do you have to offer?"

His adrenaline from a moment ago turned to anger and frustration. "I put everything I had into buying the land and fixing up the place. I've paid for marketing, a website, direct mail. We've got a real chance of making this work." He raked his hands through his hair. "It has to work."

"I'm not about to…" She stopped and cocked her head.

"What? Not about to what?"

"Do you hear that?"

A sudden sound of pounding filled the air.

"That sounds like—"

He turned as Buster, his oversize bloodhound, charged down the hall, galloping toward the kitchen.

"Buster, sit." The dog slid across the hardwood floor and ran smack into Josh's legs, all enormous paws and wiggly bottom.

"Buster's harmless."

He looked back at Sara, now crouched on the butcher-block counter with wide eyes. "Keep that thing away from me."

He felt a momentary pang of sympathy for her obvious fear, then glanced at Buster and smiled. "Looks like I've got you right where I want you, Hollywood Barbie."

Chapter 2

So much for being cool, calm and in control.

"This isn't funny." Sara hated that her voice trembled.

Josh bent to rub the giant beast's belly. The dog was deep brown with a wide ring of black fur around the middle of its back. Its eyes were dark, at least what she could see under the wrinkles that covered its head. It yawned, displaying a mouth full of teeth and flopped onto the wood floor. One pancake-size ear flipped over his snout. Outstretched, it was nearly as long as she was.

"This is *Buster*," Josh said with a laugh. "He wouldn't hurt a fly."

"That dog looks like he could eat me for breakfast."

"Lucky for you, it's nearly lunch."

"You are *so* not helping here."

"I like you better up there. You're not chewing me out."

"I wasn't chewing—" She stopped and met his gaze, now lit with humor. "You're living in my house."

"I explained that."

"I need to sell it."

"Sell it to me." He stepped closer. "At the end of the summer."

Fear had taken most of the fight out of her. "What am I supposed to do in the meantime?"

He held out a hand. "You could start by climbing off the counter."

She watched Buster, who'd begun to snore. "I don't like dogs."

Josh's low chuckle rumbled through her. "I never would have guessed."

She didn't move from the counter. "The fourth season of the show, I got a dog." She closed her eyes at the memory. "My character, Jenna, got a dog. It hated me on sight. The first day on set it bit me. Twice. I wanted to get rid of it, but the director's girlfriend was the dog trainer. She said it could sense my fear. That it was my fault the dog growled every time I came anywhere near it. Of course, the thing loved Amanda. Everyone loved Amanda."

"Who's Amanda?"

"Amanda Morrison."

"The movie star?"

"Highest-paid woman in Hollywood three years running. Back in the day, she was my sidekick on the show."

She expected a crack about how far the mighty had fallen. He asked, "How long was the dog around?"

"Lucky for me, the director was as big of a jerk with girlfriends as he was with me. By the end of the season, the dog was gone."

"Did it ever warm up to you?"

She shook her head. "I got faster at moving away after a scene. I never realized how much my fingers resemble bite-size sausages." She blew out a breath. "Animals and me, we don't mesh."

She looked away from the sleeping dog, surprised to find Josh standing next to her beside the kitchen island.

This close, she could see that his dark brown eyes were flecked with gold. A thin web of lines fanned out from the corner of them. He was tall, well over six feet, with broad shoulders that tapered into a muscled chest under his thin white T-shirt. Unlike most guys in Southern California, Josh didn't look like he'd gotten his shape with an expensive gym membership or fancy trainers. He'd clearly worked for it. Real sweat kind of work. He wasn't bulky, but solid. Although he wore faded cargo pants and gym shoes, he still gave off a definite cowboy Mr. Darcy air.

If Mr. Darcy had an unnervingly sexy shadow of stubble across his jaw, a small scar above his right eyebrow and a bit of a crook in his nose like he'd met the wrong end of a fist one too many times. A dangerous, bad boy Mr. Darcy.

It was one thing to slip on giving up chocolate; bad boys were quite another. She'd had enough of bad boys in her time. They swarmed L.A. like out-of-work actors.

His gaze caught hers, and it took her a moment to remember what she was doing in this house in the mountains, cowering on the kitchen counter.

He reached out a hand and she took it, still a little dazed. "It's not going to come after me?" she asked, throwing a sharp glance at the dog.

"I'll protect you," he answered, his tone so sincere it made her throat tighten. Among other parts of her body.

Off balance, she scrambled down, the heel of one shoe catching on the corner of a drawer and sending her against the hard wall of his chest. She stepped back as if he'd pinched her, but he didn't release her hand.

His calloused fingers ran the length of hers. "Nothing like sausages," he said with a wink.

She snatched her hand away and moved to the other side of the island, thinking the altitude was making her light-headed. Praying it was the altitude.

"Where's Claire's mother?" she asked. As she'd hoped, the spark went out of his eyes in an instant.

"She was having some problems—personal stuff— needed a little time to get herself back on track. So Claire's here with me."

"For how long?"

He shrugged. "As long as it takes. Why do you care?"

"I have experience with bad parents. It can mess with you if you're not careful."

"Are you careful, Sara?"

"I'm broke," she said by way of an answer. "Like I said before, I need the money from the sale of this house."

He hitched one hip onto the island. "You own the house, but it's only on a quarter-acre lot. I've got all the land surrounding it. Your part isn't going to be worth much without the land."

Crenshaw hadn't mentioned that. "Then why is my mother's latest boyfriend so hot for it?"

Josh took a moment to answer. "Basically, I'm hosed without the house. I can't run a guest ranch without a place to put the clients. If he gets you to sell to him now, I won't have an income stream this summer. And without money…"

"I know what happens without money."

"Right. Here's the deal. Assuming things go well when the season starts, I can pay you double the mortgage for the next three months. That should get you through until I can secure the loan."

"Why should I do it your way?"

He lifted one brow. "Because you're a kind and generous soul," he suggested.

She answered with a snort. "Is that the best you've got?"

"It will make your mother crazy mad."

"That's a little better."

"Listen, Sara. Your gran was one of the best. She was nice to me when I was a kid and a good friend since I got back. While I don't know the terms of her will, it doesn't surprise me that she left you the house. She loved this place and she talked about you a lot."

"I barely knew her."

He nodded. "One of her biggest regrets was that she didn't do more for you. Help you out when things got rough."

"Woulda, shoulda, coulda," Sara said, but turned away when her voice cracked. "You know, I spent a summer here right before the show got picked up."

"Trudy told me."

"It's funny. I don't remember a thing about that time."

"Look around the house…maybe it will come back to you. I'm going to find Claire. Whatever you decide, Sara, your grandmother did love you. You should know that."

She waited until his footsteps faded, then let her gaze wander after quickly checking that the dog remained sleeping on the floor.

The house was more an oversize log cabin, exposed beams running the length of the walls and across the ceiling. Their honey color gave the interior a cozy warmth in the late-afternoon sunlight. Across from the kitchen was a family room with high ceilings and a picture window that framed a million-dollar view of the craggy peaks surrounding the valley.

An overstuffed sectional and several leather armchairs sat in front of a wall of bookshelves with a large flat-screen TV in the center. Nothing looked the least bit familiar to her, and she wondered whether Josh had gotten the new gadgets or if her grandmother had been into cutting-edge electronics.

Did all of it belong to her, or would he strip the house if she sold? Maybe she should have spent a little more time with the attorney. Sara had been so angry when her mother had shown up that she clearly hadn't gotten the whole story about this place.

Couldn't anything be easy? she wondered as she made her way up to the second floor. She peeked her head into the first bedroom. Posters of pop stars and young actors lined the walls. A blue-and-purple comforter with peace signs covered the bed. Claire's room.

Next to that was a bathroom, and then came the

master bedroom. She stayed at the threshold, not wanting to venture into the room where Josh slept. Even from the doorway, she could smell the same scent he'd had today—a little woodsy, a little minty and totally male. She didn't want to be affected by his scent, by anything about a man who was entirely too rugged and rough for her taste.

She stepped quickly to the end of the hall. The final bedroom had soft yellow walls with lace-trimmed curtains, a four-poster bed and an antique dresser next to a dark wood ladder-back chair. She took a breath as she walked to the front of the dresser, skimming her fingers across the lace doily that covered the top. Framed photos lined one side, mostly her grandmother with people she didn't recognize, friends probably.

A few showed her mother as a girl, and in one she was a young woman carrying a baby: Sara. Sara was just a toddler in the photo and she smiled at the camera, one hand raised in a wave. Sara didn't remember a time before the endless rounds of auditions, cereal commercials and eventually prime-time celebrity. She'd been ten when *Just the Two of Us* first aired. The next seven years had been spent in a constant cycle of filming, promotions and off-season television movies.

It surprised her that her grandmother had none of her promo photos displayed. The only photos Rose had framed in their two-bedroom condo were publicity shots. Sara's hand trailed over a photo album that sat in front of the frames. She traced the jeweled beads that had been glued to the cover in the shape of her name. A sliver of memory trailed through her insides.

She sat down on the bed and flipped open the album. Her heart skipped a beat as she gazed at the first page.

It was a picture of her holding a giant ice-cream bar, mouth covered in chocolate, grinning wildly at the camera. In the next picture, she was on a trail, her blond hair pulled back in two pigtails and wearing an oversize cowboy hat. Her jaw dropped as she continued to turn the pages. Pictures of her feeding horses, a shot of her curled in a tight embrace with her grandmother. She read the caption below the photo: "Sara's first annual summer visit" written in Trudy's loping penmanship.

As she'd remembered, her mother had gotten a small part in a blockbuster Steven Spielberg movie that year. A part that had ended up on the cutting room floor. Shortly after that movie, Rose had switched her considerable energy to Sara's career. Which explained why first annual had quickly become one and only. Although Sara had no memory of this place, clearly she'd spent some happy times here.

And that was what her grandmother knew of her: Sara as a normal girl, before Rose had created Serena Wellens, deeming Sara too basic a name for the superstar she was destined to become. Even at the height of her fame, Sara had never identified herself as Serena. She'd been content with plain old Sara, although her mother had reminded her on a regular basis that fresh-faced Saras were a dime a dozen in Hollywood.

She'd had to become someone else, someone more special than who she was.

Being Sara wasn't enough.

She sniffed as a tear fell onto the photo, then wiped at it with her thumb. Taking a deep breath, she stood. One thing she had in common with her more glamorous persona was that neither one of them did tears.

She placed the album back on the dresser and started down the hall, but her gaze caught on a poster on the far side of Claire's bedroom wall. It was a picture of Albert Einstein with a famous quote underneath.

Sara wasn't one for inspirational quotes. Actions spoke louder than words in her world. She didn't know any details of Josh and Claire's relationship, but it had been very clear that it wasn't good. As she looked around the bedroom, she wondered what would happen if they didn't get this summer together.

She shouldn't care. Neither of them were her business. A month ago when she'd landed back on the tabloid covers and lost her most recent waitressing job, she'd vowed to mind her own business. Take care of herself. She was number one.

But she'd seen something in Claire's eyes that she hadn't remembered feeling for way too long. Hope. Even as the girl had looked at Josh with anger and resentment, there'd been a spark of something that said *don't give up on me*. Josh didn't seem like a quitter, so maybe they'd have a chance. The chance Sara had never had for a normal life.

How could she take that away?

Her heart raced as she made a decision. She hurried down the stairs and out the back door before she came to her senses.

Josh, Claire and April were walking across the field behind the house. She waited until they got close. "Good news," she announced. "I'm staying."

Josh stopped dead in his tracks. "What do you mean *staying?*"

"Here. For the summer. I'll make sure you have a good season, and then sell it to you in September."

Claire did a little dance around him, making his head spin more than it already was. "That's so great," she gushed. "Now maybe this summer won't be as awful as I thought."

"Hey," he said, pulling her around to look at him. "You think it's going to be bad?"

She shrugged then wiggled out of his grasp. "Not as much as before."

He squeezed his eyes shut for a moment and counted to ten. When he looked at Sara again, she'd walked toward April and taken the other woman's hands in hers. "I know I messed up and I'm going to make it right for you. The cowboy here offered to pay me double the mortgage for the next three months. That should at least cover your expenses for the summer. If Ryan ever calls…"

He didn't bother to try to follow their conversation. "I said I'd pay you double to *leave*. Go back to California. Let me run things here. You'll get your money."

She shot him a dubious look. "Hell, no, partner. I'm sticking right here, and I'm going to make sure things go right."

"I've got it under control," he ground out.

"Oh, yeah? That kitchen looks pretty decked out. I'd guess my gran was going to do the cooking."

He nodded, not liking where this conversation was going.

"Best blueberry muffins ever," Claire added.

"And now?"

"I'm interviewing people," he admitted. "Do you cook?"

She rolled her eyes. "That's not my point."

"Which is?"

"You need help."

"Not from you, I don't."

"I could handle the kitchen," April offered quietly. His gaze shot to April, who was looking at Sara.

"You don't have to do that," Sara told her. "You have a life."

April smiled. "I could use a little break, and I'm sure I can sublet the beach house for the summer."

"Is this because of losing the studio? You could teach some other place. Rent another space. You know your clients would follow you anywhere."

"That's the beautiful thing about yoga. I can take it anywhere, too." She gave Josh a hopeful smile. "I could even offer a few classes on the ranch. To start the morning, maybe."

Sara glared at him over April's shoulder, nodding vigorously. "That would be perfect," she said. "Your veggie burgers are the best. Josh, is there a Whole Foods anywhere around here?"

"A whole what?"

"They just opened one on the way to Aspen," Claire piped in. "But Dad only shops at the Red Creek Market."

April nodded. "It's important to support local businesses. I'll drive into town tomorrow morning and see what we can work out."

"When are the first guests arriving?" Sara asked no one in particular. "We'll need time to plan out the right menus. Do you have lists of food preferences and allergies? That sort of thing?"

"Hold on," Josh bellowed, raking his hands through his hair. "Hold on! No one is making veggie anything at my ranch. People book trips looking for action and adventure, not airy-fairy spa treatments and yoga classes. They want to fish and race ATVs, hike fourteeners and mountain bike the local trails. I'm the boss around here. I do the hiring. I make the plans. I'm the one—"

He looked at the three women, April's gaze a little hurt, Claire's eyes narrowed and Sara shaking her head just a bit as she chewed on her full lower lip.

"I'm the boss," he repeated quietly, willing it to be true.

"Don't be a hater," Claire mumbled.

"A what?" He rubbed his temples. "Never mind."

"You don't have a chef, do you?" Sara asked, her voice too knowing for his taste.

"I'm interviewing cooks."

"And who's planning all the so-called adventures?"

"I am."

"And leading the fun?"

Was it his imagination or did her gaze stray to his knee? "That's me, too. Got a problem?"

She took a step closer to him. Across the bridge of her nose, under who knew how many pounds of makeup, he could see the faint outline of freckles. Distracting freckles. Freckles he wanted to trace, wondering if her skin was as soft as it looked.

"Face it, cowboy," she said, bringing him back to the moment, "you need us."

"I don't need anyone."

He heard Claire snort.

"Jerk," Sara said under her breath.

A dull pounding started behind his left eye, matching the throbbing of his leg. "Fine. But this isn't the Ritz. If you're here, you work."

She tossed her streaked hair. "I've been working since I was eight years old."

He suppressed a growl. "Not the kind of work that involves a catered lunch."

"You think you know me so well."

"I know your type."

"We'll see about that." She gave his shoulder a hard flick. "I'll give it until Labor Day, Lone Ranger. If you can't get the bank loan approved by then, I'm taking the next best offer."

He studied her luminous blue eyes, their depths cold as an alpine stream. "Deal."

They glared at each other, and though he kept his eyes on her face, he noticed that her chest rose and fell unevenly and a soft pink flush rose to her cheeks. His own breath quickened, and without knowing why, he leaned in and enjoyed watching her big eyes widen.

The hippie chick clapped a few times, breaking the weighted silence. "If that's settled, we should think about planning. I'll start with dinner."

He forced his gaze from Sara's. "The local diner has decent takeout."

April laughed. "I'll cook tonight. Think of it as an official interview."

He nodded. "There are six smaller cabins on the property. Four of them are two bedrooms. You can have your pick."

"Can't they stay in the house with us?"

"No," Josh and Sara said in unison.

"Whatever," Claire mumbled.

Sara turned to his daughter. "Would you show me the other cabins?" She glanced warily at the thick pine forest that surrounded his land. "I want the one least likely to be invaded by critters."

Josh expected Claire to offer up one of the flip comebacks she gave him every time he asked for her help. To his surprise, she gave Sara a genuine smile. "Sure. Will you tell me about all the stars you know in Hollywood?"

A momentary cloud passed through Sara's eyes before she smiled brightly. "Oh, sweetie, I've got some stories for you."

Claire giggled. Actually giggled as she led Sara toward the row of cabins that sat in front of the small stream at the back of the property.

"Unbelievable," he said under his breath.

He heard April laugh again and whirled on her. "What?" he demanded. "What is so funny?"

She took a step back, palms up. "Nothing at all. Do you want to discuss menus while I check out the kitchen?"

Josh recognized a peace offering and was smart enough to take it. "Let's go," he said, and headed for the house.

Chapter 3

Sara glanced up from the computer in Crimson's small-town library. It had been three days since she and April had arrived in Colorado. Word spread fast that former starlet Serena Wellens was in town for the summer. A steady stream of locals had stopped by the ranch for neighborly visits. Of course the disappointment in meeting a once-upon-a-time celebrity in real life had been obvious from the comments she'd received.

"You looked taller on TV."

"You were so pretty when you were younger."

"Do you still talk to Amanda? Can you get her autograph?"

Her favorite had been from the town's mayor, who'd blurted, "I read you overdosed a year ago. I think I sent your gran flowers as a condolence."

It was a good thing the ego had been pummeled out of her years ago. Otherwise, the blatant disapproval might have done her in.

She watched a couple of teenage boys stare at her from behind the bookshelves at the far end of the room. She pulled off her headphones and winked in their direction. Her smile broadened as they ran away, books clattering to the floor in their wake.

"You enjoyed that a little too much."

She started at Josh's deep voice and swiveled her head to see him approach. Quickly, she clicked the mouse to minimize the screen and turned to block his view completely. "The picture-book section is on the other side," she said with a huff.

To her dismay, he gave her a knowing grin. "Whatcha doin', Hollywood?" His lazy drawl made her insides twist in a way she didn't like.

She shrugged in response. "Checking out the gossip sites. A little Facebook. April's meeting with the owner at the market to arrange food deliveries to the ranch so I'm killing time."

He craned his neck to peer over her shoulder. "I think you looked me up on Google."

"You wish," she sputtered as a voice sounded through the headphones that she'd dropped to the desk.

"Josh Travers does it again. It's a new record and another amazing showing from bull riding's reigning king." Applause and cheers echoed in the background.

Heat rose to her cheeks as Josh arched a brow.

"Fine. I was curious. So what. Don't tell me you haven't looked me up, too."

"I wasn't sure which site I liked better—serenawellensforever.com or sarawellsstinks.com."

"*Just the Two of Us* fans didn't love it when I changed my name. They thought they knew me when I was Serena. Like my name mattered."

"It mattered to you."

"Reigning king, huh?" she asked.

"That was a while back," he said with a smile, as if he knew she was changing the subject.

She studied him for a few moments. "I saw pictures of your accident."

His back stiffened. "Pictures exaggerate."

"The bull landed on top of you."

"They got him off quick."

"Does your knee still bother you?"

"Not really."

"Liar," she whispered. "Do you miss it?"

"Not really."

"Did you ever see that Jim Carrey movie *Liar, Liar* when he can only tell the truth?"

He scratched his jaw. "I don't think so."

"It's an interesting idea, don't you think? Even if he tried to tell a lie, it wouldn't come out of his mouth."

He just watched her.

"I'm kind of babbling."

"Yep."

He did that to her, she thought. He was such a presence. Big and broad and totally in his space—in her space. People in L.A. were always planning what came next, even if it was a trip to the mall. But Josh stayed in the moment no matter what he was doing. He kept busy, and to her eternal gratitude, she hadn't seen much of him other than watching him walk across the property early in the morning to take care of the horses, then catching glimpses of him throughout the day.

Yesterday, he'd spent most of his time on the roof of the largest cabin, replacing worn shingles. When the sun moved high overhead and the temperature rose with it, he'd taken off his shirt. Much to her dismay, Sara found herself staring out the window in the office far too often. It had been a while since she'd had a man in her life, but she figured she could get her wayward hormones under better control than that.

Here in the quiet intimacy of the library, those little buggers took flight again. With Josh standing in front of her, his faded T-shirt stretched over his chest and sculpted arms, she could imagine...

Nope.

She *did not* imagine. She'd given up her imagination when she'd abandoned her dreams, around the time she began filling in *waitress* under the occupation heading on paperwork.

This man was all that stood in the way of the possibility of reclaiming her life, or at the very least, creating a new one. The money from the sale would allow April and her to start over. The only view she'd let herself imagine was Josh Travers disappearing in her rearview mirror.

"So what *are* you doing here? Did they run out of *Playboy*s at the general store? I don't think the library has a subscription."

He shrugged then held out a book. The cover read *Talk To Your Teenager Without Losing Your Mind.*

"That's a mouthful."

"The librarian recommended it."

"It's nice that you're willing to read a parenting book."

"Claire hates me."

"She doesn't hate you," Sara argued as she stood and gathered her things.

"This morning after you and April left I asked her to help me feed the horses. You would have thought I was waterboarding her." He scrubbed a hand over his face. "I thought all girls loved horses."

"Not *all*," she clarified.

"Thanks, I've got that now. One of the mares sniffed her and she freaked out. I laughed a little."

"You laughed at her?"

He smacked the heel of his hand to his forehead. "So shoot me. I didn't mean it. She threw a bucket of grain at me, screamed that she hated the ranch, she hated her mother and most of all she hated me. My dad would have whipped my butt if I'd thrown a fit like that."

"What did you do?"

"Nothing. She ran back to the house. I finished in the barn and came here."

Sara led the way out of the library and into the warm afternoon air. She glanced up at the bright blue sky, still surprised at how much this small mountain town resembled a movie set. "She doesn't hate you," she repeated.

"Did you hear anything I just said?" Josh asked, his face incredulous.

"She's a teenager. Hormones running rampant and in a new place with a parent she barely knows. Give her time."

He looked like he wanted to argue then took a breath. "Time. Right. When are you coming back?"

Sara checked her watch. "I'm supposed to meet April in a half hour."

"What's the deal with the two of you? She was willing to follow you to Crimson and seems happy to do her part at the ranch. That's quite the package deal."

"I don't know much about the rodeo circuit, but in Hollywood finding someone who truly cares is a rarity." Sara took a breath before continuing. "I met April about the time my career was starting to tank and my personal life was just as messed up. She stuck with me through the bad stuff, and I did the same with her when she had her own troubles. She doesn't belong in L.A. anymore. If a summer at the ranch can help her see that, all of this would be worth it. She deserves happiness more than anyone I know."

He studied her for several moments. She struggled not to fidget under his scrutiny. "You're a good friend," he said finally.

"Oh, I'm the bee's knees, and don't you forget it." She laughed, trying to ignore the intensity of his gaze. "I need to stop by that clothing store at the end of the block. My L.A. wardrobe doesn't really work here."

Josh took a long look at the outfit she wore today. A shapeless black-and-white-striped sweater dress over skintight black jeans that zipped from knee to ankle. Her shoes, Converse trainers, were at least more practical than the heeled boots she'd worn yesterday. Without the heels, she was pixie-size, and if it wasn't for the heavy makeup lining her eyes and dark wine-colored lipstick, she might have passed for a teenager herself.

A lock of neon hair slipped from her newsboy cap, and she tucked it behind her ear. Josh's gaze locked on the soft blond wisps at the base of her neck, and he was momentarily fascinated to imagine her natural honey color.

That was the kind of woman he was drawn to: natural, sweet and compliant. A woman who'd bake pies from scratch with strawberries fresh from the garden. The kind of woman he could grow old with, reveling in a normal, boring, run-of-the-mill Ozzie and Harriett life. Not a bitter, bossy, snappish former diva.

No attraction to that type.

Not at all.

He fell in step beside her.

"You mean Feathers and Threads?" Other than T-shirt shops and the fishing shop, which sold outdoor gear, that was the only women's clothing store in town.

"I prefer to think of it as Cowgirl Duds R Us."

He chuckled. "It's not bad. Do you think you could help me pick out something for Claire? Maybe a necklace or earrings?"

She slanted him a curious look.

"A peace offering. For this morning."

"Buying your way out of the doghouse?"

"Whatever it takes." They reached the end of the block. "I need to stop in at the fly shop first. I ordered vests and waders for the ranch."

She didn't slow her pace. "See you in a few."

He watched her walk away and couldn't help but notice that the way her hips swayed under the striped dress was all woman.

Damn.

The bells over the door of Feathers and Threads chimed as he walked in fifteen minutes later. He glanced around but didn't see Sara. Maybe she was in the dressing room.

"Hey, Rita," he called to the shop's owner, who stood behind the counter with a young salesgirl and a cluster of customers.

He'd brought Claire here when she'd first arrived in town. His daughter had taken one look at the racks and announced she'd be buying her clothes from the Hollister website. The morning after, he'd taken Rita to coffee as an apology for Claire's rudeness.

Too bad she'd read more into that than he'd meant. She'd all but suggested a quickie in the back room of the store. When he'd refused, she'd still found excuses to stop by the ranch several times, dropping off sparkly tops and hand-knit sweaters for Claire. To his relief, Claire had kept her snide comments to herself, and he'd been able to avoid Rita as much as possible. That was another reason he wanted to come in here at the same time as Sara—someone to distract Rita.

"Hi, Josh," she cooed. "Can I help you with something?"

"I'm picking up a gift for Claire. I'll look around."

"Let me know if you have questions," she answered and turned back to her conversation.

He silently congratulated himself and headed toward the jewelry case at the back of the store. Rita and her gaggle of customers laughed softly as he walked by. Snippets of conversation drifted his way.

"...rode hard and put away wet."

"No wonder she can't get work. Who'd want to see that on the big screen?"

"Is it just me or has she had her lips done?"

"Doesn't belong in Crimson, that's for sure."

Josh concentrated on the necklaces as unease skated around his chest. He glanced in the small mirror above the jewelry case and spotted Sara standing behind a sale rack.

As Josh turned toward the group of women, the conversation behind the counter continued, louder now. The women made no attempt to be discreet.

"I read she was into drugs for a while," one of the customers offered, bending forward so that Josh got too much of a view of her ample backside.

Eyes widened within the group. "Did you see track marks?"

"I can't get past those raccoon eyes," another woman said with a snicker.

"It looks like she hasn't seen the sun in years," Rita answered. "Maybe we should send her down to Nell's salon for a makeover."

Maybe you should shut your mouth, Josh thought. He glanced at Sara in the mirror, expecting to see steam rising from her ears. He was surprised she hadn't come out swinging already. Instead, he watched her swipe under her eyes and return a blouse to the rack, her hand shaking a bit.

"I wouldn't wish that hot mess on anyone," the younger salesgirl said, sending the other women into peals of laughter.

Josh felt his blood pressure rise along with the volume of giggles. He looked back to Sara, and her gaze met his in the mirror. For a single moment her eyes were unguarded and he saw pain, raw and real, in their depths. She blinked and shuttered them, turning the glare he'd come to know so well on him in full force. She shook her head slightly and backed away from the clothes rack.

Now, he thought. *Cut them down now.* She turned to a display of knit tops and picked one out at random. He watched her carry it to the front of the store. The women looked her up and down, not hiding their judgment and contempt.

"Just this," she said quietly, keeping her eyes forward. "You have some lovely things in the store."

"They all have security tags," Rita answered as she punched a few keys on the cash register.

"Of course."

Josh's temper hit the roof. How could Sara let that group of catty witches fillet her without defending herself? Where was the sarcastic, no-holds-barred woman he'd already come to expect? Hell, he hated to admit it, but he actually looked forward to their verbal sparring to break up the monotony of his day.

But this? This was total and complete bull. He grabbed two necklaces from the rack and stalked to the counter.

"What do you think of these?" he asked as he slammed them onto the glass top.

Rita jumped back an inch then pasted on a broad smile. "With Claire's gorgeous skin the turquoise will—"

"I'm not talking to you," he interrupted, unconcerned with how rude he sounded. "Which one, Sara?"

"The butterfly charm," she answered immediately. "The turquoise on the other one is dime-store quality."

"I beg your pardon?" Rita sputtered.

Sara didn't make eye contact with either of them, only dug in her purse for a wallet.

That a girl, Josh thought. *Just a little more.*

"Claire trusts your opinion," he continued conversationally. "I think she was sold the moment Gwyneth called to see what she should wear to her movie opening."

"Gwyneth Paltrow?" the salesgirl asked, her tone taking on a fraction of respect.

Sara's fingers tightened around her purse and she sliced a dead-meat look at him.

He forced a chuckle. "It's like Hollywood is one big sorority." He pointed to Sara. "Her phone is ringing every ten minutes. Julia needs to know where to find some kind of boots. Sandra's texting about a brand of fancy-pants jeans."

Rita raised an eyebrow at Sara. "And they're calling *you?*"

When Sara didn't answer, Josh spoke quickly, "Like you wouldn't believe."

Sara pulled out cash and handed it to Rita. "For the sweater." She didn't acknowledge Josh's comments or Rita's question.

Rita took the money, studying Sara. "I'm ordering for fall in a couple of weeks. Maybe you could stop by and take a look at the lines. We're not as exclusive as Aspen, but I still want to offer current trends. I'd appreciate a fresh opinion."

"Fresh?" Sara questioned. "As in fresh off heroin?" She yanked her sleeves above her elbows and held out her arms for inspection. "No track marks, ladies. Needles were never my thing."

Two of the women giggled nervously and backed away from the counter. After an awkward pause Rita said, "If you've got time, stop back later in the month."

Sara blew out a breath. "Give me a break," she mumbled, and left the store, leaving the bagged sweater and change Rita had placed on the counter.

Josh quickly paid for his necklace, grabbed Sara's

bag and followed her into the warming afternoon. He caught up with her half a block down the street.

"What happened in there?"

She rounded on him. "Why don't you tell me, Mr. Name Dropper?" She jabbed at his chest, her voice rising. "Since when are you an expert on celebrity fashion? Not one damn person has called my cell phone since I got here, famous or otherwise. And you know it."

"Excuse me for trying to help. Those women were out for blood, and you were about to open a vein for them."

"You should mind your own business," she countered.

"Who *are* you right now?" He took a deep breath, needing to clear his head. It didn't work. Not one bit. "All you've done since the minute you walked into my house—"

"My house."

"*The* house," he amended. "All you've done is bust my chops. If I look at you wrong, you read me the riot act, give me one of those snide remarks or smart comebacks you're so damn good at." He pointed in the direction of Rita's store. "You didn't say one word to those ladies in there."

She rolled her eyes. "You took care of it all on your own."

"Somebody had to. It was too painful to watch your slow death."

"Julia, Gwyneth? Even if I was in L.A., do you think one of those women would give me the time of day? They are A-list, Josh. I'm beyond Z. You have no idea what you're talking about."

"Rita didn't know that."

"*I* know it." She scrubbed her hands over her face. "I'm a has-been. A nobody. You don't get it. What those women dished out was nothing compared to what I hear every single day in California. At the grocery. The dry cleaners." She laughed without humor. "At least back in the day when I could afford dry cleaning. I've been a waitress now for the same number of years I was a paid actress. Do you know how many customers gave me career advice, hair tips, dissed my makeup, my boyfriends, all of it? Nothing was off-limits. I can take it, Josh. I don't need you to swoop in and rescue me."

"Excuse me for trying to help."

"I don't *want* help. This isn't *Pretty Woman* meets mountain town. I'm not Julia Roberts shopping on Rodeo Drive. You're not Richard Gere on the fire escape."

"Why do you do that?"

Her eyes narrowed. "Do what?"

"Throw out movie plots like they compare to what's happening. This is real life, Sara."

"I'm well aware."

He shook his head. "I thought you were a fighter."

"No," she said quietly. "I'm a survivor." With that, she turned and marched down the street away from him.

Chapter 4

Sara didn't say much on the drive from town, content to let April ramble about her meeting with the man who ran the local farm cooperative. She gazed at the tall pines that bordered the winding highway, continuing to be awed by her surroundings. The vivid colors, woodsy smells—the vast magnitude of every inch of this place.

She thought about Josh's "real life" comment. Sara knew real life. Real life was struggling to meet her rent every month, praying each time she used her debit card that her bank account wasn't overdrawn. She had to admit there was something about Crimson that felt— well, authentic. In L.A., life was about who you knew, where you could get a table, which plastic surgeon you frequented. She glanced in the rearview mirror, wondering for a moment about the last time she'd gone anywhere without full makeup. Her war paint, as she'd come to think of it.

Was it possible she could have a brief reprieve from battle in this small mountain community?

As Sara drove down the narrow driveway toward the ranch, she spotted a large black SUV parked in front of the main house.

"If that's my mother…" she muttered under her breath.

April patted her knee. "You can deal with your mother. You're a fighter."

The car almost swerved into the ditch. "Did you talk to Josh?" Sara accused her friend once she was back on the dirt road.

"No," April answered slowly, her dark eyes studying Sara. "What's going on with you two?"

"Nothing."

"I can feel the vibes. They aren't *nothing*."

"You're imagining it."

"He's hot."

"Go for it," Sara suggested. "Maybe he'd relax if he got a little something."

April chuckled. "You know that after my divorce I swore off men, at least until I've found someone who's worth the time and effort. So I don't *go for it* anymore. Besides, maybe *you* could relax if…"

"Not going there."

"We'll see."

"You think you know me so well."

"I've known you since you were fourteen."

The studio had hired April to be Sara's fitness coach when she'd put on a few pounds during puberty. Sara counted that decision as one of the few blessings from her years as a sitcom star. Without April's gentle guidance, Sara might have added "eating disorder" to her long list of personal issues.

Nine years older than Sara, April had quickly become Sara's soul sister and best friend. When April's stuntman husband left her a few years later during April's grueling battle with breast cancer, Sara had been more than willing to see her friend through months of chemotherapy and radiation treatments and the nasty divorce that resulted.

Neither woman had been lucky in the relationship department—another fact that, despite their different outlooks on life, bonded them deeply.

"You only think you know me. I'm a mystery wrapped in a puzzle clothed in an enigma," Sara told her friend with a wry smile.

"Right."

Sara parked the car next to the SUV. "Are you trying to distract me from the probability of another scene with *Mommie Dearest?*"

"Is it working?" April asked, reaching for the door handle.

Sara grabbed her arm. "Have I told you today how sorry I am you're in this predicament with me?"

April shrugged. "Things happen for a reason."

"Don't go all *Sliding Doors* on me. The reason your savings account was wiped out and you lost the yoga studio is because I'm a gullible idiot, a loser and the worst friend in the world. We're stuck in high-altitude Pleasantville for the summer, thanks to me."

"Sara…" April began, her tone gentle.

Sara thumped her head against the steering wheel. "Maybe I was wrong to agree to Josh's plan for the summer. If I sold to Mom's latest sugar daddy we could be back in California next week."

"Back to what?"

"Our lives."

"Neither of our lives was that great to begin with, and you know it. Besides, what about Josh and Claire?"

"Not my problem."

"I guess that's true," April admitted. She pushed open the passenger door. "But we're not going to get anywhere sitting in this car. If you want to hear your mom out, that's your decision. You have to take control of this situation."

"Lucky me," Sara answered, and started toward the house.

Sara walked through the front door, waiting for the scent of White Diamonds, the perfume her mother had worn for decades to hit her. She smelled nothing.

She turned the corner from the foyer and stopped so suddenly that April knocked into the back of her. She stood perfectly still for one moment, then launched herself across the family room at the man who stood on the other side of the couch.

"I'm going to kill you," she yelled, reaching out to wrap her fingers around his neck.

Strong arms pulled her away and she was enveloped in a different scent—one that even in her anger still had an effect on her insides. "Settle down," Josh whispered in her ear.

"Let me go," she said on a hiss of breath. She fought, and his arms clamped around her, pressing her against the solid wall of his chest. After a minute she stopped struggling. "Let me go," she repeated. "I'm not going to hurt him."

Slowly, Josh loosened his hold on her. For the briefest second, Sara fought the urge to snuggle back into the warmth that radiated off his soft denim shirt, to bury her face into the crook of his neck and simply breathe.

She stepped away, needing to break their invisible connection, and straightened the hem of her long shirt. "You've got a lot of nerve showing up here, Ryan. Unless you've got my money and April's, too, you can crawl back under the rock you came from."

"Hi, Sara." Ryan Thompson, her onetime business partner and long-ago ex-boyfriend flashed a sheepish smile. "I came to apologize." He held out his hands, palms up. "To beg your forgiveness. Go ahead, attack me if you want. I deserve it. Whatever it takes to put this behind us."

Sara felt her temper building but kept her voice steady. "What it will take is you handing me a check for two hundred thousand dollars. The money it will take to repay April for losing the studio."

Ryan looked past her to April. "Do you, at least, forgive me, April? You understand, right?"

"I understand *you,* Ryan" came April's taut response.

His brows furrowed and he turned his attention to Sara again. "I messed up. I'm sorry. I'm going to make it better."

"By writing a check?"

He sighed. "You know I can't do that."

Sara knew a lot about Ryan Thompson. They'd met when she was nineteen.

Her career had stalled; audiences did not want to see another childhood star grow into a bona fide actor. She'd had a couple of box office flops, lost roles in several Lifetime movies to former cast members of *90210* and could barely get casting directors to meet with her for even supporting roles. She'd briefly thought of applying to college until her mother had informed her that with the quality of on-set tutoring she'd received, she'd been lucky to get her GED.

Her mother, who was still managing her at the time, had come up with the brilliant idea of sending Sara to rehab for undisclosed reasons.

Although the closest she'd come to an addiction was a great affinity for Reese's cups, Sara had been legitimately exhausted for months and welcomed a break from the Hollywood rat race.

Rose thought the publicity would make people see Sara as an adult, and if they didn't get specific about an addiction, the backlash would be manageable. The whole Drew Barrymore comeback—maybe even a book deal.

It hadn't worked. At all. She'd been blacklisted by every major studio, and her stalled career had gone down the toilet completely. But she'd loved her time at the secluded facility, morning meditation classes and long walks through the desert trails. On one of those solitary walks, she'd met Ryan, a hot young director who'd blown a huge wad of his last project's budget on his gambling addiction. The producers had sent him to the Next Steps treatment facility for a month-long program. As far as Sara could tell, he was the only other patient at the center not half crazed with withdrawal symptoms or buying drugs from the cleaning crew.

They'd been fast friends and had even tried a romance for about a millisecond. Ryan was prettier than Brad Pitt in *Thelma and Louise* and higher maintenance than a full-blown diva. He loved women, could flirt the pants off the Pope's sister and was as good at monogamy as he was at staying away from the blackjack table.

They'd remained close, and while he'd had a couple of critical and box office hits, Ryan continued to be a master of self-sabotage, finding it impossible to resist the lure of Las Vegas's shiny lights.

He'd been clean a year and a half when he'd approached Sara about forming a production company together. She was at the end of her rope with bad waitressing jobs and potential projects falling through. He presented a well-thought-out business plan, complete with spreadsheets, a list of potential investors and a movie script that had *award* written all over it. One with a lead role that made Sara literally salivate with need.

She'd agreed, and for months they'd hit the pavement, calling and setting up meetings to try to make this new dream a reality. After one of the major investors backed out, Sara'd complained to April, who'd offered to take a second mortgage on her yoga studio and give the money to Sara. April had a solid client list of California high rollers and had even been offered her own DVD series working alongside one starlet yoga devotee.

At first Sara had resisted her friend's offer, but April was confident in Sara's ability to make the production company a success. April was the only person who knew that Sara had been taking classes part-time at UCLA and was close to earning a business degree.

She and April planned on franchising the studio, and April's particular brand of yoga and one hit movie could help finance the expansion. Sara saw her chance to create a career away from Hollywood that would both fulfill her and give her the respect she craved.

That was before Ryan fell off the wagon again, blowing all their money on a weekend in Vegas. In less than a month, Sara had lost her savings, her apartment, her latest job and almost her friendship with April.

Now Ryan stood in front of her, offering to *make it better.* She'd trusted him once and wouldn't make that mistake again.

"If you can't write a check, how could you possibly make anything all right again?"

"The financing is almost set. I've got a new director interested. One who wants you for the lead. He's in Aspen for a few weeks. I just need to get hold of his people and set up a meeting with the two of you." His eyes shifted to April. "I'll get your money back. All of it."

Sara shook her head. "No way. We're done, Ryan. I don't trust you. I don't want to work with you. I don't want you anywhere near me."

"Sara, please," he pleaded, his voice a soft caress just short of a whine.

"She said no, bud." Josh had been so quiet where he stood a few feet behind her, she'd almost forgotten he was there.

Almost.

"I wasn't talking to you, Roy Rogers."

Sara saw Josh's fists bunch at his sides. "Well, I'm talking to you," he said, and took a step forward.

She put up a hand. "It's okay, Josh."

She'd been friends with Ryan long enough to know the pain and regret in his eyes were real. She wouldn't admit it, but it got to her. That was Sara's problem. She was a sucker for lost causes. Having been one for so many years, she could smell desperation on a person like some people could sniff out a good barbecue.

"I'm sorry," Ryan said again.

"You didn't even call. I had to find out from your assistant."

"I went straight from the casino to another stint in rehab." He offered a sheepish smile. "I'm a little more self-aware now, at least."

"Some good it did me."

"Give me a chance, Sara."

She blew out a breath and tried to ignore Josh seething next to her. "Fine. Call me if you get a meeting."

Ryan gave her a bright smile. "That's great. I'll—"

"In the meantime, you can help out around the ranch. Aspen's not that far and I know you have time on your hands. There's lots to do before the guests arrive."

"Hell, no." Josh sliced the air with one hand. "He's a lazy, no-good, designer-jeans-wearing pansy, and he's not touching anything in my house."

Sara whirled on him. "As I remember, this is *my* house."

"You know what I mean."

"I do," she said with a sniff. "And I don't like it." She turned to Ryan. "You'll work, Ryan. And not as in making reservations. The real thing. Start paying off your debt."

The frown he gave her said he wanted to argue but knew he didn't have a leg to stand on. "Sure. I'll do it. This is a guest ranch, right? What do you need? Someone to charm the clients. A wine sommelier, perhaps?"

She grinned. "A prep cook."

"A what?"

"Someone to help April in the kitchen."

April coughed loudly. "No, no, no. I don't need him, don't want him, won't have him."

Sara studied her friend. April was the kindest person she'd ever met. She didn't have a bad word to say about anyone. She'd give the coat off her back to a complete stranger. She'd expected April to take on Ryan like another one her charity cases. After all, April had been taking care of Sara for close to a decade. April's typically peaches-and-cream complexion had gone almost beet-red, and her chest rose and fell in frustrated huffs as she glared at Ryan.

He'd cost April her business and most of her savings, but even when Sara'd first shared the awful news, April had taken it in stride. She never lost her temper or got ruffled.

Until now.

She waited for Ryan to turn on his almost irresistible charm, offer April one of his trademark lines, smooth talk her into agreeing. Instead, he looked at Josh.

"Could you use a hand with maintenance?"

Josh shook his head.

"Grass to cut?"

"Nope."

"Horse droppings to scoop?"

"Nothing."

Ryan's squeezed shut his eyes. "I can't be completely useless. I'm done with useless."

Sara threw a sharp glance in April's direction. "Come on," she mouthed silently.

April growled low in her throat. "You can help. But you'll do what I say, which mainly involves staying out of my way."

To Sara's surprise, Ryan nodded, then stepped forward and wrapped her in a tight hug. "I *am* sorry."

"Make it better with April," Sara whispered.

"She hates me."

"Do you blame her?"

"I'm a good guy. With a little problem."

"Ryan."

"I need to get back to Aspen today." He leaned back and scrubbed his hand over his face. "But I'll be back and I'll try."

Sara glanced to where April stood, but her friend was gone. "Try hard," she told Ryan. "April deserves to be happy."

He ran a finger across her cheek. "We all do."

"If you say so," she answered. They both knew she didn't mean it.

Josh watched Ryan head toward the front door. His plan had seemed so simple a few months ago. Move back to his small hometown and make a new life on this secluded property. Work at the ranch would give both he and Claire the home and stability he needed. He'd be able to forget his past, the pain of his accident and losing his career—the only thing he'd ever cared about in his life.

With enough hard work, he'd be so exhausted he wouldn't miss the smell of the arena, would stop aching for the feel of a thousand-pound bull beneath him and the adrenaline rush that came with those seconds in the ring.

With enough patience, his daughter would stop looking at him like he was the enemy.

Now he had three California misfits crowding his space. Josh didn't do people and their problems. He had friends, sure. Other bull riders who were like him, happy to spend time drinking beer and watching old footage. Once guys left the ring and made homes and families for themselves, he usually lost touch. He was a loner and liked it that way. No complications.

The woman who walked over to the picture window at the far end of the family room was the biggest complication he'd ever met. She complicated his life. What happened to his insides when he watched her was a problem he sure didn't need.

He took a few steps toward her, not close enough to smell the scent that always surrounded her—some strange mix of honey and cinnamon—sweet with a bit of kick. But close enough that she couldn't *not* be aware of him. He wanted her to notice him as much as he did her.

"Do you two have a thing going?" he asked casually.

She looked over her shoulder at him. "You mean Ryan?"

"Who else?"

"Does it matter?"

A muscle ticked at the side of his jaw. "Stop answering my questions with questions." He hooked his thumbs into his belt loops. "My thirteen-year-old daughter is right down the hall from him. I don't want her waking up to any moaning and groaning next door."

One side of her mouth kicked up. "What if Ryan's at my cabin?"

He fought the urge to growl. "I don't need a soap opera played out in front of the clients."

She turned to him fully. "I don't do soap operas." Her eyes narrowed. "What makes you think I'm a moaner?"

Only the fact he'd spent the past three nights imagining the sounds she'd make when she was in his arms, under him, wrapped around him.

He took a step closer, so near that her subtle scent surrounded him and he could feel her breath against his jaw. His fingers reached out and pushed a wayward lock of streaked hair behind her ear. He'd only meant to touch her that little bit, but she turned her cheek, ever so slightly, into his palm. Her warm skin tempted him, called to his inner need. It wasn't a fight he could possibly win.

He brought his other hand up to cradle her face, tracing the edge of her lips with a calloused thumb. Her eyes remained glued to his mouth, and as he came nearer they drifted closed.

The desire to kiss her raced through him like a runaway train, almost knocking him back with its speed and strength. He needed to know if she tasted as sweet as she smelled, if her mouth was as soft as her skin. This prickly, snappish woman who played it so tough on the outside had sparked something in him he'd never felt before. Because he had a feeling that on the inside she was soft and warm. He craved knowing that side of her.

Josh tried to pull away, but he'd never been much

for self-preservation instincts. This moment was no different.

She made a noise somewhere between a sigh and a moan.

He was a goner.

"I knew it," he whispered against her mouth.

"Why are you still talking?" she asked, her eyes dark with the same desire he knew was reflected in his.

He pressed his lips to hers. Although he'd known she'd taste amazing, he wasn't prepared for his body's reaction to her. Electricity charged through him as he brushed his tongue across the seam of her lips. He forced himself to keep the kiss gentle when what he wanted was to wrap his arms around her and carry her to his bedroom.

"I don't want to do this," she said on a ragged breath.

He stilled. "Do you want me to stop?"

"Lord help me, no." Her arms twined around his neck, drawing him closer.

What a hypocrite, to complain that his daughter might catch wind of her and Ryan when Josh was ready to get naked in front of an oversize window.

The window. Claire. The thought of Claire seeing him play tonsil hockey with Sara made him pull away from her.

"What's the matter?"

He rested his forehead on hers and drew in several steadying breaths. "Everything. This summer is about Claire. About starting over with her. A second chance."

"Second chances," she said, her voice impossibly quiet. "I get that." The next moment she pushed hard on his chest. "You know what you are, Lone Ranger?"

He shook his head as she started past him, wondering how she could go from soft and pliant to prickly in less time than he could stay on the meanest bull. "What's that, Hollywood Barbie?"

"A tease."

Fighting words. She'd probably chosen them purposely to break the spell between them, but he couldn't let it go. He grabbed her wrist and swung her around to face him. "You'd better take that back. Now."

She shook free of his grasp. "You won't let anyone in and you'll throw out any excuse in the book so you don't have to." Her eyes glinted, daring him to argue.

His gaze locked on hers, and he let her see how much he craved her. Her breath caught. She took a small step back.

"Do you want in, Sara? Really?"

She looked at a point past his shoulder for a few moments, and when her eyes finally found his, she shook her head. "I want out. Out of Colorado. Out of debt. Out of owing people."

The right answer for both of them, Josh knew, but a sliver of pain sliced across his chest. He wasn't the kind of man women took a chance on. He had nothing to offer except a wild night between the sheets and a wave in the morning.

Even if she didn't know it, he could tell Sara needed a man who would stick.

Joe Hollywood upstairs wasn't it, but neither was Josh.

"It's better this way," she told him. "No complications."

Right.

She tapped her fingers against her jaw as if deep in

thought. "I don't like you that much anyway," she said finally. "You're not my type."

"Could you stop waving red flags in front of me?" He dug his hands deep into his pockets to keep from reaching out to her again. Every time she made some kind of ridiculous comment, he itched to prove her wrong. Over and over again.

As if sensing his intentions, she took another step away. "Sorry. No red flags. I have some voice mails to return, so I'll see you later. Or not. Probably not."

"Are we still in good shape?"

Her brow arched.

"Bookings," he clarified. "Guests. Good shape with actually making money this summer." He hadn't wanted to turn the office side of the ranch over to her, but as the start of the season got closer, it became harder to balance the preparations on the property with the work involved in making reservations and talking to potential customers. Sara had insisted that customer service was her strong suit, and despite her sassy attitude with him, so far she'd been a whiz. In less than a week, she'd organized the jumble of paperwork in the office, confirmed their current reservations and followed up with a half-dozen prospective clients.

The best part was that Josh's cell phone, where he'd had the office calls forwarded, had stopped ringing every ten minutes. He'd actually been able to get a lot of projects done. He felt almost ready for guests to arrive.

"We're in better than good shape. I just confirmed a family reunion for six nights at the end of June. There's only one weekend in July still open and August is full." She studied him. "You did an excellent job with the marketing. I guess there was a write-up in *Sunset* magazine recommending the ranch. That's quite a bit of publicity."

He shrugged. "I know an editor there."

She leaned in closer. "Must be an ex-girlfriend because you're blushing."

"I don't blush."

That elicited a full-blown laugh. "If you say so."

The sound of her laughter flowed through him. He grinned back at her. The moment grew quiet again, just the two of them watching each other. The heat in his cheeks took a nosedive south.

She blinked and her lips thinned. "I'm going to the office now."

"Gotcha."

"Don't follow me."

He tipped his head. "Wouldn't dream of it."

She headed for the other side of the house and the two rooms he'd converted to central operations with a little too much speed for a natural gait.

It looked as if she was running away.

Good. Maybe that would save them both.

Chapter 5

The crash from the floor above made Sara jump out of her seat. She rubbed her eyes and bent to retrieve the stack of papers that had spilled off the desk.

After spending the past few days buried in the office or driving back and forth to town for supplies before the first guests arrived, her eyes felt like sandpaper and her back ached. The time sequestered away from everyone was necessary, she told both herself and April, who'd brought trays of food into the office at regular intervals. For the most part, April had kept her opinion to herself, only dropping one or two pointed questions about the real reason Sara was in self-induced isolation.

Sara wasn't ready to admit she was avoiding anyone in particular. Definitely not Josh. Or Ryan, with his continuous stream of apologies and the puppy-dog eyes he kept shooting her.

Another loud thud came from upstairs, this one actually shaking the framed pictures on the office walls. It had to be Ryan, Sara thought with an accompanying curse. He must know she was working, and she guessed this was his ploy for her attention. She'd convinced herself it wasn't going to work until the telltale clatter of glass breaking reverberated through the ceiling.

She muttered another curse and stalked up the stairs. As she made her way down the hall, the sound of muffled crying came from behind one of the closed doors. Claire's room.

Sara knocked softly, then peeked in when no one answered.

"Claire, are you okay?"

Claire sat on the floor at the foot of the bed, her head resting against knees drawn tight to her chest. "Go away," she whispered, her voice clearly pained.

Good idea, Sara thought. That was exactly what she wanted to do, retreat back to her own office and not get involved in one more person's life. Her gaze caught on the nightstand that had been knocked on its side. That explained the crash. Next to the broken lamp was a framed photo, broken glass surrounding it. Claire smiled from the picture, cradled in the arms of a woman—a drop-dead gorgeous woman—who seemed vaguely familiar.

Sara stepped into the room for a closer look. She recognized Jennifer Holmes, international supermodel. In the past decade, Jennifer had graced the covers of countless fashion magazines and several Victoria's Secret catalogs.

"Is this your mother?" she asked, carefully lifting the frame from the carpet. "She's beautiful." She found a wastebasket beside the dresser and dumped the pieces of glass into it.

"I hate her," Claire mumbled. "She doesn't care about me at all."

"From this picture, she looks like she does."

"Duh." Claire lifted her tearstained face. "She's a supermodel. She can make herself look however she wants for a camera. That isn't real."

Sara knew there could be a big difference between what the camera showed and reality. "What makes you think she doesn't care? Tell me what's real, Claire."

The girl stared at her for several seconds, mouth pressed tight together. Then her eyes filled with tears. "What's real is that she's on some yacht in France with her new rock-star boyfriend. She told me she was getting help. For her drinking and stuff. She's supposed to be putting her life back together so I can live with her again." Claire sucked in a ragged breath, her words spilling forth like the tears that ran down her face. "And she's not. She won't. She doesn't care."

"Maybe she's—"

"I saw it on a gossip website. Pictures of her in a bikini with a guy's hand on her butt. I called her cell phone. She tried to tell me she was at the rehab place." Claire stood and flopped onto the bed. "*After* I saw the website. She's a liar. I asked her if I could come to where she was and she said no. She needs a break." Claire hiccupped and swiped at her cheeks. "A break from *me*."

Sara's heart melted. "Claire, I'm sorry—"

"I hate it here. I don't know anyone. I don't have any friends. Dad act likes we're going to do all this bonding, but he's always working. He barely says two words to me when he's around. It's like he doesn't know what to talk about." She shook her head. "How can I be so bad that neither of my parents want to be around me?"

"Oh, honey." Sara sat down next to the bed and wrapped one arm around the girl's shaking shoulder. Claire stayed stiff and then, with a sigh, sank against Sara.

"It's me," she repeated.

"It's absolutely not you." Sara gave Claire's arm a gentle squeeze. "I know for a fact that your dad loves you very much. He works so hard so he can make the ranch into a home for the two of you."

"It's not going to be much of home when you sell it," Claire said miserably.

Touché, Sara thought with a mental groan. "Whatever happens," she answered without addressing Claire's comment, "he wants to be with you. He's trying to do what's best because of you."

"He doesn't even like to be around me."

Sara squeezed her eyes shut, thinking of the love, longing and confusion in Josh's eyes when he looked at his daughter. "How long did your dad ride bulls?"

"I don't know. Forever," Claire mumbled. "I think since he was like seventeen or something."

"That's only a few years older than you. And how old was he when you were born?"

"Eighteen. My mom was, too."

"Yeah, well. Take it from someone who knows— young parents don't always know what they're doing. Your dad is trying. That has to count for something."

"Was your mom young when you were born?"

"Nineteen." Claire sniffed, and Sara dug in her pocket for a tissue. "Here, use this."

Claire blew hard then said, "She's really pretty. Your mom. She came to the ranch a few weeks ago. Tried to kick Dad and me out."

"That sounds like Mom."

"Are you close with her?"

Sara laughed softly. "Not exactly. You're changing the subject."

"I'm good at that." Claire shifted away from Sara and smiled a little.

"Me, too." Sara reached out a finger and ran it along Claire's cheek. "Have you talked to your dad about how hard it's been here for you?"

Claire shook her head. "I can't."

Sara watched her without answering.

"I don't want to make it a big deal. I guess it's not that bad," Claire said with a sigh. "I mean, I like the mountains. And how the air smells. Like it's..."

"So clean it almost hurts," Sara finished.

"Exactly." Claire picked at an invisible spot on her jeans. "And Brandon's okay."

"The kid who helps your dad in the barn?"

"He's fifteen. His family owns the property across the highway. He's kind of nice."

"And cute."

Claire looked up, pink coloring her cheeks as she met Sara's gaze. "Do you think so?"

"He's got those great big blue eyes, right?"

Claire sighed. "And that smile. He'll actually talk to me. But he's got a girlfriend, I think."

"You can still hang out when he's here. Just friends. I bet your dad would love an extra hand in the barn."

"I don't know anything about horses."

"Just like he doesn't know anything about what

teenage girls are into. It's up to you, but I know your dad does care about you. He wants you around. That counts for something. Maybe if you seemed interested in something he knew about, it could help with that bonding you mentioned."

"I wouldn't be in the way?"

Sara smiled. "April and I get in the way. Ryan is always in the way. You're the one Josh wants around."

"I think he wants you around, too," Claire said softly, then asked, "Is Ryan your boyfriend?"

"Absolutely not."

"Do you have a boyfriend?"

"Nope."

"Do you want one?"

Josh's face came to mind, and Sara tried to ignore the shiver that curled through her belly at the thought of his mouth on hers. "I've given up on men."

Claire studied her, looking suddenly older than her thirteen years. "Aren't you a little young for that?"

"I'm twenty-eight. That's like one-foot-in-the-grave time in Hollywood."

Claire nodded as if she understood. "My mom turned thirty-one last year. That's when she started to freak out. Party more. She gets Botox and some other wacky stuff." Claire stood and looked in the mirror above the dresser, pinching two fingers to the bridge of her nose. "She said I could have my nose done as a sweet sixteen gift. That'll be cool. I might look a little more like her and she'll..."

Sara turned Claire to face her. "Listen to me. You are perfect the way you are. Plastic surgery isn't going to change your relationship with your mother."

"You don't know—"

"I do know. I spent years jumping through hoops to win my mother's approval. Guess what? Never happened. Maybe it never will. I hope it does for you, Claire. I hope your mom gets healthy and realizes how precious you are to her. Until then, I know your dad loves you. Even if he isn't great at showing you how much."

"I just want to fit in here," Claire said miserably, her green eyes, so like Josh's, welling again.

"I know, sweetie."

"Would you take me shopping sometime?" Claire asked. "None of my clothes are right for Colorado, you know?"

Sara thought about the women in Feathers and Floss. "Are you looking for Wranglers and studded belt buckles?"

"No." Claire laughed. "Just clothes to hang out in. If you don't have time, I understand."

Sara gave her a quick hug. "I have time. How about before the weekend? I'll drive us down to Denver. We can make it a girls' day out. Go to lunch. Get our nails done."

"Really?"

"Of course, I may only be able to afford one sock, but we'll do our best."

"Dad has money. I could ask if we can use his credit card."

Sara almost choked from laughing so hard. "I bet he'd love that." She pushed the hair off Claire's innocent face. "I pay my own way. But, heck, yeah, we'll get his card for you. A shopping trip is one thing dads are always good for."

"Was your dad good for that kind of stuff?"

Sara's father had been a nameless stuntman on one of her mother's B movies. An on-set fling for Rose, who hadn't even told him she was pregnant and had never shared his identity with Sara.

"I don't know my father."

"Oh. I guess it's good that Josh wants me to live with him anyway."

"He doesn't like it when you call him Josh."

Claire grinned. "I know."

"How much did you see him before this summer?"

"A couple of times a year when he had time off from the tour. He'd come to my school and take me out to dinner. He sent me presents from the road. Lots of stuffed animals and things like that. I'd never been to the rodeo until..." Claire wrapped her arms tight around her chest. "The accident was my fault. Did you know that?"

Sara had read a half-dozen articles about the horrific accident that had ended Josh's career. It still made her sick to her stomach to think about the images she'd seen on YouTube. But none of the reports had mentioned Claire. "Why do you say that?"

"I was there." Claire scrunched up her face. "Mom was having a bad time. It was winter break and she was stuck with me. She found out there was an event a few days before Christmas and flew us both down there. I think she wanted to dump me with him for the holidays. She didn't tell him we were coming. Right before he came out of the gate, he looked up and saw me. It broke his concentration." Claire drew in a shaky breath. "They let the bull go right at that moment and..." Her voice broke off as she shook her head. "The whole arena was silent when it happened. I thought he was dead. The bull was so big and it landed right on him."

"Claire." Sara drew the girl into another tight hug. Sara had been through some bad stuff as a kid, but this poor girl gave her a run for her money in the bad-childhood department.

"They took him to the hospital straight from the event. I didn't see him again until he showed up on the last day of spring semester." Claire wiped her cheek against Sara's sleeve. "If I hadn't been there, he'd still be riding."

"It wasn't your fault," Sara whispered against the girl's head. "It was a terrible accident. But not your fault. Not your fault."

"But I—"

"Have you and your dad talked about what happened?"

Claire didn't answer.

"I'm sure he doesn't blame you."

"He should."

"You need to talk to him."

"No," Claire whispered. "I don't want to hear him tell me I ruined his life."

Josh sagged onto the wall outside his daughter's bedroom and swallowed against the bile that rose in his throat. He'd come to find her minutes ago but stopped short when he'd heard her conversation with Sara.

He didn't blame Claire for the accident. His break in concentration was his own fault. He'd been riding bulls long enough to know his focus should be zeroed in on the thousand pounds of angry animal between his legs. But when he'd seen Claire, he'd been thrown. Literally and figuratively.

Apparently, they'd both paid a price for his lapse in focus.

In his mind, he'd hoped she hadn't seen much or understood how bad it had been. Hoped her mother would whisk her away before she realized how serious it was. Jennifer had probably been too tipsy to understand the extent of the damage. But not Claire.

He had a hazy memory of trying to smile even as he felt his leg shatter, thinking that if his daughter could see him he didn't want to frighten her. He hadn't wanted her to know how scared he had been. Even now, that thought kept him rooted to his spot in the hall when his heart knew he should be the one with his arms around her, comforting and soothing her.

He'd waited until he could hide his injury before he'd come to see her, thinking that would be easier for both of them. Since he'd brought her to the ranch, sometimes he'd catch her staring at his right knee, especially toward the end of the day when exhaustion and overuse made it more difficult to hide his slight limp.

He wanted to be strong for her, not weak and half-broken. Bending forward, he rubbed at his leg, willing the pain to go away. He straightened and thumped on the wall as he walked to the end of the hall. "Claire," he called, coming back toward her room. "Are you up here?"

He made some more noise before poking his head in her room. She sat on the edge of the bed with Sara next to her. While she smiled at him, her eyes were red and puffy from her tears. "Hey, Dad," she said cheerfully, a sure sign that things were very wrong.

Sara watched him as if his face gave away the fact that he'd been eavesdropping. Impossible, he thought, but kept his gaze on Claire. "It's a gorgeous day," he said to his daughter. "I thought we could take an ATV up to Bitter Creek Pass, check on the trails and maybe have lunch."

Her smile faded. "I don't think so."

He took a breath and made his tone light. "Come on. It'll be fun. Just you and me and a ton of horsepower."

She scrunched up her nose. "Those things are so loud and they go really fast."

"That's supposed to be the fun part," he said, trying not to sound frustrated.

He let his eyes drift to Sara, who looked at him with a hint of sympathetic smile. "Can I come, too?" she asked.

As much as his body ached to be near Sara, part of him was angry his daughter had confided her pain to someone besides him. And he wanted her to know it. "There's only room for two on the ATVs, Hollywood."

"Einstein in a Stetson, aren't you? Thanks for pointing that out. I was thinking I'd have my own four-wheeler."

Her attitude made him grin despite himself. "You think you can handle it?"

She matched his smile. "Oh, yeah. I can handle it."

Claire cleared her throat, and Sara turned that million-watt grin on his daughter. "What do you say? I bet I can beat you and your old man to the top of the pass."

"He's knows a lot about ATVs."

Sara tossed her hair. "I'm not scared of his ego."

Claire gave a tiny giggle. "We're going to kick your butt," she said quietly.

"Oh, smack talk," Sara said with a loud laugh. "Guess the cowboy isn't the only one in the Travers family with a healthy ego. I love it. I'll help April pack a lunch while you two get the equipment ready."

Claire popped up off the bed and took two steps before Josh saw her realize her part of the deal. She slowed, dragging one bare foot across the carpet. "I guess that would be okay."

Josh didn't wait for her to change her mind. "Let's go, then," he said, hoping he sounded enthusiastic and not as scared as he was to mess up this chance with her. "We'll make sure Sara gets the slow one," he added in a stage whisper.

"Dad, that's not fair." Claire wiggled a finger at him.

"Right. Sorry."

"I mean, we're going to beat her bad enough as it is." Claire's eyes danced as she grinned at him and his heart skipped a beat. Her smile was so like his sister, Beth's. A smile he missed like he missed riding.

"You bet we are," he agreed, and motioned her to lead him out the door.

As she walked past, he met Sara's gaze. She arched a brow.

"Thank you," he mouthed.

Instead of the sassy comeback he expected, she only nodded and shooed him after Claire.

Chapter 6

"**G**et her!" Claire yelled in his ear over the roar of the four-wheeler's motor. "She's killing us."

Josh smiled as he hit the gas. He watched Sara's jeans stretch tight across her perfect bottom as she leaned into a turn on the narrow trail. He couldn't muster one bit of temper at getting his butt kicked by Hollywood Barbie. He was simply having too much fun racing up the mountain with his daughter's laughter filling him and her small arms wrapped around his waist as though she was totally comfortable in the moment. As though she trusted him.

He pushed hard on the throttle because the one thing Claire trusted him to do right now was catch up to Sara.

This day was another revelation about Sara. He'd expected her to be hesitant and unsure on the ATV, since she said she'd never ridden one before. But after a few minutes of instruction and warm-up, she took off on the dirt road that led from the property to the forest service trail as though she'd spent her life on the mountain.

Between the pain in his leg and Claire's extra weight behind him, it had taken Josh longer to find his groove. By that time, Sara was at least three hundred yards ahead of them.

She looked back over her shoulder, and her grin widened, hair escaping its ponytail under the helmet to whirl around her neck. He felt something unfamiliar around his stomach as he followed her, the powerful ATV vibrating under him, and realized it was happiness—an emotion he hadn't experienced in far too long.

Most of his last two years on the PBR tour had been spent defending his title and reputation from a new crop of upstarts willing to risk life and limb for a steady paycheck and an adrenaline rush. Green kids, the same as Josh had been when he'd first gone pro, with nothing to hold him down or back in his quest for fame and what little fortune there was to be had in the arena. Years on the back of a bull had taken its toll on his mind and body. He still felt the repercussions as he maneuvered around a fallen log, his back screaming as his knee throbbed.

"We're gaining on her," Claire yelled in his ear. "Go, Dad, go! You can do it!"

A surge of power coursed through him. Who needed Advil when he had his daughter's confidence?

"Hold on tight," he answered, and took a sharp left onto a single-track trail invisible to anyone unfamiliar with this mountain.

They sped along rocks and exposed roots. Hundred-year-old pine trees rose on either side of the trail, the smell of the woods thick and warm on this beautiful afternoon. It reminded him of all the reasons he'd come here with his daughter, why he believed—with enough time and patience—this place could heal them both.

Claire let out a delighted screech and Josh's smile spread. "Almost there."

He made another turn and the forest cleared. They raced into a high country meadow, bathed in sunlight. The Rocky Mountain peaks towered in the background, their tips still covered in snow. At this altitude, Josh still felt a slight chill to the air as he slowed the ATV in the middle of the clearing.

Claire hopped off and looked around. "We did it," she screamed.

At the same moment, Sara's four-wheeler came into view. She stood up from her seat as she got closer, shock and amusement clear on her face.

Skidding to a stop in front of them, she cut the engine and sank back onto the machine, gasping for breath. "How in the world did you beat me?" she asked with a laugh.

"Shortcut," he answered simply.

Claire danced a circle around Sara's ATV. "We won, we won," she chanted, and did a complicated series of dance moves that made Josh smile.

"Nice work." Sara gave Josh a small nod as she climbed off the machine. "You did good."

Another surprise.

Josh didn't often encounter good sportsmanship, so he expected at least a little pouting or fuss. Nothing. It was like she didn't care a bit about winning. For so long Josh had been focused on competing it was hard to change gears and enjoy something just for the fun of it.

Sara seemed to appreciate his daughter's buoyant mood as much as he did. Claire wrapped her arms around her. "That was awesome!"

"It sure was." She released Claire after a long hug, and Josh watched her take in the scene in front of them. She sucked in a breath. "Wow. This is amazing."

"Yes, it is," Josh agreed, but continued to watch her.

Sensation rippled across Sara's stomach as she felt his gaze. She was careful not to look at him, afraid of what she'd see in his stormy sea eyes and what her own might reveal. She prided herself on staying in control of her emotions, and had the hard-won walls around her heart to prove it. But she'd left that self-possession somewhere on the mountain and needed a few moments to regain it.

She turned a circle to see the full meadow view, then took another deep breath and closed her eyes. Her whole body tingled from the excitement of the ride. Yep, she told herself, it was an adrenaline rush and nothing more. Not her reaction to Josh.

Not at all.

It had been years since she'd let herself go all out like she had on the mountain. She'd left the world and its troubles behind and simply felt free.

When was the last time she'd truly felt free? She honestly couldn't answer that question.

Still not trusting her emotions, she busied herself removing a backpack from the rack of the ATV. "I've got sandwiches and drinks here," she called over her shoulder.

"I'm spreading the blanket," Claire answered from the middle of the meadow.

"Is everything okay?"

Josh's voice so close to her made Sara practically leap out of her skin. "Good gravy," she said, thumping her heart with one hand. "Sneak up on a person much?"

"Avoid eye contact much?" he countered.

Sara knew a challenge when she heard it but didn't rise to the bait. "I'm trying to help out, you know, get your kid fed."

He spun her around to look at him and lifted her sunglasses onto her head. Her eyelids fluttered shut as his finger traced her eyelashes. "You left off the heavy makeup today. It's nice."

She batted at his hand. "I should have known you'd be a sucker for plain Janes. Trust me, I won't tempt you again."

"There is nothing plain about you, Hollywood." His voice was a caress that made her insides warm and gooey. She swayed just a little. "Besides which, you tempt me each and every time I lay eyes on you. Now, tell me what's going on."

"Nothing," she said, an obvious lie. "I'm just a little light-headed, probably the altitude. Food will help."

"This is why I want the ranch to work."

She stared at him. "To make people sick?"

His mouth twitched but his eyes remained serious. "To take them out of their comfort zone," he said, dropping his arms to spread his hands wide. "These mountains change people. Inspire them. Make them see the world and their place in it in a different light. Sometimes there's no other way."

She nodded, although she didn't know if he was

talking generally or about her in particular. Either way, she understood down to her soul what he meant.

"I want to do that for the people coming here. When someone books a trip with us, it's not like heading to Disney World or Fort Lauderdale at spring break. It means something. To them. To me."

"I get it," she answered automatically, taken aback at his emotion.

"Do you? Do you understand how precious these mountains are? How few truly wild places there are left in this country? I want to celebrate that, help people appreciate it."

"A cowboy environmentalist?" Her lame attempt to lighten the moment fell flat.

He shook his head in clear frustration. "Do you think your mother's fast-talking boyfriend is going to give a rat's behind about the beauty of this place when he builds his luxury condos?"

"Rich people can have breakthroughs, too, you know."

"Not with what he has planned. Have you seen them? The plans?"

"No."

"He's going to level the trees that surround your grandmother's house. Put in a competition-size swimming pool under a huge bubble. Sure, he'll have a couple miles of paved trails—wouldn't want to scuff your running shoes on actual dirt."

"He's not going to demolish the entire forest," she argued.

"It changes things, Sara. Crimson is special. We don't need another Aspen-type playground for the rich and famous. Can't you see that?"

She did see it, but the knowledge left her in a precarious position. "What I see is that I need money and Richard Hamish has it. I haven't sold yet. You still have time, the entire season, to line up financing. But if not, you know what I have to do."

He crossed his arms over his chest. "Spoken like a true Californian."

"Was that the reason you let me come today, to prove some kind of point?" Despite her rising anger, her heart hammered in her chest anticipating his answer.

He stared at her, then sighed and said, "No. I wanted you to see this because it's amazing and breathtaking. I thought you'd like it. Both you and Claire." Reaching out, his thumb trailed across the skin exposed above the collar of her V-neck sweatshirt. "I wanted you here."

She itched for a fight, a reason to funnel her traitorous emotions into anger. She needed to pull away, from this man and his daughter, from the house that her grandmother had loved. The place that, despite her best efforts, Sara had quickly come to consider home. The honesty of his response and the warmth in his gaze melted away her defenses, and she felt herself more drawn to him than ever.

Her hand lifted to his, her fingers rubbing his calloused palm. "Let's focus on that, okay? Just for now. Can you do that? We'll have lunch, make Claire happy and deal with the rest later."

Her own version of a peace offering.

He lifted her fingers to his mouth and rubbed his lips across her knuckles. Butterflies flitted along her spine in response. "Later," he murmured.

Somehow she didn't think he was talking about their problems.

Which scared her even more.

* * *

Sara left Josh and Claire in the equipment garage two hours later and brought the backpacks into the kitchen to clean up. The afternoon had been perfect, relaxed and easy, with dad and daughter actually having a real conversation about Claire's homesickness for her old friends. Josh had suggested setting up Skype on the office computer so Claire could stay in touch, which had made Claire happy.

Neither had brought up Claire's mother or her dubious summer activities. The question remained what would happen once school started. But that was another issue to deal with later. And not hers, she reminded herself.

She couldn't quite wipe the grin off her face and was relieved April didn't seem to be around to ask questions about the afternoon. She bent forward to put the leftover apples back into the fridge.

"You're avoiding me."

At the sound of the voice, Sara jumped, banging her head on the top of the refrigerator. "Then take a hint, Ryan," she said, rubbing the bump.

"We need to talk." He stood, one hip hitched up on the counter, wearing a wrinkled polo shirt, cargo shorts and flip-flops.

"I don't think so." She pointed at his feet. "What kind of help can you be on a ranch wearing those?"

"I had a meeting in Aspen earlier." He raised a brow. "Besides, I saw you take off with Josh. Looks like I'm not the only one playing hooky today."

She blew out a breath. "He wanted to take Claire for a ride. It made her more comfortable if I came, too."

"You're still as much of an addict as me, Sara."

"I was in that rehab center for publicity and you know it. I am *not* an addict."

"I'm not talking drugs or alcohol. People and their problems. You're addicted to fixing other people's issues. Makes it easier to ignore your own."

"You're crazy."

"Tell me why you're here."

"Because this house belongs to me now," she said, holding tight to the refrigerator door handle but unsure why she needed the support. "I can make more money from a successful season than a bust."

"And what will you do then?"

"Repay April the money that you gambled away. Finally start the yoga center she wants."

"Her dream. Her problem."

"She's my friend, Ryan. The only one who's stuck with me all these years. And I want to run a business. I want to *do* something. Something real. Can't you get that?"

"Read for the part. That's real. Do you really think you can go back to L.A. and run an exercise studio? Cater to whatever star of the week flounces through the front door looking to use yoga as a front for her latest eating disorder?"

Her eyes narrowed. "It would sure beat waiting tables and clearing up their plates of barely touched food."

"You're an actress, Sara. It's in your blood. You have something to prove still. I know it. Don't give up on your dream."

"Acting wasn't my dream, Ryan. That one belonged to my mother." It was true, but so was his comment about Sara having something to prove. She hated that her career had fizzled so publicly. If she'd been able to walk away on her own terms, with some of her pride intact...well, maybe that would have made a difference. She didn't know. What could she do about it now? Read for a part and open herself up to more ridicule? She'd swallowed loads of that in the past and wasn't sure she could stomach any more.

"Your mother's here right now."

Her gaze flicked to Ryan's face. He looked guilty and sheepish. "Why?" she said on a growl.

"To help you. Sell this place to her boyfriend. He tells me he made you a pretty good offer."

"It's not worth what he plans to do to this place. It was my grandmother's house, Ryan. Her home. I may not have known her well, but I have to respect what she built here. I can't let it be destroyed without at least trying to save it."

Her mind strayed to the photo album on the dresser upstairs and the genuine smile on her eight-year-old face sitting on that porch swing. She thought about the pure joy she'd felt racing through the forest earlier, the way the mountain peaks felt like they cradled this valley and the peace it brought her. A feeling she hadn't known for years, if ever.

Ryan's voice broke through her reverie. "He wants the property, Sara. He's going to get it one way or another."

"Not from me." Sara didn't have much to hold on to in her life, but that feeling of peace was worth fighting for. She wouldn't give it up. She glanced at the doorway to the family room. "Is she waiting?"

"In the office."

She released her death grip on the refrigerator, flexing her cramped fingers. "Put some decent shoes on and go find April. Whatever she's doing, I'm sure she can use some help."

Ryan's full mouth twisted. "She doesn't like me."

"Do you blame her?"

"I'm a cad. That's my deal. But women still like me. They can't help themselves. She's different."

Sara stifled a laugh. "I can't believe you just said that line out loud. This isn't the nineteenth century. *I'm a cad.* So what? You can't flirt and charm your way out of what you did to April. This time you may have to actually work at making things better." She paused. "Trust me, Ryan. It's worth it."

He scrubbed his hand over his face. "Fine. You deal with your mother. I'll face the wrath of the hippie princess."

"You're so brave." Sara patted his cheek as she passed him.

He held on to her wrist. "I really am sorry, Sara."

"I know. Now go make it better." She slipped from his grasp and walked out of the kitchen, hesitating at the doorway to the office.

Go make it better.

Could she take her own advice? Was it possible to make better all the things that were wrong in her relationship with her mother? Did she even want to try? Since her career had gotten so far off track, Sara hadn't seen Rose often. She'd quickly tired of the never-ending litany of advice and criticism. Without the spotlight, Sara didn't have much to offer her mother. Rose was a stage mother in the worst sense of the word—Sara could give Lindsay Lohan or Brooke Shields a definite run for their money in the bad-mama department.

As awful and contentious as their relationship had become, some part of Sara still craved her mother's approval. That knowledge upset her more than anything. The fact that Rose could still send her into a tailspin with a well-chosen dig or subtle jab ate at her self-confidence before either of them spoke a word.

Laughter rang down to where she stood. Not her mother's voice. Claire. Sara took the steps two at a time but slowed in the hallway outside Claire's bedroom.

"That's right, dear," she heard her mother say. "Look over your shoulder. Just the hint of a smile. Make them want more of you."

Sara's stomach lurched. She'd listened to that same litany of advice for years. Before every Hollywood event, premier or even trip to the mall Rose had coached her on what to wear and how to carry herself. According to Rose, being an actress was a 24/7 occupation. Sara had never been allowed to be truly off. Even now she'd catch herself doing an unconscious hair toss when someone recognized her. Maybe the training had served her well, she thought, as it was the one thing that had made her hold her head high in the face of many moments of ridicule.

But that had nothing to do with Claire.

"What are you doing?" she asked, bracing one hand against the door frame.

Claire beamed at her. "Auntie Rose is giving me lessons on how to be a star." The girl breathed the word *star* with such reverence it made Sara's teeth hurt.

"Auntie Rose?" She flashed a pointed glance at her mother.

"Do you know who Claire's mother is?" Rose asked by way of an answer.

Sara nodded and tried not to roll her eyes.

"Jennifer Holmes, the supermodel," she answered anyway. "The girl has an *in*. You know how much that can help, Sara. How my fame opened doors for you."

Give me a break, Sara thought to herself. "Claire doesn't need doors opened for her, Mom. She's thirteen."

"I know it's a late start." Rose walked around the desk and stood next to Claire, running one finger along her cheek. "But look at her bone structure. She was meant to be on screen. The camera will love her. I have a friend over at Disney. They're always looking for the next big thing." She tipped Claire's face to hers. "You could be it. Can you sing?"

"I think so," Claire said, looking dazed.

"Mom! Stop." Sara stepped forward and pulled Claire away from Rose. "She has a life here. A good, normal life. She's not going to California or anywhere with you. Leave her alone."

"Just because you crashed and burned..." her mother began.

At the same time Claire asked, "Don't you think I'm good enough?"

Sara squeezed her eyes shut and tried to block out the sharp stab of pain Rose's words caused. She focused on Claire. "Honey, of course you'd be amazing. That's not the point. It isn't all fun and glamour. It's not a good place sometimes. There are a lot of bad people in show business." She threw a glare at Rose. "People who only care about themselves."

"Maybe it would give me something in common with my mom. If I was famous she might come be with me instead of…" Her voice trailed off and she swiped under her eyes.

"Oh, Claire." Sara enveloped in her in a tight hug. "Why are you doing this?" she asked her mother over Claire's shoulder.

Rose smiled sweetly. "I came here today to talk to you about this house. Richard wants to stay in Colorado until you decide to sell. I need a something to keep me busy. Claire is a lovely girl. Maybe she's it."

Sara's throat tightened. "Leave her alone, Mom."

"You know how to get rid of me," Rose said softly, and tapped the corner of the bed where a stack of paperwork sat. "Are you ready to sign?"

Chapter 7

Sara swallowed against the lump of regret balled in her throat. She'd spent years avoiding Rose, and now she wanted nothing more than to get rid of her mother. But not at the expense of her grandmother's dream. Selling would be simple and give her the money she desperately needed to repay April and get her own second chance.

Yet what would it cost her soul?

She'd given up on so much in her life, compromised her hopes and values to make life easier. She was done running from the hard stuff or letting other people bully her. If nothing else, being in Colorado had made her see that she could live life on her own terms. She had something to contribute. Her mother wasn't going to rob her of that so soon.

"I'm not selling, Mom. Not now. Not to Richard."

Rose's delicately arched eyebrows lifted. "Well, then—"

"And you're not spending any more time here. I want you to leave."

"This was my childhood home, Sara." Rose dabbed at the corner of one eye.

"You hated it here. Counted the moments until you could leave. I know the story by heart, so don't try to change it."

Her mother's eyes narrowed briefly. "You always were an ungrateful child," she said on a huff of breath. "Because of me you had every opportunity to succeed."

"Because of you I didn't have a childhood."

"Don't be dramatic, Serena."

"I quit being dramatic years ago, Mother. Now I'm trying for normal."

"Normal is boring."

"I'll take that, too."

Rose made a sound somewhere between a sigh and a growl. She wrapped one arm around Claire's small shoulders. "I'm so looking forward to getting to know you better, dear," she said, and flashed a smile at Sara. "I'll make a few calls to agents this week, then see if I can find a decent photographer to do some head shots of you. I bet the camera will love you the way it does your mother."

"That would be great."

Sara opened her mouth to argue but before she could get a word out, Josh appeared next to her. "There won't be any photographers or agents for my daughter, Ms. Wells." His voice was controlled, but Sara could see a muscle tick in his jaw.

Her mother's smile broadened. "Mr. Travers, how

nice of you to join us. Have you been listening from the hallway?"

"Long enough to know this discussion is finished, ma'am. And I'd appreciate if you'd stop filling my daughter's head with your celebrity mumbo-jumbo."

"She has star potential," Rose cooed.

"I believe Sara asked you to leave."

"Daddy, don't be rude," Claire said, crossing her arms across her chest. "Sara's mom wants to help me."

"You don't need her kind of help."

Tears welled in Claire's wide eyes. "You don't understand anything," she yelled, and tore past Josh, her angry footfalls echoing from the stairs.

Rose pressed her soft pink lips together. "Well, that's unfortunate. How do you think her mother would feel about a chance at Claire making it in the big time?"

Josh felt his blood turn from boiling to ice-cold. He knew exactly how Jennifer would feel—thrilled about an opportunity to meet bigger Hollywood A-listers and score better drugs. While Claire's mother was still one of the most beautiful women in the world, she'd lately gotten more press for her partying than her photo spreads. She'd even lost her contract as the face of one of the big cosmetic companies because of her extracurricular activities.

The only saving grace was that the further she spiraled out of control, the less Jennifer took an interest in Claire. Josh planned to go back to court and file for sole custody once the ranch was stable and profitable. He didn't figure Jen would fight him, but that would change if she thought Claire was useful to her.

He took a step toward Rose. "Stay away from my

daughter and out of my family's business," he commanded, not trying to hide his anger.

To her credit, the older woman didn't flinch. "It's
too bad you're building your business in a house that
should rightfully belong to me." She tapped one finger
against her mouth, a slight smile playing at her lips.
"Claire really is lovely. Plus she has a budding flair for
the dramatic. I like that in a girl."

Sara moved in front of him before he could wrap
his hands around Rose's birdlike throat. "Enough,
Mother. The house belongs to me. I'm telling you to
leave. Now."

Rose backed away, palms up. "I can take a hint,
honey. But I'll be back. One way or another, mark my
words."

"This isn't *The Terminator,* Mom." Sara leaned in
and said softly, "Are you so desperate to keep your
boyfriend that you'll stoop this low this to get what
you want? I always thought you had a replacement
guy waiting in the wings. I guess things get tougher
as you age. How sad."

Josh watched Rose's perfectly bronzed cheeks turn
a deep shade of pink. "I don't know what I did to deserve such an awful daughter," she said with a sput-
ter. "I gave up everything for you and this is how you
repay me? You were a horrible, colicky baby and a demanding child. You couldn't even make something of
the career I practically gift wrapped for you. Does it
make you happy to watch your own mother struggle
when we both know you could help me if you wanted
to? You make me sick."

He saw Sara's sharp intake of breath as Rose

stormed past them both, slamming the door shut in her wake.

"Okay, then," Sara whispered after several moments, her back still to him. "That was fun and a great trip down memory lane." She said the last with a laugh that caught in her throat and turned into a strangled sob.

Josh reached for her and slowly turned her so she was facing him. His gut twisted at the tears that filled her eyes. "I'm sorry," he told her. "You don't deserve that."

She shook her head. "I'm the one who's sorry. That she's giving you so much trouble. For ideas she may have put into Claire's head." She swiped her hands across her face. "I'll do whatever it takes to make sure she doesn't corrupt Claire, Josh. She's an amazing girl. I know you only want what's best for her."

He trailed a thumb across a stray tear that ran down her cheek. "Even if I'm an idiot about knowing how to talk to my own daughter?"

She sniffed. "All men are idiots sometimes." Holding up her fingertips, she cringed. "I can't cry anymore. My makeup is going to run all over the place."

He wrapped his hands around hers. "Why do you wear so much makeup anyway? You don't need it." As soon as the words were out, he regretted them. Jeez, maybe he should ask her if she was pregnant next or say her thighs were fat. He really was an idiot.

She stared at him for what seemed like minutes as he braced himself for an explosion. Instead, she said softly, "It makes me feel protected—like armor. People see the goop and not me. I like it that way."

The brutal honesty of her words contrasted with the stark vulnerability in her eyes. His breath caught and his cold, hard heart melted. She leveled him. He bent forward and dropped a soft kiss on each of her eyelids. Up close she smelled like cinnamon and honey, sweet and spicy at the same time.

"I see you," he whispered against her forehead.

"That's a James Cameron line," she answered, her voice not quite even. Her hands pressed against his chest as she pressed into him. "From *Avatar*."

He smiled and brushed his mouth across hers. "You know a lot of movies."

"Uh-huh."

"And you talk too much."

"Probably. I think it's because—"

He covered her mouth with his, ran his tongue along the seam of her lips until she opened for him. Everything about her drew him closer. He savored the feel of her in his arms. His hands trailed up and down along her back, played with the soft strands of her hair. Her whole body pressed into him, and for a moment he tried to hide the evidence of his desire. Then she moaned into his mouth and he lost all coherent thought.

She pulled his shirt out of his waistband, and her long fingers were cool on his skin. "Good lord," he muttered as what was left of his brain cells took the fast train south.

He tugged at the top of her shirt and trailed kisses from her jaw down her neck and across her collarbone. Just as he moved aside her bra strap, a horn honked from the driveway below. He bolted upright. The horn blared again, this time followed by a chorus of loud whooping and slamming doors.

"Travers, where the hell are you? Let's get this party started, man!" a deep voice called.

Josh met Sara's gaze, knew his eyes were as hazy as hers. He stepped away and cursed under his breath, dug the heel of his hand into his forehead, willing his brain to start functioning again.

"Who is that?" she asked, her voice shaky as she readjusted her shirt.

He cursed again. "Our first guests."

"Your friends from the rodeo? I thought they weren't coming until next week."

"Sounds like they're early."

She blew out a breath. "Right. We can do this. I'll find April and have her whip up something for dinner. Most of the things on the itinerary can be moved up to the next few days. I'll make calls once everyone is settled. Ryan can at least put sheets on a few beds." She turned toward the door, all business.

He tugged on her arm, pulling her back against him, and wrapped his arms around her. "Are you okay?" he asked, his lips just grazing her ear.

"No, I'm freaking out. These are the first paying guests. Things have to be perfect."

"As long as we have cold beer and lots of food, they'll be fine. I mean, are *you* okay?"

She stiffened in his arms and he held her tighter. "I'm fine. I'm sorry about my mother. I'll try to control her better."

"You're not responsible for your mom. She shouldn't have said what she did to you. It will work out in the end. I'm not giving up." He paused then asked, "Are we okay?"

She wiggled until he released her. "There is no *we,* Josh."

Irritation bubbled in him. "That's funny, because I don't think I was kissing myself just now."

She threw him an eye roll over her shoulder. Her big blue eyes held none of the spark he'd seen earlier. She'd been so relaxed on the mountain, more of whom he believed she truly was. Not the guarded, fragile woman who stood before him now. "We were both upset. No big deal. It was a kiss, not a marriage proposal."

Her attitude got under his skin and he couldn't help baiting her. "Are you looking for a marriage proposal, Sara?"

"Not from you, cowboy," she answered with a scoff, but her shoulders tensed even more.

He wanted to grab her, kiss her until she was once again soft and pliant in his arms. The horn honked for a third time and he heard a loud knocking at the front door.

Sara smoothed her fingers over her shirtfront. "Go greet your buddies. I'll get everyone moving."

"This conversation isn't finished," he told her as he headed for the stairs.

"My end of it is," he heard her say under her breath.

He smiled despite his frustration, wondering how the fact that she always had to get in the last word could be so endearing to him. He shook his head, making a mental note to start thinking with his brain rather than other parts of his anatomy.

Sara came through the back door of the main house an hour later. Music streamed into the kitchen as April appeared from the family room, two empty platters in her hand.

"You'd think those guys hadn't eaten in months,"

she grumbled. But Sara noticed her grin and the light in her eyes. April was at her best when she could take care of people.

"I've got the two big cabins made up. That should hold everyone. Do you need anything?"

"I've got another batch of wings ready to come out and a vat of queso dip almost heated. I'll need to run to the grocery tomorrow. We should at least make it through breakfast."

Sara glanced at the spotless counters. "Can I help clean up?"

April gave her a knowing look. "Go introduce yourself. They're rowdy but seem nice enough. Four guys and one girlfriend. Her name is Brandy. She's a looker in that farm-fresh way."

Sara took a tube of deep plum lipstick from her jeans pocket and applied a liberal layer to her mouth. "I don't want to interrupt."

"It's a party in there," April countered. "The more the merrier."

"Has he told them who I am?"

April's smile turned gentle. "I don't think so. It's not a big deal, you know. Maybe they won't recognize you."

"How old is Brandy?"

"Early twenties."

"Unless she was raised without a TV in the house, she'll know me."

"It doesn't matter."

"It doesn't matter in L.A. Much. I can blend in a little in the land of falling stars. Especially with a new crop of beautiful losers coming through every year. But here it's just me—the only big fat failure for miles."

April took a pot holder and opened the oven to pull out a baking sheet of wings. They smelled delicious. "Did you ever consider you might be the only one who believes you're a failure?"

"My mom thinks I'm a failure," Sara said with a shrug.

"Your mom is a witch."

Sara snorted. April didn't call people names. Ever. "Whoa, there, lady. Them's fightin' words."

"Bring it," April said as she dumped the wings into an oversize basket. Her hands free, she turned and hugged Sara. "I'll take down your mother and the broom she rode in on."

"You're a Buddhist."

"I'll make an exception for her. And you. Go out there for a few minutes. Have fun tonight, Sara. You deserve it."

"What would I do without you?" Sara gave her friend one last squeeze and walked into the family room.

Josh and his four friends sat on the sofas and chairs surrounding the coffee table, filling the large room with their presence. Three of the men looked around Josh's age. The last one was so young he seemed barely out of puberty, despite having the broadest build in the group. Two were clearly brothers, both blond, tall and lanky. The third had a thick head of midnight-black hair and deep brown skin. The young one reached for another handful of chips, a shock of red hair falling over one eye. As a whole, they were tough, rangy and utterly male. Something Sara was unused to in Hollywood.

"It's enough testosterone to choke you," a voice said close to her ear.

Sara turned to see a young woman standing at her side who was as "farm fresh" as April had described. Her light brown hair was pulled back in a plastic clip and cascaded in healthy, unprocessed waves to the middle of her back. She wore little makeup other than a hint of lip gloss, and her soft denim shirt was tucked into a pair of high-waisted jeans. Actual Wranglers, if Sara guessed right.

"You must be Brandy," she said and held out her hand. "I'm—"

"Serena Wellens," the woman finished, her eyes widening.

"I go by Sara now. Sara Wells is my real name."

Brandy pumped Sara's hand at fever pace. "I loved *Just the Two of Us*. My sister and I lived for Tuesday nights."

"Thanks," Sara said weakly, her stomach beginning to churn. She braced herself for the questions about her career, her fall from stardom, her stint in rehab. She waited for criticism to cloud Brandy's gaze.

Her eyes clear, Brandy glanced around the room. "Josh said this house belonged to your grandmother."

That was it? Where was the third degree she was so used to from people she met in L.A.? She answered, "I didn't know her well, but she left it to me when she passed."

"It's a great setup and really nice of you to help Josh make it work this summer. Having a place of his own for Claire means the world to him."

Her mother's refrain from her childhood filled Sara's mind: "the world doesn't revolve around you."

Based on life in Crimson, that might really be the case. Maybe outside the dysfunctional Hollywood bubble, people didn't care about her past. She wanted to keep the conversation away from her personal life so she asked, "Do you know Josh well?"

"Those four are like brothers." Brandy nodded. "Manny and Josh started the circuit at the same time. Noah and Dan are the only ones related by blood, ten months apart. Irish twins, if you know what I mean? Noah doesn't actually ride. He does search and rescue up here in the mountains, but he's an honorary member of this crew. I've been dating Dave, the older one, for about five years."

"You don't look old enough for that."

"We met when I was sixteen at a county fair in Indiana. My dad's a big-time doctor so it about killed him that I had it bad for a bull rider. He'd expected me to follow in his med school footsteps. But I graduated high school and got a job at a preschool so I could have summers off to be with Dave."

"How'd your dad take that?"

"He was on fire for a while, but in his heart he wants me to be happy. He learned to live with it. You know how it goes."

Sara only wished that were true.

"We're getting married this fall." Brandy held out her left hand where a small diamond ring glittered on her finger.

"Congratulations. I hope you have a great life together. What about the baby-faced redhead?"

Brandy smiled. "That's Bryson. He's new this year and the guys have taken him under their wing. He was dying to meet Josh so came with us to the ranch. I'm sorry if getting here early made extra work for you."

"It's no biggie." Sara watched Josh throw back his head and laugh at something Manny said. "He seems happy tonight."

"He seems happy here," Brandy corrected. "We weren't sure whether he'd recover from the accident."

Sara turned her attention more fully to the other woman. "I didn't realize his injuries were life threatening."

"The physical part was bad, but the worst part was losing his career and the life he'd known. He took it hard. If it wasn't for having to get things together for Claire, I'm not sure he would have made it."

Sara had assumed Josh's leg and the surgeries he'd endured to fix it had been the worst of his struggles. She knew a thing or two about losing a career and the emotional damage it could inflict. She hadn't considered she and Josh might have that in common.

"I'll introduce you." Brandy walked forward into the room, clearly expecting Sara to follow.

"You all need a chance to catch up," Sara said, suddenly feeling out of place in her low-slung jeans, tight T-shirt and heavily made-up face. Even the streaks in her hair made her feel like an outsider. It was one thing to wear her carefully crafted mask in California, but these people were real. She felt like a huge phony.

"Come on." Brandy's smile was open and friendly. "They know me too well to be on their best behavior. Without backup, I'll be stuck judging burping contests, or worse."

Sara couldn't help but return Brandy's smile. "For a few minutes, I guess."

"Hey, y'all," Brandy announced over the music. "This is Sara. She's keeping Josh's tight buns out of trouble this summer. And she's taking care of all you yahoos while we're here. Try not to make her regret the hospitality."

Sara felt a blush rise to her cheeks as the attention turned to her. That and the mention of Josh's buns. Good gravy.

All four men jumped to attention. "Nice to meet-cha," Dave said, coming around the coffee table to shake Sara's hand before draping a long arm across Brandy's shoulders. "Thanks for taking us in early."

"No wonder you look so dang happy," Noah told Josh as he came to stand in front of Sara. "You are the prettiest thing I've seen in ages," he said to her, making her color deepen. She put out her hand but he swatted it away, instead grabbing her up in a bear hug and twirling her in a fast circle.

"Put her down," Josh ordered.

"Oh, darlin', you smell so good. Sweet as my mama's apple pie." He nuzzled his face into Sara's neck. She heard Josh growl behind him.

"I mean it, Noah. Enough."

Manny stepped in front of Josh. *"Señorita,"* he crooned, pulling Sara away from Noah's tight embrace. "You make us crazy hombres act even more loco." He took her hand, but instead of shaking it, brushed his lips across her knuckles.

"You've got to be kidding me," Josh grumbled.

"Wow," Sara whispered. She hadn't experienced anything like this in years. To be the center of attention for these men was strange and exhilarating, like the first time she'd flipped through channels and watched herself on TV. She felt strangely exposed, but not in a bad way like she had so many times in L.A.—still safe, although not quite herself. It gave her a dizzy sort of feeling.

"You guys are funny," she said with a giggle, then cupped her hand over her mouth. Sara was not a giggler by nature.

Manny released her hand as Noah stepped forward. "I feel like I know you from somewhere. Do you have a twin sister?"

Sara's shook her head as her grin evaporated. *Here it comes,* she thought.

He paused and wiggled his eyebrows. "Then you must be the most beautiful girl in the world," he said to a chorus of groans from the rest of the group.

Josh gave him a quick thump on the head. "Knock it off, bozo."

"Who died and made you boss of me?" Noah countered, his good-ole-boy ease replaced with six feet of tall, angry man. Josh's shoulders stiffened.

"It's okay," Sara said, stepping between the two.

"Not to me," Josh answered. It felt like all the air whooshed out of the room at the intensity of his tone.

Noah studied Josh. "Is there something you're not telling us? You guys have a fling going on here?"

"No," Sara and Josh answered at once. Josh continued, "I don't want things complicated while you're here."

"Uncomplicated," Dave said, giving Noah a soft elbow to the back. "That's us."

"Dinner," April announced in the ensuing silence.

As quick as that, the mood changed again. "I'm starving," Noah said, heading for the dining room.

"With service like this, we may never leave," Manny agreed with a wink at Sara as he passed.

When everyone else had left, Sara turned to Josh. "I know they're just joking with all of the compliments. Trying to be nice."

"Those guys don't do nice." He scrubbed one hand across his face.

She put her fingers on his arm, shocked at the tension in his corded muscles. "What's the problem?"

"Is Noah your type?"

"What?" The question took her aback.

"At first I thought it was Ryan, the slick Hollywood bit. But maybe you'd like slumming with a bad boy. Tell me, which way is it going to go?"

Sara sucked in a breath. "You are way out of line, Josh. My idea was to spend the night holed up in my cabin. Alone. But April convinced me to come out here to meet your friends. It was hard as hell since I was sure they'd give me the same once-over I get every day in L.A. then make a big deal about who I used to be. But you know what? Those guys were nice. And sweet. And funny. I don't get that a lot and would appreciate if you'd stop raining on my parade with your bad attitude."

She whirled away but he held her wrist. She wouldn't turn around but felt his heat against her back. "I'm sorry," he said finally.

"Fine. Now let go."

He didn't release her. "You deserve someone nice, sweet and funny. You deserve someone whole. I hope you find that man. Even if it's one of those guys. Any of them would be lucky to have you."

She looked over her shoulder and her breath caught

at the stark pain in his eyes. "What do you mean *whole?*"

He dropped her arm. "Never mind. Let's go eat." He moved past her without another word.

As he walked from the room, her gaze caught on the slight limp in his gait that became more pronounced at the end of a long day. She couldn't answer for herself, but she was certain he didn't deserve the self-inflicted solitude he seemed to carry as his burden. He'd had everything in his life taken from him. Not the slow unraveling that marked her failure, but one instant that stole his future and challenged a reputation he'd built for years.

At least she knew that she could go back to acting if given the chance. His days on the back of a bull were done. She couldn't imagine the strength it had taken him to move on, to start over on the ranch and with Claire. How could he think he was anything less than whole? His strength of character was deeper than most of the men she'd known combined.

The question remained: What did she want in a man? Her eyes roved over his strong body as he disappeared around the corner, a shiver dancing along her spine. It had been years since she'd considered dating after a string of relationships with would-be actors had left her hollow inside.

Josh was 100 percent real man. As she followed him into the dining room, the thought crossed her mind that she might not even be up for the challenge that he held.

Once again, she reminded herself it was a good thing she was only on the ranch for the summer. For any number of reasons.

Chapter 8

Josh sat through dinner with a chip on his shoulder and a pit in his stomach that prevented him from enjoying any of the delicious food April had prepared. Not so for his friends, who dug into heaping dishes of enchiladas and all the trimmings with the gusto of a pack of NFL linebackers.

What ate at his gut even more was the way Noah and Manny continued to flirt with Sara right in front of his face. Her rich, musical laughter filled the dining room as she immediately slid into the rhythm of their close circle as if she'd been a part of it for years.

That got him, too, because she was so different from any of the girls he'd met on the circuit. The ones he'd known his buddies to date throughout the years. The "buckle bunnies," as they were called, were a special brand of groupies, and it was rare to find a true love, like Dave and Brandy, when you were on the road in cheap motels and seedy diners for weeks at a time.

He took another pull on his beer and groaned inwardly when he heard the front door slam shut. One more complication for his evening.

"Daddy? Sara? Whose truck is that in the driveway?"

Claire came into the dining room, and out of the corner of his eye, Josh saw Bryson sit up straighter.

Down boy, Josh thought to himself, giving a mental eye roll at how much he sounded like an old geezer.

He got out of his chair to stand next to Claire. "Claire, I think you've met Dave and Brandy. The guy who looks like his twin is his little brother, Noah. That's Manny at the end of the table and Bryson next to him. Everyone, this is my daughter, Claire." He pointed a finger in Bryson's direction. "Off-limits," he ordered, placing a protective arm around Claire's shoulders.

"Dad," Claire said with a groan, "don't embarrass me."

"Hi, sweetie," Brandy crooned. "It's so good to see you again."

"Hey." Claire gave a small wave and shifted uncomfortably next to him. "I'll just go up to my room."

He wondered what could be wrong with Claire. There wasn't a more welcoming group than this bunch, but he got the sense that Claire was ready to bolt. Sara stood before Josh could answer. Her eyes met his for a brief second before she turned to Claire. "Did you have a good time with your friend?"

"Sure, I guess."

"Come and sit next to me. We can be newbies to this group together."

After a little push from Josh, Claire shuffled toward Sara and sank into the empty chair next to her.

Noah took up the conversation without a beat. "Did you hear about the last event?" he asked Josh.

"I don't get a lot of bull-riding news out here," Josh said without emotion. "And that's the way I—"

"It was awesome, man. I rode Big Mabel and after six seconds she really let loose. I hung on like never before, legs back and chin down just like you taught me. You wouldn't believe the high. I was in the zone like never before. You have no idea."

"I have an idea," Josh grumbled as he took his seat again.

"Five thousand dollars, dude. The biggest purse this season and it was all mine."

Manny leaned over and thumped Noah on the head. "Shut up, amigo."

"No, it's fine." Josh took another drink of his beer. "I want to hear everything." He turned to Bryson. "How's your first season going?"

Sara rubbed her hand along Claire's back as she kept one eye on Josh. "Are we still going shopping this weekend?" she asked quietly.

"Sure."

"What's wrong, honey?"

"Do you think they blame me for what happened to Dad? I mean, maybe they hate me. It was my fault he—"

"Stop," Sara said, hoping to soothe the young girl before Josh noticed her distress. "What happened to your dad wasn't your fault. We've been over this. These are his friends. I think he'd want you to enjoy tonight, not to beat yourself up."

"You're right." Claire smiled, although it looked more like a grimace.

Sara laughed softly. "That's a start." She grabbed the plate of brownies April had brought out a few minutes earlier. "Let me share something I've learned over the years. Chocolate is often the best medicine."

Claire's smile turned genuine. "I like that philosophy."

With Claire happily nibbling on the brownie, Sara turned her attention back to Josh. His full focus was on Bryson as he nodded at something the young bull rider said. To a casual observer he'd looked relaxed, but Sara noticed the tension that radiated from his jawline down through his shoulders. His fingers gripped the beer bottle with a white-knuckled grasp.

It must be so difficult for him to listen to stories from a new crop of bull riders. She knew what it was like to have failure tap you on the shoulder and ask for advice in the form of a new generation of rising stars.

Sara stood without thinking. "How about a game of charades?" Everyone at the table looked at her like she'd grown a horn. "You know, the game?" she clarified.

Continued silence and stares. Finally Dave cleared his throat. "Cowboys don't usually play parlor games, darlin'."

Of course not. Sara felt color creep into her cheeks once again. She glanced at Josh, who'd finally loosened his grip on the beer bottle. Too bad for the cowboys, she thought. If it could keep these guys distracted and give Josh a little breathing room, she'd push them into it one way or another.

She leaned over the table toward Dave. "What's the matter? Afraid of being beat by a girl?"

Brandy gave a quiet snort of laughter. "I'm on Sara's team," she announced.

"Women against men," April added as she came into the room. "Perfect."

Josh pushed away from the table. "I don't think—"

Sara made squawking noises and flapped her elbows.

Josh's eyes widened. "Are you calling me a chicken?"

Sara smiled broadly. "If the feathers fit."

"Come on, boys," Josh ordered. "Into the family room. These ladies are begging to be trounced."

"Charades," Dave mumbled, but stood without argument. "This has to be a first."

"Should I come, too?" Claire asked.

"It wouldn't be a girls' team without you," Sara told her, meeting Josh's gaze for a brief second. She thought she saw gratitude and maybe a little relief before his mask snapped into place.

"Let's do this." He hustled the other bull riders out of the dining room, grumbling all the way.

Sara didn't make it back to her cabin until close to eleven, way past her bedtime with the early-morning hours on the ranch. She'd helped April clean up in the kitchen after Brandy and Claire had gone to bed, leaving the guys to relive old stories around the fire pit on the side patio.

To her surprise, Ryan had seemed to find his place in the overtestosteroned group, happily sharing stories of which Hollywood starlets had what body parts surgically enhanced.

She smiled to herself at the stories she could tell if she wanted, then jumped at a noise from the trees next to her front door.

"Heart-attack central over here," she squeaked as Josh stepped out of the darkness.

"Sorry." He didn't look sorry. He looked big and gorgeous in his soft flannel shirt, faded jeans and boots. A light was on in her cabin, its glow illuminating the front step enough for her to see him clearly.

Late-night stubble shadowed his jaw, defining it even more and making her wonder how that roughness would feel across her skin. She quickly pulled her mind away from that train of thought. No good could come from there.

"Expecting someone else?" he asked.

"Yogi Bear?" she answered, still trying to catch her breath. "Or Grizzly Adams, maybe?"

One corner of his mouth hitched up, matching the catch in her throat. "Noah likes you."

"I got the impression Noah likes anyone with breasts and a pulse."

That drew a laugh from him. "Probably. The question is, do you like him?"

Something in his tone of voice put her on edge. "I don't think that's any of your business." She took a step toward her door but he blocked the path.

"It is if you're going to mix business with pleasure."

She eyed him for a moment then swallowed, too tired to play games or even put up a fight. "I'm not interested in Noah."

He watched her.

"Or Manny. Or Bryson."

He continued to stare.

She huffed out a breath. "I'm not after your friends. Why do I feel like there's still a problem?"

He blinked several times then mumbled, "Thank you."

"I'm having trouble following you."

"For tonight. You made Claire feel comfortable, and I have a feeling you suggested the stupid game to do the same for me."

"Everyone had fun playing the game," she said, letting a little temper seep into her voice. "I was just keeping the guests entertained. I'm sure you can handle your own feelings."

"You're right—it wasn't stupid. We did have fun. Because of you."

The cool night air licked across her bare arms and goose bumps tickled her skin in its wake. She took another deep breath, hoping the scent of the surrounding mountains would calm her. Josh's gaze fell to her chest, which had the exact opposite effect on her jumbled emotions.

His eyes squeezed shut. "I don't know how to do this."

"Do what?"

"Want you so badly and not act on it."

She knew that feeling. "There are a lot of reasons we shouldn't be together."

He nodded but said, "Tell me why I shouldn't kiss you right now."

Every shred of rational thought dissolved from her brain. Without meaning to, she swayed a tiny bit closer to him. "I don't want to."

"You don't want to kiss me?"

"I don't want to give you a reason not to," she said on a shaky laugh.

He laced his fingers with hers and tugged her closer. With his other hand he cupped the back of her head, bringing her mouth against his. Like before, his kiss mesmerized her. Her defenses, her protective walls—everything inside her loosened and traveled south to parts of her body that hadn't been lit up for years. Those bits were glowing now as he claimed her, pulling her against him and deepening the kiss.

A shiver ran across her back and he wrapped his arms tightly around her. She snuggled into the heat that radiated from his body, losing herself in his spicy scent.

Tugging at the hem of her T-shirt, his warm hands pressed against her skin for several minutes before his fingers worked at her bra strap. *Yes, yes, yes,* her reawakened senses shouted in her head. At the same time, a trickle of unease danced across her conscience.

Darned conscience.

She didn't do casual flings. That was one of the few standards she'd held true to, both in and out of the spotlight. L.A. was filled with relationships built on nothing more than mutual attraction and soul-crushing loneliness. Sara hadn't given her body or her heart in a moment of weakness in the past. She wasn't going to let her hormones take over now. She knew how badly that could play out in the morning, and she wouldn't risk her pride, no matter how good it felt.

The silent snap of her bra opening brought her fully to her right mind.

"Stop." She wasn't sure if she'd said the word out loud until Josh's hands stilled on her waist.

He buried his face in the side of her neck. "Is this what you call a dramatic pause?" he asked, his voice ragged.

"We shouldn't do this."

"I hope you mean we should take it inside your cabin instead."

Sara gave him a small push and he immediately moved back. "I mean, the two of us is a bad idea for a lot of reasons."

"If I'd known you'd actually muster an argument, I'm not sure I would have asked the question."

"What do you want out of this summer, Josh?"

He tilted his head, massaged his thumb and index finger above his eyes. "Money," he answered simply.

"Is that all?"

"Give me a break on the twenty questions, Sara. My brain isn't firing on all cylinders right now." He sighed. "I want a future for Claire and me. I want this ranch to feel like home for her."

She nodded and tried not to admit that the truth in his words stung. She was used to not being a priority to anyone, even herself. But it still hurt to hear it out loud. "It's about Claire for you. For me it's about a second chance of a different kind."

In a way, things had been easier in California. The day-to-day struggle to make ends meet had left her little time to ponder the sad state of the rest of her life. Now that she had that time, it was up to her to protect herself. No one else was going to.

She liked to believe that her grandma would have fought for Sara if her mother hadn't made sure they never returned to Crimson. Maybe her grandmother would have been the positive role model Sara had so desperately needed.

She wanted to think that was why Gran had left her the house. An olive branch of sorts. Sara had no intention of letting it go to waste.

"I want the money and the fresh start it will give me. I'm going to get it one way or another. Even if that means..."

The lingering heat in his eyes went instantly frosty. "Even if that means crushing my future to guarantee your own."

"I want both of us to get what we want. I really do. But at the end of the summer, that might not be possible. I'm going to sell this house. I hope it's to you. I'm working to make sure that happens. But getting involved is a complication I'm not willing to risk."

"And that's what this is? A complication?"

"I don't know. I think so."

"What about Claire?"

"I'd never hurt Claire. You know that."

"She feels close to you. It will break her heart if you throw us over."

"That's not fair, Josh. Whatever happens, I've been honest about my intentions. I'm not going to mess with you and Claire."

"Why does it feel like you already are?"

His anger felt like a slap in the face.

"You don't understand."

"Explain it to me, then." Frustration radiated off him, hitting her like rolling waves.

She opened her mouth but couldn't think of how to tell him how scared she was. How frightened her feelings for him and his daughter made her.

As she'd done so often in her life, she took the coward's way out. "It's late. We're both tired. You should go."

"That's what you want?"

No, no, no. "Yes." She stepped aside to let him pass.

He moved past her, but at the last moment, swept her into his arms and claimed her mouth in a kiss she felt all the way to her toes. When he finally released her, she stumbled back against the door of the cabin, her knees as wobbly as a newborn foal.

He didn't look any more in control than she did, but his voice was steady as he told her, "You think too much, Hollywood," before turning and disappearing back into the darkness.

Chapter 9

Josh finished wiping down the last ATV and leaned back against the machine's front tire. Massaging his fingers against his leg, he thought about how happy everyone had looked coming back from last night's sunset ride.

The weather had been perfect for the past three days and his friends had taken full advantage, spending as much time as possible hiking, biking and fishing on the mountain. Yesterday afternoon, they'd ridden the four-wheelers up to the old mining town on the other side of the peak. He'd even convinced Claire to come along.

Things were exactly the way he'd pictured them for the summer. Except for watching Noah and Manny continue to flirt with Sara while Bryson made cow eyes at his daughter. That wasn't part of the plan.

Neither was the way his knee throbbed after several days of constant action.

The door to the equipment barn squeaked. "Josh, are you in here?"

Josh straightened as Dave shuffled into the barn. "I'm just cleaning things up a bit."

"That ride was killer today. The views from the top are definitely worth the price of admission."

"Yep." Josh rubbed the towel across the seat of one ATV. "Brandy seemed happy."

Dave snorted. "She's happy anytime I let her drive. That woman has the heaviest lead foot in history."

"I'm glad it's working out with the two of you."

"Me, too." His friend studied him. "Sara's pretty great."

"It's business, Dave. Nothing more."

"You don't look at her like it's business."

Josh flipped the towel onto the workbench and turned. "She's going to sell the house at the end of the summer and head back to L.A. If I can't get the bank to finance me, there's a decent chance all my work will have been for nothing."

"Really?" Dave whistled under his breath. "She seems happy here. Not a Hollywood type. Have you thought about asking her to stay?"

"Why would I do that?"

"Because you're crazy about her."

"That'll pass."

"How long have I known you, Josh? More than ten years, right? We started the circuit the same season. I remember how bad things got with Jen, how hard you tried to make it work."

"Not hard enough."

"Sara isn't your ex-wife."

"Thanks for the insight. But I'm making a life for Claire. One that will keep her safe and out of trouble."

Dave's eyes widened a fraction. "This is about your sister," he whispered.

"Don't go there."

Dave ignored the warning in Josh's voice. "You'd been gone three years when Beth died. The car accident was stupid and tragic but not your fault."

"I should have been there for her," Josh argued, shaking his head. "I knew how bad things were between my parents, what kind of hell that house was to live in every day. I could take out my anger in the ring, but she didn't have that option. If I'd been around to help, maybe she wouldn't have been drinking that night. Maybe she'd have been strong enough to not get in that car."

"Not your fault," Dave repeated.

"It doesn't matter." Josh opened the barn door, letting bright light flood the sawdust floor. He stepped into the warmth and took a deep breath. "I have a chance to make things right for Claire. I'm not going to blow it."

"Part of Claire being happy is you being happy. Sara does that. Everyone can see it except you. Your daughter is a teenager. She needs a woman in her life who isn't as messed up as her mother. You don't have to do it alone."

Josh let his eyes drift closed. He'd done things alone for so long he wasn't sure if he knew another way. He saw how much Claire was drawn to Sara. More often than not he'd find her curled in the overstuffed chair in the office while Sara was on the computer.

At first he hadn't wanted his daughter to have anything to do with Hollywood Barbie. As time went on, he could see Sara's influence on Claire's behavior in good ways. Claire seemed less sullen and moody. Hell, she'd even smiled at him a couple of times—a big improvement over the start of the summer. He'd felt the change, hard as it was to admit, in himself, as well. Something about Sara gave a lift to his heart. Her unflagging energy and upbeat spirit drew him out of the fog that had become a constant in his life since the accident.

Could it be something more? She said she was leaving at the end of the summer, but he knew she was happy on the ranch. She also said she didn't do casual relationships. If he offered her something more, he might have a chance of changing her mind about the future.

Sara and Claire were leaving this morning to go shopping in Denver. He checked his watch and pulled off his work gloves, tossing them to Dave.

"Can you guys handle a day on your own?"

Dave nodded. "The plan was fishing, and Noah can get us to the best water."

"Then do me a favor and close up the barn. I've got someplace I need to be."

Sara stepped out of her cabin at the sound of a horn honking. *Not more unannounced guests,* she thought, then stopped at the sight of Josh's enormous black truck idling in front of her.

Claire opened the door and scrambled into the backseat. "Dad's coming with us," she called over her shoulder. "He's got his credit card. Woo-hoo!"

"Don't get too crazy," Josh told his daughter, then patted the seat next to him. "Are you ready?" he called to Sara.

To spend three hours next to him in the front seat? No way, no how.

"Sure." She walked toward the truck. "What made you decide to spend your afternoon shopping?"

He looked at her through aviator glasses so dark she couldn't see his eyes. "I have a couple of parts to pick up from a mechanic in north Denver. Thought we could stop by on the way to Cherry Creek."

Sara's stomach gave a lurch at the mention of the upscale shopping area. She was bound to be recognized, which had seemed bad enough with Claire, but to add Josh to the mix was almost too much. She had no control over the things complete strangers were willing to say to her, most of them embarrassing.

She hesitated, then hoisted herself into the truck. She could handle whatever came her way, she told herself. This summer was about taking back her power, and dealing with public attention was part of that.

She glanced in the backseat, where Claire had already popped in a pair of earbuds. She gave Sara a thumbs-up and returned to mouthing the lyrics of the song from her iPod.

Buckling her seat belt, Sara turned to Josh. "I think we're set."

He continued to watch her, then lowered his glasses to the tip of his nose. "You're not wearing makeup again."

He'd noticed. Damn. Sara had put her hair in a long braid and applied just a touch of mascara and gloss, hoping to blend in more with the other shoppers and avoid recognition. She forced a casual smile. "I am, just not as much. Thought I'd give my skin a rest. A little detox for the pores, you know. I think…"

Josh's hand on her wrist stopped her nervous babble. "You look beautiful," he said softly, rubbing his thumb across her knuckles.

"Oh" was all she could manage. She looked down at his fingers the way she might eye a rattlesnake on the trail. Without thinking, she snatched her hand away and dug through her purse for her own sunglasses.

He gave a deep chuckle and switched the truck into gear. "Is country music okay?"

"Fine." Anything to fill the charged silence.

He swung onto the road and turned on the radio, drumming his fingers on the console in time with a song.

Sara kept her gaze focused on the scenery rolling by and soon lost herself in the beauty of the mountains. Driving in from California, she'd been so consumed with what she'd find that she'd given little thought to the jagged peaks that framed the interstate. Now she had time to take in the mountains that had been carved out to create this road through them. She thought about the hours of work it must have taken—the blood, sweat and tears of the men who built it. Her own life felt even more insignificant in comparison.

"It's humbling, isn't it?" Josh asked, as if reading her thoughts.

Sara blinked several times. "How did you know that's what I was thinking about?"

He pointed toward the front window. "It's hard not to, driving through here. The majesty of this place takes my breath away every time."

Sara nodded. "That's exactly right. It makes me feel so small. But in a good way. Like nature is protecting us with its very mass. The things that make me feel little in my life don't seem to matter when I'm faced with this type of beauty."

"I feel the same way," Josh answered, his voice so soft she barely heard him.

Sara felt the warmth of his glance and squirmed a bit in the seat. What happened to his anger from before? Anger was clear-cut, no questions. Not like the feelings his kindness produced in her.

"Are the guys having a good time?" she asked, hoping for an easier subject.

He smiled. "The best. Everything you planned is perfect."

A little zing tripped along her spine. "The questionnaire helps narrow down their interests. Your friends were easy. Anything loud, with lots of adrenaline."

"When does the next group come in?"

"This weekend, only one day between them and your crew. It's the family reunion. Age range from toddlers to the patriarch in his seventies."

"The old man who wants to catch a trout with his great-grandson as part of his bucket list?" Josh laughed. "No pressure on me."

"You have a gift for leading the groups, Josh. Everything will be fine."

"I hope it's enough to make it work."

She sighed. "Me, too," she answered, unsure if she was talking about the ranch or her life.

They talked easily the rest of the drive, about his life on the tour and the places he'd seen in his travels. The way he described them, those seconds in the ring reminded her of the way she felt the moment a director called, "Action," the spotlight on her with adrenaline pumping. While a scene wasn't life-or-death high stakes the way a ride on a thousand-pound animal could be, it had the same emotional letdown when it was over.

Talking to Josh made her remember how much she'd loved the actual acting part of her job if she could leave behind the baggage that crowded her life.

By the time they got to the shopping area, Sara felt relaxed. Claire's excitement about the boutiques that lined the streets was contagious to the point that she'd almost forgotten her trepidation about a public outing.

Josh dropped them along the block that looked the most interesting to Claire and went to park. Sara followed Claire into a store and to a rack of colorful sundresses near the front.

"I love this," Claire said on an excited breath, holding up a low-cut V-neck sundress with a deep back.

Sara stifled a laugh at what Josh would think of that choice. She thumbed through the dresses and pulled out two with a more modest neckline. "I think one of these would be perfect."

Claire hesitated, then put the first dress back. "The blue one is pretty."

Sara's sigh of relief was interrupted by a voice behind her. "Let me know if I can be of any help," a saleslady purred. "We're having a great summer sale on all dresses in the store."

Sara turned and met the woman's critical gaze with a bright smile. "Thanks. Are the dressing rooms in the back?"

To her surprise, the woman returned her smile. "Yes. Can I take those dresses for you?"

"The blue one," Sara answered, and released the breath she hadn't realized she was holding. Okay. That went well. One stranger down, dozens of others to go. She hated feeling so nervous and out of sorts, especially when Josh was along to watch her squirm.

Claire's squealing caught her attention.

"This one," the young girl said on a rapturous breath. Sara's grin broadened at the soft pink fabric draped across Claire's arm.

"It's beautiful," she agreed.

"What's beautiful?" Josh asked at her shoulder.

"Dad, look at this dress. I love, love, love it."

"Try it on then. Let's see how it fits."

Claire practically ran toward the dressing room. "Be right back," she called over her shoulder.

"I don't get women and shopping."

Sara turned to Josh, who looked more than uncomfortable standing between racks of feminine clothes. He adjusted the bill of his baseball cap lower on his face.

Sara studied the color that crept up his neck. "Are you blushing?" she asked, and followed his gaze. "At a mannequin wearing a bra and panties?"

"I don't blush," he argued, adjusting his cap again. "And I like to see a real woman wearing a bra and panties." His gaze raked her. "I'd like to see you in a bra and panties." He paused, then added softly, "Or out of them."

She swayed forward a fraction as her southern hemisphere revved to life. Glancing over her shoulder to make sure no one else had heard him, she pointed a finger at him. "You can't say that here. Your daughter's in the dressing room."

"I know where she is, and I can say whatever I want." His big shoulders shrugged. "I've got to think of something interesting to keep me going today. You need a distraction, too. You're wound like a top."

"I am not." She followed his gaze and quickly let go of the wad of fabric bunched in her hand, placing the dress back on its hanger and smoothing her hand over it. "What happened to your attitude from the other night?"

A Cheshire grin spread across his face. "I got a better one."

"I'm not sure this is any better. We agreed nothing will happen between us."

"You agreed." He took a step toward her, his hand brushing her bare arm. "I might buy you something to model later for me."

Sara coughed and sputtered at his brazen words. "I don't need you to buy me anything, and I'm not anyone's model."

Josh winked. "That's more like it. I like you all full of spunk."

"Okay, I'm ready," Claire called from the back of the store.

Sara narrowed her eyes as Josh walked toward the dressing rooms but couldn't quite stop herself from smiling.

He did that to her.

Their easy banter felt strangely right, and her whole body tingled at the message in his eyes when he looked at her. His attitude might be joking but his energy was intensely serious.

As she followed the sound of Claire's voice, the saleslady grabbed her arm and pulled her behind a bathing suit display. "Just a minute," she whispered, her head bobbing over the shelves to make sure they couldn't be heard. "I need to ask you something."

Here it comes, Sara thought, tension curling tight in her chest once again.

"Is that Josh Travers?" the woman asked, her eyes bright with expectation. "Are you with *the* Josh Travers?"

Sara blinked and looked over her shoulder. He had to have put the woman up to this. "*The* Josh Travers?"

The saleslady nodded. "He's the retired PBR champ, right?"

Sara racked her brain. "Professional Bull Riders," she said, almost to herself. "Yep, that's him."

"I knew it." The woman patted her chest. "He's even hotter in person than on TV."

Sara felt her jaw drop. "Are you for real?"

"Ever since they put the tour on cable, my husband's been addicted. He grew up down in Calhan, so even though we're in the big city he's a cowboy at heart. He likes me to watch, too—makes him feel like I get him."

She leaned closer and squeezed Sara's arm. "Let me tell you, it's no chore sitting on the couch watching those gorgeous boys do their thing. Josh Travers was the best of the best. It does my heart good to see him getting around, looking so happy and in love."

Sara's mouth dropped farther. "In love? Oh, no. We work together. We're here with his daughter."

"Whatever you say," the saleswoman said with a knowing smile. "You look like a nice girl."

"Sara, where are you?" Claire's voice came from the back of the store.

"Let's see how that young lady did with her choices." The saleswoman pulled a stunned Sara toward the dressing room. All that worry and someone recognized her as Josh's girlfriend?

Unbelievable.

The rest of the afternoon was just as surreal. Sara noticed several people staring and a few pointing at her as they meandered up the tree-lined streets. Each time it happened, Josh gave her hand a gentle squeeze, told a bad joke or generally teased her to distraction.

Claire did her best to put a generous dent into Josh's credit balance, growing happier with each store they entered. Sara felt the same way but for a different reason. Away from the looming tension about the fate of the ranch, she and Josh relaxed into an easy camaraderie that made hope bubble in Sara. She hadn't felt the sensation in years: the possibility of a normal life.

She floated along on that feeling until they stopped for dinner at a quaint bistro at the edge of the shopping district.

The young man at the host desk informed them that without a reservation, the wait for a table would be over an hour. Claire gave a sigh of disappointment, as the cozy restaurant had been her first choice.

As Sara turned to scan the street for nearby options, a gray-haired woman approached her from the sidewalk. "Are you Serena Wellens? The one who used to be a movie star?"

Sara sucked in a breath, unused to hearing her failure phrased quite that way. She forced a smile. "I guess you could say I used to be Serena Wellens. And yes, I was an actress. I go by Sara now."

She waited for the criticism to come—as it always did. It was human nature, Sara thought. People loved to sit in judgment of others' lives. The explosion of the internet and media outlets made it easy to feel like you had insight into someone else's business, no matter how untrue so much of what was published could be.

Josh's warm hand pressed against the small of her back, reminding her to take a calming breath. "Is everything okay here?" he asked.

Claire came to stand beside her, grabbing hold of Sara's hand. "Let's find another place," she said, and gave Sara a small tug.

Sara glanced at Claire and leaned against Josh ever so slightly. *He and Claire have my back,* she thought. *They literally have my back.* One thing about being in L.A. that she'd hated was the feeling of being alone against the world, as though she had no one but herself to depend on. She'd never been her own best defense. April had been there, but in the past few years had gone through so many of her own troubles, Sara hadn't wanted to be a burden with her own insignificant worries.

Still she stood transfixed by the stranger in front of her, like a deer in headlights. "We should go," she whispered.

"Wait." The woman took a step forward and Josh moved even closer. "I have to thank you first. My daughter, she's in college now, but when she was younger her father and I got divorced. It was messy and she was caught in the cross fire."

"I'm sorry," Sara responded automatically.

"Jessica, that's my daughter, closed off emotionally. She'd barely even look at me. But she loved your show. So every week we'd watch together. It was the only time she'd let me sit next to her. We'd talk during commercials. I swear *Just the Two of Us* saved our relationship." The woman dabbed at her eyes. "I'm sure that sounds stupid to you but it's the truth."

Sara reached out and took the woman's hand. "It doesn't sound stupid. I'm flattered that you told me."

"So thank you. We've been following Amanda's career since the show ended. Not hard since she's everywhere these days."

"She's had an amazing career," Sara agreed woodenly.

"When are you going to make your comeback? You were a much better actress than she was on the show. I'm sure that hasn't changed."

"My life has gone in a different direction."

The woman let out a bark of laughter. "I read the tabloids but I don't believe half of it. It'll happen when you're ready. You have a natural gift. Always have."

Emotions clogged Sara's throat. "Thank you again," she whispered.

The maître d' from the restaurant peeked around Josh. "Ms. Wellens?" he asked. "The manager has found a table for you."

"I'll let you get on with your evening," the woman said, and with a last squeeze of Sara's arm, scuttled down the sidewalk.

Sara met Josh's questioning gaze. "That was different, even for me," she said, trying to make her tone casual.

He gave her a knowing nod. "Looks like Serena got us a table."

"She's good for something, at least."

Chapter 10

Josh rubbed his hand over his face and gave a weary look around yet another store filled with racks of women's clothes. How many different shops had he been into today? More than in the past ten years if he had to guess. After eating, Claire had led them from one end of the ritzy neighborhood to the other.

She'd promised this would be the last one, and Josh couldn't be finished soon enough. His knee ached, his head pounded and all he wanted was to get out of the city and up into the mountains again. Sara had gamely kept up with Claire's boundless energy, but even she'd begun to wilt a little as she'd followed his daughter back to the fitting rooms.

He'd also noticed that in the whole day, Sara hadn't purchased one thing for herself. All of her attention remained focused on Claire's needs. He knew Claire had never had that with her own mother, and it made his heart open to Sara all the more.

"I'm not sure that's your size," a voice said next to him.

Sara stood just to the side of a rack of dresses, eyeing him with a smile.

He looked down at the soft fabric he clutched to his chest, then held up the dress. "It would look good on you," he said softly.

Her eyes sparked, whether with humor or temper he couldn't tell. "Today isn't about me."

"You haven't seen anything you want?"

"Doesn't matter." She sighed. "I don't have the money for new clothes."

He ignored the way his gut tightened at her comment. "I thought maybe Colorado wasn't trendy enough for you."

"What do you know about trendy?"

"More than I ever wanted to after today." He held the dress out. "Try it on," he coaxed, suddenly wanting to see her in something other than her chosen uniform of jeans and shapeless T-shirts.

"No point," she answered, but he thought he saw a sliver of longing in her gaze. Josh knew all about longing these days. Although he found it hard to believe, Sara had almost as many walls built up as he did. Right now, he wanted to crash through each and every one of them.

"You're right, though," he told her. "It doesn't matter what you wear. The bottom line is you're beautiful."

She took a step toward him and reached for the dress. "I'm not sure—"

"What do you think?"

He and Sara turned as Claire came from the back of the store. Josh felt his eyes widen. "I think you have thirty seconds to take that off and put on a decent outfit."

Sara's mouth dropped open as her gaze traveled up and down Claire. The saleswoman who'd followed Claire from the dressing room quickly backed away as Sara shot her a glare.

His daughter wore a skintight, black lace concoction that revealed more skin than it covered. Suddenly, he saw her not as his little girl but as a woman, one who was quickly going to rival her supermodel mother in the looks department. He had a visceral need to polish a shotgun or move to Tibet. Anything to avoid what the next few years held for him as a father.

"That's not the dress we'd picked," Sara said carefully.

Claire did a quick twirl, and he realized the dress was practically backless. He growled low under his breath. "No. Way."

"Dad," Claire whined, her bright smile turning to a pout. "Don't be a stick-in-the-mud. I saw Mom wearing something like this in a magazine last month. I want to have something she'll like when I go to visit her before school starts."

"You don't have a trip planned to see your mother," Josh argued. "And you're not going anywhere in that dress."

Claire's tiny hands came to rest on her hips. "I want to see her. I texted this morning and asked when she'd be back in New York. I could fly out next month if it works for her."

"What did she answer?"

Claire's mouth thinned, and she didn't meet his gaze. "She hasn't responded yet. But she will. You know how Mom does things last minute. I want to be ready."

"You aren't going to 'fly out' to be with her. We're spending the summer in Colorado."

Claire shook her head. "You can't stop me."

"The hell I can't," he shot back.

"You're not the boss of me."

"I'm your father and you'll do as I say."

"She's my mom. You can't keep me from her."

He couldn't think straight with Claire in that dress, looking so grown-up and out of his control. He had to keep her safe. He'd do anything, say anything to make sure she stayed with him. "I'm not keeping you from her," he yelled. "She doesn't want—"

He broke off, knowing the words were a mistake as soon as he said them.

"Me," Claire finished on a sob. "You think she doesn't want me."

He watched his daughter's eyes fill with tears and cursed himself for being the biggest idiot on the planet. "Claire, I didn't mean—"

She shook her head. "You're wrong," she said quietly, the pain in her gaze cutting a deep hole in his heart. "I hate you. Mom is going to take me back. I know she will." She turned and ran for the fitting room, silence filling the small store.

He took a step forward, but Sara put a hand on his arm. "She needs some time."

"I can't let her be with Jennifer. Too many bad things could happen."

Sara shook her head. "Then don't push her away."

She was right, but that only fueled his frustration more. "What do you know about protecting the people you love? From what you've told me, April is the only friend you have and you lost her entire life savings. If you and your mother hadn't put thoughts of another world in Claire's head, we wouldn't be here today. She'd be on the ranch. She'd be safe." His hands balled into hard fists. "Only I can keep her safe."

Sara sucked in a breath as if he'd slapped her. He waited for her to argue, to fight back. His words were untrue, but he'd baited her on purpose. He needed a good fight right now, a way to get rid of the fear crawling through every pore, making him feel weak and defenseless.

Instead, she looked away. "I'm going to get Claire. Pull the truck out front. I think this day is done."

"Sara," he called out as she walked away. She shook her head and kept moving, leaving Josh alone. His gaze dropped to the dress he held, a wrinkled, balled-up mess in his hands.

A lot like his life right now.

Sara followed Claire into the kitchen at the ranch three hours later. Three of the longest hours of her recent life. She was on edge down to her teeth after the tense ride back from Denver.

Claire had spent the entire time with her earbuds shoved in her ears, heaving dramatic sighs from the backseat as she furiously texted on her phone. Josh had turned the music loud, not the lulling country tunes from the morning but a pounding heavy-metal station that had only served to intensify Sara's headache.

She'd leaned her head against the cool window glass

and tried to tune out everything around her. It was a trick she'd learned as a girl on set, the ability to ignore the world and crawl into her own internal life.

But with Josh's hulking presence next to her, it felt like all her other senses became more attuned to him when she closed her eyes. His clean, male scent. The hot tension curling from him. She could even sense the pattern of his breathing and wasn't surprised when she opened her eyes to see that his chest rose and fell at the same rate hers did.

Although the words he'd spoken were the truth, he'd hurt her feelings. Still, she wanted to reach out and comfort him. He was a bumbling bull in a china shop when it came to Claire, but at least he cared. That was more than Sara had ever gotten from either of her parents, and she knew how much it mattered.

She also knew, because April continually reminded her, that she was a sucker for lost causes. Maybe it was because her secret dream had always been that someone would care enough to rescue her. She gave the best parts of herself to people who couldn't return the emotion. Part of her fresh start, her second chance, had been the opportunity to finally take care of herself. To make herself whole and right so she could move forward with her dreams. If she let herself get too involved with Josh and Claire, all her careful plans could slip through her fingers.

She might, once again, be left with nothing.

Regardless, she couldn't stand to see either of them in this kind of pain.

"He didn't mean to hurt you," she said to Claire's back as the girl grabbed a bottle of water from the refrigerator.

April walked in from the family room. "How was the shopping trip? Do I get a fashion show tonight?"

Claire slammed shut the fridge door and whirled. "I'd like to burn every single piece of clothing my jerk of a dad bought today." She swiped at her cheeks, her desperate gaze swinging between Sara and April. "He's wrong, you know. My mom loves me. She's busy, but she loves me."

"I know, honey," Sara answered. "He knows it, too. You scared him in that dress."

"I looked scary?" Claire's voice rose to a squeak.

Sara pressed her palm to the girl's face, smoothing away a tear. "You looked gorgeous and grown-up. That's the scariest thing a father can face. It makes them a little crazy."

"A crazy jerk," Claire mumbled.

A door slammed at the front of the house. Claire looked around wildly. "I don't want to see his friends tonight. I don't want to see anyone."

Sara glanced at April. "Are you making dinner?"

"Everyone is going into town. Ryan made reservations."

"Ryan is entertaining a group of cowboys?"

April nodded. "He stopped by earlier, looking for you. He's adamant that you be there, too. For moral support."

"I'm staying here if Claire wants company."

April stepped forward. "I'll keep Claire company." She smiled. "I made chicken soup and an apple crisp earlier. I happen to know there's a Jane Austen marathon tonight. *Emma* and *Sense and Sensibility,* two of my favorites. Does that sound okay, Claire?"

The girl nodded then gave a tiny hiccup. "I'm going

to take a shower. I'll be down when everyone else is gone."

She gave Sara a quick hug. "I had a good time with *you*. Sorry Dad ruined it for both of us."

"I enjoyed the day, no matter what."

"I'll get fresh towels for you," April said, and took Claire's hand, leading her up the back stairs.

Sara braced her hands on the counter and leaned forward, dropping her head to stretch out some of the tension in her neck.

"Now I ruined the whole day?"

She looked up as Josh filled the doorway leading to the front hall. His broad shoulders looked as tense as hers felt.

"You need to apologize," she answered.

"To Claire or to you?" He crossed his arms over his chest, his dark eyes unreadable in the shadows of the soft evening light.

"I'm not important here." She straightened, wiping an imaginary crumb from the counter. "Your daughter is."

"You're important to me," he said quietly.

"Don't do that, Josh."

"Do what?"

"Care."

He took a step forward at the same moment the back door of the house burst open.

"Come on, you two," Ryan said. "I've got the masses corralled into the Suburban. We need to make it to town before the poor vehicle implodes from the force of all that testosterone."

Sara saw his eyebrows raise as he studied both Josh

and her. "Whatever's going on here can only be helped by a drink and some food. Let's go."

Before she could argue, Ryan took her hand and pulled her out into the night.

Josh emptied his second beer and set it on the table. He looked down to where Sara sat, Manny and Noah on either side of her. He made eye contact with the waitress and lifted his finger to order another round.

"Rough day with the girls?" Dave asked from his seat next to him.

"I'd rather spend an hour in the ring with the orneriest bull you can find than another minute shopping."

"Amen to that," his friend agreed. "But I sure do like the results."

Josh followed Dave's gaze to where Brandy did a quick two-step with young Bryson on the dance floor. She wore a short skirt and a colorful blouse that flowed as she spun to the music. "How do you two make it look so easy?" he grumbled.

"I'm smarter than you," his friend told him sagely. "I keep my mouth shut unless I'm giving her a compliment."

Josh's laugh turned into a coughing fit as Noah leaned in close to whisper in Sara's ear.

He started to stand but Dave cuffed him on the shoulder. "He's doing it to get a rise out of you."

"Looks more like he's trying to get a rise out of himself."

"It's freaking him out being in town again, but we wanted to make sure you were doing okay. Neither of us planned on ever coming back to Crimson until we heard you'd settled here."

"Wasn't my plan either, but I'm going to make it work."

"Have you seen Logan and Jake recently?"

Josh took a breath at the mention of his two brothers. "Jake was here for Mom's funeral a couple of years ago. We both stayed less than twenty-four hours. Long enough to hire someone to clear out the old house and get it on the market. He flew off to whatever country needed doctors again after that. Logan...well, he couldn't exactly get away at the time."

"I'm sorry, man. About a lot of things."

Josh did stand now. He wasn't ready for this conversation. "I'm going to stretch my legs while doing my best to ignore your brother."

He got his beer at the bar and tried not to watch his two so-called friends flirting with Sara. It wasn't any business of his what she did with her time, but it still grated on his nerves.

His eyes strayed to the woman next to him, or at least to her hands, which were busily building some sort of structure out of a pile of matchbooks. "That's quite a building you've got there," he said, focusing all his wayward attention on the intricate display.

The woman jumped three feet in the air at his words, the house of matchbooks crumbling onto the bar.

"Sorry," he said with a wince. "Looks like that took some time."

He saw color rise to her pale cheeks. She turned and gave him an embarrassed smile. "It's a silly pastime." Her light brown hair was pulled back into a tight bun at the back of her head. She began stacking the little cardboard boxes into neat rows. "You're Josh Travers, right?"

He nodded. "Have we met?"

She shook her head. "No, but my husband grew up here, so he's mentioned you." She glanced over her shoulder. "He told me Serena Wellens is staying with you for the summer."

"Her name is Sara Wells now," Josh said, his protective instinct kicking in. "Who is your husband?"

The woman closed her eyes for a moment as if she'd said too much. Just then a firm hand clasped Josh on the shoulder. "Travers, it's been a while. How's it hangin'?"

Josh turned to see Craig Wilder, one of his least favorite people in all of Crimson, Colorado. Craig had been an insufferable prig as a kid. His family was the wealthiest in town, and they'd made sure everyone else knew it. Craig had had no time for any of the Travers kids, who were way below him on the social totem pole. Since Josh had come back, not much had changed. He knew Craig had become mayor last year, and he'd heard rumors that he'd bought the election. But Josh hadn't had a conversation with him for years, and he didn't want to start now.

One more reason he kept to himself out on the ranch.

"It's hanging fine," he said through clenched teeth.

"I see you met my wife, Olivia." Craig glanced at the woman. "Seriously, you aren't making those stupid houses again, are you, Liv?"

"No," she mumbled, and gave Josh an apologetic smile.

"I'm going to head back to the table," Josh said quickly. "Dave and Noah are at the ranch this week."

Craig stepped in front of him. "I hear Serena Wellens is there, too."

"She prefers Sara Wells," Olivia interjected.

Craig shot his wife a silencing glare. "You may have heard that in addition to my duties as mayor, I bought the old community-center building in town. I feel as though it's my civic duty to bring some culture back to Crimson. There are plenty of people who'd drive over from Aspen with the right incentive."

Josh took a slow pull on his beer. "You think Sara is the right incentive?"

"A D-list celebrity," Craig said with a chuckle, "is better than no celebrity at all."

Without thinking, Josh reached out and grabbed the other man by his shirtfront, pulling him close enough to see the whites of his eyes. "You're not using Sara for anything, Wilder. Don't talk to her. Don't even look at her. You were a slimeball when we were young, and I don't see that much has changed."

Craig fidgeted. then narrowed his eyes. "You're going to need the support of this town and the visitors' center to draw people to your ranch. Don't forget that."

Olivia stood and smiled at Josh. "I volunteer at the visitors' center. I'll make sure you get whatever publicity you need, Mr. Travers."

"Shut it, Liv," Craig said on a hiss of breath.

"I'll wait for you in the car," she answered, and turned away.

Josh released Craig and stared as he stomped off after his wife. He couldn't imagine all the things wrong in that marriage, but he'd meant what he said. He wouldn't let anyone use Sara for her fame. She deserved much more than that.

His eyes tracked to where she sat at the table. A man he didn't recognize sat next to her now, with Ryan standing between them, his face alight with excitement. The other man was clearly another Hollywood type. A shaggy beard covered his jaw, but his button-down shirt looked like some sort of expensive fabric. and a heavy gold Rolex flashed on his wrist.

Crimson had seen its share of wealth and fame. The town's close proximity to Aspen drew enough moneyed tourists to keep the town thriving. He'd been able to ignore them growing up and hoped that wouldn't change. The who's who wasn't the crowd he hoped to attract to the ranch—his ideal guests were people who'd appreciate the beauty and majesty of the mountains as much as he did. People who wanted a true Colorado vacation experience. But money was money, and he'd take what he could get if it meant having enough savings to buy the ranch at the end of the summer.

Watching Sara smile at Ryan and the other man made him wonder what she truly wanted. He was only guessing at the things that made her happy.

He had trouble believing all she cared about was selling her grandmother's house. Already she was an important part of his daughter's life and had captured a big part of his heart, even if he didn't want to admit it. But he couldn't blame her for wanting to reclaim her life on her own terms. He only hoped he could convince her there was room enough in it for him.

Chapter 11

Sara twirled the stem of the wineglass between her fingertips as she looked up at the stars dotting the Colorado night sky. It was well past midnight, but she wasn't the least bit tired.

She'd feigned a yawn when the group had gotten back from town, needing to be alone to sort out her thoughts. Her emotions were a jumble, and something about sitting under the vast expanse of stars calmed her frazzled nerves.

Footsteps echoed across the flagstone path that led from her small porch to the main house. She half expected Ryan to seek her out and thought about retreating into her cabin, unwilling to submit to his relentless pressure any more tonight.

But the way the hairs on her neck pricked as the figure drew closer made her think of beating a retreat for an entirely different reason. Instead. she remained rooted in her chair as Josh's tall figure came clearly into view.

"I saw your light on," he said simply as he hoisted one hip onto her front porch rail. Buster trotted forward out of the darkness, sniffed at her leg and plopped onto the ground.

"I couldn't sleep yet," she answered. "I have a lot on my mind."

He glanced up at the sky above them. "This is as good a place as any to work things out."

Her mouth curved into an unwilling smile at how succinctly he'd guessed her reason for being outside tonight. Still, she shivered as a sudden breeze whipped up from the creek bed behind the property.

"Your grandma loved that robe," he said as she cinched the belt of it tighter.

"I found it in her bedroom." She smoothed her fingers across the soft folds of chenille and cotton. "I hope you don't mind that I took it."

He waited until she met his gaze. "Everything in that house belongs to you, Sara. Don't forget that."

"It doesn't feel like mine." She shook her head. "You and Claire belong here, Josh."

"If I don't push her away." He repeated her words from earlier.

"Like you said, what do I know about making relationships work?" She tried to laugh but it caught in her throat. She wanted to muster the righteous anger she'd felt earlier but didn't have the energy or inclination for it.

"I'm sorry," he said softly. "I didn't mean that." He stood, walking to the edge of the porch. "It scares the hell out of me to think of Claire with her mother. Jennifer wouldn't know a maternal instinct if it bit her on the nose. Claire was an easy little girl, quiet and bent on pleasing whomever she was with at the time. Jennifer could send her off to school then shuttle her around on breaks, parading her in front of the media for a photo op before pawning her off on nannies or lackeys or whoever was available at the time. She let me have Claire more as she got older and had needs of her own. Now that Claire's on the verge of becoming a woman, I'm afraid Jen will treat her as a young protégé, using Claire to get into clubs or entice men." He ran a hand through his hair. "If I'm not there to protect her, there's no telling what could happen."

"Claire has a good head on her shoulders." Sara didn't know how to assuage his fears. "You've raised an amazing daughter and you have to trust she'll make the right decisions."

"I can't," he whispered miserably. "The stakes are too high. If I let her go..."

"You don't know—"

He whirled around. "I do know, Sara. My sister died in a car accident because I left her behind. I didn't take care of Beth, and I'm not going to make the same mistake with Claire."

She stood, wanting to reach out to him. For the first time she saw the stark pain his strength hid so well. Now it made sense to her. It was in the hard line of his jaw, the square set of his broad shoulders, the sharp pull of a mouth she knew to be soft as a butterfly kiss. All of that hid the pain and guilt he felt over his sister's death.

She knew what it was like to hide your true self

so thoroughly that you almost believed the mask you wore was real. She knew the emotional risk involved in revealing the wound behind it.

"Tell me," she whispered.

He turned away again.

For a moment she thought he'd leap off the porch and disappear into the black night. When he didn't move, she came slowly toward him, wrapping her arms around his strong middle. Her cheek pressed against the back of his denim jacket. She breathed in his scent as she willed away the tension pouring off him. Willed him not to leave.

After a moment, his warm hands enveloped hers and he took a deep, shuddering breath. His muscles remained tight but he stayed with her. That was enough for now.

"Tell me," she said again. "Please."

"My father was a mean drunk," he began. "My mom, she both loved and feared him. I'm not sure which one made her stay. In the end, it didn't really matter. There were four of us kids. My brother Jake is two years older than me. When I was four, the twins were born. Beth and my other brother, Logan. My mom did what she could to keep us in line. My dad worked construction, mainly over in Aspen. The more time he spent building mansions for rich people, the more bitter he became about our tiny, run-down farmhouse. And the more bitter he became, the more he drank. Then..."

Sara laced her fingers in his. "What happened?"

"It's not an uncommon story in the mountains. As beautiful as it is up here, it's isolating, especially in the winter. Especially when there's not much work or a man can't hold a job because he's too tempted by the bottle. When we were young, my mom tried to keep us away from him when he was in a mood. That didn't always work with three boys underfoot. Beth was the only one of us he ever seemed to care about. She was shy and quiet. A hell of a lot easier to be around than the rest of us."

He squeezed her hands. "As soon as Jake and I got big enough to fight back, Dad left us alone. He'd take out that anger on Mom when we weren't around. She'd hide the bruises, but we knew. She never sent him away or thought of leaving. Said he needed her too much. More than we needed a decent life.

"Jake got a college scholarship and never looked back. I started on the circuit soon after. I sent money back to Mom when I could. Jake and I both did. But without us in the house to temper his behavior, Dad got even worse. Beth was so quiet, and Logan was a scrawny, sickly kid back then. Mom eventually kicked the jerk out, but it was too late. Beth and Logan were running wild. Beth had an older boyfriend. One night there was an accident. Beth and a group of friends had been drinking—the boyfriend was driving drunk. He hit an elk crossing the highway and…"

Sara wrapped her arms tighter around Josh's waist as he spoke. The anguish and guilt were clear in his tone.

"It wasn't your fault," she whispered.

"I left her here. I left both of them here. I was so intent on getting out, I deserted them. The twins weren't like Jake and me. They needed someone to protect them." He paused to drag in a miserable breath. "I should have protected them. If I'd been here…"

Sara unlaced her fingers from his and scooted

around to stand in front of him. She took his face in her hands and tipped it down so he had to look her in the eyes. The pain she saw there tore at her heart. "That's why you want to keep Claire away from her mother."

"Claire was the same age as Beth when I left. I can't take the chance that something in my daughter could change. What if something happens and I'm not around to make it okay?"

"You should explain that to Claire." Sara drew her fingers through the soft hair along Josh's neck, wanting to relax some of his tension. "Right now she thinks you want to squash her fun. If she understood the reasons why you're protective of her, it might help."

"How can I admit that to her? I'm supposed to be the dad, the one with all the answers."

"You're the dad who loves her with your whole heart. That doesn't always mean you have the answers." Unable to resist, she reached on tiptoe and kissed the corner of his mouth. "You're human, Josh. Not a superhero. You know that, right?"

"If my injury has taught me anything, it's that I'm all too human."

"Human is good," she whispered. "Flesh and blood makes things more interesting."

His eyes darkened as a slow smile broke across his face.

"What did I say?"

"Flesh."

"And blood," she offered.

"Right now, I'm focused on the flesh." He drew his palms up her arms and across the front of the soft robe, rubbing his thumbs against her exposed collarbone. "Yours in particular."

As much as his touch made her skin tingle, she shook her head. "Will you talk to Claire?"

"Will you kiss me again if I say yes?"

"One doesn't have anything to do with the other," she argued, but leaned into him just the tiniest bit.

"I know," he agreed. "Yes, I'll talk to Claire."

She nodded. "You do look a little like a superhero, you know. Like you could handle the weight of the world because you're so strong and tough."

"You're talking movies again. You must be nervous."

She huffed out a breath. "I'm not nervous."

His eyebrows lifted in disbelief. "Anxious, then?" He lowered his head and touched his lips to the curve of her neck. "Or excited?"

He traced a path of kisses along her jaw, then whispered in her ear, "Wondering what it will be like between us?" His teeth grazed her earlobe gently.

Goose bumps rose along her heated skin. "We agreed this was a bad idea."

"I didn't agree to that." His fingers undid the knot of the robe's sash, then moved under the tank top she wore, massaging her back.

Her eyes drifted closed from the pleasure of his touch. She felt each of her arguments fade away in the riptide of desire building throughout her body. It was dangerous, she knew, because she felt more for this man than simple physical attraction. He'd wound his way into her heart with his quiet strength and deep commitment to doing the right thing. Sara hadn't had a lot of experience with men who were truly good, and she found it to be a heady thing and not easy to resist.

"I want you, Sara. From the moment you walked

through the door, I've wanted you." His mouth moved to hers and she felt the smile on his lips. "If I were a superhero, the type who could fly and leap over tall buildings, you'd be my one weakness."

"Did you just make a movie reference for me?" She melted against him a bit more.

"Officially, it was a comic book reference, but you can interpret it any way you want. *If* it means you'll invite me in."

"Come in, Josh," she said as a sigh against his mouth.

A groan of pleasure escaped his lips as he lifted her into his arms and turned for the cabin.

She wrapped her legs around his lean waist as they all but crashed through the front door. His kisses became hotter and more demanding, drawing from her a need she hadn't known she could feel. Pleasure and passion banked inside her for years bubbled to the surface demanding a release.

Josh slammed shut the door then pressed her into it, balancing her weight with his own body as his tongue swept between her lips, mingling with hers in a dance that made her body ache with longing for him.

"Bedroom," he said on a moan.

"Can't wait," she answered, frantic to touch and be touched by him in this moment. Not wanting to delay her need one second more.

Her legs dropped to the floor, and she pushed against him while tugging at the hem of his T-shirt until he flung it off. The robe fell to the ground as they found their way to the couch. Her mouth went dry as he stripped off his boots and jeans, taking her hand as he sank onto the cushions.

She straddled his legs, feeling the evidence of his desire press against her. The realization his reaction was all for her gave Sara a feeling of power she savored, much as she did the warmth of his skin under her hands. She ran her fingers through the short hair on his chest and felt his stomach muscles contract when her tongue skimmed across his nipple.

His hands ravaged her hair, tugging gently until she looked up at him. "You're overdressed," he told her.

She stood and shimmied the pajama pants down past her hips. Then with a breath she lifted the tank top over her shoulders. Sara knew she had a decent figure—although in L.A. even the geriatric set had decent figures. She was well aware what a perfectly sculpted body looked like and just as aware that hers didn't fit the bill. She stood in front of him for a moment, hands held over her breasts in only her cotton panties, wishing she'd had the foresight and budget to buy something more worthy of the moment. But the way Josh's eyes darkened then sparked reminded her that this wasn't Hollywood.

Maybe a real guy wanted to be with a real woman after all.

The thought gave her confidence a boost at the same time as another layer of her heart's armor unfurled for this man.

She took a tentative step closer, and he moved forward to the edge of the sofa. He reached out and cupped her thighs, causing her to shuffle forward until her knees grazed the front of the couch. His mouth pressed against her stomach, drawing small circles of kisses as his fingertips mimicked the pattern on her legs.

Slowly, he gripped the sides of her underpants and

smoothed them down until they fell in a puddle on the floor. He pulled her closer until she was once again on his lap, this time only the thin fabric of his boxers separating them.

"You're the most beautiful thing I've ever seen," he whispered as he took her breast in his mouth, loving the sensitive tip with his tongue. Her back arched against the pleasure he was giving her. He lifted then gently lowered her onto her back on the couch.

Sara felt open and vulnerable, unable to resist her desire in the moment. But when she looked into his eyes, there was something more. An answering need that had nothing to do with a physical release. It was as if he was claiming her with every kiss, every touch. Marking her body and soul as his. She'd never belonged to anyone, and the thought of giving herself now in that way both terrified and exhilarated her.

"You've got a pretty darn good superhero impression going tonight," she said, trying to ground herself with humor.

But the light in his eyes only glowed deeper. "And we haven't even started to fly."

He kissed her again and his hand moved down her bare skin to the place where her body needed him the most. His fingers found her core, stroking her center until her legs would barely hold her. Slowly, he lowered her to the sofa. His mouth found hers as his fingers continued to drive her wild with pleasure.

When she was so close to the brink she wasn't sure she could take any more, she turned her head. "Inside me," she whispered on a tortured breath. "I want you inside."

He lifted away from her for a moment, time enough

to strip off his boxers and pull his wallet out of his jeans, yanking a condom wrapper from the side pocket. Sheathing himself, he covered her once more, his elbows resting above her shoulders as he cradled her face between his hands. "Open for me, Sara."

And she did, biting down on her lip as he filled her completely.

His lips found hers, soothing the place she'd just bitten with his tongue. Her arms wrapped around his shoulders, her fingernails grazing across the corded muscles in his back as he began to move. She moaned, or maybe it was him. Sara was so lost in the pleasure of how he made her feel she couldn't tell.

An intensity built in her body, a golden light filled every fiber of her being. He whispered her name over and over in a voice so full of reverence it made every inch of her tingle in response.

She gripped him tighter as the waves of pleasure washed over her and felt him shudder in response, his body releasing a desire that matched her own. After several minutes, they both stilled, Josh's face nuzzled into the crook of her neck. He kissed her softly, as if to soothe her fractured nerves and emotions.

"I've never felt…" she began, hardly able to put a sentence together. "That was…"

"Amazing, epic, mind-blowing, incredible," he supplied, kissing her once for each adjective he offered.

"All of the above," she admitted when she could form a coherent thought. "I don't know how else to describe it."

"No movie references do it justice?" He lifted his head to look into her eyes.

She saw a hint of amusement but also a question

there. "This is better than the movies," she answered simply. "It's real."

He kissed her deeply again, an exclamation point at the end of her sentence, then cradled her in his strong arms.

Josh used one finger to trace the beam of moonlight that made a sliver of Sara's back gleam in the darkness. She gave a contented sigh and turned her cheek on the pillow.

"How was round two? Better than the first?" she asked, her voice a husky growl that gave him a satisfied tug low in his chest.

"We're a good fit," he answered.

She lifted her head to look at him. "In the bedroom, we're a good fit," she amended for him.

"Not bad on the sofa, either." He tried to ignore the shadow that crossed her face. He knew what she meant but wasn't ready to let reality intrude on this night quite yet.

"I still want to sell the house," she said quietly.

He groaned. "Don't tell me you think we made love so I could convince you not to sell the house."

"I just mean…"

"Because that would make me a royal jerk and you a bit of a hussy. Neither one of those is the case." He propped himself up on his elbow, his hand stilling on the curve of her waist.

"I know you've got goals for the summer and I've got—"

He held one finger up to her lips. "You're trying to pick a fight and it won't work. Tonight was amazing. That's enough. Let me wallow in my undeniable sexual prowess for a few minutes more. It's been a while, you know?"

Her head flopped back down onto the pillow. "I don't want your expectations to change."

"Have you ever been with a guy who hasn't wanted something from you after?"

She squeezed her eyes shut tight.

"Sara, answer me," he prompted.

"My track record with men isn't exactly stellar. Most people I know live their lives wanting something from others. For a while, I couldn't tell if men were interested in me or the doors I could open to parties, premieres and the like. Let's just say I had a lot less offers once my star began to fade."

"Nothing about you is faded," he said, and placed a kiss on the inside of her elbow. He felt her gaze on him but didn't look up. He was too afraid of what his own eyes might reveal.

He didn't expect to change Sara's mind about selling her grandmother's property, but at the same time he still wanted...more. He wanted more for her and from her. He wanted her to see what he saw when he looked at her: a smart, beautiful woman who had so much to offer.

He knew what it was like to believe you were a one-trick pony. When he'd gotten hurt and realized he'd never ride competitively again, he figured he had nothing more to give anyone. The only thing he'd ever been good at in his life was bull riding. In the ring, nothing else mattered. Not his messed-up family, his sister's death, the tenuous relationship he had with his daughter. For those few seconds, his concentration had been completely focused on staying on the back of one thousand pounds of angry animal.

With that gone, he'd wondered what else he had in life. Then he'd gotten another chance with Claire and he'd realized that the time in the ring wasn't as important as he'd once thought.

What mattered was each tiny moment in life and how you lived it. He'd made up his mind to do better, both for Claire and himself. Slowly, he was coming to realize the accident had been an opportunity. A second chance to live life on his own terms.

He wanted Sara to realize that she was more than the on-screen persona created by Hollywood. She had choices and didn't have to prove her worth to anyone but herself.

"I got offered the audition."

He realized his hand had tightened on her hip when she fidgeted underneath it. His mind raced, then he remembered a moment from earlier in the night. "The bearded guy you were talking to at dinner?"

She nodded. "He's a hot director right now. Most of his work has been in television, but he's agreed to make Ryan's movie his first big-screen project."

"Congratulations," he said, unable to muster much enthusiasm for the word.

"Aren't you going to ask why he wants me to read?" Her eyes held a hint of accusation.

"I watched *Just the Two of Us*," Josh answered honestly. "Back when it was a network show and recently, too. Claire's been ordering each season online."

Sara swallowed and looked away. "I didn't know that."

"You were a good actress, Sara. You may be out of

practice, but I doubt that has changed. You had some bad luck, but it doesn't diminish your natural talent."

A lone tear dripped from the outside corner of her eye, and he brushed it away with his lips. "Why don't you seem happy about this?"

She blinked several times. "I stopped believing I had any talent," she told him. "The washed-up child star is such a familiar cliché in Hollywood. Why should I be any different?"

"Because you're an original." Josh took her chin in his fingers and turned her to face him. "You're better than they gave you credit for. You're more than Serena Wellens ever dreamed of being." He studied her for a minute, then added, "You know you don't have to prove anything to anyone? Not your mother, not the critics. Not Ryan or your former friends. Not even me."

"Thank you for saying that," she whispered. "How did you know Ryan is pushing me so hard?"

"That guy is full of bad ideas."

That coaxed a bit of a smile from her. "He knows the director, Jonathan Tramner, from a project they did a few years back. They reconnected because Jonathan has a place in Aspen. He was a fan of my show and, when he heard I was in Crimson, asked Ryan to set up a meeting."

"Which is why Ryan wanted to take us all out to dinner last night," Josh guessed.

"Yes." She shrugged. "The casting people will flip, but Jonathan wants me to read for the lead. He's only in Aspen through next week, so I'm supposed to get the script tomorrow." She glanced at the clock on the nightstand. "Later today, I guess. If I'm interested, I have to meet him at his place on Saturday."

"No way."

She drew back. "No way, what?"

"Even I've heard stories about what happens on casting couches. You're not going to his place alone."

That produced an actual laugh from her. "Trust me, I'm fairly long in the tooth by Hollywood standards. If Jonathan Tramner wanted to make a pass at an actress, he could find a more nubile victim than me."

"Trust me, you're plenty nubile." He scooped her up until she was pressed across the top of him, her long hair tickling his skin. "Are you sure this is what *you* want?"

She rested her arms across his chest, cradling her chin in her hands. "It's been so long since I had a chance to act, it's hard for me to know. But I loved it once. In the midst of all the other crazy in my life growing up, the actual work was good. I know you say I don't have anything to prove, but you're wrong. I have something to prove to myself."

He nodded, leaning up to kiss her on the tip of the nose. "I get that." His stomach burned at the thought of her back in Hollywood. Yet he couldn't blame her for taking another shot at the life she once loved.

Hell, what did he have to offer her here anyway? Running a guest ranch in a tiny mountain town couldn't compare with being on a movie set.

As if reading his thoughts, she said, "It's a long shot, and I'm still committed to making this summer work. To you and Claire."

"I'll drive you to the audition."

Her big eyes widened a fraction. "You don't have to do that."

"You're not alone here, Sara. I—"

Before he could say more, she kissed him sweetly on the mouth. "That's the nicest thing anyone has said to me in a long time."

He could hear the emotion in her voice and it pulled on his heart. He couldn't afford to give himself to this woman but couldn't seem to stop the tumult of emotions she created in him. Running his hands up her bare back, he deepened the kiss. "There's time before I need to go back to the main house," he whispered to her.

She wriggled her hips against his. "Let's make the most of it, then."

Chapter 12

"You're ready."

"I'll never be ready." Sara slumped her head onto the kitchen table and thumped it several times.

"I agree with April," Claire told her, scooping a spoonful of peanut butter from the jar. "We've been practicing every day for the past week. You're perfect for the part of Amelia. They'd be crazy not to hire you."

The more Sara thought about the audition, the more she was afraid Jonathan Tramner would be crazy if he actually did hire her. Yes, she'd rehearsed the lines, tapped into the emotion of the character, a single mother fighting for custody of her autistic son. Both April and Claire had read through pivotal scenes in the script with her dozens of times. But was she really ready to put herself out there in this way again?

Luckily, she hadn't had much time to ruminate over

her doubts. After Josh's friends had left, the family reunion checked in, and she'd been busy arranging activities and making sure the needs of guests ranging in age from three to seventy-eight were met.

The family members were lovely, especially the grandparents. They'd been thrilled to share stories of their courtship and fifty-plus years of marriage. Although it was clear their children had heard the tales many times, they gamely listened over and over, adding funny commentary about childhood antics, long-ago vacations and good-natured sibling rivalries.

Being on set during her childhood had been the closest Sara had ever come to feeling like she had a family. During her summer hiatuses, she'd count down the days until she could get back to filming, the only time her life seemed to make sense. As she glanced up to her grandmother's warm, welcoming kitchen and her friends here supporting her, she thought maybe she didn't need a set to give her that sense of normalcy any longer.

"Get a new spoon," she said automatically to Claire as the girl began to dip her used one back into the peanut-butter jar.

Claire pulled a face but tossed her spoon into the sink. "You'll be great at the part of the overprotective mother," Claire said as she pulled a clean spoon out of a drawer. "You already sound like one half the time."

Sara stood and claimed a spoon for herself then dipped into the jar over Claire's shoulder. "What if I do get it? What if I don't? I can't decide which is scarier."

"You'll know what was meant to be when it happens," April counseled as she dried dishes from breakfast and put them away in the cabinets.

"How are we friends when you're always so darn zen?"

"It's the yoga," Claire told her. "You should do it with us in the morning."

"I need my beauty rest more than I need to turn my body into a pretzel." She met April's gaze over Claire's head and felt a blush creep up her cheeks at her friend's raised eyebrows.

April had been leading 7:00 a.m. yoga sessions for the guests to start each day. Sara would normally be a part of each one. Now, thanks to Josh, the early mornings after he left her cabin were the only rest she was getting. Maybe he wasn't turning her body into a pretzel each night, but she was certainly moving in ways she hadn't for a long, long time. She thought they'd been discreet about their relationship, but from the look on April's face, her friend knew exactly what was going on.

"Have you and your dad made things right?" she asked Claire, wanting to turn the attention away from April's inquisitive gaze.

"I guess," Claire mumbled around a mouthful of peanut butter. "I'm mainly ignoring him. It's easy because he's so busy with the guests."

"You need to talk to him." She wrapped one arm around Claire's small shoulders. "He loves you, sweetie."

"Your mom came by the other day," Claire countered.

Sara heard April cough to cover a laugh. The girl was young but she was good. "Yes, I know. She texted me later."

"She said there's a photographer in Aspen who does

great head shots of models and actresses. She offered to drive me over."

"Your father isn't going to allow that."

Claire shrugged out of Sara's embrace. "What if I don't tell him?"

"Then I will," Sara said, her eyes narrowed. "Trust me, my mother is not someone you want in your life."

"She seems nice and she believes in me," Claire grumbled. "It's about time someone did."

"Your father believes in you. He wants to keep you safe so you have a decent future. You have choices, Claire. You can be whoever you want."

"As long as I do exactly what my dad says. How is that a choice?"

"Talk to him. Tell him how you feel."

Claire swiped a hand across her cheek. "He doesn't care about how I feel. He wants me to be the no-trouble little girl I used to be, playing quietly with my dolls in the corner. It stinks to get older."

"Amen, sister," Sara whispered, then caught herself. "You're barely a teenager. This is new territory for both of you. I know your dad loves you. Even if he's stumbling around how he shows it."

Buster galloped into the room and nudged his big head under Claire's arm. Her eyes widened and she shook her head. "I'm crying and Dad's here. I don't want him to see me like this."

Sara took hold of her arm. "He knows you're upset. He is, too, Claire. He's driving me to Aspen this morning for the audition. Why don't you come with us?"

"Not a chance," Claire said, shaking off Sara's grip. "I'm going to hang out with friends all day."

"What friends? Where will you be?"

"Friends," the girl repeated. "I'll be around town." She took a step toward the back door. "You're not my mother, Sara. You don't need to act like you really care."

Before Sara could argue, Claire had run out of the house, Buster following close on her heels.

Josh walked into the kitchen at that moment, his gaze swinging between Sara and April. "What's going on in here?" he asked, brow furrowed.

"Hormones," both women said at once.

Josh took a step back. "Should I wait for you in the car?"

Sara shook her head. "It's Claire. I pushed her to talk to you. Probably too far." She pointed a finger at Josh. "Why haven't you made things right with her yet?"

He threw up his hands. "I've tried. She locks herself in her room anytime she's in the house and tells me she has a headache. With guests coming and going, I've barely had time to take a breath, let alone pin her down."

"It's important, Josh."

"I know."

"Maybe you should stay here instead of going to Aspen with me. Rent a bunch of vintage John Hughes movies. Anything with Molly Ringwald. Might give you a sense of what you're dealing with."

"Your audition is important, too." His brows knit in frustration. "And there's no way in hell I'm watching teeny-bopper flicks from the eighties."

Sara bit down on her lip. "I can manage the audition." She didn't want to admit how embarrassed she'd be if she bombed the read-through. The thought of Josh seeing her at her most vulnerable made her chest tighten.

"Let him take you," April told her, sliding one arm around Sara's shoulders. "You're not alone, Sara."

Sara glanced at her friend, the one who'd been at her side through both her slow descent into obscurity and self-sabotaging attempts to ruin her own life. April had stayed with her no matter what. There was no one Sara trusted more.

"Am I good enough?" she whispered, too desperate for the answer to care that Josh could hear her pathetic question.

"You're better," April assured her. She turned to Josh. "I'll be at the house all day, so I can keep an eye on Claire. I'll suggest that her friends come here to hang out."

"Thanks," Josh said gruffly. "I have a van coming to pick up the family reunion for the airport later this morning. We have a couple of days until the next guests arrive." He glanced at Sara. "I'll take Claire out on the ATVs tomorrow, spend the whole day with her on the mountain." He took a breath, then added, "I'll make things right."

Sara nodded. "Good. Then let's get this over with."

With a last hug for April, she made her way to the front of the house and Josh's truck. She put her hand on the door but before she could open it, Josh spun her to face him.

His lips met hers, and he kissed her for several moments, his palms encircling her face. His touch helped to melt away the anxiety she'd felt since the morning, giving her a sense of delicious pleasure that curled her toes.

"Not here," she told him when she finally broke the connection. "Claire could see us. Anyone could see us."

"I don't care," he answered, and kissed her again. "We shouldn't have to hide." He dipped his head until his eyes were level with hers. "Never think for a minute that you're not good enough, Sara."

Her gaze dropped to the ground, but he tipped up her chin until she met his eyes again. "That director would be lucky to have you on his movie, just like we're lucky to have you at the ranch. You have a place here. No matter what happens. This is your grandmother's house and it belongs to you. You belong."

A light breeze blew in from the hills behind the ranch. The swirling gray clouds in the sky matched her tumultuous emotions. As much as she didn't appreciate it when she'd first come to Colorado, the crisp scent of pines in the air had become a salve to her frazzled nerves. In more ways than one, she was acclimating to life in this small town. The very thought scared her to her core. She'd never had a true home before and wondered if she was made to last in a place like Crimson.

She bit down on her lip and nodded. "Thank you" was all she could say in response.

He opened the door and she climbed into the truck, emotion welling in her throat. Raindrops began hitting the windshield, large drops of wetness that turned into a deluge by the time he was at the end of the driveway. He didn't say anything more as they pulled out onto the two-lane highway that led to Aspen. Sara was grateful. She wasn't sure she could manage a single word right now without bursting into tears.

The sound of the rain lulled her into a quiet trance. The sudden storm was so heavy, Sara could barely see beyond the rain-soaked windows to the valley beyond. Was this a good omen? Mother Nature washing away all the old gunk she harbored? Or a bad one, the mile-high version of *The Perfect Storm?*

"Are we going to make it?" she asked, only half kidding as the rain turned to hail. A ferocious rhythm pounded outside, echoing in the truck's interior.

"A normal summer storm, that's all," Josh answered with a wink. "To make sure I'm paying attention."

She closed her eyes as he took her hand in his, soothing her with his gentle touch. It was dangerous to have her emotions this close to the surface before she went into an audition. She needed to stay professional. She concentrated on breathing, pulling air in and out of her lungs as she thought about the character she was reading for, what made the single mother tick and how Sara could use her own experience to enhance the lines she read as Amelia.

After a few minutes, her mind cleared and all that was left was the character. This was the part she loved about acting, pushing off reality and turning herself into someone new.

By the time they wound their way into downtown Aspen a half hour later, she was in the zone, despite the continuing rain. Jonathan Tramner was staying at one of the upscale boutique hotels just off the town's center. Josh pulled the truck to a stop under the building's front canopy, ignoring the valet who came around the vehicle.

"I don't want to hover like a helicopter parent today," he said with a sheepish smile. "I'm learning something from my time with Claire."

Sara turned and gave him a small smile in return.

"Thank you for bringing me here. I'll go up to the audition on my own. I need to do that. Dust off my Serena Wellens attitude in the elevator."

"Leave Serena behind, sweetheart. You don't need her anymore." Josh lifted the hand he still held to his mouth, grazing a long kiss across her knuckles. "I have some things to pick up at the hardware store just outside of town. I'll be back in thirty minutes and waiting in the lobby."

She grimaced. "Are you sure you want to come back so soon? These things can sometimes take a while."

"I'll be waiting," he assured her. "And don't forget, you've got this."

I've got this, Josh thought to himself more than an hour later as he shifted in the overstuffed chair at the side of the hotel's lobby, where he was out of the way but still able to see the bank of elevators in the back. He'd thought about heading to the bar, but since it was only noon and he still had to drive back to Crimson, that didn't seem like the best idea.

He picked up his cell phone and gave it a hard shake, but the screen remained dark. Thanks to his nerves, he'd spilled an entire cup of coffee on the damn thing shortly after dropping Sara off earlier. He wasn't sure whether he was more nervous that she'd get the part or she wouldn't. Either way, his heart hammered in his chest each time the elevator doors slid open.

He believed in Sara without question and hoped that whoever this *hot* Hollywood director was would be able to see what Josh did. He'd heard her rehearsing with both April and Claire over the past week, and the emotion in her voice had made a shiver roll down his spine.

If she was as good as he thought, then in no time she'd have a better offer than anything he could give her. He wasn't sure what she wanted from her next chapter in life, doubted she knew herself. His heart couldn't help hoping it would somehow involve him.

His head lifted as the elevator dinged. Before the doors had opened fully, Sara bolted out. Her wild eyes scanned the room then landed on him.

"We need to go," she yelled, and motioned him toward the front entrance. "Now."

He sprang out of the chair and caught up to her within a few strides. "What happened up there? Did he do something to you?"

"Where's your phone? Why isn't it on?" she asked, not stopping to look him in the eye.

"Sara, what's the problem?" He swung her around to face him, trying to figure out why she looked so panicked. "How was the audition?"

She shook her head. "I left in the middle of it." Her hand squeezed his arm. "It's Claire. There's been an accident. We have to get to the hospital."

Josh's mind reeled like he'd taken a sucker punch to the jaw. Her words played through his head in slow motion.

Claire. Accident. Hospital.

He turned and ran through the sliding doors leading to the street. He'd parked his truck around the corner, not wanting to bother with the valet. He reached it in seconds and fumbled for his keys, his fingers shaking uncontrollably. He took a breath and steadied himself. He'd do his daughter no good if he was too crazed to get to her.

The rain had slowed to a light drizzle, and he hit

the wipers to clear the windshield as he turned the key in the ignition. Sara climbed in next to him, breathing hard from following at his breakneck pace.

He pulled out onto the street, mentally calculating the route to the hospital in his head. The facility was located between the two towns, which would put him there in about twenty minutes. Fifteen without traffic. His mind saw the stretch of highway they'd drive in detail, from the tight curves to the areas where water was likely to pool after a storm. His focus was absolute, much like it had been during his bull-riding days. That had been Josh's gift in the ring. His ability to visualize the entire ride, anticipate how the animal was going to move before it did.

Control the situation.

His current life left him feeling more out of control by the day. All his well-crafted plans amounted to nothing when his daughter was in trouble.

"What happened?" he asked, his gaze remaining fixed on the road. "Is Claire okay?"

"I don't know," Sara answered, and his knuckles tightened on the steering wheel. "April said something happened at the creek. I had terrible reception in the hotel suite so the call dropped. Why didn't you pick up your phone?"

"Spilled coffee and fried it."

"She was trying to reach you for a while before she called me." He saw her glance at the phone held tightly between her fingers. "Do you want me to try her again?"

He shook his head. "We'll be there in minutes." If his head didn't explode from the pounding inside it first. Claire needed him and he couldn't be reached.

Wasn't the whole point of returning to Crimson so he'd be around to keep his daughter safe?

Now the one time she needed him, he'd failed her. Like he'd failed his sister.

Sara reached out and placed a hand on his arm. "I'm sure she'll be fine. April would call back if there was anything else to report."

"I have to get to her," he whispered, not hiding the emotion that choked his voice. "I have to know."

Sara squeezed his arm but said nothing more. Josh knew how fast the creek on the far side of his property flowed after a heavy rainstorm. The water could go from a soft trickle to a raging current within minutes. That was how it was in the mountains. He hadn't expressly warned Claire to stay away from the creek because they hadn't been getting much rain this summer. She wasn't much inclined to be outside when she didn't have to be anyway. He should have thought of it, though. His job as her father was to think of everything he could. Josh knew all too well how losing your concentration for even a moment could cost a person. It was a lesson he didn't want his daughter to learn.

Within minutes, they pulled into the hospital parking lot. He threw the truck into Park, not caring that he'd stopped in the fire lane, and headed for the entrance.

"Claire Travers," he said to the receptionist behind the desk in the E.R. lobby. "I'm her father."

The woman barely glanced from her computer screen. "Exam Two, down the hall to your right."

Sara was beside him as he raced down the hall. At the room marked Two, Josh swung open the door. His heart skipped a year's worth of beats as he saw

Claire in the bed, her eyes closed. A white bandage wound around her head and her arm was casted up to the elbow.

He must have choked out a sound because she blinked and turned her head on the pillow. "Daddy," she whispered, her voice scratchy and slow.

But she'd said his name. Her eyes were focused on his. That had to be a good sign, right?

He took two steps toward the bed, then noticed April in the chair at the corner of the room. "She's okay," the woman told him, clearly reading the panic in his expression.

"I'm fine," Claire added groggily. "Just clumsy." She must be on some heavy painkillers.

As he got closer, Josh noticed the scratches all along her knuckles and a large bruise forming on one cheek. He clenched his jaw with a mix of worry, frustration and anger. He hadn't been there and she'd been hurt. He wanted to punch his fist into the wall, to feel a tenth of the pain she felt.

Even more, he wanted to know how to make it better. He'd not been around enough to kiss away boo-boos or mend scraped knees when she was younger. Maybe if he had, he wouldn't be so traumatized now.

He couldn't speak, couldn't move. She looked so fragile, her face pale against the white sheet. He lifted his hand then lowered it again, not sure what to do with his mixed-up emotions.

Sara took his arm and gently led him to the side of the bed, pushing him to sit next to Claire.

"What if I hurt her more?" he said through gritted teeth, making to stand again.

"You won't," Sara assured him. She moved to stand

next to him and took the hand from Claire's uninjured arm, wrapping Josh's fingers around his daughter's.

He swallowed around the lump in his throat. Claire's skin was cool to the touch, and instinctively he grasped her hand tighter, rubbing his fingers back and forth until warmth began to seep into her fingertips.

"You don't have to talk, sweetheart," Sara said, soothing her thumb across Claire's forehead below the bandage. "We're so happy you're okay."

Claire gave Sara a wobbly smile then her gaze turned to Josh. "I'm sorry I worried you. I knew it was stupid to go down to the creek after such a hard rain. Some of the kids thought it would be cool." She made a tiny sound that might have been a laugh. "I could hear your voice in my head telling me not to." She coughed, wincing from the effort.

"Don't talk," Josh told her, dragging in a shaky breath. "Rest now. I'm here. You're okay." He said the words as much for his own benefit as hers.

"She slipped on a rock and went down in the creek," April said, coming to stand at the foot of the bed. "The current was pretty strong, but she held on to a branch until one of the boys she was with could drag her out. She told me they were walking to a neighbor's house." April's breath hitched. "I'm sorry, Josh. You left me in charge and this happened. I'm so sorry."

April shook her head, then turned and left the room.

"It's not her fault," Claire said, squeezing Josh's fingers. "I lied about where I was going." She coughed again.

"Hush now," Josh told her softly. "I'm not mad at April." He lifted Claire's hand and kissed the inside of her wrist. "Or you, even though I probably should be." His voice caught as he added, "I'm just so damn glad it's not worse."

He watched as Sara bent to give Claire's cheek a gentle kiss. "I'm going to find April. You get some rest, and soon we'll take you home where you belong."

As she turned to leave, Josh caught her hand. "Thank you for taking that call," he said, and leaned up to kiss her quickly on the mouth. Her cheeks immediately turned a bright shade of pink as she glanced over her shoulder at Claire, who was now watching them with an interest that belied the effect of the painkillers.

"I'll be in the hall," Sara said, and left the room.

"So the two of you…" Claire began as Sara left the room.

Josh couldn't help but return his daughter's smile. "We'll talk about that later. We'll talk about a lot of things later. Right now, do as she said and rest. I want you out of here as soon as can be arranged."

Claire took a deep breath. "I love you, Daddy," she whispered as her eyes drifted shut.

"I love you, too, Claire-Bear," Josh answered, for the first time in years using the nickname he'd given her as a young girl.

One corner of her mouth kicked up, but within moments her breathing had slowed to an even rhythm that told him she was asleep.

He sat there for several more minutes, drinking in every one of her features. In sleep, she looked more the child than a girl on the cusp of becoming a woman. If only he could keep her small, maybe he'd be able to avoid the gray hairs he could imagine sprouting at the moment. How did any father of a teenage daughter ever sleep at night?

She'd said she could hear his voice in her head, but she'd made the bad choice anyway. That was exactly how he'd been as a teen, almost eager to thwart his mother's advice and his father's commands at every turn. He knew all about the trouble that could come from wanting to rebel against your parents. He'd seen it in each of his siblings, and had no doubt it had contributed to his sister's tragic death.

He wasn't kidding when he'd said he was going to talk to Claire later. About everything, just like Sara had originally advised. He couldn't stop Claire from making bad decisions, but if he was honest about his own feelings, maybe she'd feel freer to share hers and not act out. It was the exact opposite to the parenting strategy his own mom and dad had taken, which led him to believe it was far more sound than anything else he could try.

At this point, Josh would try anything to avoid his past from making trouble in his present life.

Chapter 13

Sara tucked the covers in tight around Claire, making the girl's slim body into a tiny cocoon, then adjusted the hot water bottle she'd placed near the bottom of the bed.

"Mmm," Claire mumbled. "Feels snug as a bug."

Hours earlier at the hospital, Sara had first comforted April, convincing her friend no one blamed her for the accident. Then she'd tracked down the doctor who'd treated Claire, making sure he discussed her injuries and treatment with Josh. The doctor reassured Josh that Claire's broken wrist was the worst of her condition and she'd recover without a problem.

Josh had been both overwhelmed and terrified at Claire being hurt. That was a normal reaction for any parent, but Sara knew that part of his anxiety had to do with memories of his sister's accident. She wanted to make sure the hospital staff didn't worry him any more than was necessary.

They'd brought Claire home just before dinnertime, and Josh had insisted on carrying her from the truck up to her bedroom. She'd been too tired to text her friends, but had begged Sara and Josh to watch part of season three of *Just the Two of Us* with her.

Unable to say no when Claire was clearly so out of it, Sara had climbed onto the bed with her while Josh hooked the iPad up to the television on the dresser. He'd positioned himself on the other side of Claire, her head resting against his strong shoulder. Sara had almost flinched when her younger self appeared on screen during the opening credits.

She'd pressed her head back against the headboard and remained resolutely still so Josh wouldn't see her reaction. They'd made it through three episodes before Claire admitted to being too tired to continue. She'd complained about a chill, and Sara'd felt almost frozen herself as she heated a water bottle and took an extra quilt from the linen closet in the hall.

Thankfully, Josh had disappeared by the time she returned to Claire's room. She bent to give Claire a kiss, surprised when the girl reached out to take her hand.

"You were a cute kid," Claire said sleepily.

"Cute only takes you so far," Sara answered.

"You're even prettier now," Claire continued as if Sara hadn't spoken. "Especially since you stopped wearing so much makeup and took the streaks out of your hair."

Sara rolled her eyes at this drug-induced critique of her beauty habits. She'd heard way worse. "I don't remember much about my gran, but I think she used to

say, 'Pretty is as pretty does.' That makes more sense
to me now than it used to."

"I'd like to be prettier," Claire answered around a
yawn.

"You're beautiful, sweetheart."

"I haven't been much in the 'pretty does' category
lately. I'm going to work on that." She tugged on Sara's
sleeve until Sara sat on the edge of the bed.

"I like you with my dad," she whispered.

Sara felt her mouth drop open. "It's not serious. I
mean, he's great. You know I'm only here for the summer and..."

She stopped as Claire's eyes closed. The girl's fingers dropped from her arm. Sara adjusted the pillow
and blankets a bit more then straightened.

Tiptoeing out of the room, she flipped off the light
and closed the door behind her.

"Not serious?" a voice asked next to her ear.

Sara jumped back, her palm landing with a thump
on her chest. "Eavesdrop much?"

Josh laced his fingers in hers. "Only when it counts."

Too tired to argue, she let him lead her down the
stairs. "We need to talk," he said quietly as they
reached the bottom step.

"I'm tired, Josh." She huffed out a breath. "If *talk* is
code for *argue,* I don't have the energy for it tonight."

"It's not," he assured her. When they stepped into
the kitchen, she noticed the large trestle table was set
for two, delicate china plates and beautiful crystal gob-
lets. Candlelight danced from two pillars near the center of the table.

"What's this? Where's April?"

"April was tired. We talked and she went back to

her cabin." He held up his hands at her look. "It's fine, Sara. I don't blame your friend and she knows it."

"Good, because April would do anything to keep Claire safe."

"Sit down," Josh told her softly. "You haven't eaten since breakfast."

"Did April…"

"I ordered carryout from the Italian place in town. They delivered."

"I love meatballs," Sara said on a tiny sigh.

Josh smiled. "April told me they were your favorite."

She glanced at him, stunned for a moment that on a day when he'd been through so much, he'd think of her preferences. So much for her comment about not being serious. Her heart was seriously flipping in her chest.

"You didn't have to do this," she said casually, not wanting him to see how much the small gesture affected her. "I can—"

He leaned forward and kissed her before she could continue. "Let me take care of you," he said against her lips. "Just for tonight."

He held out a chair for her and she sat, biting on her lip as she looked at the spaghetti, salad and garlic bread in bowls on the table.

Josh scooped noodles, meatballs and the rest on her plate. She unfolded the delicate linen napkin before her and spread it on her lap.

"It smells delicious," she said, breathing in the tangy scent of the food.

"It tastes even better," Josh answered, serving himself generous portions of everything.

Sara cut off a chunk of meatball and brought it to her mouth. Josh was right; the food was divine. As soon as she swallowed the first bite, she realized how hungry she was. All she had at her little cabin was granola bars and an overripe banana, so she was especially grateful for this feast.

"Tell me about the audition," Josh said after a few minutes.

The meatball that had moments earlier tasted like a little piece of heaven turned dry in mouth. "I wasn't right for the part after all," she said simply.

"You left because of Claire." Josh studied her over the rim of his wineglass.

Sara didn't drink often, but she took a big gulp of her own wine to wash down the bite of food lodged in her throat. "It doesn't matter."

"You were up there for a while. Did you read at all?"

She nodded. "Jonathan was on a call for a long time when I got there. We talked about the character for a bit. I told him how I saw Amelia. We read a small piece from the script, but I couldn't concentrate because I could feel my phone vibrating in the purse at my feet. Finally, I took the call. Then I left." She lifted her hands and forced her lips into a smile. "End of story. Not a big deal."

"It is a big deal." Josh's gaze was sympathetic. "I know how hard you worked for this reading. How much you wanted it."

"Bad timing. Story of my life." Sara pushed away her plate, her stomach suddenly rolling precariously.

"Will you get another chance?" Josh leaned forward and tried to take her hand.

She folded her arms across her chest. "This *was* my other chance."

He shook his head. "That can't be the end of it. It wasn't your fault. I'll call. Ryan can call."

She tried to laugh. "Since when are you so ready to be rid of me? I didn't think you were excited about the audition in the first place."

"I'm not. But I want you to know that you're good. Whatever the future brings, you deserve it to be on your terms. You sacrificed a lot for Claire and me today."

"I told you it wasn't a big deal."

"I know it was a very big deal." His eyes turned dark as he watched her. "A serious deal."

"Why did you kiss me in front of Claire at the hospital?"

One broad shoulder lifted. "Because I wanted to kiss you."

"Oh" was all she could manage.

He stood, his face lit by the glow of the candles. "I want to kiss you now."

"Oh," she repeated.

"Do you want it, too?"

Her heart fluttered in her chest. She nodded, and he drew her out of her chair and into his arms, his mouth melding over hers as if his lips had been expressly formed for hers.

"I know you're not staying past the end of summer," he said, drawing back to look into her eyes.

Ask me to stay, a voice whispered inside her head.

"I can't give you the life you want here."

What if all I want is you? the voice asked silently.

She focused her gaze on his mouth, not wanting him to read the emotions she knew clouded her face.

"My priority has to be Claire."

She gave a brief nod. When would Sara ever be someone's number-one priority? His comment didn't surprise her; she couldn't blame him for it. Still, a tiny pit of despair opened in a corner of her heart. She made to turn away, but Josh held her close.

"Unless we could be enough for you."

Her gaze snapped to his. She saw a flame flickering behind his eyes that stoked a thunderous wildfire in her body.

"Would you consider making Crimson your home?" he asked softly. "I want you here. With Claire and me. It's not glamorous and there's still a long way to go before the ranch is set. But you make it better. Claire loves you and I..."

Sara held her breath as she waited for the words she hadn't known she longed to hear.

After a moment Josh continued, "I think we make a good team."

I love you. I love you. I love you. The voice in her head had gone from a whisper to a full-out yell. But she didn't say those three words. She wouldn't take the chance of scaring him away. She knew a good offer when she saw it. It was a perk of wading through bad ones for so many years.

"I think I might like that," she answered carefully. Which was only part of the truth. What she'd like was for Josh to drop to his knees and proclaim his undying love for her. She'd never ask for that. Sara tried never to ask for anything, too afraid of being disappointed.

Unaware of her inner turmoil, he bent and claimed her mouth once again. If he wasn't actually able to say the words, his touch certainly communicated the deep feeling she longed for from him.

This is enough, she counseled her inner voice. More than you ever expected.

Apparently her inner voice was a bit of a floozy, because it gave a small sigh then commanded her to concentrate on the kiss.

Which she did without hesitation.

Josh's touch was pure magic. He wrapped his arms around her waist as her hands twined through his thick hair. She loved being enveloped in his strength. The heat radiating from him warmed all the cold, lonely places in her soul.

"Upstairs," he said as his mouth grazed her ear.

She pushed against his shoulders with her palms. "We should clean up down here. If April comes in…"

"April won't be back tonight," he assured her as a devilish gleam lit his gaze. "Which gives me a better idea for right now."

He kissed her again, and at the same time lifted the hem of her blouse up over her head.

Sara's eyes widened. "We can't. Not here."

"Why not?" His grin turned wicked. "All the guests are gone. Claire is fast asleep and the pain meds will almost guarantee she stays that way through the night. It's only us. You own this house, Sara. You can do whatever you want with it and in it."

He stepped back, and she knew he was putting the power to decide where this night went next in her hands. Sara relished the feeling of being able to control something in her life, even if it was this one moment.

Her fingers reached behind her back and unclasped the strap of her bra. She let the satin fabric drop from her arms and smiled a bit as Josh sucked a breath. Slowly, she undid each button on her jeans, using her palms to slide the material over her hips and down her legs.

"You're going to kill me," Josh said, his voice ragged.

She straightened, wearing only her bright pink panties. "There are worse ways to die," she told him, making her tone sympathetic.

His hungry gaze rolled over her from her face to her toes then came to rest on her hips. "Put me out of my misery," he whispered. "Please."

The raw desire in his eyes made her want to run into his arms. Instead, she looped a finger through the thin waistband on either side of her underpants, bending forward a little as the small piece of fabric fell in a puddle at her feet.

"Is this what you want?" she asked, coyly placing her hands on her hips.

"You have no idea how much," he answered, and ate up the distance between them in two steps.

The moment he touched her, she realized she'd either been acting or fooling herself by thinking she was in control of this situation. Her whole body tingled in anticipation of being with him.

She tugged at his shirt but he circled her wrists in his fingers. "Not yet," he breathed against her breast before taking the puckered tip in his mouth.

Her head arched back with pleasure as he pushed her arms behind her, giving him better access to her sensitive flesh. An instant later, she let out a gasp as her bottom touched the cool granite counter.

"Right where I want you," he said, and dipped his head to place a line of kisses down her belly.

"Josh, this isn't…"

The protest died on her lips as he ran his tongue along her inner thigh. "We need to be quiet," he whispered. "No noise."

Right. Claire upstairs sleeping. April in the nearest cabin. Quiet. She could do quiet.

But when he kissed the center of her being, Sara almost had to bite down on her arm to keep from crying out. The way he touched and tasted her was perfect, as if knew her body's needs better than she did. She felt the pressure build throughout her limbs, and when the release burst over her it was like the Fourth of July, New Year's and all the other holidays rolled into one. Fireworks exploded behind her eyes and a delicious tremor coursed the length of her body.

But it wasn't enough. "Need you," she said, gulping for air. "Now."

Immediately, Josh straightened and shed his shirt and cargo pants in an instant. He fumbled with the condom packet and gave a harsh laugh. "My fingers aren't working right at the moment."

She took the foil from his hands, then wrapped her fingers around his hard length, rolling the condom over his tip. When she glanced up and winked, he gathered her into his arms, lifting her to the edge of the granite as he sheathed himself in her. Her arms wound around his shoulders. She buried her face in the crook of his neck, biting down softly on his skin. He increased his rhythm, and she matched him stroke for glorious stroke until they dived off passion's cliff together. He murmured her name over and over, his warm, calloused palms stroking up and down her back.

After a few moments, they stilled, holding each other without moving. She wished she could give her heart the same release as her body, leave it blissfully content. Instead, the dumb thing continued to pound against her chest even after her breathing had slowed.

She knew the reason, even if she didn't want to admit it. She was in love. A litany of silly movie lines rang through her tormented mind: "You had me at hello," "You've consumed me body and soul," "You make me want to be a better..." Well, maybe she'd draw the line at Jack Nicholson.

Sappy chick flicks had been her favorite before this summer. She wondered if she'd even be able to watch one again. Because she suddenly understood the sentiment behind every tear-jerking scene. Hell, if she got the chance she should audition for one of those roles. She had a wellspring of lovelorn angst to tap.

He'd asked her to stay. Said they made a great team. Wasn't that enough?

But now that she'd really felt what it was like to be head over heels in love with someone, could she settle for anything less?

"Are you okay?" Josh drew back to look at her. He placed his hand across her chest. "Your heart's beating like crazy."

"Altitude adjustment," she said dismissively, scooting out of his grasp and bending to pick up her clothes. "That was quite a workout."

He took his own T-shirt from the chair where it had landed and pulled it over his head. "Stay with me tonight?"

Sara swallowed, then waved at the table. "We need to clean up."

"Clean up. Then stay," he told her. "At least for a few hours."

He looped his arms around her waist. "Please."

Knowing he couldn't see it, she squeezed her eyes shut tight. "You have good manners for a cowboy." She made her tone light. Perhaps she really was a decent actress.

"Is that a yes?"

She nodded, unable to resist. Was there anything he'd ask of her that she could say no to? April had always told Sara she needed to be better about guarding her heart. But when a person spent their life with little encouragement or true affection, it was hard to stand strong when a man offered her any little bit.

She'd gotten used to living on emotional crumbs. While Josh hadn't exactly baked her a cake, he was a good man. He was doing the best he could. She couldn't fault him for that.

Why not enjoy the ride, as long as it lasted?

Sara stepped into the Crimson visitors' center later that week. She'd just picked up the new brochures for the ranch from the printer and wanted to deliver them personally.

The latest guests had left for the airport that morning, and a new crop was arriving in a few days. She was taking this, her one off day, to run errands and arrange a few promotional things in town.

She tried to let April do most of the work with the locals, still not sure of the reception she'd receive. So far today, people had acted normal, no snide remarks about her career or how she didn't fit in here in the mountains. A few of the townies at the post office had asked about the ranch, appearing pleased when she told them their booking rate. Apparently, a lot of people had been rooting for Josh and her gran. It made Sara proud to be part of the ranch's success.

Ryan had been livid when she'd explained what had happened at the audition, but that wasn't her problem anymore. She'd done what she needed to in the situation. If she'd lost her best chance at regaining her career, so be it. Other than the cast on her arm, Claire had recovered nicely. Josh had taken her out for a picnic at one of the nearby waterfalls today. He'd invited Sara to come, but she knew that father and daughter needed time for themselves.

A slender woman with a severe ponytail looked up from a computer as the door jingled. Her mouth dropped open, and Sara recognized her as one of the women who'd been in the clothing store when the shopkeeper had been so rude.

"Hello," Sara said, stepping forward while ignoring the potential awkwardness of the situation. She could make a scene, but that wouldn't do anything to help the ranch. Despite her years in showbiz, Sara'd never been one to play the drama-queen card. "Who do I talk to about these brochures for Crimson Ranch?"

"I'm sorry," the woman answered immediately.

Sara waited for her to continue with, *I don't want to promote anything you're involved in*.

Instead, the woman said softly, "For that day in Feathers and Threads when you first came to town. I shouldn't have listened to Rita gossiping about you like that. I wanted to stand up to her but..."

"I'm not used to people standing up for me." *Josh had done just that,* her irritating inner voice piped up. "Don't worry about it."

"That doesn't make it right." The woman held out

a thin hand. "My name is Olivia Wilder, and I hope you'll accept my apology."

Sara's first reaction was to make a sharp comeback, probably aimed at herself. Josh had told Sara she was a difficult person to compliment. That was true, she realized. She also didn't take apologies well. It felt like letting her guard down. She'd learned long ago the negative consequences that came from that.

Olivia looked sincere, however, and Sara was growing tired of the energy it took to keep the walls built up around her. "Sara Wells," she answered. "Nice to meet you. I appreciate the apology."

Olivia's face broke into a wide smile, and Sara was amazed at the transformation. When Olivia Wilder stopped looking like she'd spent the day sitting on a large stick, she was quite lovely.

"We'd be happy to display your brochures here." She shuffled through some papers on the desk. "I also have a mailing of promotional materials going to several different cities around the state and the Midwest. A few to Texas as well, since they're a big part of our tourism business." She picked up a pen and did some quick calculations. "If you can get me an extra five hundred by the beginning of next week, I'll include you in what I send out."

"That would be fantastic," Sara said, doing a mental fist pump. "Do you manage the visitors' center?"

Olivia's mouth opened and shut a few times. "Not exactly." She tucked a stray strand of hair behind her ear. "I'm an artist, a painter. My husband is the mayor, and he likes me to stay busy with activities he deems appropriate and productive."

"Huh," Sara answered slowly. "That's funny, because you seem like a grown woman fully capable of deciding how you want to spend your own time."

"Yes, well...marriage is about compromise, I guess." Olivia flashed a smile that was anything but happy.

Sara placed a stack of brochures on the desk. "If it's what you want," she said, not believing for a minute that this woman was happy being her husband's puppet. Maybe it was because Sara had spent so many years doing other people's bidding with no concern for what she wanted from life. She could smell dissatisfaction like a bloodhound.

"I've convinced him to redo the community center," Olivia said by way of an answer. "Have you seen the building on the edge of downtown?"

"The one with scaffolding covering it?"

Olivia nodded. "It's going to be great. We'll have art classes, yoga, a camp for kids and..." she paused and pressed her lips together. "There will be an auditorium with a stage. I'd like to revive Crimson's community theater group."

"I didn't know this town had a theater group," Sara said, straightening the brochures. She looked up at Olivia and did a double take at the other woman's hopeful expression. "Oh, no. You don't expect me to get involved?"

"Craig thinks..." Olivia paused. "Of course not. Why would you give your time and talent to a small-town group? I'm sure you have more important ways to spend your time."

Sara cringed. She could tell Olivia was being sincere, but the truth was Sara didn't have anything more important to occupy her time. And nowhere to go at the end of the summer where she was really needed.

Claire needed her. Josh, too, even if he couldn't admit it. He wanted her to stay. If she could prove that she fit into his life, maybe they'd really have a chance.

Despite her fear, that was what she wanted more than anything.

"I don't have much experience in live theater."

"Most of us don't have any experience at all," Olivia answered with a smile. "I'd take any advice or help you're willing to give. There's a small improv group in town, but I think we could get a lot more people involved."

Sara nodded. "I'm not sure how long I'll be staying in Crimson," she said slowly, hating how hard those words were to choke out. "I'm happy to pitch in where I can."

Olivia's smile widened. "Craig would love to meet with you about his ideas—"

"I thought you were heading things up?"

"Well, I'm doing most of the work. But Craig likes to personally handle the VIPs."

Sara choked out a laugh. "I'm a VIP?"

"Of course."

"Do you only want me for the tiny bit of name recognition I have left?" she asked, raising her eyebrows. Better to know up front if she was being used or not.

Olivia shook her head. "You're a good actress. You have experience. I want the community center to be a success. I don't exactly understand what motivates my husband. But I'm not going to use you for publicity, if that's what you're asking. And I won't let him, either."

"You're tougher than you look," Sara observed.

"You're smarter than your reputation," Olivia shot

back, then clapped a hand over her mouth. "Sorry. Shouldn't have said that out loud."

"I take it as a compliment," Sara told her. "You don't strike me as a local."

"I'm from St. Louis. Craig and I met in college. This is his hometown. He has big political dreams and thought being mayor would be a good place to start." She paused, then added, "I'm not sure I fit into his plan the way he wants me to."

"I don't fit into anyone's plan," Sara answered. "I've gotten used to making my own way." She glanced at her watch. "I'm not expected back at the ranch for a few hours. Would you want to grab a bite to eat?" She bit down on her lip as she waited for Olivia to refuse. Sara didn't have any girlfriends outside of April. She'd found that once her fame died, so had her appeal as a friend.

"Really? You want to have lunch with me?" Olivia seemed shocked.

"I do." Sara realized she truly meant it. It was time to start living outside of her own doubts. "Then I think we should do a little shopping."

Olivia gave a knowing smile. "At Feathers and Threads?"

"Exactly," Sara agreed. She glanced around. "Can you leave for a bit?"

"Absolutely. It's a slow day."

"Great. It will be nice to know a friendly face in town."

They picked a Mexican place just off Main Street that Olivia said was the best. Sara noticed a few questioning looks as the mayor's wife walked in with her.

Olivia ignored them, choosing a table on the crowded patio out front.

"Are you sure you don't want something a little more secluded?" Sara asked as she slid into her seat.

"Are you embarrassed to be seen with me?"

"Very funny," Sara mumbled, but one corner of her mouth curved. She felt relaxed with Olivia, much like she did with April, and was grateful for the possibility of a new friendship.

"If you're thinking of staying in Crimson or spending any time here in the future, the town is going to have to get used to you being around. We've had our share of celebrities wander over from Aspen, so it's not too far out of the norm."

"It's silly," Sara admitted. "Being a celebrity has a way of creeping into every aspect of your life. A lot of stars claim they want their privacy but turn around and court the fame with the vacations and outings they choose. It gets to the point where you can't live with the recognition, but you don't know how to live without it."

Olivia nodded. "My father was a U.S. senator when I was younger. He loved the attention he received from everyone in our hometown when he was back there or on the campaign trail. I know it's not the same thing, but I have an idea of what you mean."

Sara breathed a little easier thinking there was someone else in town with whom she could be honest. That was a gift she hadn't received very often in recent years.

The waiter came and took their orders. Sara thought back to her last waitressing job, the latest in a long string of them. It had paid the bills, mostly, but she hadn't taken pleasure in it. She actually enjoyed the work she did on the ranch. She liked working with guests to pinpoint activities that would make their vacations perfect. She was good at coordinating and the customer-service part of it and wanted to make a difference for them. Most people who came to Crimson, Colorado, did it because they craved an adventure. Josh was well equipped to meet their needs. Sara balanced his resources by figuring out exactly what those needs were.

They made a good combination. She wondered if her gran would have been happy with Sara's contributions to the ranch and liked to think she would have been proud.

She and Olivia ate and talked. Olivia was a few years older than Sara, and her childhood had been very different from Sara's own: daughter of a prominent senator, private school then a prestigious Midwestern college. Still, they had an easy rapport, and Olivia had many kernels of wisdom to offer about fitting in in this small mountain community.

As their plates were cleared, a shadow fell over the table. "Olivia," an icy voice said. "You didn't tell me you'd be having lunch in town with Ms. Wellens today."

Sara looked up to see a thin, blond-haired man standing just on the other side of the gate surrounding the patio. He placed a hand on Olivia's shoulder and squeezed, but the gesture didn't look at all loving.

Sara disliked him on sight and even more when she noticed Richard Hamish, her mother's land-developer boyfriend, standing next to him.

The older man tipped his cowboy hat in her direction. "Afternoon, Serena. I've been meaning to pay a visit to Rose's family home to talk to you again about that offer."

"Her name is Sara Wells," Olivia told both men, shrugging out of her husband's grasp. "This lunch wasn't planned, Craig. Sara came into the visitors' center."

"You should have called me to join you," he said with a smile that didn't reach his eyes. "Or better yet, I could have taken her to lunch. It's not very responsible for the mayor's wife to leave her post unattended. What will visitors to our town think of that kind of welcome?"

Olivia cringed and Sara plastered a smile on her face. "They'll think whoever works at the visitors' center needs to eat and maybe the town should make arrangements for better coverage."

She turned her gaze to Richard. "Don't bother coming to the ranch. It's my home now. I own it."

"For now," the cowboy said with a smirk. "I'll send you my latest offer. I have another group of developers interested in the property. I can make you a good deal, Sara." He didn't try to hide his derision. "One that can get you out of the deep financial hole you're in."

Sara grabbed her wallet and took out a wad of bills. "It was lovely meeting you, Olivia. I hope we can schedule some girl time again." She gave Craig an icy stare. "I need to get back now."

The other woman quickly stood and gave her a quick hug. "I'm sorry," she whispered.

Sara returned the hug then turned to the two men. "I hope *not* to see either of you again anytime soon."

"I'm the mayor," Craig said coolly. "You'll see me everywhere if you have plans to stick around."

"Sara doesn't stick," the cowboy put in. "That's not the Hollywood way."

We'll see about that, Sara thought to herself. But that nagging voice inside her head suddenly sounded a lot like her mother.

If you'd only tried harder. You give up too quickly. Who are you if you're not on screen?

She glanced between the cowboy's knowing gaze, the mayor's smug smile and Olivia's sympathetic eyes.

The sympathy was the worst of it. Sympathy felt a lot like pity to Sara. She couldn't stand to be the object of anyone's pity.

She hooked her purse over her shoulder and headed for the exit, unwilling to make eye contact with anyone else. Needing to get to her car, to be alone.

When she finally did, the tears came fast and furious. Years ago, she'd vowed not to let anything make her cry, but she couldn't seem to help herself. She cried for the childhood she'd never had, for the lost innocence and all of the times she'd had to swallow her pride and self-respect. For all of the times one of her mother's boyfriends had made her feel less than who she wanted to be.

For all the times she'd made herself feel even worse.

Could this town really give her the second chance at the life she craved? It was different from the future she'd planned. Yet so far, all she'd gotten from her best-laid plans was a big pile of disappointment and failure.

She loved the acting part of the job, becoming a different character, bringing to life the words on the page. She might be just as fulfilled working in a tiny community theater as she was on a TV or movie set. She'd never know whether she was good enough to make a comeback in Hollywood, but she hoped that after a while that wouldn't matter to her any longer.

She hoped life in Crimson, Colorado, would be enough.

Chapter 14

A week later, Josh watched as Sara greeted each of the ranch's new guests with a warm hug. She had a way of making every person feel comfortable and welcome. It was a gift she shared with her grandmother. Part of why he'd wanted Trudy as a partner on the ranch from the beginning had been the way she put people at ease.

Josh could lead a trail ride or a hike or a four-wheeler drive over a mountain pass, but he was often awkward with casual conversation. He preferred doing to talking. Sara filled in the gaps naturally, both with the guests at the ranch and with Claire.

His relationship with Claire was on the mend, and a large part of the reason why was Sara's encouragement. Josh had some rough edges left over from his days on the circuit and Sara smoothed them, helping him to become the father his daughter needed him to be.

Tonight, Sara's blond hair hung in soft waves around her shoulders and the pale yellow shirt she wore made her eyes seem an even deeper blue. He was glad she remained mostly makeup-free. It was as if she was finally willing to let people see who she truly was instead of her carefully cultivated mask.

Josh would never admit it to her, but a small, selfish part of him was secretly relieved nothing had come of the audition. He didn't know how to compete with her former life. He understood a little bit about the lure of lights and fame. If Sara had to make a choice between her career and life on the ranch, he couldn't imagine she'd choose him. At least not yet. They needed more time for her to really see this was where she belonged.

She drew Claire forward and introduced her to the teenage son of one of the families checking in this week.

Their occupancy was full, and to celebrate, they'd decided to have a big cookout on the patio outside the main house. April had created one of her usual amazing feasts, and Sara and Claire had handled the decorations. Tiny lights glistened from strands wound through the wrought iron gate around the edge of the patio. They'd set the tables with colorful tablecloths and mason jars filled with wildflowers picked from the meadow near the pond. The mountains provided a commanding backdrop, especially now as the sky above them turned a dozen shades of orange and red. The sun was close to dipping behind the highest peak.

This was one of Josh's favorite times on the ranch. The moment when day slipped toward evening and all the colors softened while the sounds of nature became more pronounced in the shadows.

A soft country ballad played from the speakers on the porch. The lilting melody made Josh want to gather Sara in his arms and twirl her across the path from the main house to her cabin. He loved the feel of her in his arms, and though he'd given up dancing long before his knee injury, tonight seemed like the perfect time to make an exception.

As if reading his thoughts, her gaze found his through the groups of guests milling about. He watched as her breath hitched and a blush crept across her cheeks. He hoped she could read in his eyes all the wicked things he had planned for her later.

She took a step toward him, and he realized that he was happy. For the first time in…forever, Josh felt content with his life. The ache for his sister was still there, deep in his heart. His knee would never be as strong as it once was. Despite what it had taken him to get here, or maybe because of it, Josh was truly happy with his life.

Sara had a lot to do with that. He thought about the hope in her eyes when he'd asked her to stay in Crimson. She wanted more from him, more than he believed he was willing or able to give a woman.

There was no doubt in his mind that she deserved more than he could ever give her. But if she wanted him, what was holding him back from making her his? For real. Forever.

He had a sudden vision of the future. The image included a family: Claire, Sara and maybe even a baby. One with Sara's blond hair and dark eyes like his and Claire's.

As if she could sense the change in him, a shy smile lit up Sara's face as she stepped closer. Before she reached him, a loud honking had everyone at the cookout turning toward the front of the house.

Josh could see a late-model sports car speeding up the long driveway that led to the main house, dust billowing behind it. Ryan's car.

A sliver of unease bracketed Josh's shoulders, but he ignored it. He didn't know what scheme Sara's former partner was cooking up tonight, but it didn't matter. Josh knew what he had to do.

He took the two steps to bring him to Sara's side. The scent of cinnamon and honey tantalized him, making his pulse stutter an erratic beat.

He wrapped his fingers around hers. "Sara, I need to talk to you."

"Sara!" Ryan's voice called from the front of the house.

She glanced up at Josh then to where Ryan was leaping onto the back patio.

"I have the most amazing news."

"Ryan, we have guests."

Ryan looked around for the first time, as if realizing there were other people at the house. Josh could sympathize. Sometimes when he looked at Sara everything else faded to nothing—that was how bright she glowed.

"Howdy, folks," Ryan said, then turned his attention back to Sara. "It's good there's a crowd. We're going to want to celebrate tonight. I talked to Jonathan Tramner today." He paused dramatically then raised his fists into the air. "He wants you," Ryan shouted. "He wants you for the part of Amelia!"

"That's impossible," Sara murmured.

Josh immediately released her hand and took a step back, feeling as though he was actually in a movie. He could see the scene in slow motion, him shouting an exaggerated no as the crowd looked on.

But this was real life and he kept his mouth shut, waiting to see how Sara would respond.

Ryan spoke before she could answer. "He loved your take on the character and said the short bit of the reading you did was fantastic." He glanced at Josh then back at Sara. "What made up his mind was the look on your face when you took the call about Claire. He said he saw Amelia in your face, all the motherly concern and love. He actually said it gave him chills."

Josh had chills right now. The bad kind, like right before you got sick to your stomach.

"I don't know what to say." Sara's hand fluttered to her chest as if to settle her breathing.

Josh kept his own breathing steady and even. Blood pumped through his veins, and he could have shot himself to the moon on pure adrenaline, but from the outside he knew he looked completely calm. It was a trick he'd mastered through decades of practice; whether it was his father coming after him as a kid or later when he was perched on the back of a bull, Josh earned a reputation for being cool under pressure.

The pressure on his heart right now threatened to overtake him.

"Say you'll accept the part. This is the kind of role that comes along once in a career, Sara. An award-winning kind of role." Ryan turned to the guests. "Give her some encouragement, everyone." Ryan's gaze met Josh's over her shoulder. "Our girl is going to be a star again."

Applause broke out around the small gathering, guests approaching Sara to offer their congratulations and words of encouragement. She might not get approval in L.A., but these people—strangers practically—were rooting for her. Josh guessed the rest of America would feel the same way. The country was built on comeback stories, and Sara would make a great one. She had talent but was smarter now. She wouldn't let anyone take advantage of her. She'd make career choices that would take her to the top.

Josh could see her future like a map and grew cold with the knowledge that it most likely didn't leave room for him.

He watched as April approached, taking Sara by the arms. "What are you going to do?" she asked softly.

"She's going to take the part," Ryan answered quickly. "She's wanted this for years. She deserves it."

"Let Sara decide," April told him sharply. "Think about it if you need to," she said to Sara in a gentler tone. "You don't have to give an answer right now."

Ryan tapped April on the shoulder. "Actually, she does. She reports to set next week."

"Next week?" Sara's gaze swung between April and Ryan. Josh felt himself sinking further into the background. Felt the walls he'd constructed for his own protection rebuilding, cutting off his heart. "Why so soon?" she asked. "I'm not ready to—"

Josh wanted to stop it, to swing her around and tell her everything he felt, all the plans he had for them. He wanted to beg her not to leave him. He couldn't, so he said nothing, stayed still as a statue while he watched her drift further away. The woman he hadn't believed would fit into his life only a month ago. Now he couldn't imagine living without her.

"Ready or not," Ryan answered. "They were already in preproduction when you met with Jonathan. He gave you a big break. The studio had a list of actresses they wanted. He fought for you, Sara. Do you know what that means?"

She nodded then turned to look at Josh as if to say, *Will you fight for me?*

Her eyes held a mix of hope, question and expectation. It was the last that did him in. After the accident, he'd felt broken and unfixable. He'd been given a second chance at life and with his daughter. But did he have enough to give to Sara, too?

He knew a life with her would mean revealing everything: his emotions, his heart. She'd want access to all the hidden crevices in his miserable soul. He could see it as he looked at her now, her gaze beginning to cloud as she read the doubt on his face. He was bound to disappoint her. He couldn't protect her, didn't have the guts to be the man she needed him to be. As much as he wished it was another way.

"Congratulations," he mumbled then forced a smile. "You deserve it."

Her breath hitched as she stared at him. All the people around them faded away as a single tear slid down her cheek. "So that's it?" she whispered.

He shrugged and ignored the pounding in his head. "Ryan's right. This is a once-in-a-lifetime chance. Take it." His throat felt like he'd swallowed a bucket of dust, but he didn't stop. "You don't belong here, Sara. I told you that from the start."

Sara clutched at her stomach, wondering if she might actually throw up. She didn't belong. Wasn't that the story of her life? Wasn't that what she thought she'd had here in Crimson with Josh? A place to call home for the first time.

Get a grip, her inner voice scolded and she bit down on her lip.

She turned to Ryan. "Make the call. I'll do it."

April reached for her hand, but she shrugged away, knowing if her friend touched her right now she might lose it completely. She'd gone soft this summer, let down her guard and her armor. That was the great thing about L.A., between the people and the traffic and the smog, she'd never questioned that every day would be a battle. She was used to it, ready to attack or go on the defensive no matter the situation.

Crimson Ranch and the mountains around it had lulled her into a false sense of security, made her believe she was safe in their shadow. She should have known better. She'd opened her heart and now she'd pay the price.

"You're crying." April handed Sara a napkin from a nearby table.

"Happy tears," she mumbled, praying she was a good enough actress to pull off this last scene. "Tears of joy for my dream come true." Her lips pulled into a wide smile. "I guess we have a real reason for a party now."

The guests cheered again, and Sara tried not to think about how much she'd miss meeting the vacationers who came to the ranch, hearing the stories of their lives. She'd already come to love the mornings when she walked across the property in the crisp mountain air to share a cup of coffee with April and any other early risers.

Yes, a part of her wanted her acting career back

on track. She wanted to prove she was more than a washed-up child star. She wanted to lose herself in bringing a character to life again, stretch her range and know she could connect with the audience in that way.

Was it too much to want it all?

"How can you leave us?" Claire's angry voice broke her out of her musings. "You're dumping us, just like my mom did, for a better offer. Why does everyone leave me like I don't matter? I thought you were different."

"It's not like that," Sara whispered in response. Her heart broke all over again for the pain in the girl's eyes. Pain she'd caused.

Claire stood in front of her, chin trembling. Her arms were crossed in front of her chest.

Josh stepped forward, his entire focus on his daughter. "Sara was never going to stay," he told her, his voice a cool murmur.

I want to stay, she wanted to scream in response.

Ask me to stay.

Give me a reason to stay.

Claire turned to Sara. "You're a liar. You used us when you had nothing. You made me think you really cared."

Sara shook her head. "I do care, sweetie."

"You're as bad as my mother." Claire's big eyes narrowed. "As bad as your mother. I hate you."

Bile rose in Sara's throat at the comparison to Rose Wells. She'd been disappointed by her mother for so many years, she felt like it had broken something fundamental inside of her. She didn't trust her own judgment, her ability to form lasting relationships, her capacity for love.

This summer had gone a long way to fix what was wrong in her life. Or so she'd thought. Now she realized this was just one more illusion, like a movie set that could be stripped away in days—or in a moment—leaving a vast emptiness in its place.

But she didn't want that for Claire. She'd only wanted to spare the girl the pain Sara had felt for so many years.

She took a step forward but Josh blocked her way, putting himself between her and Claire, his back to Sara. Just like that, he cut her off from the two people she'd come to think of as hers. Guests drifted to the far side of the patio, making her feel even more alone.

"*We're* going to make this place work, Claire. You and me." Sara watched as he put his large hands on each of the girl's thin shoulders. "This is our home now. I'm not going to leave you. We're a team."

Sara had to physically restrain herself from rushing forward and wrapping her arms around them both. She ached to be part of their "team," as Josh called it. But here she was, once again on the sidelines.

Claire threw herself against her father's chest and sobbed out loud. The irony of the embrace wasn't lost on Sara. It had taken the two of them having a common enemy—her—for Claire to lean on Josh the way he'd wanted. She took no comfort in pushing the two of them together at last. Her pain was too raw for that. There was too much hurt between them all for her to believe this was the best ending to their story.

With his arm around Claire's shoulder, Josh led her from the porch.

Sara whispered his name and he turned. Fool that she was, she still held out a glimmer of hope that he'd call her to him and they'd work together to make this right.

Instead, his eyes held only derision as he looked at her. "You need to be out of here by tomorrow. I'll handle the bookings for the rest of the summer."

Pride made her chin notch up an inch. "It's my house."

A muscle in his jaw knotted. "I'll find a way to buy it from you. Before the end of the season."

No, she wanted to scream. That wasn't what she meant. "Josh, I don't..."

Her voice faded as she realized she was talking to his back. He and Claire disappeared into the house. Sara turned to April, miserable and needing her own comfort.

Even her best friend looked disappointed, as if Sara could have done better. How? How was she supposed to fight for something that wasn't hers to begin with?

Ever the peacekeeper, April turned to the guests, who'd gone silent. "It's still a beautiful night," April said, making her tone encouraging. "And we're happy each of you is here. I've got dinner ready in the kitchen." She smiled, and only Sara could see it didn't reach her eyes. "Who wants to load up a plate?"

The guests smiled and clapped and Sara felt a palpable easing of the tension. If April happened to be an X-Men type mutant under her braids and patchouli-scented sundresses, Sara would guess her superpower was making people feel better. She'd blessed Sara with her gift too many times to count, but never had she needed it more than now.

So when her friend turned and enveloped Sara in

a hug, Sara sagged against her, wanting reassurance that she'd tried her best.

"What else could I do?" Sara asked, swallowing against the catch in her voice.

April pulled back and cupped Sara's face gently between her palms. Sara held her breath, waiting for the words of encouragement, the slant on the situation that would make Sara feel like a happy ending was still within reach.

"Make it right," April said simply, then turned and walked into the house to help the guests.

Sara whirled on Ryan. "What does she mean, make it right? I'm not the one who said I don't belong. I'm trying to make it right. I'm trying to resurrect my career, to pay her back the money you lost. I want the ranch to succeed. I want Claire to be okay. I want it all and I don't know how to get any of it. And she tells me to make it right?" She threw her hands in the air. "How do I do that, Ryan?"

He gave her a hug. "You start with what you should have done years ago. What I should have helped you accomplish. You take care of yourself."

The next morning, Sara folded her clothes and returned them to the suitcase she'd stowed in the back of the closet in her cabin.

She didn't go to the main house for breakfast, too emotionally drained to make small talk with the guests and too much of a coward to face April in the daylight.

As much of a nurturer as her friend was, April had made no secret last night that she thought Sara was making the wrong decision. Even if she hadn't said it out loud.

To Sara's surprise, April had told her she was going to stay on the ranch for the rest of the season. Apparently, Sara wasn't the only one who had experienced the healing power of the high mountain air. Sara had suggested that April contact Olivia Wilder to see about teaching yoga classes at the community center when it was complete.

Community.

It was a word that had held little meaning to Sara before this summer. With good reason, she realized now, since she clearly wasn't meant to be a part of this one.

Ryan was picking her up this morning to drive her to the airport, where she'd board a plane for the movie set. She was arriving a few days before shooting started, but an apartment had been rented for her and she wanted a chance to settle in before the rest of the cast and crew arrived. She also needed to get away from Colorado, from Josh and the dreams she'd been foolish enough to believe could come true for the two of them.

When a knock sounded on the door to the cabin, she called, "Come in," expecting to see Ryan. He was bringing by the contract and official paperwork for her to sign before they left.

Instead, her mother's voice rang out from the front room. "Serena, where are you? We need to talk."

Sara closed her eyes and took a steadying breath. The last person she wanted to speak to right now was her mother. But she walked from the bedroom into the main room of the cabin.

"Word travels fast," she said to Rose, who rushed forward to give her a hug.

"I'm thrilled for you, darling." Her mother smoothed

back her hair with a frown and slight tsk of dissatisfaction. "We're not going to let this opportunity go to
waste."

"*We're* not going to do anything," Sara replied, stepping out of her mother's embrace. "This has nothing
to do with you."

"It has everything to do with me." Although Rose's
voice was soft, Sara heard an edge of steel underneath.
Her stomach did a slow roll, the same visceral reaction she'd had to her mother's unspoken demands since
she was a girl.

"I'm your biggest fan," Rose continued. "Your first
manager, you'll remember." She combed her fingers
through her bangs. "It's time for me to get involved in
your life again."

Sara's head snapped back as if she'd been slapped.
"Not going to happen in a million years."

"Oh, yes. I think I may come to stay with you on
set, for moral support and to make sure no one takes
advantage of you. You're in a precarious place emotionally, since this is a chance you never thought you'd
get." Her mother leaned forward. "Truth be told, you
look quite ragged. Perhaps we could get you in for a
bit of Botox before filming begins?"

Sara threw her arms into the air. "Mom, what are
you talking about? I'm not getting Botox. You're not
coming to the set."

"I have nothing else to occupy myself right now,"
her mother said with a sigh. "I'd planned to help Richard with plans for the condo development. I've always
had an eye for interior design." She shrugged. "But
since you won't sell the house yet, his deal has stalled.
That leaves me free to focus my attention on you, my

darling daughter." She tapped her finger on her upper lip. "And maybe Josh's daughter. I really do see potential in her. She obviously needs some maternal guidance."

"Leave Claire alone," Sara said on an angry hiss of breath. Temper flared to life inside her. "And get out of my life while you're at it."

"Give me a reason to," Rose shot back, the smile never leaving her face.

"Really, Mom? You're going to try to blackmail me now. That's a new low. It doesn't matter. I'm not afraid of you anymore and I don't need your approval. I haven't needed you for a long time."

Rose had the gall to look offended. "You'll always need me. I gave you the career you had."

"I worked for my career," Sara told her. "I had the talent you never did, and I worked for all the success I had. Unfortunately, I was naive enough to listen to you back then, to think you had my best interests at heart. Trust me, I won't make that mistake again."

She brushed past her mother and opened the front door. "I'm not going to sell the house, and there isn't a damn thing you can do about it. Now get out. For good, Mother. I don't want to see you here again."

"Don't do this, Sara," Rose said. Her voice turned to a pitiful whine. "I love Richard, but things are rocky between us since the land deal isn't working. I need you to help me."

Sara squeezed her eyes shut. This was the first time since she'd been a girl that her mother had called her by her given name. But even that small concession was too little, too late. "Get out," she repeated, sweeping her hand toward the porch.

With a dramatic sob, Rose rushed forward. "You'll change your mind," her mother called over her shoulder. "You can't do it on your own. You're not strong enough. You never were."

Sara sank onto the edge of the sofa, not bothering to shut the door behind her mother.

Those last angry words echoed through her as her head dropped to her knees, tears spilling down her face, soaking her bare legs. All the emotions, the hurt and betrayal, the disappointment over what would never be poured out of her.

After minutes, she gulped in an unsteady breath and raised her face, wiping her hands to clear the wetness.

"She's wrong," a voice said softly from the porch. Claire stood in the doorway, clenching her fingers at her sides. "You're strong enough. I believe in you, Sara."

Tears came again as Sara propelled herself off the couch, wrapping her arms around the girl. "I'm so sorry, sweetie. I never wanted to hurt you in all of this. I do care about you, Claire. I promise. Just because—"

"I know," Claire interrupted. "I was mad last night. I'm pretty sure the therapist my mom made me see would tell you I have some wicked abandonment issues." She laughed softly.

"Join the club." Sara pulled back. "We should introduce my mother to yours. They could start a mutual narcissistic personality club."

"If it keeps them busy…" Claire started.

"And off our backs," Sara finished.

They both laughed and Sara hugged her again. "You can call me on set. And text. And tweet. And Facebook. And whatever other ways to communicate they invent in the next five minutes. I'm sorry this summer didn't work out the way any of us planned, but I'm still your friend."

Claire nodded and blinked several times. "My dad isn't great at relationships. He won't let himself be vulnerable," she said, sounding far more mature than her thirteen years.

"Your therapist talking?"

"My mom. She talked a lot about him, mostly complaining. I think that's part of why I'm so hard on him. Years of conditioning, you know?"

Sara knew all about years of conditioning. That might explain why she was so hard on herself.

"He's a good man, Claire." The words ripped open a fresh flash of pain across Sara's heart. It made her ache to think of Josh, which was hard not to do on the ranch, when every smell and sound was bound together by her time with him. "He loves you."

"He loves you, too," Claire said firmly. "I know he does. He's just too much of a…man…to admit it."

"Common problem," Sara answered. "There's practically a whole subgenre of movies based on unhappy endings—*Gone with the Wind, Shakespeare in Love, Casablanca.*" She waved her hand, trying to be flip, then realized her fingers were trembling. She tucked her arm behind her back. "Our lives are too different to make it work."

"What about *Notting Hill?*" Claire's chin jutted forward at a stubborn angle. "Julia Roberts and Hugh Grant made it work."

Sara couldn't help but smile. "I like the way your mind works, but this isn't the movies." She watched

Claire push the toe of one shoe into the floor. "I promise you'll be okay. Your dad will make sure of it."

"I wish you didn't have to go," Claire said, hugging her again.

Sara willed herself to remain strong when all she wanted to do was melt into a weepy puddle once again. "Maybe you can come to the movie premiere." She paused, then added, "If your dad agrees."

Claire smiled through a hiccup. "If I'm on my best behavior, maybe he will." Then she giggled. "Do you think you could introduce me to Justin Timberlake?"

Sara laughed in response. "If I ever meet him, you bet."

Chapter 15

"Can I go look at clothes?" Claire bounced on the tips of her toes as she smiled and nodded at Josh.

"At Feathers and Threads?" He arched a brow at her. "I thought you'd rather be seen in a potato sack."

"Don't be dramatic," his daughter answered, but her smile remained. "Sara told me they're carrying a couple of new lines." She bit her lip and glanced away.

Something that felt a lot like regret scraped across his insides at the mention of Sara's name. "I know you still talk to her and text. I monitor your phone even if I don't read them all, remember?"

"So annoying," Claire mumbled. "Can I go?"

"Sure." Josh glanced at his watch. "I need to load the rest of the wood into the truck, then I'll be down to pick you up."

"Thanks, Dad."

He watched his daughter cross the street toward the boutique on the corner. He felt a lightness fill his chest at the change in his relationship with Claire. It was followed quickly by the weight of knowing that Sara had a lot to do with the progress.

It had been three weeks since she'd left Crimson. Almost a month filled with emptiness and a constant longing to be with her again. He hoped it would fade soon, or he thought he might go mad from the pain of it. Pain he knew he'd caused himself.

He knew what she'd wanted that night on the patio. Her eyes had held a hope that he'd offer more. He'd wanted to, planned on it until Ryan had come in with his big announcement. How could Josh compete with the bright lights of Hollywood?

He cursed under his breath. When had he ever backed away from a fight? He knew it was a mistake, but in that moment he couldn't stop himself from making it.

He wouldn't ask her to give up another chance at her career. Yet he hadn't been able to offer her the relationship she deserved, because he was too afraid that when she was away filming, he couldn't protect her. It hadn't worked with his sister or with his relationship with Claire's mother. Here in Colorado, on the ranch, he could make sure everything was okay for the people he loved. He was in charge of his life and emotions. Things were simple, just the way he liked them. He was too afraid of losing her when she left him. Too scared she'd eventually choose her career over him.

As much as he knew now that he loved Sara with his whole heart, he'd tried to convince himself it was for the best. The whole reason he'd returned to Crimson was to protect Claire, to give her the normal life he'd always craved. Not to let the outside world seep in and destroy them.

It was irrational, he knew. Sara had been a positive influence on his daughter from the start. But he held on to his fear like an anchor and only now worried it might take him down, as well.

"You got a lot of posts there. Not sure you'll need that many."

Josh looked up into the face of Richard Hamish, partially shaded by the large Stetson on his head. "You have no idea what I need, Rich." Josh took a pair of work gloves from his back pocket and slipped them on. "Go play intimidating cowboy with someone else. It's wasted on me." He hefted several boards into the truck bed. "If you haven't heard, Crimson Ranch is having a great first season. I'm going to secure that loan and buy the house come fall."

"Not if she sells it to me first."

The older man sounded as if it were a done deal, confidence dripping from every syllable.

"You're bluffing." Josh kept working on loading fence posts into the truck, needing to keep his hands occupied so he wasn't tempted to wrap them around Richard's craggy neck. "Sara isn't going to sell you the house. Not now."

"Rose flew down there and is working on her as we speak."

Josh stilled. "On set with Sara?" He knew how much being near her mother upset Sara. She didn't need that kind of distraction when she was filming a movie.

"I sure as hell don't want Rose around me until this deal goes through." Richard spit a wad of tobacco into the street. "Dang woman talks my ear off. She meddles into every detail of a man's life. It's about time she uses her energy on someone other than me. She can wear that girl down. I'd bet my belt buckle on it."

"You think Rose will convince Sara to sell?"

"Her mom will head back here once Sara agrees."

"She won't do it." Josh wanted to be sure, but how could he? He'd given Sara no reason to believe in him. Why should she stick to their bargain at this point? If she wanted to get on with her life, the easiest path would be to sign the house over to her mother.

"If she wants to keep that fancy new movie role, she will."

"Sara earned that part. Even if her mother is an annoyance, she's not going to cost her the job."

Richard's smile was too confident. "Sara's had a bumpy few years. There's a lot of pressure trying to restart a life. You should understand that better than most. Who knows if she can handle it? She may crack, go back to using drugs—"

"She didn't use drugs and you know it."

"Doesn't matter what I know. The important thing is what the American people believe. One story in the tabloids and that production company will drop her in an instant."

Josh took a step forward, stripping off his gloves and grabbing Richard by the collar of his custom Western shirt. "You wouldn't..." His voice was a low growl.

"Who's going to stop me?" He pulled away from Josh's grasp. "Son, you've been outplayed."

Without thinking, Josh slammed his fist into the other man's jaw. Richard staggered back into the brick storefront. Several men rushed out of the hardware store to see what the commotion was.

"This isn't a game, you old coot." Josh shook out his hand, glancing at his knuckles where a few trickles of blood pooled.

"It's her life. And to answer the question of who's going to stop you?" He came close to Richard, who cradled his face in his palm. "That would be me."

Sara held her fingers to her ears, but even that couldn't drown out her mother's incessant rambling.

"I talked to craft services about your food allergies and exactly what they need to stock for you."

Sara's head shot up. "I don't have food allergies."

"Sensitivities, then."

"I'm only sensitive to your voice." She got up from the couch in her on-set trailer. "When is this going to end, Mother?"

When Rose had first arrived three days ago, Sara had refused to let her on set. But Rose took matters into her own hands, meeting with the director and one of the executive producers to spin a tale of Sara's fragile emotional state and how Rose wanted to make sure she didn't cost them money on the movie.

What Rose was going to cost Sara was her sanity.

Thanks to Sara's less-than-stellar reputation, the men had believed it. Rose had become a constant presence during filming. It was hard for Sara to stay connected with the character of a hardworking mom when all she wanted was for her own mother to leave her the hell alone.

"You know what it takes," Rose said simply, turning to the small bank of cabinets she was rearranging.

Rose had even gotten Jonathan Tramner, the director, to suggest to Sara that her mother stay with her in the studio apartment at the end of filming each day. Sara got no break, which was making her crazy.

"Why is Richard Hamish so important that you'll do anything to make me sell Gran's house to him?"

"I love him."

"It would be a revelation if you loved your own daughter half as much."

Rose didn't turn around, but her shoulders stiffened. "I do love you, Serena. I devoted my life to making your career a success. You owe me for that."

"I paid the bills for a decade." Resentment rose hot and strong in Sara. "I more than paid my debt to you." When her mother didn't turn around, Sara's gaze fell to the line of glass bottles on the small cabinet.

"Why is all that liquor in here?"

"One of the men helped me unload it." Her mother's voice was emotionless. "I explained to them that you might need a little something to calm your nerves."

"My nerves wouldn't be so shot if you'd leave. And you know I do yoga for…" Her voice trailed off as realization dawned. "You're going to make it seem like I'm a drunk?" She stood, pacing the small room. "Do you have needles stashed somewhere, too?"

"Sell the house." Rose spun around, her finger pointed in accusation. "Why are *you* so devoted to a man who doesn't want you? You're going to save his ranch and let my dream for a happy life be thrown in the trash. You shouldn't be protecting him. He doesn't care about you, Serena. You're not important to him. When are you going to stop being a doormat for people who are only using you?"

The air whooshed out of the room, and Sara thought her knees might buckle. Her mother was right. She was a doormat. No matter how tough she talked, how insolent her attitude, she let people take advantage of her. Her mother was first in that line.

Maybe that was what Josh had been doing, wooing her in Colorado to ensure her loyalty. It didn't matter anymore. Her time with him had given her the confidence to believe in herself again. Even if he didn't believe in the two of them, he'd given her a gift she could never repay.

"Good point, Mom." She pushed open the door to the trailer. "First I'm going to stop being a doormat for you."

"I didn't mean…"

"I don't care." She lifted her hands. "I don't care if you ruin my career. Again. If they fire me, I'll find another job, another path. Even if it isn't in Hollywood. I love acting, not being a celebrity." She thought about Olivia's offer to help with the community theater in Crimson. "I can make my life a success. I deserve happiness, and I'm not going to let you rob me of it for one second longer."

"You don't know what you're saying."

"She does."

Sara whirled as Josh filled the tiny doorway of the trailer. His gaze was fixed on Rose. "She should have said it a long time ago. I should have said it for her. To her." He turned to Sara. "You deserve happiness."

Rose stalked forward. "You only want the house. You don't care about her."

His eyes never left Sara's. "Sell the house."

She shook her head.

"I mean it," he said, and took her arms between his hands. Close enough that she could see the tiny flecks of gold in his dark eyes. Close enough that the smell of him wound through her senses like a drug. "Sell the house if it will make you happy."

"It's your future," she said softly.

"I'll make a different future," he answered. "With you, if you'll have me. No piece of property, no business is worth anything without you in my life to share it. I love you, Sara. I think I have since the moment you jumped on the counter and spun my world out of control."

She drew a shaky breath, unable to believe what she was hearing. "But you like control."

"I thought I needed it," he said, pushing a stray hair behind her ear. His touch made a shiver run through her. "I'm sorry for hurting you and letting you walk away." He dipped his head so he was looking directly into her eyes. "I was wrong about a lot of things. But one thing I'm definitely right about is that nothing is worth losing you."

She choked back a sob and tried to look away. He held her head steady. "Claire loves you. I love you. We both need you in our lives so damn much. Please give us another chance, Sara. Name the terms. Anything you want."

She shook her head. "I can't cook," she mumbled.

One side of his mouth kicked up. "We'll order takeout."

"I'm opinionated."

"I want to hear every thought in that beautiful mind."

Her eyes searched his. She saw the truth of his

words, of his love for her. Still, she was so scared to risk having her heart and dreams crushed once more. She didn't know if she could survive again.

"I want to act," she told him, wondering if it would be the nail in the coffin.

He leaned forward and ran his lips against hers. "I'll be at every premiere and production. I'll help you learn lines. I'll come to you wherever you are." His soft breath fell against her mouth. "Because I'm nothing without you, Sara. Wherever you are is where I want to be. Forever."

Her arms wrapped around his waist, and he pulled her to him, deepening the kiss until she was lost in sensation. "I love you, Josh," she said after a moment. "Forever."

"Well, that was a scene worthy of a Lifetime movie if I've ever seen one."

Her mother's sarcastic voice cut into Sara's bliss like a blade.

Josh held her to him, dropping a kiss on her forehead. "It's real, Rose. You wouldn't recognize real love, and I'm sorry for that." He met her mother's angry gaze. "I love your daughter and I won't let you hurt her anymore."

"Easy to say when you get what you want in the end."

"What I want is Sara's happiness."

"What you get is the house that should have been mine."

He looked down into Sara's eyes. "I meant what I said. Sell the house if it will make things easier for you. I'll find another property. We'll rebuild. As long as you're with me, I can make it right."

She shook her head. "It's right just the way it is."

Turning to Rose, she said, "I'm not selling, Mom. You can't blackmail me into it. You can't threaten. I'm not giving you power over me again."

"We'll see what happens when Richard takes control of this," her mother spit out, pulling out her cell phone and punching in numbers. "You always were ungrateful."

"I don't think you'll get a hold of him right now," Josh said casually. "He flew down to Houston this morning to see his wife."

Rose's hand stilled in midair. "Wife?"

"You didn't know? Yes, his wife of twenty-five years lives in Texas. Didn't you think it was odd how he never took you with him when he flew down there?"

"Those were business trips," Rose said woodenly.

"You were the one being used, Mom," Sara said. "I'm sorry."

Rose shook her head. "I don't need your pity."

"I don't pity you," Sara explained. "I'm sorry you think so little of yourself that you let a man treat you like that."

"That house should still be mine."

"It's not and it's never going to be. Move on, Mother."

Rose looked around the trailer as if not really seeing anything. "I need help. I need the house."

"Yes," Sara agreed. "You need to learn to stand on your own two feet. Trust me—that's the best help I can give you."

Rose's spine stiffened. "Once I walk out that door, you're dead to me, Serena. Be careful what you choose right now."

Sara didn't hesitate in her response. "I choose love," she whispered, and pressed her cheek against Josh's warm chest.

With a muttered curse, Rose fled from the trailer, slamming the door behind her.

Josh tipped her head up. "Forever?"

She nodded. "I choose you, Josh Travers. Forever."

* * * * *

She rose from her seat of slab rock. "We'd probably better
be going. We still have one more hiking trail to cover before
we hit another set of campgrounds."

While she gathered up her partially eaten lunch, Sawyer
left his seat and walked over to the edge of the bluff.

"This is an incredible view," he said. "From this distance,
the saguaros look like green needles stuck in a sandpile."

She looked over to see the strong north wind was hitting
him in the face and molding his uniform against his muscled
body. The sight of his imposing figure etched against the
blue sky and desert valley caused her breath to hang in her
throat.

She walked over to where he stood, then took a cautious
step closer to the ledge in order to peer down at the view
directly below.

"I never get tired of it," she admitted. "There are a few
Native American ruins not far from here. We'll hike by
those before we finish our route."

A hard gust of wind suddenly whipped across the ledge and caused Vivian to sway on her feet. Sawyer swiftly caught her by the arm and pulled her back to his side.

"Careful," he warned. "I wouldn't want you to topple over the edge."

With his hand on her arm and his sturdy body shielding her from the wind, she felt very warm and protected. And for one reckless moment, she wondered how it would feel to slip her arms around his lean waist, to rise up on the tips of her toes and press her mouth to his. Would his lips taste as good as she imagined?

Shaken by the direction of her runaway thoughts, she tried to make light of the moment. "That would be awful," she agreed. "Mort would have to find you another partner."

"Yeah, and she might not be as cute as you."

With a little laugh of disbelief, she stepped away from his side. "Cute? I haven't been called that since I was in high school. I'm beginning to think you're nineteen instead of twenty-nine."

He pulled a playful frown at her. "You prefer your men to be old and somber?"

"I prefer them to keep their minds on their jobs," she said staunchly. "And you are not *my* man."

His laugh was more like a sexy promise.

"Not yet."

Don't miss
A Ranger for Christmas *by Stella Bagwell,*
available December 2018 wherever
Harlequin® Special Edition *books and ebooks are sold.*

www.Harlequin.com

HARLEQUIN®

SPECIAL EDITION

Life, Love and Family

Save **$1.00**

on the purchase of ANY

Harlequin® Special Edition book.

Available whever books are sold,
including most bookstores, supermarkets,
drugstores and discount stores.

Save **$1.00**

on the purchase of any Harlequin® Special Edition book.

Coupon valid until February 28, 2019.
Redeemable at participating outlets in the U.S. and Canada only.
Limit one coupon per customer.

52616105

Canadian Retailers: Harlequin Enterprises Limited will pay the face value of this coupon plus 10.25¢ if submitted by customer for this product only. Any other use constitutes fraud. Coupon is nonassignable. Void if taxed, prohibited or restricted by law. Consumer must pay any government taxes. Void if copied. Inmar Promotional Services ("IPS") customers submit coupons and proof of sales to Harlequin Enterprises Limited, P.O. Box 31000, Scarborough, ON M1R 0E7, Canada. Non-IPS retailer—for reimbursement submit coupons and proof of sales directly to Harlequin Enterprises Limited, Retail Marketing Department, 22 Adelaide St. West, 40th Floor, Toronto, Ontario M5H 4E3, Canada.

5 65373 00076 2   (8100)0 12397

U.S. Retailers: Harlequin Enterprises Limited will pay the face value of this coupon plus 8¢ if submitted by customer for this product only. Any other use constitutes fraud. Coupon is nonassignable. Void if taxed, prohibited or restricted by law. Consumer must pay any government taxes. Void if copied. For reimbursement submit coupons and proof of sales directly to Harlequin Enterprises, Ltd 482, NCH Marketing Services, P.O. Box 880001, El Paso, TX 88588-0001, U.S.A. Cash value 1/100 cents.

® and ™ are trademarks owned and used by the trademark owner and/or its licensee.

© 2018 Harlequin Enterprises Limited

HSECOUP04506

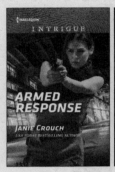

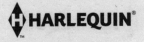

Love Harlequin romance?

DISCOVER.

Be the first to find out about promotions,
news and exclusive content!

EXPLORE.

Sign up for the Harlequin e-newsletter and
download a free book from any series at
TryHarlequin.com.

CONNECT.

Join our Harlequin community to share
your thoughts and connect with other
romance readers!
Facebook.com/groups/HarlequinConnection

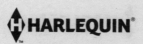

**ROMANCE WHEN
YOU NEED IT**